POWER
CRAZY

OTHER BOOKS BY KARL GROSSMAN

COVER UP: What you *are not* supposed
to know about Nuclear Power

The Poison Conspiracy

Nicaragua: America's New Vietnam?

POWER CRAZY

By KARL GROSSMAN

GROVE PRESS, Inc./New York

First Grove Press Edition 1986
First Printing 1986
ISBN: 0-394-55461-2
Library of Congress Catalog Card Number: 86-3159

First Evergreen Edition 1986
First Printing 1986
ISBN: 0-394-62222-7
Library of Congress Catalog Card Number: 86-3159

Library of Congress Cataloging-in-Publication Data

Grossman, Karl.
  Power crazy.

  1. Long Island Lighting Company. I. Title.
HD9685.U7L664   1986   363.6'2'0974721   86-3159
ISBN 0-394-55461-2
ISBN 0-394-62222-7 (1st Evergreen ed. : pbk.)

Designed by Dave Miller
Printed in the United States
Grove Press, Inc., 196 West Houston Street
New York, N.Y. 10014
5   4   3   2   1

To my parents, Herbert and Ruth Grossman

▼

CONTENTS

▼

PREFACE

The American electric utility industry is in worse shape than it's ever been. It demands sky-high and still-rising rates, builds nuclear plants with huge cost overruns and little regard for public safety. Utilities across the country make ambitious expansion plans that go wildly off-course. Added to that is a pattern of lax governmental supervision—based on common vested interests and the "revolving door" between government and industry—and of attempts by the industry to undermine the democratic process.

All U.S. utilities are not the same: some are better or worse than others. But few are worse in the area of malfeasance than Pennsylvania's Metropolitan Edison Company. Met Ed pleaded guilty to a criminal charge of corporate misconduct involving the accident at the company's Three Mile Island 2 plant.[1] As far as economic disaster is concerned, the Washington State Public Power Supply System (WPPSS) is notable for a 500 percent cost overrun on a five-plant nuclear project.[2] That publicly owned utility's misjudgment led to most of the project's being scuttled and to a multi-billion dollar default.

But leading the U.S. utility industry in all categories of mismanagement, ineptitude and worse is the Long Island Lighting Company (LILCO).

For example:

• Although other U.S. utilities have built expensive nuclear power plants, LILCO has built per proposed kilowatt *the most expensive nuclear plant in the world.*[3]

• Although in nuclear power plant construction there have been cost overruns of 30 percent and 50 percent and 100 percent, indeed even WPPSS' 500 percent, LILCO's cost overrun on its Shoreham nuclear plant is 7,600 percent![4] And it is still rising.

• Other U.S. utilities have high rates, but LILCO's, now the second highest in the nation, could jump 81 percent if Shoreham goes into operation—making LILCO electricity the most expensive in the U.S. by far.[5]

• Although shoddy, slipshod construction is far from unknown in nuclear plant construction, LILCO at Shoreham—according to former Shoreham inspectors and workers on the project—has set a new low. One high supervisory inspector—a veteran of the nuclear industry—says that of hundreds of thousands of mistakes and violations of standards at Shoreham, fewer than half have been corrected. "You wouldn't believe what went on there. . . . As God is my judge, if that thing is permitted to operate, a lot of people are going to die."[6] Also attesting to widespread problems at Shoreham are documents— including more than 1,000 reports from the plant found at a Long Island garbage dump.

• Although organized crime influence in unions is not unknown in the U.S., five of the principal unions on the Shoreham project have been linked by law enforcement authorities to organized crime.[7]

• Although many utilities have ties to the U.S. government's energy "establishment" of national laboratory and federal energy agency bureaucrats, none has more intimate links than LILCO.[8] The utility's current chief is the former assistant director of Brookhaven National Laboratory—whose scientists had a role in inspiring and have been leading the promotion of LILCO's nuclear program.

• State regulatory commissions have begun to impose sizeable penalties on utilities for mismanagement, but LILCO has received the record penalty imposed by state authorities—$1.395 billion—for pervasive mismanagement of Shoreham construction.[9] But other than levying that penalty, the New York State Public Service Commission has looked the other way on LILCO and provided a case study of, as one PSC member phrases it, "regulatory neglect."

• Other utilities in precarious financial shape have been aided by banks, but LILCO has been kept, barely, from bankruptcy with massive assistance from America's top banks—indeed, from some of the world's top banks, led by Citibank of New York. Citibank, the biggest bank in America, has been tied closely with LILCO for decades.[10] In the 1950s, LILCO, with a history of poor management, in large part came under the financial oversight of what was then the First National City Bank and became involved with some of the most powerful financial forces in the U.S., which have had a strong commitment to nuclear power. LILCO could easily become the first private utility in U.S. history to go bankrupt.

• Other utilities have taken advantage of the system of government regulation that usually allows them to charge ratepayers the full cost plus a profit for any capital project undertaken. LILCO has attempted to make lavish use of this system not only on its nuclear plant program but for such a scheme as investing $126 million in a purported uranium mine in New Mexico that has not produced an ounce of uranium and is now flooded and abandoned.[11]

• Although takeovers of other companies have not been unusual in the U.S. utility industry, hardly a company has been as voracious as LILCO. It has gobbled up virtually every independent utility in an area of 1,230 square miles with a population of roughly three million. Furthermore, its nuclear program has been aimed not just at supplying Long Island with electricity but at making LILCO the power broker—through nuclear power—of the U.S. Northeast.[12] Shoreham was planned as the first of a series of seven to eleven or more nuclear plants.

• Some utilities have influence on media that cover them. LILCO has enormous leverage with two of the most prestigious newspapers in the U.S., *The New York Times* and *Newsday.*[13]

• Other utilities have engaged in heavy political action, but none as intensely as LILCO. On its home territory, it has become the central corporate actor, so powerful that the charge is regularly made that it could become "government by LILCO" on Long Island. Nevertheless, public sentiment is overwhelmingly against LILCO and its Shoreham project—proportionally more so than against any other nuclear project anywhere else in the U.S. In late 1985, a poll[14] showed that in Suffolk County—the county of 1.3 million people where the Shoreham plant is located—77 percent of residents were against Shoreham operating, only 15 percent for it. Some 71 percent of Long Islanders were for a takeover of LILCO by a public power entity. Shoreham has been the scene of one of the largest demonstrations at a nuclear plant site ever held in the U.S. Some 15,000 people took part; over 600 were arrested.

• Despite LILCO's aggressive lobbying, large numbers of public officials on Long Island and in New York State have been fighting the Shoreham project. The Suffolk County Legislature (which has a Republican majority) and New York State Governor Mario Cuomo (a Democrat) have led the political battle. The clash over Shoreham with local and state governments on one side and the federal government on the other is regarded as the most intense government-against-government conflict over nuclear power in U.S. history. The issues on which it is being fought, home rule and the feasibility of evacuation in the wake of a serious nuclear plant accident, have become critical in the debate over nuclear power in the U.S.

• In Washington, D.C., LILCO's political operations have included use of former federal officials such as Lyn Nofziger, who had been President Reagan's chief political aide, to push for its Shoreham project (Nofziger, according to the New York State Consumer Board, has received $500,000 from LILCO since he was hired by the utility in 1984 as a LILCO "governmental affairs consultant").[15] LILCO has used its relationship with the U.S. government energy "establishment" for the same purpose. A LILCO friend at the highest level of the Reagan administration is Central Intelligence Agency Director William Casey, who left his seat on the LILCO board of directors, where he was a staunch promoter of Shoreham and LILCO's overall nuclear power program, when he went to run the CIA. The federal government has, meanwhile, picked LILCO's Shoreham plant as the symbol for the nuclear industry's future, despite its being among the most outrageous examples of nuclear technology, a symbol of the worst about nuclear power.

"The Shoreham plant must open!" declared U.S. Energy Secretary John S. Herrington at a Nuclear Power Assembly in 1985 in Washington, D.C. "If it doesn't, the signals will be the low point in this [nuclear] industry's history. If it does, we are going to begin a brand new era."[16]

Yet another distinction: If Shoreham goes into operation and a major mishap occurs, the consequences because of Shoreham's placement would be far more serious than a similar incident at most other nuclear plants. It is 50 miles east of the biggest city in the United States, New York City, and midway out on a densely populated island.

The most recent U.S. government study of the consequences of a severe accident at a nuclear plant, done at Sandia National Laboratories and issued in 1982, projects that a core meltdown at Shoreham stands to leave 40,000 "early fatalities," 75,000 "early injuries," 35,000 "cancer deaths" and $157 billion in property damage.[17]

However, Dr. Richard E. Webb, an expert on nuclear plant accident hazards, who was involved in the earliest federal government hearings on Shoreham, says these calculations "do not consider the worst accidents that can occur." The Sandia report, he says, "does not consider the potential of a massive reactor explosion, a massive, complete exploding apart of the containment building by several different possible mechanisms" including a nuclear runaway in which a nuclear plant can erupt in a huge, instantaneous steam explosion. Dr. Webb says that "if the plume" of radioactive poisons that could be discharged in a catastrophic accident at Shoreham "moved on New York City, the number of deaths could be many fold greater than the estimate in the Sandia report. There could be several hundred thousand deaths or maybe close to a million."[18]

The Chernobyl nuclear plant catastrophe in the Soviet Union, involving an explosion and a massive plume of radioactive poisons moving over Europe, showed these concerns to be very real. If there is to be a disaster like Chernobyl—or worse—in the United States, LILCO's Shoreham plant is a prime candidate.

LILCO has, with its Shoreham project, managed to combine the negative aspects of many electric utilities—and outdone all the competition *in extremis.*

Thus the story of how LILCO became the way it is today and where it is heading provides a clear picture of the forces at work throughout the U.S. utility industry.

It is a story not just involving electric power. It is about political power—and of profound threats to both democracy and human life.

KARL GROSSMAN
Sag Harbor, New York
1986

NOTES

1. The criminal charge of corporate misconduct Met Ed pleaded guilty to was for falsifying test data on leaks of irradiated water from the cooling system of its Three Mile Island 2 plant between October 1978 and March 28, 1979, when the plant underwent a partial meltdown. As part of the plea to the felony, the company agreed not to contest additional charges. It had been indicted in November 1983 on 11 counts of falsifying test data. *The New York Times*, February 19, 1984: "Plant Operator Ready to Admit Report's Faulty."

The New York Times, March 1, 1984: "Utility Pleads Guilty to Nuclear Violation." *The New York Times*, September 1, 1985: "Tips at Atom Plant: Keep Inspectors in Dark."

2. Coverage of the WPPSS situation has included a comprehensive week-long series of stories in *The Oregonian* of Portland, Oregon, between September 13–20, 1981. In a segment headlined, "Management Fueled Soaring Costs," the series noted:

In the early 1970s when the Washington Public Power Supply System decided to build five nuclear power plants at once in Washington state, the total cost was estimated at $4.1 billion. . . . Since then, the estimated costs have ballooned. The latest figure is $23.9 billion, a staggering 483 percent increase in seven years.

3. Declared the executive summary of report entitled *Investigation of the Shoreham Nuclear Power Station* issued in February 1984 by the New York State Public Service Commission staff: "Shoreham is the most expensive per kilowatt of rated capacity to date." This was confirmed by Charles Komanoff, a specialist on nuclear power economics, in an interview with the author, January 1986. He added that Shoreham has also become "the most expensive commercial power plant of any kind per kilowatt ever constructed."

4. This is calculated by comparing what LILCO originally projected Shoreham would cost—"in the $65–75 million range" (LILCO press release distributed as LILCO officials announced the Shoreham project on April 12, 1966) with the 1985 disclosure that the plant's price had grown to $5.7 billion. *Newsday*, September 16, 1985:

The Long Island Lighting Co. plans to spend $1.167 billion on capital construction at the Shoreham nuclear-power plant over the next decade, state Consumer Protection Board head Richard Kessel said yesterday. Kessel said the proposed spending would bring the total cost of the plant to $5.7 billion. . . . LILCO outlined its spending projections in a plan to phase-in rates over 10 years to cover Shoreham costs. . . . The total had climbed to an estimated $4.55 billion before LILCO announced its latest spending plan. . . . Elaine Robinson, a LILCO spokeswoman, confirmed that the company had budgeted $1.167 billion for "post-operational capital costs."

5. The account, headlined "LILCO Rates Listed 2nd Highest" (*Newsday*, December 12, 1981), was based on a survey done by the National Association of Regulatory Utility Commissioners. Only the Consolidated Edison Company of New York was listed as having higher rates than LILCO. Of the six utilities with the highest rates in the U.S., three were in Hawaii. LILCO's most recent proposal for a "phase in" of costs for Shoreham into its rate base, if the plant goes into operation, provides for a 40 percent increase in rates, according to the New York State Consumer Protection Board. A PSC majority on May 14, 1986, gave approal to a plan under which LILCO could increase rates as high as 81 percent to pay for Shoreham. With compounded interest, the "phase-in" of higher rates means consumers' bills would double. Earlier, in a series of decisions, the PSC allowed LILCO to include $1.8 billion of Shoreham costs into its rate base.

6. Interview with the author, February 1985. He asked that his name not be published because he feared retaliation against his family and himself if it were.

7. Links to organized crime of five principal unions at Shoreham—Local 66 of the Laborer's Union, Teamsters Union Local 242, Boilermakers Union Local

5, Operating Engineers Union Local 138 and Local 1, Power Plant Police & Security Officers—have been alleged in various FBI and U.S. Department of Justice depositions and/or claims by organized crime specialists in law enforcement in New York City and Long Island. A segment of Chapter 2 deals with this issue.

8. The links between LILCO and the U.S. government's energy "establishment" is the subject of Chapter 6.

9. *The New York Times*, June 27, 1985: "This was the largest disallowance of costs ever imposed on a utility by a regulatory agency in the United States." Until Shoreham, the biggest such penalty was levied by the Missouri Public Service Commission against the Union Electric Company: $384 million of the $3 billion cost of its Callaway nuclear plant. The charge that the New York State Public Service Commission, otherwise, has shown "regulatory neglect" towards LILCO was made by Commissioner Anne Mead in an interview with the author, December 1985.

10. *Newsday*, February 13, 1986: "Citibank has overtaken Bank of America as the nation's largest bank ranked by deposits. . . . Citibank has long outranked BankAmerica Corp. as the nation's largest bank holding company and had assets of $173.6 billion at the end of 1985." Corporate connections between LILCO and Citibank were explored in *Newsday*, March 22, 1973: "LILCO's Ties That Bind," part of a series entitled "Corporate Closness." There were also outlined in "Competition in the Nuclear Power Supply Industry," a 1968 report prepared by Arthur D. Little, Inc. of Cambridge, Massachusetts, for the Atomic Energy Commission and the U.S. Department of Justice. These links are examined in Chapter 3.

11. A section of Chapter 5 concerns LILCO's Bokum uranium mine venture.

12. This point is explored in Chapter 3.

13. This point is examined in Chapter 8, which includes complaints about *The Times'* handling of the Shoreham story by Frances Cerra, who said this caused her to resign as a reporter for the paper. Cerra made her charges in a letter published in *The Quill* (March 1984), the magazine of the journalistic fraternity, Sigma Delta Chi. She further commented on the situation in an interview with the author, December 1984. Former *Newsday* national editor Ernest Volkman alleged that *Newsday* has limited its LILCO coverage in an article entitled "Nuclear Reaction: How They Didn't Bring the News from Shoreham to Long Island," *Media People* (November 1980).

14. Poll commissioned by *Newsday*, reported on November 17, 1985. Further details on the poll are included in Chapter 9.

15. *Newsday*, August 8, 1985.

16. Tape recording of John Herrington's remarks in a speech entitled "The Challenge for Nuclear Power" made at a Nuclear Power Assembly held on May 8, 1985, in Washington, D.C.

17. From calculations done for *Technical Guidance for Siting Criteria Development*, a report prepared by Sandia National Laboratories, Albuquerque, New Mexico, for the U.S. Nuclear Regulatory Commission, 1982. (NUREG/CR-2239)

18. Dr. Richard Webb in interviews with the author, 1985–1986.

▼

─────────────

ACKNOWLEDGMENTS

With many thanks to my wife, Janet, who, as always, was with me every inch of the way, and our sons, Kurt and Adam. To Barney and Lisa Rosset, whose idea this book is, my editor John G. H. Oakes, Fred Jordan, Jennifer Atkinson, and all the people at Grove Press. And, to Dr. Richard Webb, Wayne Prospect, George Henry, Richie Kessel, Irv Like, Tom Twomey, Warren Liebold, John Rather, Herb Brown, Larry Lanpher, Greg Blass, Lorna and Eric Salzman, Anne Mead, Mat Chachere, Murray Barbash, Marty Bergman, Ron Stanchfield, John Matthews, Steve Liss, Paul Harenberg, Bob Clifford, Vic Yannacone, Bill Chaleff, Ralph Herbert, Kathy Boylan, Father Bill Brisotti, Esther Pank, Richard Lercari, Charlie and Audrey Raebeck, Ann and Bill Carl, Charlie Komanoff, John Mullen, Dale Bridenbaugh, Greg Minor, Dick Hubbard, Pat Bower, Van Howell, Jane Alcorn, Jack Everett, Jock McCrystal, John Huber, Leon Campo, Nora Bredes, Marge Harrison, Bill Chaleff, Steve Latham, and so many others.

▼

INTRODUCTION

By RICHARD KESSEL

Executive Director,

New York State Consumer Protection Board

My experience with (or against) the Long Island Lighting Company began back in the early 1970s, while I was running for the post of state senator of New York at the ripe age of 24. Here I was ready to tackle the world—talking about such important issues as Viet Nam, Cambodia, and cancer research—when someone mentioned to me that there was a LILCO rate hearing in Mineola.

Curious, I headed off to the Nassau County seat, and what I saw when I got there started me on my new career of consumer advocacy. There was a room filled with television cameras, notebooks, pencils, public officials, and some ordinary citizens, ready to tee off on a LILCO rate increase. What fascinated me was the fact that every one of the first two dozen speakers was an elected official who had something negative to say about LILCO. Yet, after each speech, the elected official did his or her radio and television interview, smiled to the public, and left, not to be heard from again until the next rate increase hearing.

At the same hearing, there were several private citizens, outraged at LILCO, who, along with me, an aspiring state legislator, stayed until the end of the day. One woman leaned over to me and said,

"Son, by the time you speak, the cameras and pens will be gone, and no one will know that you were here." How right she was. Yet, the day after I lost the election (and boy did I lose, being a Democrat in a heavily Republican county), I vowed to stick with those private citizens who didn't want their rates to go any higher. A journalist looking into all of this was Karl Grossman, the author of this important book about Long Island's "favorite" utility.

Now, some 12 years later, Karl and I are still there, seemingly fighting the same LILCO dragon, seeing a new breed of public officials uttering the same criticisms.

As a member of the Cuomo administration, serving as head of New York's consumer protection agency, I see the same frustrations as I did many years ago when I helped coin the phrase "Say NO to LILCO."

The LILCO story is one that never seems to end. The rates go up, Shoreham stands there, unopened, and the people of Long Island get angrier and angrier.

It is amazing that with all of the opposition to LILCO and Shoreham, the utility survives and continues to believe that Shoreham will open, rates will stabilize, and Long Island will be healthier because of LILCO. The old leadership, the new leadership, all believe that what's good for LILCO is good for Long Island. How wrong they are.

These days, there are many ratepayer heroes—Governor Cuomo, State Senator Kenneth LaValle, Nora Bredes and her Shoreham Opponents Coalition, attorney Irving Like, Suffolk Legislators Wayne Prospect and Gregory Blass, and citizen activists like Marge Harrison and Leon Campo, who have all stood up to the company. Despite this strong anti-LILCO movement, the LILCO machine moves forward, getting renewed energy from regulators and banks that seem to care more about their investments and the nuclear industry than they do about the safety of the people of Long Island.

LILCO, a company that fired over 500 of its hard-working employees—people who, by the way, take too much of the blame for a problem that is clearly not their fault—has, in order to stave off bankruptcy, been able to come up with millions of dollars to hire the best political and public relations gurus in the country to sell Shoreham to a public that wants no part of it.

Yet, with all of the battles—the $1.395 billion prudency fine levied by the state's Public Service Commission; the myriad of rate increases doled out by a passive PSC to help investors and hurt ratepayers; the specter of LILCO spending hundreds of thousands of dollars trying to create a grass-roots citizens group, Citizens to Open Shoreham, to con the public—with all of this, public anger simmered under the surface until *she* entered the picture. The *she* was Hurricane Gloria.

Gloria arrived on a Friday in September 1985, knocking out power to over 750,000 LILCO customers for up to 12 days. People from Malverne to Montauk weren't buying the LILCO story that the hurricane was totally at fault for the extensive power outages. In fact, as people started to dig out and notice the untrimmed trees, the rotting poles, and hard workers from other utilities expressing amazement at the deteriorated condition of the LILCO system, they soon realized that the LILCO line that they had been hearing was no longer believable. Could it be that LILCO spent so much money on Shoreham that it failed to maintain its system properly?

The answer to many was an obvious yes. The fact was what all of us who followed the sorry LILCO saga were saying for years: that the LILCO system was being ignored at the expense of the utility's single-minded desire to open Shoreham. LILCO denied this, time and again, but Gloria made the truth came out.

The LILCO drama continues to unfold as Karl Grossman writes this important story. The Grossman book is compelling, driving, certainly a document of historic proportion.

Governor Cuomo and most members of the Suffolk County Legislature continue to fight for the safety of the people of Long Island, claiming that Shoreham cannot open because a viable evacuation plan cannot be developed. And the current administration in Washington, led by the utility-oriented Nuclear Regulatory Commission and Federal Emergency Management Agency, tries to force Shoreham on a public that does not want it. The Reagan notion of ending federal government interference in our lives obviously doesn't apply to Shoreham, where Washington wants to get the plant opened even if it means overriding state and local prerogatives regarding safety.

Where it all ends no one knows. Does Shoreham open? Or is it relegated to the scrap heap as a symbol of utility arrogance and mismanagement? Does LILCO continue as a private company? Or is a public takeover in the cards, as suggested by public officials from both sides of the aisle? And who pays for all this—the ratepayers? The stockholders? The taxpayers?

Power Crazy, the story of a utility gone mad, is an important, timely book that must be read by everyone living on Long Island and everyone who wonders about the powers of a utility. As usual, Karl Grossman doesn't pull any punches—he tells it like it is.

One can only hope that this time, the public and their elected representatives will have the staying power to once and for all say no to LILCO. Long Island's future—the country's future—may be at stake.

POWER
CRAZY

1

"THEY
CAN'T
RUN ANYTHING"

"With LILCO, there has to be something basically wrong," Mike Loos says in the living room of his family's darkened home.[1] His wife, Eileen, is in the kitchen pouring water hauled from a nearby pond. They, like two and a half million other people on Long Island, have not had electricity this week.

It is a rainy Saturday. Hurricane Gloria struck nine days before, on September 27, 1985. As the first winds buffeted Long Island, LILCO electricity on most of Long Island went dead. Now service is still in the process of being restored, slowly.

"That storm wasn't that severe," says Loos, "but, you know, a good thunderstorm and LILCO goes out. I've never experienced such regular losses of electricity before moving out to Long Island."

Loos speaks of the frequent losses of LILCO electricity at the die-casting shop where he works. Machines at the shop have digital readouts, and "we're always having to reset the readouts. They go back to zero with outages. Resetting the readouts all the time, that's a nuisance," says Loos. "Being without electricity now for well over a week, that's more than an annoyance and, in my view, is completely unnecessary."

There was only a "minor interruption" in telephone service after Gloria hit, notes Loos. "The phone company has buried most of its lines. LILCO hasn't had the sense to do that." (According to a spokesman for New York Telephone, 96 percent of the company's subscribers received uninterrupted service during the storm, due to the system of underground telephone cables.[2])

1

He recalls comments made by out-of-town linemen who helped restore electricity on Long Island. "They say that the LILCO system is in terrible shape, is antiquated, and should have been replaced years ago. And that there's a very small inventory of spare parts here, no connecting clips, for instance, not even transformer parts."

As an example of how LILCO has drained sparse resources to Shoreham, Loos points to the seemingly brand-new trucks and equipment of the out-of-town crews. "I haven't seen any new LILCO vehicles. They're vintage mid-1960s."

An electric clock on a kitchen counter is stopped at the time—11:13—when about 80 percent of LILCO's 925,000 commercial and residential customers lost their electricity nine days ago.

Eileen Loos' mother, Sonia Schrottke, straining her eyes playing a game of solitaire on a table in the living room, tells of the hurricane of 1938, the most severe hurricane to hit Long Island in the twentieth century. It was "many, many times worse than Gloria," says Mrs. Schrottke. "We were living two blocks from the ocean, at Coney Island. The ocean came up to near our house. A tree fell down on the electric lines in front of our house. But we didn't lose electricity then. The electricity in our neighborhood stayed on in thirty-eight."

Coney Island, in Brooklyn on the western portion of Long Island, is provided electricity—as is nearly all of New York City—by the Consolidated Edison Company of New York. New York City, including its boroughs of Brooklyn and Queens on western Long Island, suffered no serious losses of electricity because of Gloria—except for the Rockaway Peninsula in Queens, which is covered by LILCO and so faced a blackout like the rest of the LILCO territory.

The Loos family lives in the hamlet of Noyac on eastern Long Island. It is provided electricity by LILCO like nearly all the rest of Suffolk County, adjoining Nassau County and the Rockaway Peninsula—in all, 85 percent of 120-mile-long Long Island. The exceptions are three villages where there are public power companies: Freeport and Rockville Centre in Nassau County and Greenport in Suffolk County.

These three public power companies, with rates half that of LILCO, are oases of light in the midst of the post-Gloria LILCO darkness. "On the North Fork, where the Village of Greenport has its own utility department with generators, residents had an opportunity to make comparisons that did not come out in LILCO's favor," reports *The Suffolk Times* (published in Greenport). "While virtually everybody else on the North Fork was wondering when they'd have lights or be able to take their next shower, almost every village utility customer had both water and power within about four hours of Gloria's exit."[3]

"LILCO won't even take care of its lines," says Eileen Loos. "We called LILCO a few years ago about a branch rubbing against a line outside. We called several times. The tree was rubbing the insulation bare. LILCO never came. Finally, one day there was a lot of sparks and the branch burned off."

A few miles down the road from the Loos home, Howard Ruths, a barrel-chested veteran lineman, the foreman of a Potomac Edison Company of Virginia crew that has come to Long Island to help restore electricity, speaks in amazement about the LILCO system.

It is a "bunch of junk," is outdated and should have been replaced long ago, he says. The equipment he and his crew from northwest Virginia have been repairing "looks like it hasn't been replaced in a long time." Ruths says it appears to him that LILCO simply has "no maintenance program."

One of Ruths' linemen, John Lewis, says that LILCO apparently doesn't try very hard to prune tree branches to prevent them from striking the lines in a storm. "They don't keep them clear like we do." There has been very little tree trimming, he says.[4]

Further, Lewis notes, LILCO also does not adhere to the practice of Potomac Edison and other utilities of placing automatic tripping devices at intervals throughout distribution systems. LILCO has installed these devices, called oil circuit reclosures, only at its substations. As a result, if a tree falls on a line, power is lost all the way back to the substation—rather than to the nearest tripping device. "It costs more money to put them on the lines," Lewis says of the automatic tripping devices. "But in the long run they pay for themselves."

Hurricane Gloria was no killer—it became "disorganized," reported the National Weather Service, shortly before coming ashore on Long Island. Alistair Cooke, the British-born author and commentator, a Long Islander who also experienced the hurricane of 1938, described Gloria as having "turned out to be a very large bluster."[5]

The major mark it left is what it revealed about the Long Island Lighting Company.

New York Governor Mario Cuomo summed it up eleven days after the hurricane when, with tens of thousands of LILCO customers still without electricity, he was asked in a television interview whether the extended blackout had reduced LILCO's credibility. "It would be difficult for it to reduce its credibility in my eyes," said the Governor, who has opposed the utility's Shoreham project for years. "There's a point beneath which you can't get." Of LILCO, he said: "They can't run anything."

Cuomo was concerned about who would pay for what LILCO claimed as the $40 million cost for restoration of electricity. "LILCO is a private corporation," he said. Its executives "get very big salaries"; there are "shareholders who get dividends. The question is, who should pay for this—a private corporation or their ratepayers? Is it fair to charge the people whose lights were out?" If the blackout was "the fault of the utility," then it should "pick up the expense."[6]

LILCO officials dealt with Hurricane Gloria and its aftermath with the same approach they have long brought to every aspect of LILCO operations: arrogance.

In the days following the hurricane, at the Loos home, at hundreds of thousands of homes and businesses on Long Island, in the view of public officials and newspapers, the company's emphasis on its multi-billion dollar nuclear project at Shoreham at the expense of maintaining its operating system was regarded as the reason for the extended blackout.

"LILCO has placed a greater priority on Shoreham than on providing reliable service to its customers," declared New York State Assemblyman John Behan (a Republican from Montauk). He asserted: "Had LILCO set its priorities straight, perhaps we Long Islanders would not be without power."[7]

State Senator Kenneth LaValle (a Republican from Port Jefferson) told of LILCO ratepayers having seen "their money funneled into a nuclear project they oppose because it represents a threat to their health and safety," and LILCO having ignored "its delivery system— while concentrating on Shoreham." He, too, spoke of the observations of the out-of-town crews who "repeatedly describe LILCO's power distribution system as 'antiquated.' "[8]

Suffolk County Legislator Patrick Heaney said that "the only thing Gloria did was highlight what would have happened eventually in an ice storm because this system was not maintained." The Republican from Hampton Bays noted his "conversations in the field with crews from West Virginia, Pennsylvania, upstate New York, Ohio and other places. Almost to a man they had the same observation: They couldn't believe the condition of LILCO's transmission system. They had never seen such utter chaos and neglect."[9]

County Legislator Gregory Blass, a Jamesport Republican, said that it was apparent that LILCO officials "have channeled all their money for maintenance into Shoreham," leaving their system "a complete mess." He said out-of-state workers he spoke with "expressed shock at the condition of the poles and the wiring, and the generally deteriorated conditions. They said they had never seen anything like it."[10]

Suffolk Life (a weekly newspaper circulated throughout the county) editorialized about the huge Shoreham financial drain having left LILCO "in a shambles. . . . This system is a victim of mindful, deliberate neglect."[11]

The Shoreham/blackout connection was also brought home—in a peculiar way—at the long lines that formed as LILCO distributed dry ice from its utility trucks to people without electricity.

To get dry ice for his warm refrigerator, Bill Wyrick, news director for WRIV Radio in Riverhead, Long Island, headed on Sunday, September 29, to the parking lot at Suffolk County Police Department Headquarters, one of the centers for dry ice distribution.

"By the time I got down there, they were out of ice. That wasn't a big deal; so I missed out on ice," he recounts. "But then I learn from people there that they had been asked to sign statements saying they were in favor of the Shoreham nuclear plant while the ice was being given out. I went into the police station to check it out, and the sergeant at the desk corroborates it: People on the dry ice line had been asked to sign a statement saying, 'Yes, I am in favor of the Shoreham nuclear power plant.' Pretty outrageous, I thought, shocking. I recognized the news value of it right away. I called the LILCO media department. They had no comment. And I went on the air with the story. This was almost using scare tactics to get signatures for Shoreham.

"You'd think the politics of Shoreham would be left out while an emergency situation was going on and people were seeking dry ice for their refrigerators and freezers," concludes Wyrick.[12]

At LILCO headquarters, Dr. William Catacosinos is absent. He is president of LILCO as well as chairman of the board and chief executive officer and, at $275,000 a year, one of the highest-paid utility executives in the United States. Catacosinos ignored the order given to all LILCO employees as the storm approached canceling leaves and vacations, and remained on vacation in Italy. He stayed overseas after the storm came and went, and through much of the blackout.

There was a strong political and public outcry over the power company chief's decision to remain in sunny Italy while there was no power on Long Island. "His absence is inexcusable, his failure to return promptly a serious disregard of his responsibility," said State Senator Caesar Trunzo, a Republican from Brentwood.[13]

Finally, a week after the hurricane, Catacosinos came back and held a press conference at LILCO headquarters in Hicksville.

He strode into the room, giving no appearance of concern about charges of mismanagement. His words buttressed the impression. He defended his own conduct and all LILCO policies. "LILCO is a super organization and an asset to Long Island," declared Catacosinos. It was being "unjustly and unfairly" criticized.[14]

Nothing LILCO did or did not do contributed to the cost of restoring electricity after the hurricane. And that $40 million price of restoration, he said, will be "part of the rate process"—LILCO ratepayers *will* have to pay it.

Reporters noted that to save money for its Shoreham nuclear project, LILCO drastically cut back on maintenance of its system, including tree trimming. The company spent the same in 1984 for tree trimming as it had in 1973, when the dollar was worth twice as much. "No amount of tree trimming could have prevented this from happening," said Catacosinos.

The year before, it was pointed out, Catacosinos instituted an "austerity program" to raise money for Shoreham that resulted in the dismissal of a fifth of LILCO's work force. Those with the job of maintaining the LILCO system were particularly hard hit. "We do not believe," said Catacosinos, "that the 1984 austerity program impacted on our performance."

LILCO, reporters reminded the president, failed to carry insurance to cover it for damage from hurricanes or other storms and instead set up a "storm restoration fund" because it was required to do so by the New York State Public Service Commission in the absence of insurance. However, company officials have admitted that LILCO had taken all the money from that fund, leaving it with a "negative cash flow" when Gloria arrived. Catacosinos said that the utility could not get such insurance—although other utilities have it. He defended the handling of the storm fund.

As to criticism of LILCO's preparation for the hurricane, "everyone is entitled to a point of view."

As to his extended absence, "I came back at an appropriate time to assess this situation."

And then he slid into a pitch for the Shoreham nuclear plant. The evacuation of residents of low-lying South Shore areas showed that "you can evacuate people around Shoreham," claims Catacosinos. "Long Island is continuing to grow, and there's a necessity for more power." Shoreham "is there; it's finished. The money has been invested." He closed by declaring that "LILCO is a good system."

In the aftermath of Gloria, he was one of the very few to feel that way.

"Long Islanders See Red in the Dark," declared the headline in *The New York Times* (October 6, 1985). Gloria, said *The Times*, "exacerbated the already strained relationship between Long Islanders and their utility."

"Paying for LILCO's $40 Million Folly" read the editorial headline in the *Smithtown News* (October 10, 1985), a weekly.

It is obvious from the "let-them-eat-cake" tone of remarks made this week by LILCO Chairman William Catacosinos that he has yet to grasp the breadth and depth of anger and frustration of LILCO customers. . . . For years, the utility has taken profits at the expense of its customers, allowing the system to become antiquated by failing to provide the kind of upkeep it requires. While its executives drew hefty salaries and perks, tree limbs went untrimmed, weak lines were not replaced and no effort was made to begin a system-wide program to put the lines underground.

Declared the *Review* newspapers (a chain of weeklies in Islip and Brookhaven towns in Suffolk): "The one good thing that came from Gloria is that many people's eyes opened to the well-known fact that LILCO is incompetent and inept." The editorial added that "we will be in big trouble" with LILCO operating Shoreham. "The way LILCO has dealt with the hurricane is a special message to all residents of Long Island."[15]

There were demonstrations in front of LILCO offices. At a protest rally in Port Jefferson Station, people chanted: "We want lights now!" and "How can they evacuate, if they can't illuminate."

Yellow ribbons were tied to poles holding powerless LILCO lines, along with placards reading: "Free Our LILCO Hostages."[16]

Everywhere, the tie was made between the hurricane aftermath and the LILCO Shoreham nuclear project. In a *Newsday* story, Judith Earle of Farmingville, her family without electricity for nine days, said: "I'll tell you one thing, if LILCO can't handle Hurricane Gloria, they sure can't handle Shoreham." The *Newsday* reporter, to give an example of the temper of the times, noted Mrs. Earles' comment when she first mistook the reporter for a LILCO representative: " 'Where's your truck?' she snapped, shaking her finger threateningly. When the reporter identified herself as decidedly not from LILCO, she said, 'If you were going to say you were from LILCO, I was going to have to kill you.' The rhetoric is escalating, the words and gestures are growing more threatening."[17]

The Southampton Press, in an editorial entitled "Latest Insult," stated:

> The storm, according to LILCO radio ads, was the worst in the century. It devastated the LILCO system. And LILCO president, Mr. Catacosinos—fresh from a lingering European vacation that even a fuzzy-chinned public relations trainee could have told him should have been cut short—brazenly announced that of course nobody but the ratepayers would be footing the massive bill for the unprecedented clean-up. Despite LILCO's radio announcements, everyone knows that Gloria wasn't the worst hurricane on Long Island in a century. There have been several storms with higher winds and tides over the years . . . the Hurricane of 1938 was the wildest of them all. If Gloria did more damage to LILCO's system than any other storm—which LILCO says it did—then there was more to the destruction than foul weather. Foul planning and short-sighted cost-cutting, all for the sake of the Shoreham nuclear power plant, no doubt had a lot to do with the devastation and inconvenience.
>
> As for Mr. Catacosinos, can't he even bother to be sensitive to the public and delicate with its sensitivities? His lack of concern for public opinion is symptomatic of the arrogance that has led LILCO to all but bankrupt itself in a blind quest to build the most expensive power plant in history and make its

customers among the most put-upon and well fleeced of all the ratepayers in the United States.[18]

The question of why LILCO had not buried its lines was widely asked. The New York Telephone Company in the early 1970s began burying its cables on Long Island because of the vulnerability of Long Island—a slender piece of land jutting out into the Atlantic—to the hurricanes that move up the East Coast with the hurricane season every year.

"We've had hardships, terrible hardships," said Edward Dyer, as he was being treated at Central Suffolk Hospital in Riverhead for dysentery from eating food spoiled in the power outage. "LILCO let us down." The company should have begun burying its lines years ago, should have realized that was necessary on Long Island, he noted, from the hurricane of 1938. "They could have done it street by street, year by year, but instead they put all their money into Shoreham," he said angrily.[19]

The LILCO/Gloria disaster led U.S. Representative Thomas Downey, an Amityville Democrat, to introduce a "Disaster Response Act" in Congress. He spoke of "the famous Boy Scout motto—Be Prepared," and asked, "What can be done about those utilities who ignore those words of wisdom?" His proposed law would mandate that "if the costs of an emergency electrical service and repair are due to poor management, they can't be passed on to the consumer" by the utility that is liable.[20]

Governor Cuomo established a Task Force on Hurricane Gloria and the Long Island Lighting Company to conduct an investigation.

Resolutions were approved by the Suffolk County Legislature that demanded LILCO bury its lines and set up a Suffolk County Commission to Study the Long Island Lighting Company's Preparation for and Response to Hurricane Gloria. A lawsuit charging LILCO with being "grossly negligent" was announced by two legislators.[21]

Meanwhile, *Newsday*, the only daily newspaper on Long Island and, for years, a staunch editorial supporter of LILCO and its Shoreham project—indeed, a key element in defending LILCO and promoting nuclear power on Long Island—ran an editorial entitled "Bashing LILCO Won't Turn the Lights Back On." *Newsday* said, ". . . it's a safe bet that thousands of Long Islanders who are still without electricity today are frustrated, annoyed, impatient and angry at the Long Island Lighting Company," but the paper's editors urged people not to "rush out to stone the nearest LILCO repair truck." And *Newsday* used the occasion of the hurricane to attack the central reason for Suffolk County and New York State opposition to Shoreham: the lack of an adequate evacuation plan. That editorial, four days after the hurricane hit, went on: "The fact is that large areas of Long Island's South Shore were evacuated smoothly and efficiently Thursday night and Friday morning, without a hint of panic or confusion—suggesting, perhaps, another subliminal message: that even a Shoreham emergency could be handled if everyone cooperated."[22]

That's optimism, to say the least. In 1983, Suffolk County concluded after a $600,000 study involving experts around the nation that evacuation was not feasible on Long Island in the event of a major accident at Shoreham. The finding was largely based on the number of people who would be involved if a major nuclear accident occurred at Shoreham on highly populated Long Island and the unique dead-ended geography of Long island and its limited road network. Long Island's one central highway is the misnamed Long Island Expressway, long the butt of jokes for being constantly jammed. The only routes off the "world's largest parking lot" are the few tunnels and bridges, also regularly packed, that link the island at its western end to the New York City boroughs of Manhattan and The Bronx. Since the 1979 Three Mile Island accident, having an evacuation plan in place and ready to be implemented, normally a function of local government, has become the legal responsibility of a company planning to operate a nuclear plant. It has been the main issue blocking the opening of Shoreham.

Newsday's assertions that the storm proved nothing did not sit well with many readers. "Once again we find Newsday snuggling up to the powers that be on Long Island, especially the Long Island Lighting Co.," wrote William Jabanoski of East Meadow in a *Newsday* letter to the editor.[23] Wrote Lester Reisch of Stony Brook: "Newsday continues to be a strong advocate of the Long Island Lighting Co. I wonder how Newsday would feel if their offices and printing plants remained blacked out as my home continues to be."[24] *Newsday* escaped the blackout. The newspaper has its own generator.

Citing "another not-too-subtle example of Newsday's pro-Shoreham and pro-LILCO blind spot," Esther Pank of the Stop Shoreham Campaign in a letter to the editor charged that *Newsday* would make us believe that moving some people away from dangerous wind and flooding conditions with up to 72 hours notice is equal to an emergency evacuation where there's no warning and where there is attendant radiation danger. Long Islanders are smarter than that and are able to make a better distinction in dangers than can Newsday. As we sat in the darkness, held hostage by a crippled utility, we had no intention of going out and bashing the nearest LILCO truck. The workers did the best they could. It is the management at LILCO that is at fault. . . . When LILCO went on austerity because of Shoreham, they mistakenly assured the Public Service Commission that it would not place the delivery system in jeopardy. . . . Just as Newsday is consistent in its praise of LILCO, even in the face of its ineptness, LILCO is consistent in asking the ratepayers to pay for LILCO's continued mismanagement. "Utility bashing" may be a popular sport because people can no longer tolerate this utility.[25]

Laurie Hennessey of Wading River wrote: "The South Shore residents had ample time to evacuate only because meteorologists were able to predict the storm's arrival, giving all of Long Island nearly a week to prepare for the worst. The evacuees also had their choice of facilities to escape to. This is hardly the scenario that would occur should a full-scale evacuation be necessary due to a serious accident at Shoreham."[26]

The *Suffolk Life* newspapers scored "Newsday, LILCO's staunchest ally," for having

. . . tried to slip in that silly logic only four days after Gloria's visit. . . . Newsday, you've got to be kidding! How can anyone equate a hurricane coming up the coast, with days of advance warning and flood waters still far away, with an accident at a nuclear plant and the release of radiation? How can anyone suggest that moving people a few blocks to higher ground is similar to moving people miles away via traffic-clogged roadways?

Suffolk Life also charged that *Newsday* was demonstrating that it

. . . has corrupted its editorial integrity for the benefit of LILCO. . . . The public has suffered enough. LILCO, Newsday, and the Public Service Commission have been partners in the actions that have bred the problems of the recent past. Their preoccupation with putting Shoreham on line has had its impact. Enough is enough. The sins of the past must be corrected. [27]

Governor Cuomo's task force established that utility bashing in LILCO's case was in order. [28] The panel criticized LILCO's management and connected the extended post-Gloria blackout to its decisions, especially the drain of funds to Shoreham. The panel warned that due to the dismal condition of the LILCO system, more storm-connected disasters could lie ahead. "Because of the extreme vulnerability of LILCO's transmission and distribution system, a major ice storm this winter could bring about a new disaster of even greater proportions."

By 1975, the task force reported, the Shoreham project was fully underway, and LILCO was straining to pay its costs. It cut back sharply on system maintenance—and has continued with deep maintenance cuts ever since. The report cited State Public Service Commission rulings and analyses that found "that the company's tree-trimming expenditures, in constant dollars, had fallen significantly in each year since 1975 and that service reliability had declined.

"Other preventive maintenance activities showed a similar pattern of decline," including "pole inspection and replacement, wire insulation and maintenance." In all these "vital areas . . . significant reductions were effected," particularly during the austerity program ordered by Catacosinos in 1984 to raise money for the nuclear project.

The State Public Service Commission, meanwhile, was regularly granting "the company emergency cash flow relief to finance its construction program" at Shoreham. A margin of profit was not the problem: "In the 12 months ended September 30, 1984, LILCO earned a return of 15.5% on its rate base, compared with an allowable return of 12.9%," says the report. "This difference represents excess earnings of approximately $87 billion."

Not only have millions of dollars needed for system maintenance gone to build Shoreham, but to promote it as well, said the task force.

LILCO's reduction in expenditures in distribution system reliability and customer services stands in marked contrast to its expenditures on political lobbying and public relations campaigns to promote Shoreham. It is estimated that LILCO has spent about $2 million on such items in 1985. That $2 million represents the approximate shortfall in 1985 tree-trimming expenditures compared with 1982 levels. Further, it is four times the $500,000 shortfall from pre-austerity expenditures on the company's distribution system improvement program. Thus, there clearly is a need to examine LILCO's spending priorities both generally and in light of the extended outages resulting from Hurricane Gloria.[29]

LILCO, because of the drain of money to Shoreham, did not have such essential replacement items on hand as poles, transformers and wire when Gloria struck, said sources in the company. And its credit with suppliers was described as being so bad that, in the days after Gloria when it rushed to obtain these items, in many instances it was asked to pay in cash and to settle old debts before sales were made.

The Suffolk County hurricane commission reported a failure in "planning and execution" by LILCO's management. "This failure at the highest levels of management at LILCO has manifested itself in the utility's fall," its report stated. "Management's lack of performance in this instance is symptomatic of a larger problem—lack of accountability," said the panel. It recommended that all of Long Island consider following the lead of the Long Island villages that had power despite Gloria and develop publicly owned utilities. It "strongly urges . . . an in-depth look at the issue of a public power takeover of LILCO."

The chairman of this commission was Deputy Suffolk County Executive Frank Jones, who said:

> There's no question in my mind and the commission's mind that LILCO . . . was grossly negligent in allowing its system to deteriorate while diverting money for Shoreham. It was grossly negligent in response to the storm, in informing governments and people on what was happening. It would not submit information to governments on what restoration was going on. In its hurricane plan it has a provision to send sound trucks though communities to tell people what is going on. It arbitrarily decided not to. People were literally left in the dark.[30]

"There was no program to contact people on life support equipment. And one woman on life support died," Jones continued. "We found a total disregard by LILCO. What we couldn't find," he said with regret, "was gross negligence in the legal sense."

The hurricane presented a "typical LILCO performance," said Jones.

> Here—as LILCO has been doing year after year—was LILCO stonewalling governments, stonewalling people, treating every-one arrogantly. It was the usual arrogant LILCO attitude that what's good for LILCO is good. That's all that concerns them. They don't want to be accountable for their actions to anybody.

Hurricane Gloria was not a natural disaster. It was—as many headlines stated in the storm's wake—a "LILCO DISASTER." It was a LILCO disaster affecting millions that had long been in the making. It was not the only disaster LILCO has been asking for.

NOTES

1. The following comments are from a visit and interviews with the Loos family, October 1985.
2. Letter from Bruce W. Reisman, Direct Manager/Public Relations for New York Telephone to the author, March 5, 1986:
   > New York Telephone began placing cable underground wherever feasible in the early 1970s in connection with a nationwide trend to avoid visual pollution and increased corporate concerns for cost-reduction. . . . Cost studies clearly indicated to us that it would simply be less costly for us over the long term to place much of our telephone cables underground. It is generally less expensive to maintain a telephone plant when it is underground. This is because underground facilities are less likely to be damaged by falling trees or branches, high winds, ice storms, etc. . . . The majority of our telephone cables on Long Island (69 percent) is now underground. This appears to have benefitted us during Hurricane Gloria. Despite the hurricane, we were able to maintain telephone service for about 96 percent of our more than one million Long Island customers.
3. *The Suffolk Times*, October 3, 1985.
4. Potomac Edison Company foreman Howard Ruths and lineman John Lewis made their comments to Peter Cunningham, a reporter for *The Southampton Press*, in article published October 10, 1985.
5. *Newsday*, September 28, 1985.
6. Gov. Mario Cuomo's remarks were reported in *Newsday*, October 7, 1985.
7. Column of State Assemblyman John Behan written for Long Island weekly newspapers for week of October 14, 1985.
8. State Senator Kenneth LaValle's comments were made in a press release he issued October 9, 1985.

9. Patrick Heaney in an interview with the author, October 1985.
10. Gregory Blass in an interview with the author, October 1985, and also in interview with John Rather of *The New York Times*, published October 6, 1985.
11. *Suffolk Life*, October 9, 1985.
12. Bob Wyrick's comments were made in an interview with the author, October 1985.
13. From Sen. Caezar Trunzo's weekly newspaper column for week of October 21, 1985.
14. William Catacosinos' comments, here and following, at his press conference upon returning from Italy are quoted from *The New York Times* and *Newsday*, October 8, 1985.
15. Editorial in the *Review* newspapers, October 10, 1985.
16. *Suffolk Life*, October 9, 1985.
17. *Newsday*, October 6, 1985.
18. *Southampton Press*, October 10, 1985.
19. Interview with Edward Dyer, *The News-Review* of Riverhead, October 10, 1985.
20. Rep. Tom Downey's comments were made in a statement released by his office, October 14, 1985.
21. A resolution introduced before the Suffolk Legislature demanding that LILCO bury its line was written by Legislator Donald Allgrove, Republican of Smithtown. A resolution setting up county commission to investigative LILCO and Hurricane Gloria was introduced by Legislators Gerald Blass, Republican of Lindenhurst, and Patrick Mahoney, Republican of Bay Shore. Both were passed on October 8, 1985. Suffolk Legislators James Morgo, Democrat of Bayport, and Sondra Bachety, Democrat of Deer Park, announced a lawsuit against LILCO in the *Review* newspapers, October 17, 1985.
22. *Newsday*, October 1, 1985.
23. *Newsday*, October 8, 1985.
24. *Newsday*, October 8, 1985.
25. *Newsday*, October 15, 1985.
26. Laurie Hennessey letter, *Newsday*, October 21, 1985.
27. *Suffolk Life*, October 9, 1985.
28. From a report by Governor Cuomo's Task Force on Hurricane Gloria and the Long Island Lighting Company, issued October 22, 1985.
29. From a report of the Suffolk County Commission Established per Legislative Resolution 868–1985 to Study the Long Island Lighting Company's Preparation for and Response to Hurricane Gloria, issued December 10, 1985.
30. Frank Jones in an interview with the author, January 1986.

2

THE MESS
AT
SHOREHAM

"No doubt about it, there is catastrophe ahead," said George W. Henry, a former LILCO quality control inspector at Shoreham. "Shoreham is a nuclear plant constructed without compliance to federal and industrial standards. It has been built the LILCO way—do it quick, get it done and the hell with standards." The plant "constitutes a grave threat."[1]

Henry testified under oath before the Suffolk County Legislature in 1985, along with a second former Shoreham inspector, Ronald Stanchfield. Both told of widespread defects in the plant and provided documents to substantiate their charges.

A third ex-inspector, who worked in a high supervisory capacity at Shoreham for nearly ten years, then came forward and made similar allegations, also providing documentation.

A number of Shoreham workers have come forward through the years also maintaining that Shoreham is riddled with defects.

Other evidence that Shoreham has widespread problems involves what became known as the Shoreham "dump documents"—more than 1,000 engineering reports from the plant, citing problems in construction and found in a box in a Long Island dump. MHB Technical Associates of San Jose, California, a firm composed of three former engineering supervisors at the Nuclear Energy Division of the General Electric Company (manufacturer of the Shoreham reactor) examined the documents. Dale Bridenbaugh of MHB said that the reports underlined to him "the importance, the vital importance, of an intense, independent investigation of that job. That is what the NRC is supposed to be doing, but they don't do very much of its."[2] Dr. Michio Kaku, professor of nuclear physics at the City University of New York Graduate Center, whom I interviewed after he studied the documents in May 1979, said: "These reports reveal an absolutely outrageous pattern of shoddy work. They are damning. . . . What are involved are most serious problems in the most sensitive areas of the reactor."

A top Nuclear Regulatory Commission inspector, James H. Conran, blew the whistle on LILCO and testified under oath at NRC licensing hearings on Shoreham in 1983 "that LILCO truly does not understand what is required minimally for safety."[3] This deeply upset the administration of the NRC staff, which has a policy of allowing utilities, by and large, to enforce regulations without outside interference. The NRC staff normally accepts whatever a utility does and bases most of its inspections not on checking work or equipment firsthand but on going through a utility's "paperwork."

A two-year investigation of Shoreham paperwork filed in a government-established "public document room" showed, according to the two persons who conducted it, "fundamental flaws in Shoreham construction" reflected in those documents.[4]

There is also the matter of allegations of organized crime's involvement in the plant's construction.

LILCO, meanwhile, has steadfastly refused to allow independent investigators into the plant to conduct a physical investigation of construction.

There is also an issue involving where the plant was built: right on top of an artesian or free-flowing well on water-saturated land highly vulnerable to earth movements. LILCO had claimed earthquakes in the area are highly unlikely, but in 1981, there was an earthquake with an epicenter in the Long Island Sound twenty-six miles from the plant. "If you searched, it would be very hard to find a worse site on Long Island for a nuclear plant," said Steven Englebright, curator of geology at the State University of New York at Stony Brook.[5]

In addition, when the plant underwent "low-power" testing there were a series of mishaps, some of which, if they had occurred when the plant was operating at full power, could have been extremely serious.

Victor J. Yannacone, Jr., is a feisty Long Island attorney who in the 1960s led the legal battle—starting on Long Island—that resulted in DDT being outlawed in the United States. In recent years, he initiated the legal action of Vietnam War veterans over Agent Orange that ended in a multi-million dollar settlement. He called to say there was someone in his office he wanted me to see: George Henry.[6]

"It's not that I'm anti-nuclear," Henry stressed, sitting on the couch in my living room with his wife, Vickiann, who, like her husband, worked for LILCO at Shoreham. He said he still supported nuclear power as long as it is "handled properly." At Shoreham, he said, nuclear power has been handled totally improperly.

Major components of the plant—including many critical safety systems—are below standards, he said. Serious defects in the plant's construction have been ignored or "rubberstamped" through.

Among the Shoreham documents Henry had with him were numerous reports of defects in Shoreham's backup diesel generators, reports made while LILCO was claiming that the diesels—which later broke down in tests—were fine. There were color photographs of Shoreham's uranium fuel rods, many of which, said Henry, have defects that could lead to catastrophic accidents but were approved for use anyway. And on and on.

"Towards the end, things really began to fall apart," related Henry. "The attitude was: 'Let's get the plant on line. The company can't afford to float this turkey any longer. If things do not meet the criteria, it doesn't matter. We are on a critical path.' "

Inspectors attempting to enforce proper standards, he said, have been routinely discharged—including, ultimately, himself. The deciding factor for him, said Henry, involved defects in the diesel generators. "I pointed to problems with the diesels for a year and a half. I wrote several violations." Then he was present when a diesel was tested in 1983, and the kind of serious problem he expected occurred. Its twenty-foot long, two-foot wide crankshaft broke in half. And he was "escorted off site" the next day. "They didn't want me there any longer pointing out the problems."

Backup diesels to generate electricity are a critical element in a nuclear plant. They must go into action at once if there is a mishap causing the normal nuclear-generated electricity operating a plant to fail. If the backup diesels also fail, the coolant water in a nuclear plant ceases to flow and other vital systems stop, which can result in a loss-of-coolant accident and core meltdown.

Henry told of going to LILCO higher-ups about what was happening on the project, but they were not concerned. He went to NRC inspectors, and "they didn't give a damn."

Subsequently, LILCO "went after" his wife, who worked at Shoreham as a documentation clerk keeping track, with a computer, of much of the paperwork on the project.

"First some of my work was pulled," Vickiann Henry said. "They kept certain documents from me. Then there was a lot of harassment." Finally, she was fired, too.

They hadn't sought out a reporter before because, like many people, neither had ever had contact with a journalist, and to arrange to see one was something outside their experience. Meanwhile, said Henry, they presumed the "big guys"—Suffolk County and New York State—would be able to deal with Shoreham. So he went to the lawyers representing Suffolk County on Shoreham and offered his expertise.

Finally, the plant had been loaded with nuclear fuel and was at the brink of operating, and as two people who have long called Long Island home, the Henrys viewed it as an imminent threat to themselves and their families. They had been seeing Yannacone on a civil legal matter, and during the course of that conference they mentioned to him that they had worked at Shoreham and spoke of some of their experiences. Yannacone urged them to call me.

I broke the Henry story and several investigations began, including one by the NRC. A week later, Ronald Stanchfield called. He had read my story about Henry, had also been a Shoreham inspector, and had "similar experiences," he said.[7]

He said he had been in engineering for fifteen years and had done engineering work at six nuclear facilities including Waterford in Louisiana, Surrey in Virginia and Braidwood and Byron in Illinois. He said he had never seen the kinds of deficiencies such as those he saw at Shoreham.

"Over the years I have been with incompetent people, but I've never seen incompetence *en masse* as goes on at Shoreham." Like Henry, he said, "I am not opposed to nuclear power, but what is going on at Shoreham is something else."

Stanchfield said he worked at Shoreham as a quality assurance engineer for two months before he was fired for complaining that people with inadequate engineering backgrounds were being hired as inspectors and then given poor training. He switched his job to electrical designer for another contractor on the project and did that for nine months.

At Shoreham, he said, he saw "numerous engineering and construction practices not consistent with nuclear plant construction standards. Shoreham is poorly conceived and poorly constructed. I've been around good plants, and the fact of the matter is that Shoreham is a real lemon." He said he "wouldn't be surprised if it starts coming apart in pieces, if they let it go on line." He said there was "no self-monitoring, no self-discipline" on the project, and he found LILCO "belligerently arrogant."

He resigned after LILCO issued a press release in the wake of the October 21, 1981, earthquake saying that no tremors were felt at the Shoreham reactor from the quake that registered 3.4 on the Richter scale. He showed me his letter of resignation to L. K. Comstock of Pittsburgh, a principal contractor at Shoreham. It declared:

> LILCO's whitewash of last week's earthquake is the final straw to my departure. I was in the reactor building when the tremors occurred and, without question, the earthquake was felt by hundreds of workers in all the buildings, including the Reactor Building. . . . As a longtime resident of eastern Long Island, I cannot let LILCO's blatant irresponsibility to the community go unanswered.

Stanchfield said he did not want to "sound holier than thou, but I have experience. And the whole thing up there at Shoreham is an absurdity."

A special session of the Suffolk County Legislature was held to hear the charges of the two former inspectors, who had not known each other at Shoreham and had not met until the day of the meeting.[8]

After being sworn in, Henry testified: "I intended to be a Long Island Lighting Company career employee, to work at the Shoreham nuclear power station. I am a science graduate of Dowling College in Oakdale, Long Island, and I have always been mechanically inclined and believed—and still do—in nuclear power as a viable source of energy, at least, if handled properly."

He said that he began working for LILCO during summers while at Dowling and, in 1980, received a full-time position as a LILCO accounts representative. Thereafter, he applied for a position as quality control inspector at Shoreham.

> I was accepted, and I reported to Shoreham in July of 1981. My training involved instruction at Shoreham and at LILCO's Hauppauge Training Center. The training included instruction

in: Magnetic Particle Testing, Liquid Penetrant Testing, Leak Testing, Welding Inspection, Visual Examination Crimping Qualification, all taught by LILCO instructors; Boiling Water Reactor Familiarization, taught by Nuclear Utility Services; Nuclear Fuel Bundle Inspection, taught by General Electric; Fire Protection for Power Plants, taught by Professional Loss Control, Inc.; and the Operational Quality Assurance Indoctrination and Training, and Basic Supervisory Training, both by LILCO.

He said he received his American National Standards Institute Level I Certification as a nuclear plant quality control inspector that year, and in 1982, he was certified a Level II inspector. He presented to the legislature copies of those certifications and also examination records from his training. The records showed grades in the high 80s and 90s.

Henry said it was during training that he "began to question the independence of the quality assurance program LILCO was conducting for Shoreham. The Code of Federal Regulations 10 CFR Appendix B—Criteria 1 states clearly that a quality assurance program for a nuclear project must be 'independent of cost and scheduling.'

"In LILCO's program, however," he said, "the inspectors-in-training, indeed graduate inspectors and supervisors, were directly manipulated by LILCO's plant management, LILCO's Start-Up Organization, plus we were all LILCO's employees. When I questioned this, I was told this is how the program is set up and the way it is run. I failed to see this as an excuse.

"Working at the plant as an inspector," he continued, "I quickly discovered how the plant was being constructed without compliance with the Code of Federal Regulations as well as the standards of nuclear plant construction set by the American Society of Mechanical Engineers, Institute of Electrical and Electronic Engineers, the American National Standards Institute, among other standards."

As an example, he cited the case of a "critical check valve, part of the hydrogen recombining system" which was found to be "in violation. The valve didn't seat properly. It was returned to its manufacturer, the Velan Corporation of Montreal, Canada for re-manufacture. However, it came back worse than before. But because it was a $60,000 valve, LILCO managers didn't want to send it back again for additional work."

The "attitude was: 'Let's get the plant on line. The company can't afford any further delays. If things do not meet criteria, it doesn't matter. We are on a critical path.' Meanwhile," said Henry, "the entire point of quality assurance is for the job to be done independently, free from cost and scheduling concerns. However, at Shoreham, inspectors were constantly being pressured, manipulated, expected to conform to a policy of approving slipshod construction— even though that construction may jeopardize the integrity of the reactor and the plant and public health and safety."

He cited the case of a motor-operated valve that was found not to open or close in the required time. "This valve is part of a critical safety system for the reactor involving high pressure coolant injection." A 1983 violation report on this valve, which he presented to the legislature, "sat in the files while there was no action to repair the valve." On May 28, 1983, said Henry, he filed a "surveillance report" describing the valve as "still unsatisfactory."

He turned over this report to the legislature, pointing out that his supervisor, Arthur R. Muller, LILCO's director of quality control at Shoreham, had written on it: "George, Cut the Shit" and then, "The CAR [Corrective Action Report] was dispositioned 11/9/83. Don't play games on QA documents. Rewrite."

"Speaking of playing games, the supposed disposition [final determination] was to be in the future," Henry pointed out, noting that "11/9/83 was six months in the future."

"I confronted my supervisor on how he could approve this valve— in the future," said Henry. Muller, he said, "claimed that the LILCO Start-Up Organization would 'take care' of the violation in the future.

"I said, 'What procedures allow quality assurance to disposition a violation based on a future possibility?'

"He could show me none," Henry went on. "The operative philosophy here, as with so much at Shoreham, was rubberstamp it, let it go through, change the procedures, if necessary, to match the violation."

Henry spoke of deficiencies in the backup diesels.

For a year and a half, I pointed to problems with those diesels. . . . I wrote several violations. I was present in August 1983 when one of the diesels was tested and the sort of major breakdown I had anticipated came to pass. The diesel began vibrating, but the test engineer refused to stop the test, maintaining that the diesel had six hours left of testing before it

ALCO

OPERATIONAL QUALITY ASSURANCE
SURVEILLANCE PLAN

STATION OQA REPRESENTATIVE(S): George W Henry

ORGANIZATION(S) UNDER SURVEILLANCE: Start-up + Plant Staff

FILE: 1A11-920-LIM-SU-001 6.942

Surv. No. 83-27

TYPE OF ACTIVITY: OQA CAR Response Follow-up

SURVEILLANCE DATE: 5-28-83

ITEM NO.	ATTRIBUTE	REFERENCE	SAT	UN-SAT	N/A	REMARKS
1	Assure that all new CARs or newly dispositioned CARs are entered in the CAR Log		X			Verified new cars 042 and 043 entered in log. Also newly dispositioned 042 and 043.
2	Verify that new CARs are responded to within a prescribed amount of time or that a letter requesting an extension is available		X			Verified new car responded to 041, 042 and 043.
3	Verify that corrective action dates are being met or that a letter requesting an extension is available			X		Verified cars corrective action dates are being met with one outstanding 040 which is not closed and no extension granted.
4	Verify that corrective action has been accomplished as stated in the response.			X		see above attribute 3 remarks.

(handwritten across reference column) George cut the Sh.t the CAR 40 was Dispositive at 11/9/83. Don't play games on QA documents Rewrite

cc GWH file

Attached copy of CAR 40 status as of 5-28-83

Fail to see justification of above comment

SUBMITTED BY:

Shoreham inspection report on which the "corrective action" was made six months in the future.

would pass the first Nuclear Regulatory Commission test run of it. The test only ended as the diesel, indeed, underwent a major breakdown. Its crankshaft severed in two.

"I was suspended," said Henry, "in my view, for being outspoken, honest, not playing an improper game—for doing my job as an inspector."

He said that in his "years at LILCO, I had an impeccable record with the company. I was sick maybe two days during my term of employment. I had excellent reviews." So he wrote to then LILCO President Wilfred O. Uhl "to see him about what was going on at Shoreham, and what was being done to me. A meeting was arranged with LILCO Vice President Matthew S. Procelli. I explained to Mr. Procelli what was happening and showed him some of the same documents I am showing you today," recounted Henry. "What did he tell me? He explained to me that what was involved was in a 'gray area.'

"Well, there is no gray area when it comes to nuclear power and public safety," declared Henry. "The procedures followed are either right or wrong. The regulations are clear and concise. Procedures, machinery must meet criteria or not.

"The meeting ended," Henry went on, "with me telling Mr. Procelli that it was obvious that the problems at Shoreham were not just at Shoreham but reflected an attitude and policy that came from the top management of the company. At Shoreham, you had the specifications and the right way to do things—and the LILCO way.

"I was informed a month later that I was being discharged from LILCO for not properly logging in and out of buildings on site," he said, adding that he then went to the New York State Department of Labor, which dismissed the claim. He handed the legislature a copy of the decision in which the administrative law judge ruled that "the evidence herein fails to demonstrate behavior on the part of claimant which amounted to misconduct in the course of his employment."

He then related going to Suffolk County's lawyers on Shoreham and how they were particularly interested in having him review testimony on quality assurance at the plant given by LILCO executives before the NRC's Atomic Safety and Licensing Board. He said he marked portions of the testimony which were "untrue."

He also told of having gone to the NRC. "I found the NRC inspectors didn't care about the serious problems at Shoreham. They had a lax attitude," said Henry. "Their view was, in effect, 'All the plants have problems. It's no big deal.' "

Since the press accounts of his disclosures, the NRC had come to him. "Now, all of a sudden, the NRC is concerned." Henry doubted the sincerity of the agency. He noted that when an NRC supervisor, Jack Strosnider called, "I told him that the first thing the NRC should do is carefully review the testimony before the Atomic Safety and Licensing Board by LILCO executives. I was told, 'Do you know how long that would take?' I told him that if the NRC had done its job, all along, we wouldn't be in this dilemma today, that it was necessary to do an in-depth audit of the quality assurance program at Shoreham—starting with the testimony before the NRC."

Henry went on to "other serious problems at Shoreham."

He spoke of "defects in the fuel rods. I was involved in inspecting the rods. Some do not have the proper zirconium cladding. Some had gouges. Some had improper spacing for water flow. Such problems can lead to hot spots, breakdowns in the rods themselves—huge problems if the rods become distorted and are not being cooled. Some of the fuel rods were remanufactured on the spot. Others were dispositioned by paperwork."

Then, there is "the matter of the decontamination area for vehicles," a parking lot built by LILCO near the plant. In the lot, "vehicles would be hosed down. The area is supposed to be lined with a catch basin of fiberglass. It is not. When the radioactive debris is washed off vehicles in that area, the radioactivity will go right into the groundwater," which is the only source for drinking water on Long Island.

He noted that he had "stressed the lack of independent inspection at Shoreham. Another example of this is the situation involving LPL Technical Services of Great Neck [Long Island], which provides inspectors for nuclear plants all over the world. At Shoreham there has been a systematic program of hiring LPL inspectors as an adjunct to LILCO inspectors, but then discharging them when they were strict on standards. Jeff Randalls of LPL once told me, 'LILCO Start-Up pulls the trigger, and away goes the inspector.' "

Henry pointed out that "Suffolk County has been concerned about the issue of evacuation in the event of a serious accident at Shoreham. You surely should be," he continued. "In 1983, I participated in an evacuation drill. Members of the Shoreham nuclear power station's Radiochemistry and Health Physics Departments were, based on prevailing winds from the west, calling for an evacuation of western Long Island. I noted that if the wind was coming out of the west, there would be an evacuation in the east—not the west. The calculations were rechecked, and it was announced that, yes, they were in error."

He spoke about sirens "which are supposed to signal an evacuation, warn the public. Don't count on them. The motor in each siren is rated at 3,500 rpm but coupled to a reduction gear rated at a maximum of 1,700 rpm. How long are those sirens going to last being driven at more than 100 percent their maximum rpm? . . .

"I began by noting that I intended to be a career LILCO employee," Henry testified. "I am ashamed of that utility. I hear LILCO management is now trying to claim I am a disgruntled employee. I am not disgruntled. I am concerned with what this company is doing to Long Island, what it is doing to itself, what by its dereliction at Shoreham it stands to do to the millions of people who live in the shadow of that improperly built nuclear plant."

He concluded: "A large majority of the people of Long Island are against the Shoreham nuclear power station, believing that it represents a threat to their health and safety. Before going to work at the Shoreham nuclear power station, I thought this was not correct. Now I know the people are right."

Ronald Stanchfield was then sworn in. He began by telling how "since 1963, I have worked for numerous engineering firms and engineering departments of corporations throughout the country." He gave a list.

In a majority of these companies I was placed for a specific period of time by a contract services firm, usually on a "task force" basis, usually with extensive overtime and usually at a premium rate of pay. My job titles have been all of the following: draftsman, structural designer, checker, electrical designer, preparer/evaluator, construction manager, project architect, project level structural designer and quality assurance engineer.

He said he has "enjoyed security clearance" from the Electric Boat Division of General Dynamics, "where I was a structural designer on the Trident submarine, and I received top security clearance on the ICBM Sentinel System at Ammann & Whitney. I hold letters of reference from some of the top engineers in the country. I count among my friends architects and engineers who are critically placed both in industry and education and who, I am proud to say, help shape our future. I have the highest respect for them and, I dare say, they respect me."

He stated that in 1980, "at a party in Southampton, I met three quality assurance engineers who were working at the Shoreham nuclear power station." He was then commuting weekly, he said, from Long Island to a job in Pennsylvania. "Having heard of my engineering background, and knowing about the inconvenience of the weekly commute . . . they urged me to submit a resumé to Courter & Company," the main piping contractor at Shoreham and their employer. "They assured me that my qualifications were ample for the job and confided to me that they, in fact, had little or no technical experience and that the same was true of 'many quality assurance engineers on site.' "

A few days after submitting his resumé, Stanchfield was informed that he was hired as a quality assurance engineer at Shoreham. "Enthusiastically, I went to work on the first day of the new job at Courter and went through the procedures of getting a badge, going through a brief orientation and being told that I would have to spend the first few weeks in classes, learning about quality assurance procedures. On the second or third day on the job, things started to become a bit questionable."

The classes given by Courter basically involved an instructor "reading from procedures and, more often than not, he would mumble through the material at a very rapid pace," said Stanchfield. "There was never any real instruction." Further, when it came time to take an examination, inspectors-to-be were told to go to a construction trailer to complete the test. At the trailer, quality assurance engineers were present and they "offered answers."

Testified Stanchfield: "At this point the entire picture became very clear to me. Through complicity, the company was hiring people with little or no technical background, walking them through the procedures, and then giving them full opportunity to pass the qualification test." Nevertheless, he said, he was "the only one to pass on that first day." However, the next day, the other six people in the class "retook and passed the examination."

He said he mentioned the casualness of the training operation to his supervisor. "In response, he took an extremely belligerent attitude and told me on more than one occasion to 'forget about it, go to your desk and shut up. This is the way we do things around here.'

The supervisor also made it clear that 'I get rid of troublemakers quickly.' "

Stanchfield said he "directed a number of official communications" about the operation up the chain of command of Courter, which has its headquarters in Brooklyn, New York. As a former Marine, he said, he has "respect for the chain of command." But, he said he "got nowhere" so he "went to the top" and wrote directly to the president of Courter. The result, he said, was that Courter corporation's overall quality assurance manager came to Shoreham to see him.

"The first words out of his mouth," Stanchfield testified, "were 'Who the fuck do you think you are, Stanchfield?' For about five minutes he continued to intimidate me, and then he introduced himself. For the next two hours I proceeded to tell him all the areas of question that I had at Courter which were directly related to the quality assurance program. I explained to him that it was my belief that a number of individuals who were now certified quality assurance engineers had probably falsified their resumés, and I gave him the names of two individuals who had told me of falsified resumés. I also told him of the lax procedures regarding testing. . . . He had, by the end of the meeting, enough information to pursue the problems that I talked about. A week later, I was fired. Because I had sensed an impending firing from Courter, I submitted my resumé to another contractor on the site, L. K. Comstock." A week after being fired from Courter, Stanchfield was hired by Comstock.

As an electrical designer for Comstock, Stanchfield said "my design responsibilities were such that I would have to climb throughout different areas" in the Shoreham reactor building "in order to best fit a new design. I began to find that items that were supposed to be in one place were in another place. Although this is sometimes acceptable, it seemed to me that it was occurring too frequently." Stanchfield said he mentioned this to his supervisor who "either didn't know of the discrepancies or didn't care about them. In some instances, he even told me that what I had seen wasn't there. When I would invite him to inspect the area I was talking about, he would decline."

Stanchfield said that as he continued "to find discrepancies in both the design and construction" of the reactor building and informed his supervisor about what he found, he faced hostility. On one occasion, the supervisor "became very belligerent to me and repeatedly poked at my shoulder and told me not to make waves. He told me also that he was going to have me fired."

On October 21, 1981, Stanchfield had been in the reactor building, and he "felt a strong quivering motion and a sudden jerk, like something had fallen. I assumed it was simply a strange construction jerking, a result of a machine falling in another area. Later in the day it was reported that an earthquake with an epicenter in the middle of the Long Island Sound had occurred. It was generally agreed that most people on site had felt it."

But on the day of the earthquake, "LILCO sent out a press release" which stated that—he produced a copy of the release and read from it—"None of the tremor from today's quake was felt in the reactor building at the Shoreham nuclear power plant."

"But I felt the tremors," Stanchfield declared. "LILCO's press release was a lie."

Also on the day of the earthquake, "in the westerly construction staircase" of the reactor building, he said, he noticed "a flood of water pouring down the stairs."

He then turned over a copy of his letter of resignation to the legislators.

He concluded:

> What I have just stated has all been fact. If you will indulge me a few more minutes, I would like to express an opinion. What happened at Shoreham, and what is probably still happening out at Shoreham, is a crime. Regardless of the nature of crime, you the legislators, you the lawmakers, must use your power to stop it. From what I understand of law and police procedures, when a crime occurs, the area is first and foremost cordoned off. Then an investigative unit is sent in to take evidence. The area in question is never left open to the alleged criminals so that they may cover up their crimes. Yet this is what is happening at Shoreham. We have been giving the criminals years and years of freedom to cover their tracks. This is absurd. And what is more absurd is that this power plant has already robbed the people of over $4 billion. And it sits there belligerently threatening our very lives. And the crime goes on.

There were questions from the legislators and answers from the ex-inspectors. Henry was asked why he had not come forward earlier. He said he had gone to Suffolk County's lawyers on Shoreham and had felt the "big guys"—Suffolk and New York State—would handle the situation. Now, however, because "we are coming down to the wire" and with the NRC ready to allow LILCO to begin operating Shoreham at low power, he felt he had a responsibility to come forward. "I happen to have the facts and information to show that the plant does not deserve an operating license and LILCO does not deserve to operate the plant," he said.

Stanchfield said that "in all probability, I don't expect to get a job in the nuclear field again."

Soon after that meeting, I received a call from County Legislator James Morgo that a former supervisory inspector at Shoreham wanted to see me.

We met at the Bayport Democrat's office with the legislator present during the interview. This ex-inspector said he did not want to be identified publicly because, he said, he believed that he and/or members of his family would be injured or killed if his identity became known.

The former inspector, a nuclear engineer with long experience in the nuclear industry—he listed a string of nuclear projects he was involved in—said that since working at Shoreham, because of his deep concern about what he witnessed there, he has gone into other engineering work. "The reason I got out of the nuclear field," he said, "is that I don't want the kind of things I saw at Shoreham on my conscience."[9]

He noted that he holds Level III Certification from the American National Standards Institute, the highest such certification given. Morgo, a teacher before becoming a legislator, said he had long known the ex-inspector as an "upstanding citizen."

The former inspector said he spent considerably more time working at Shoreham than did Henry and Stanchfield, almost ten years, and the situation, he said, was even worse than they knew. Fewer than half of the mistakes made and defects found at Shoreham—he said there were hundreds of thousands registered on various "deficiency" and "nonconformity" reports and "engineering and design coordination reports"—have been corrected. "They've been phonied up, covered up, dummied up."

He charged:

• The main feedwater system that is to bring coolant water from the Long Island Sound into the plant's reactor is defective. Welds of the copper-nickel pipe "never could get through inspection; the welds kept cracking." Concrete was poured over the pipe and it was buried.

• Although the American Society of Mechanical Engineers' standard calls for no more than three attempts to repair any one weld on a pipe—after that the pipe must be cut and a new piece of pipe welded in—routinely at Shoreham "welds were gone over six, seven, nine times" and often still were not repaired and were left faulty.

• "Half the pumps at Shoreham have defects," particularly cracked castings, and a similar percentage of valves have major problems including "the four main steam valves."

• The stainless steel shield wall built around the reactor pressure vessel and containment is "totally inadequate. Heat could never be maintained for proper welding on that shield wall. There were numerous cracks," which, he said, were not repaired per standards.

• Many top officials on the project have had no experience in nuclear construction, and the same with many workers. He cited the case of a file clerk who became supervisor of welding. He spoke of the steamfitters on the job, "who came out of New York City putting steam lines into buildings. Because they knew nothing about nuclear plant construction, for five years they used chloride pens to mark pipes even though the NRC prohibits such pens in nuclear plant work because they have a corrosive effect on piping."

He had with him a box of documents from the project. He pulled various documents out to buttress his points.

The former inspector emphasized: "I have nothing against LILCO and nothing against nuclear power—if done right." At Shoreham, he stated, as Henry and Stanchfield also maintained, government and industrial standards have not been followed, and that has occurred on a widespread basis.

"That place needs to be physically examined, and not by LILCO," he said. An NRC inspection would also prove meaningless. "The NRC is a big farce." An inspection should be done by people "who can't be reached."

Morgo asked: "Is this why LILCO hasn't wanted an independent inspection?"

"That's right," he replied.

Morgo and I, repeatedly during the interview, asked the former supervising inspector to come forward by name. "I can't," he said. "I won't. I could name you fifty other guys who also have this kind of information. They can't come out in public either. They fear for their families. They fear getting a bomb through a window. Jim, you know me. I don't BS. I don't play games. I'm dead serious. We're talking about billions of dollars and racketeers."

Before we parted, the ex-inspector made reference to the Shoreham "dump documents" that I had written about a few years earlier. "I remember reading LILCO's comment that they were just copies of documents at the plant," he said. "You should know, those documents were dumped."

Besides the three inspectors, Shoreham workers that have come forward to blow the whistle on the nuclear plant's construction have included John Everett, a shop steward for the Suffolk County District Council of Carpenters, who left the project in 1976 because, he later said, he could "no longer work at a power plant I believe is not safe." Everett testified at a trial in 1979,[10] the first for one of the more than 600 persons—including himself—arrested at Shoreham on trespassing charges on June 3 of that year, part of the demonstration at Shoreham that drew 15,000 persons and was among the largest demonstrations at a nuclear plant site in U.S. history.

Those arrested had been involved in sit-ins in front of the plant's gates or had symbolically "gone over the fence" at Shoreham. They claimed there was legal "justification" for their civil disobedience because of the dangers posed by Shoreham, and they wanted to prove it in court.

Under oath in the courtroom, Everett said Shoreham "was not being built to specifications." He told of the use of defective concrete at the nuclear project and shoddy methods of pouring and forming concrete resulting in cracks and "honeycombing" (air bubbles) in the concrete that were cosmetically "covered up" with mortar. Attempts were not made, he said, as they were supposed to have been, to examine the imperfections closely, to probe into the cracks to see how deep into the walls they extended. He said the defects could mean that the concrete would be unable to take much stress. Much of it was critical to the plant. "I'm talking about the pedestal walls which hold up the reactor vessel." The violent pressure of a "blowdown," the first stage in what could be a loss-of-coolant or "China syndrome" accident, could cause improperly built pedestal walls to "collapse and drop the reactor vessel, which could cause a meltdown."

Cracks also constantly formed in the primary containment structure, the cylinder and dome that cover the reactor, which is supposed to contain any releases of radioactivity. These cracks, too, he said, were simply mortared over.

Concrete was poured in subfreezing weather when it was unable to set properly, he testified. Heaters were supposed to be used to allow the concrete to cure in such weather, but workers routinely turned off the heaters "when they went home," he said. "You could come to work the next morning and there actually would be ice on the walls from the water that had been pushed out of the concrete. The next day when the sun came out, the concrete would crack." Also, forms used to hold concrete in place until it cured were removed in a single day instead of the seven he said were required.

Workers without proper credentials were put to work doing critical tasks, he said. Everett said he himself failed a welder's certification test seven times but was given welding duties at Shoreham.

Everett, the son of the union's business agent, said he took "this particular job" at Shoreham "because there's been a lot of underhanded practices in the union" at Shoreham and he thought he could "straighten them out." But at Shoreham, he said, he found poor construction practices overwhelming. "I complained and complained, but they told me to go away."

The day of his testimony, Everett was told—by his father—that he was being dismissed from his present job as a shop steward at Brookhaven National Laboratory because of his testimony on Shoreham. James Everett said he warned his son the night before that if he went ahead and testified, he would be finished as a shop steward. "I told him he would be replaced because a shop steward represents the union, and we can't have our representative testifying on the quality of a contractor's work. That's not our job. Unfortunately, it's my own son." He fired his son on orders from the president of the Building and Construction Trades Council of Nassau and Suffolk Counties.[11]

The younger Everett said he had decided to go ahead with his testimony despite the threatened loss of his job because "my life is at stake if Shoreham goes into operation."[12]

As a result of his testimony, Everett was unable to work again as a carpenter on Long Island. "The union kept saying a job might come up, but of course it never did."

"It was after the trial that the death threats came," said Everett, "plus other nice things like guys calling me and saying they were going to beat the hell out of me." Once he was shot at, another time his truck was sabotaged. "Somebody cut the clutch rod on my van and left it hanging by just enough so that when I was going down the road and hit the clutch, there was no clutch. This stalled my engine and I lost my power steering. Luckily, I had the presence of mind to jam it into neutral and restart the engine."

He left Long Island and moved to Florida.

Jock McCrystal also testified at that trial, and before other forums including before the NRC.[13] He worked at Shoreham for Courter & Company. It was his function "to check the paperwork of the construction workers and pass out the proper materials." Routinely, he said, wrong materials were used. This was particularly common, he said, with welding wire. Welding wire has numerical designations for the type of weld it is to be used for. Some wire is earmarked for joining "similar metals," and some, for "dissimilar metals—i.e., stainless steel to carbon steel or copper-nickel alloy and other metals." He came upon "repeated instances" of the incorrect type of welding wire having been used for a weld, and "workers refused to return to redo" the work.

He testified about a major crack in a feedwater condensor jacket—a critical system that helps cool the reactor core. The eighteen-foot-long crack was hurriedly patched by workers of the contractor that caused it. Meanwhile, a second contractor, responsible for the component, was not informed because if this contractor knew, it "would have raised the issue of the integrity of the entire jacket."

At Shoreham, "surface appearances . . . became the method used for all levels of personnel to pass inspection—from the construction workers' dealings with on-site quality-control quality-assurance personnel to LILCO's elaborate masquerading before the NRC."

At one point, McCrystal said, he told NRC inspectors about the poor construction practices at Shoreham, and they promptly "sabotaged" the investigation. He said he "furnished the NRC with a list of site personnel" who could corroborate what he was reporting—but he was to remain anonymous. "Within two days I had heard from two people on the list that they knew I had named them. It put my life in danger. . . . The NRC is a disgrace." And Shoreham construction, he said, has been "an absolute shame."

McCrystal, in 1982, reviewed his charges about poor construction on the project before an NRC panel as the agency began considering granting LILCO an operating license for Shoreham. He remarked to the three hearing officers that in the context of what they heard, if they allowed Shoreham to operate, they would be personally responsible. The warning drew grimaces from the three NRC administrative judges.

John Huber, a steamfitter for more than twenty years who supervised 800 steamfitters, plumbers and millwrights at Shoreham, told the same NRC panel that the plant "is not really safe."[14]

He charged there "are glaring construction and design defects" at Shoreham. He listed numerous instances of defective cement at the plant grouted with mortar and told of deep voids in the cement of the reactor "pedestal" and support wall. He alleged there were widespread defects in piping in the plant, cuts in reinforcement bars and improper welding. He said there had been improper hydrostatic testing of valves involving the emergency core cooling system.

Of LILCO, Huber said, "They can't construct it [Shoreham], so how are they going to operate it?"

Soon after, a tire on Huber's car was slashed while the auto was parked in the Shoreham plant's lot. And he was fired from his Shoreham job.

In 1983, he went to the NRC's regional office in King of Prussia, Pennsylvania, and gave testimony before NRC inspectors there. He told of controls for a hydrogen recombiner being manufactured by a company that "had since gone out of business and, that being the case, there were problems in getting information, getting spare parts and getting the machine to perform . . . as specified." He said that "drilling into reinforced concrete and cutting the rebars [steel reinforcement bars] inside" was commonplace. "At one point in the job there was no documentation. We were given free rein to do whatever we wanted, wherever we wanted to do it, as far as drilling was concerned." He spoke of numerous instances of "honeycombed" concrete, according to the official NRC transcript of the interview.

Huber said that "off-site quality control quality assurance" of fabricators of components for Shoreham was even worse than that at the nuclear plant project. "What goes on in the fabricators' plants? It's been my experience that they are pretty much left to their own. . . . Quality control off site, I think it's probably nonexistent."

Huber said that when LILCO started to get "unhappy" in the middle 1970s with its Shoreham architect-engineer and construction manager, Stone & Webster, because of "the job falling behind and things taking longer than expected," and LILCO "took a little bit more responsibility for what was going on," proper construction standards were even further ignored. More "corners started to be cut."

He expressed concern about expansion joints often poorly installed, he said, on critical piping. He spoke of one situation in which "they just yanked the pipe over with chain blocks and come-alongs, got the alignment, tacked it, welded it, released everything and let it go its merry way. What that expansion joint's lifetime is, it's going to be severely reduced because of that," if "it will function at all."

He said contractors such as the one that was his employer, Courter & Company, would not complain about what was going on at the project.

Courter & Company is not going to go in and start complaining about the fabrication coming in from another vendor because that's not in the interests of the utility. Courter is there serving at the whim of the utility. They are not going to do that type of thing. . . . It's not in their business interest to do that. If it's good enough for the utility, what does Courter care?

Meanwhile, Huber told the NRC inspectors, "The problem is that if something is safe, it's safe. And if it's not safe or not good, it's not good."

In all the cases—Henry, Stanchfield, the supervisory inspector, Everett, McCrystal, Huber—the NRC announced it would conduct investigations, and then subsequently announced that it found little or nothing improper at Shoreham, or asserted that what had been improper was no longer so.

As Hugh L. Thompson, Jr., director of the NRC's Division of Licensing, Office of Nuclear Reactor Regulation, wrote on September 6, 1985, in a memo to the NRC's five commissioners, the NRC "staff has found that most of Mr. Henry's technical allegations accurately describe conditions that existed at Shoreham but they were properly identified, documented and dispositioned by LILCO."[15]

"A whitewash!" declared Stanchfield after he received a letter back from the NRC on his allegations. "Once again, I would like to thank you for discussing your concerns regarding the Shoreham nuclear power station with the NRC," read the letter from Jack Strosnider, chief of the Projects Section of the NRC Region I's Division of Reactor Projects.[16]

"The NRC is not a watchdog of the nuclear industry. It is a function of the industry," said Stanchfield. "Its purpose, obviously, is to have the industry continue—as is."[17]

Legislator James Morgo said that when he turned over the documents provided by the supervisory inspector to Keith Christenson of the inspection staff at the NRC's Region I office, "I got the clear impression from him that he was doing a thankless job. He explained that his group was terribly understaffed—only three investigators for the entire Northeast. I got the sense that inspection was certainly not a priority for the NRC but a stepchild. It was for appearance that they had this group. They didn't take it seriously."[18]

An NRC inspector who dramatically stepped out of the NRC line on Shoreham was James H. Conran, a senior engineer at the NRC considered a top federal safety expert.

At a 1983 set of NRC hearings on granting Shoreham an operating license, Conran testified, "It is now clear that LILCO truly does not understand what is required minimally for safety."[19] He was sharply critical of what he described as LILCO's failure to classify equipment "important to safety," including equipment necessary to shut the reactor down.

He urged that, as a result of this lack of comprehension by LILCO concerning safety, no operating license be granted for Shoreham.

In a sworn affidavit he submitted, he underlined words for emphasis. He declared: "LILCO truly does not understand what is required minimally for safety by NRC under the regulations, i.e., what is considered necessary and sufficient to provide reasonable assurance of no undue risk to the health and safety of the public in the operation of a facility." He told of "considerable effort" being made by "counsels for the [NRC] staff and applicant . . . to resolve what was perceived as resolvable language differences as contrasted to fundamental lack of mutual understanding regarding what is required minimally for safety. I participated in those efforts. . . . I recognize now, that we are, in fact, not near a meeting of the minds on the very important fundamental safety concept at root in this matter."

Further, he wrote, the differences, it had become evident, do not involve "a language problem. . . . My concern at this point is more serious." There "appears to be a substantive defect in applicant's true understanding of what is really at a minimum necessary to protect public health and safety."

LILCO officials were shocked at Conran's testimony. "This is one man's opinion," claimed Jan Hickman, a LILCO public relations person.

Conran maintained his position. Higher-ups at the NRC, however, quickly attempted to undercut him. Five high-ranking NRC officials, including Roger J. Mattson, director of the NRC's Division of System Integration, and Richard H. Vollmer, director of the Division of Engineering, sent the licensing board their own affidavit a week later which asserted: "It is the staff's judgment that the proper design and construction, coupled with [LILCO's] programs for operating the facility, demonstrate that [LILCO] understands what is minimally required to operate the facility without undue risk to the health and safety of the public."[20]

"We're gratified," announced LILCO public relations person Judith Brabham.[21]

Deputy Suffolk County Executive Jones said, "It would appear to me that LILCO and the NRC staff are trying to line up to attack the whistle-blower in the NRC."[22]

The Shoreham "dump documents" were found by a person who refinishes furniture on Long Island and regularly goes to town dumps looking for pieces that he can work on and sell. The box of Shoreham reports was found at the Southold Town dump, thirty miles east of Shoreham.

The scavenger turned the papers over to Judy Ahrens, a photographer with *The Suffolk Times*, and her husband, William Morris, because he knew of Ms. Ahrens' newspaper connection. "He thought what he found might be something important," said Ahrens.[23]

They brought the reports to me. "He told us he found them by some bushes, tucked away," said Ahrens, as she, her husband and I examined the papers in my living room. "Why at the time of the Three Mile Island incident did they get rid of all their paperwork?" asked Morris. It was early May 1979, just a few weeks after the March 28 accident at Three Mile Island.

Someone asked why the documents were not shredded or burned at Shoreham. It was noted that LILCO seems to have problems "doing anything right."

Morris, a plumber, who thus had a basic knowledge of construction plans, said that in looking through the papers he was "amazed to see how this thing is built as it goes along; they do the plans as they go, with problems all over the place, nuclear safety-related problems, as the reports say."

Each document was headed "Stone & Webster Engineering Corporation, Engineering & Design Coordination Report, Shoreham Nuclear Power Station—Unit 1, Long Island Lighting Company."

On each document was a space for "Problem Description" and another space for "Problem Solution." There were boxes to check as to whether the problem was "Nuclear Safety Related" or "Not Nuclear Safety Related." Of the more than 1,000 reports, we counted 416 on which the box "Nuclear Safety Related" was checked.

The reports were dated January and February 1979. A few concerned December 1978. Morris said that the scavenger said he had seen another box of reports that was in the process of being buried, and there were additional 1978 reports scattered around.

The reports were all stamped: "Received Document Control" and the date, "Construction Office Shoreham Project," and then there were spaces for various signatures including those of the "Project Design Engr.," "Equipment Specialist," "Qual. Sys. Div.," "Eng. Assur. Div." and "Materials Engr." There was a box for "Client Approval" and thirty-two separate boxes to be checked by people at Headquarters," reached through "Field Distribution," and "Const. Supervisors."

I spent several days going through the documents that showed below-standard construction on the nuclear plant—construction that deviated from engineering drawings, with the consistent remedy that the "specs" and drawings be changed. The documents gave a picture of a nuclear plant being designed while being built, with frequent references to items not in conformance left as is.

I sent copies to MHB Technical Associates because its principals, Dale Bridenbaugh, Richard B. Hubbard and Gregory C. Minor, could be regarded as top experts in the nation on the type of nuclear plant at Shoreham because they had been employed by the reactor's manufacturer, General Electric, as engineering supervisors in its nuclear division. They also had been consultants to Suffolk County on Shoreham. They have also served as consultants in the evaluation of nuclear programs to the NRC, the U.S. General Accounting Office, the Congressional Office of Technology Assessment, to states including Massachusetts, Illinois, Texas, California, New Jersey, Connecticut, Vermont, Oklahoma and Ohio, and to the governments of Norway, Spain, Germany and Sweden. I also sent copies to Dr. Michio Kaku of the City University of New York, regarded as highly knowledgeable in the field of nuclear physics. In recent years, he co-edited the book *Nuclear Power: Both Sides* (1981).

I called Stone & Webster, meanwhile, and Martin Reynolds, a public relations person, declared after a day of "looking into" the matter that Stone & Webster executives "are stunned" by the reports having ended up in a dump.[24]

June Bruce, chief of media relations for LILCO, said: "These things indicate what tremendously careful, meticulous and painstaking quality control is being done on the Shoreham site."[25]

Some of the Shoreham problems cited in the reports—all described in the documents as "nuclear safety related"—and comments of Bridenbaugh and Hubbard on them are:[26]

• Problem Description: "Stiffeners cannot be installed due to concrete interference" in the "Hanger Program Turbine Building," declares one report. The Solution: "OK to eliminate stiffeners." Hubbard was particularly concerned about what the report described as "verbals" for this change, declaring that government regulations require a "documented basis for quality assurance."

• Problem Description: "Discrepancies exist between S & W pressure test diagrams, LDT's and the Dravo piping isometrics regarding design conditions," says another report. Declared the Problem Solution: "It should be understood that press-temp. conditions as stated on isometric dwgs. were established very earlier in design and are no longer valid." Said Bridenbaugh: "Have they gone up or gone down?"

• Deviation: "Embedment supports" of "housing restraint" were "installed at incorrect elevation and azimuth location. . . . Disposition: S & W engineering has approved and completed the following modifications . . . Sim using 3/4" PLT. . . . Modify the remaining brackets." Said Bridenbaugh: "It's a case of if it's already cast in concrete, leave it."

• Problem Description: "The number and size of drain holes on the quencher assembly drawing does not agree with the requirements of the specification," said a report about quenchers for discharge lines. The Problem Solution: "The specifications will be revised." Said Bridenbaugh: "It's easier to change paper than quenchers. This is a typical solution."

• Problem Description: "Maintainability of check valve 14"-WCF-90FA-2 cannot be performed because pipe support PSSP800 interferes with the required removal space for the valve," said a report. The Problem Solution declared that "relocation" to "make room for valve maintenance is not required." Said Hubbard: "Are they building a plant difficult and dangerous to maintain?"

• Problem Description: "Anchor bolt location violates E & DCR P29406 Section 3.2. Due to extreme difficulty in locating acceptable holes in area, field requests to leave anchor bolt hole in violation as is." The Problem Solution: "Verbal accepted with the addition of

△5210.49B

STONE & WEBSTER ENGINEERING CORPORATION REACTOR

ENGINEERING & DESIGN COORDINATION REPORT

PAGE 1 OF 1

NO. F-16879.A

PROJECT / CLIENT:	SHOREHAM NUCLEAR POWER STATION-UNIT 1 LONG ISLAND LIGHTING COMPANY HYDRO	JOB NO. 11600.03

AREA 7

REFERENCES:
1P41-PSST 516; REV 0

PROBLEM DESCRIPTION:

1P41-PSST 516 WILL INTERFERE WITH INSTALLATION OF
1P41-PSSH 832/PSSP 821/831.

RECEIVED

FEB 2 1979

REPRODUCTION

SUGGESTED SOLUTION:
DELETE SUPPORT DUE TO PROXIMITY OF 1P41-832/821/331.

PB1-16

TELECOPY DATES (REQUESTING PARTY)
Sent:
Rcv'd:

Requested By: Paul R Jacobs	Dept. or Div. Const	Tele. Ext. 482	Date 1/12/79	Needed By: 1/26/79

PROBLEM SOLUTION:

DWG 1P41-PSST 516 IS ~~DELETED~~ PER
STRESS SUMMARY MSK-133B. SUPPORTS
PSSP 821, PSSP 831 & PSSH 832 ARE SHOWN
AT THIS PT. (81)

RECEIVED
DOCUMENT CONTROL
FEB 9 1979
CONSTRUCTION OFFICE

TELECOPY DATES (RESPONDING PARTY)
Sent:
Rcv'd:

AFFECTS WORK UNDER SPECIFICATION SH 1- 068

IMPLEMENTATION VERIFICATION ☐ IS / ☒ IS NOT REQUIRED   VERIFIED BY LHM

Furnished By: A. KAHN	Date 1-25-79	Responsible Lead Engr. P. Patel for S. Yerandi	Date 1-25-79

☐ INFORMATION ONLY	Project Design Engr. C. Breland	Date 1-30-79	ESAR CHANGE ☐ Yes ☒ No
☒ DRAWING CHANGE 60.51			
☐ SPECIFICATION CHANGE	Equipment Specialist NR	Date	CLIENT APPROVAL:
☐ PROCEDURE CHANGE			☐ Required ☒ Not R'qd.
☐ ENG. SERV. SCOPE OF WORK CHANGE	Qual. Sys. Div. or Eng. Assur. Div. NR	Date	Obtained Date:
Change will ☒ be incorporated in the will not ☐ following documents:			Reference:
1P41-PSST-516	Materials Engr. NR	Date	

CLIENT DISTRIBUTION—CLIENT HEADQTRS

☒ Nuclear Safety Related (QA Cat. I)
☐ Not Nuclear Safety Related (☐ QA Cat. II / ☐ QA Cat. III)

Project Engineer Approval & Date
C Akawson for E J Brabazon 1/31/79

☐ Engineering ____
☐ Project Manager ____
☐ ____

HEADQUARTERS	FIELD DISTRIBUTION	CONST. SUPERVISORS
☒ Proj. Engr. — ☐ Chief ___ Engr. —	☒ Originator — ☐	☐ Structural — ☐
☒ Proj. Des. Engr. — ☐ Chief _ Des. Engr. —	☐ Client QA Mgr. — ☐	☐ Mechanical — ☐
☒ Resp. Engr. — ☐ Supt Const. Serv. —	☐ Client Const. Insp. — ☐	☐ Electrical — ☐
☐ Equip. Spec. — ☒ Ch Engr - EA Div. —	☒ S&W FQC — ☐	☒ Piping TESCO — ☐
☐ Mat'ls Engr. — ☒ G. ARENA —	☒ S&W Res. Engr. — ☐	☐ Welding — ☐
☒ QA - Qual. Sys. D. — ☒ J. BUSA —	☐ Fld. Des. Engr. — ☐	☐ Instrument — ☐
☐ QA - PQC Div. — ☒ G. PRUNIER —	☐ Hedd-Fld. Ext. O. — ☐	☐ Planning — ☐
☐ QA - FQC Div. — ☒ PRASAD (LD CHK) —	☒ EOS REHL — ☒ MERRILL —	☒ SUPPORTS — ☐

T. LATHAM

NOTED JAN 19 1979 I.W.Luthan

One of the "dump documents."

gussets." Said Bridenbaugh: "Was this cranked all the way through the design process? Has the seismic analysis been redone as a result of this?"

Other problems in the plant detailed in the reports, each problem also designated as "nuclear safety related," included one in the reactor building: "Problem Description: Field requests approval to eliminate the . . . L braces. . . . These members cannot be installed without infringing upon the area required for the reflective insulation. . . . Problem Solution: This is acceptable."

There was a problem with flexible metal hose connections. "Problem Description: Field requests further relaxation of guidelines for supporting flexible hose connections. . . . Problem Solution: Acceptable as shown for this case only."

There was a problem in the reactor's suppression pool.

Problem Description: E & DCR14836 states that to repair the gauge in DP-52 a backing strap will be tacked in place. . . . An additional problem arises in that the downcomer has been hydro tested and accepted. Field requests to grind the strap with a $1/8"$ radius and to accept the tacked condition as is. . . . Problem Solution: The requirements for seal welding of backing strap . . . is waived.

There was a problem with the reactor fueling bellows.

Problem Description: A crack at Az. 175. In the refueling bellows to RPV weld. . . . Suggested Disposition: Stop holes $1/8"$ dia. will be drilled $1/8"$ beyond the crack. Precautions shall be taken to ensure that the penetration is limited to the plate thickness plus $1/10"$. On the lower end of the bellows, the cracked weld shall be excavated for a distance of $2"$ and $1/8"$ stop hole drilled as described above. Recommend that a $1/4"$ thick plate $2"$ wide be welded over the cracked shop weld.

The "Far filter" had a problem.

Problem Description: Attached please find the test data. . . . Please approve a specification change with the requirements given on the attached data sheets. . . . Problem solution: The attached test data . . . *is approved.* . . . Maximum leak rate increased from .05% to .075% of rated flow.

There was a problem with an "RCIC pump."

Problem Description: Referenced E & DCR does not have SK #112278A attachment as noted per drawing on mounting details for RCIC pump. In addition, this drawing is not clearly readable. LILCO has recommended that the hole depth on SK #1L1778 be reduced to avoid any possible damage to thrust bearing. Please resolve.

The Problem Solution: "Hole depth for sensor mounting on HPIC pump is reduced to 0.40". Bottom tapping must be utilized for this hole. . . . This E & DCR supersedes in Part E & DCR F-16509."

There was a problem with a "quencher." "Problem Description: In order to expedite delivery, the stainless steel portion of the inlet pipe assembly has been changed to carbon steel." The Problem Solution: "Specification will be addended." And a problem with struts. "Problem Description: The following dwgs. call for power strut channels but actually unistrut channels were installed." The Problem Solution: "Unistrut channels in place of power strut channels are acceptable."

There were problems in the reactor building. "Problem Description: Floor drain sump and pump tanks IG11-TK-050A, TK-050B, TK-056A & TK-056C have been installed incorrectly—turned 180°." For Problem Solution, a supplementary sheet was referred to, but was not attached.

"The attitude through the documents is one of, 'Let's just sand it smooth and pass it on,'" said Kaku. They are full of examples of "shoddy workmanship."

He said he was particularly concerned about admitted violations of the American Society of Mechanical Engineers standards on welding of piping that is supposed to withstand pressure. Improper welding, he said, can lead to a break in such "pressure pipe . . . and if it's in a primary circuit, that's it. A loss of coolant accident, a catastrophic meltdown can result."

There were a number of documents Kaku noticed concerning "rebars" or reinforcement bars—the pieces of steel imbedded in concrete to give it strength. "The reports concerning rebars are most important," said Kaku. Rebars "are not supposed to be hit or cut, or the tensile strength of the concrete is reduced. In one document, in ten incorrect tries to make a hole, seven rebars are hit."[27]

Kaku also expressed concern about documents reflecting mistakes in the construction of "the primary containment—what actually holds the uranium fuel rods—there is no more crucial area in a reactor," and reports about errors made in the construction of the "residual heat remover" system. "This is an area which malfunctioned at Three Mile Island."

Said Kaku: "These documents make you jump up and down and ask, 'What are they doing?' "

LILCO public relations person June Bruce, meanwhile, issued a second statement. "Shoreham has been built almost twice. It was originally designed before the [federal] hearings [on granting LILCO a construction permit] took place and, because the hearing was dragged out for three years, a truckload of new regulations relating to construction that developed during that period had to be satisfied. Therefore, some of the normal problems of design had to be resolved during the actual installation of the equipment."[28]

The statement also maintained, "These papers are undoubtedly routine interoffice memos on file in Shoreham. I don't know how they got there [in the dump]. They were probably duplicates picked up by the normal carting company. There are voluminous quantities of these reports."

I was asked, along with Kaku, to appear before the New York City Council's Environmental Protection Committee.[29] I explained how the box of documents was discovered and read from a number of reports. Dr. Kaku gave his explanation of what the documents signified and said he believed that the builders of Shoreham should be held "criminally liable for deliberately violating codes on the construction of nuclear plants."

Queens Councilman Arthur Katzman (Democrat), the committee's chairman, declared that in light of the "dump documents," the Shoreham plant "poses a threat of disaster to people living in New York City, Suffolk and Nassau." He scored the NRC for "sleeping in the same bed with utilities. They don't monitor the utilities. They let them do what they wish. I can't understand why Congress lets this go on."

The documents were numbered from the middle 16,000's to slightly over 18,000. I spoke to Albert Toth, the Shoreham project inspector for the NRC, about examining the engineering design and coordination reports from the very first up to those found. Toth said he thought the files with these reports were kept by LILCO "on the site."[30] He said it would be up to LILCO to let me see them.

My interview with Toth also provided insight on what sort of investigatory oversight the NRC had over Shoreham—and other nuclear plant construction projects.

Toth said over the telephone that he was not only responsible for inspection of Shoreham construction but he was the project inspector for the Millstone III nuclear plant being built in Connecticut, and he had just ended inspection supervision for the Salem II nuclear plant in Lower Alloway, New Jersey, with the completion of that plant. Also, said Toth, he was in charge of inspection of "preconstruction" activities on nuclear plants then planned for Montague, Massachusetts, and at Jamesport on Long Island, a twin nuclear plant LILCO project.

Speaking from the NRC's Region I office in King of Prussia, Pennsylvania, he said he went "to the Shoreham site once a month." He had a bachelor's degree in mechanical engineering, but no advanced degrees. He said he had gone, in the early 1960s, to a "school run by the government" at Oak Ridge National Laboratory, the Oak Ridge School of Reactor Technology. It was "not a formally accredited institution," he said, "and was suspended in 1964."

Toth said dealing with problems in the construction of a nuclear plant was "basically the responsibility of the licensee." He said he examined some reports when he went to a nuclear plant site, reports such as those found in the dump.

As to the reports themselves, he said, "Every time they run into a glitch or find something wrong, they look at the mistake and say, 'Can we rework it?' Sometimes it's a matter of some money and engineering constraints. And they come up with economical engineering dispositions." He said the NRC doesn't get copies of construction reports.

As to how the Shoreham reports ended up in a dump, Toth said, "There is no prohibition against taking papers off the site. Someone may have taken these reports home for his kids for scrap paper."

I made a request to LILCO to look at the earlier 16,000 records. "We will make them available to the NRC but not to you," Ira Freilicher, LILCO's vice president for public affairs, told me. Freilicher, who has an active sense of humor (he once commented that after LILCO he would represent Idi Amin), joked: "If we only could have persuaded the East End towns to go for resource recovery [in which garbage would be burned], we wouldn't have this problem."[31]

I filed a request under the U.S. Freedom of Information Act with the NRC to "inspect any and all notes and correspondence the NRC has" on the earlier documents. I got nowhere.

The U.S. Environmental Protection Agency asked the NRC to specifically investigate welding violations and the cutting into reinforcement bars at Shoreham in view of the information in the "dump documents." Paul Giardina, EPA radiation officer for its Region I, said he was concerned about "certain discrepancies in various codes and safety criteria."[32]

Suffolk County, in papers filed with the NRC, said that a "complete physical inspection" of the Shoreham plant by the NRC was "imperative" because of what the documents showed.[33] The county demanded to know whether it had "inspected Shoreham drawings against complete systems installed to insure that the drawings reflect the 'as built' system, that the original design quality requirements are not violated and that the procedures specified by the drawings are followed." The county also called for an explanation of "LILCO's practice with respect to the disposal of documents. Does LILCO claim that such disposal is permitted by any regulation of the NRC? If so, cite the regulation."

As with the Shoreham whistle-blowers, the NRC turned a deaf ear to the issues raised by the Shoreham "dump documents." Two months after papers were found, it declared: "Conditions were encountered in the field which were properly referred to the appropriate engineers for resolution. The engineers determined that the conditions were acceptable."[34]

There have been others coming forward about Shoreham, other documents examined indicating serious problems at the plant, and more evidence of the government's generally lax attitude toward poor nuclear plant construction.

"Inside the Nuclear Industry's Heart: Construction Workers Talk About the Monster They're Building at Shoreham" was the title of an article published in the magazine *Seven Days* (October 26, 1979). It was prepared by Gloria Jacobs and Barbara Ehrenreich, two senior editors of the magazine, and was based on their interviews with several people with personal knowledge about the building of Shoreham, including five construction workers on the project and a quality-control engineer.

The piece began with a quote from one of the workers: "This construction site has to be, without a doubt, the world's biggest flea market. It makes no difference what you have to sell, what you have to give, what you're looking for—it's there. Drugs. There's a constant underground throughout the entire complex. Horse racing, numbers." The workers said sex could also be obtained "on your lunch hour. It's a casino. It's a circus," he said of Shoreham.

With the pay of workers at Shoreham "sometimes rising as high as $2,000 a week," the article reported, "and the boss telling workers to shut up or get out, there are few gripes. Anyone who talks and gets found out by the union or the contractor will never work in the Northeast again."

But the Three Mile Island accident had unnerved the workers who came forward to be interviewed. They were "angry, and fearful about talking. They'd already tried to tell LILCO about construction problems." Meanwhile, "word was out on the site that 'tattlers' were looking for trouble. Our informants' greatest fear was that others working at the Shoreham site would discover who had been passing information."

One worker said: "My life would be on the line because I'm threatening someone else's job. All they've got to do is drop one piece of metal and you're dead." Thus the workers were not identified by name.

They gave accounts of improper work and untrained workers. "I've seen welders teaching guys how to do the job—while they're working," said one. "They were teaching them as they went along, how to hold the rod and everything," He said "some of these guys" were hired "because they were friends of the boss."

As to why LILCO would allow what was happening to go on, the workers said that their understanding was that because utilities are allowed by state regulatory commissions to "pass their costs on to customers, the company isn't paying" and thus did not care.

"None of the men we talked to are anti-nuke," said the article. "They're convinced that following the rules would make nuclear plants safe, but they've seen incredible mismanagement on the [Shoreham] job." There was "divided" opinion on what would occur if the plant is allowed to begin operating. "One side believes so many little things will go wrong first, the reactor will probably be shut down before it had a chance to blow up," while the other anticipates a disaster. "I'll probably go lay down on the bed and watch TV and wait for it to come and hope it's fast," one worker is quoted as saying. "There's no sense in running because there's no way you're going to get off this island."

The Shoreham quality-control engineer maintained that many of the problems at Shoreham had to do with the plant being designed and partially built for a 500 megawatt reactor. However, a project of the New York State Electric and Gas Company to build a 820 megawatt nuclear plant in upstate New York, on Lake Cayuga near Ithaca, had been cancelled and LILCO was able to get a "good deal" on the reactor that was supposed to be installed there. Installing this larger-than-planned reactor into Shoreham, explained the engineer, led to many major changes "made as the work goes along."[35]

Warren Liebold, an energy analyst, and Matthew Chachere, at whose trial for civil disobedience at Shoreham Everett and McCrystal testified, conducted a study between 1980 and 1982 of government and LILCO records on the Shoreham project going back to 1972. These papers were part of a Shoreham collection established by the government at the Shoreham-Wading River Public Library.

In a report, they charged that the records showed "fundamental flaws in Shoreham construction" and "consistent and dangerous deficiencies in the NRC's and LILCO's oversight."[36] They said "only 5 to 10 percent of the plant has ever been physically inspected by the NRC; most of the plant has been inspected only once and by LILCO." The report, issued by the Shoreham Opponents Coalition, of which both are directors, listed 250 Shoreham flaws. It contained copies of pertinent documents on which the charges were based.

One item concerned the dome of the Shoreham reactor building that, according to the documents, to make transportation easier, was sent to Long Island in four pieces after it was fabricated at the Pittsburgh-Des Moines Company in Pittsburgh, Pennsylvania. Employees of that firm then attempted to weld the four pieces together at Shoreham, but the welding was botched—"temperatures were held too high for too long," said government reports. So the welds had to be removed, along with what was described as "base material"—up to two feet of dome on each side of each weld. That made each segment smaller, so a fifth piece had to be made and inserted when the dome was rewelded. LILCO, meanwhile, did not tell the government about any of this and was cited, said a government document, for "failure to report a significant construction deficiency." The company "failed to report extensive damage to the removable head of the containment structure due to improper post weld treatment of certain weld seams."

Another item involved anchor bolts that are crucial for support. A LILCO document said that over a third of the anchor bolts installed to support "the primary shield wall" in the reactor building "were inadvertently damaged when adjacent plates were flame-cut to correct an installation error." A consultant recommended "mechanical corrective action"—reinstallation of the bolts, the LILCO report on the problem went on. But LILCO rejected that idea and instead ground down the damaged bolts, deciding the bolts that remained were sufficient.

Another item involved blueprints for the plant's construction. The government cited LILCO twice with violations, according to NRC documents, for failing to supply supervisors with "latest, revised design drawings." And some of the drawings that were available could hardly be used. In one government document, an inspection is described in which it was found that "a significant percentage of the drawings in the Courter & Company master file were torn and illegible. These drawings are used on a regular basis by the engineering and drafting staff for the construction of the plant."

Patricia Bower, an artist and writer, decided to independently interview Shoreham workers about construction defects. In 1983, she advised the NRC that a number had spoken to her anonymously, and she passed on their information.

> Following is a list of allegations made by technicians and engineers at the Shoreham nuclear power plant. I have been speaking with these men during the past six months. To my knowledge, these are new causes for additional concern about the safety of the Shoreham plant and require both investigation and response. It is especially important to note that the initial response of the plant employees was hostility towards me; they were supportive generally of the nuclear industry and specifically of Shoreham.[37]

However, she said, they started to talk perhaps partly because "I am a member of neither anti-nuclear nor anti-Shoreham groups but, simply, a resident doing independent research in order to gain understanding of the issues under discussion."

The list of allegations of workers that she related to the NRC included problems "in the hydrogen recombiner . . . hangers and anchors are improperly spaced. Specific comment: 'With sufficient thermal expansion, those pipes could explode.' Further, 'I worked at Limerick. Comparing the two, there is terrible quality control here. . . . I have never seen such a lack of quality control.' " In the ventilation system, workers said that "electrical routing is 'outrageous,' cable trays are unsupported . . . nipples and covers have been omitted—wires go unprotected from one tray to another." Bower quoted a technician as saying, "It is impossible to keep the venting system clean—there is low-level leakage of ionizing radiation at all times."

Another worker, she said, told her, "Data is continuously fudged. . . . GE and Stone & Webster drawings don't corroborate, are off in some instances by 180°. Air pressure gauges are off, showing 3 percent pressure when pressure is actually 100 percent. Too many technicians are untrained. Here at Shoreham they don't need, or don't have, prior nuclear experience."

Several NRC inspectors came to Long Island to interview Bower. But, she said, they were "mostly interested" in "getting the names of the people who spoke to me."[38] They finally told her, she said, "if I wouldn't give the names I could be subpeonaed and forced by a judge to give the names." She said at the time of the NRC inspectors, "They were suppressive and coercive. There are real bad things at the plant, and they don't seem to want to know about them."

Bower asked two friends to accompany her to the first meeting with the NRC inspectors. The inspectors objected to that and to her taping the meeting, claiming, she said, that the motel conference room where they told her to meet them was "too small" and that a tape recorder wouldn't "pick up the conversation." One friend who came to the meeting with Bower, despite the prohibition by the inspectors, was Van Howell, also an artist and writer. He said afterwards that the NRC inspectors acted "like interrogators, almost as if we were accomplices to a crime." They "refused to deal with any substantive information. They wanted only to know the sources of information. It looked like they were trying to plug up all the leaks of information, even to themselves."[39]

At a second meeting, Bower took a lawyer with her "because the NRC inspectors were so intimidating." Upon arriving home after the second interview, she found that her house had been broken into and a set of documents that the Shoreham workers had given her were missing.

"It's distressing," she said then, "but I can't allow myself to become really upset. It would be very easy to withdraw and say this is getting too dangerous. I will not do that."

Bower was to fall in love with one of the Shoreham workers who served as a source for her. She said recently, "He was one of the first persons I interviewed. Because of his credibility and honesty I was immediately attracted to him." They were married in 1985 and moved off Long Island. She said her husband, an instrumentation control technician, is now working on the Hope Creek nuclear plant project in Salem, New Jersey, but they hope he soon will be out of the nuclear industry.

"He's completely disenchanted with the nuclear industry," she said. Her husband has been finding at the project on which he is now working some of the same types of poor construction practices he encountered at Shoreham. A foreman at Hope Creek 2, as he was at Shoreham, he recently "refused to sign off on systems that violated safety standards" at Hope Creek and ended up being "demoted on a trumped-up charge of low productivity. He took it to the labor department, which investigated and cleared him."

Said Bower, "The minute you open up your mouth and express your concerns about safety at any of these plants, they get after you. What is true of Shoreham is true for every one of these plants."

Organized crime is an element in many construction projects in the United States, including the building of nuclear plants. But, according to police specialists, on no nuclear project has organized crime been so pervasive as at Shoreham.

Indeed, the CBS News program *60 Minutes* broadcast a report in 1985 that highlighted this aspect of Shoreham.

"I would say the unions actually ran the show at Shoreham," and in "many instances" these are organized crime-linked unions, said Lt. Remo Franceschini of the New York City Police Department on *60 Minutes*. One major union involved in Shoreham construction has been the Laborer's Union, members of Local 66 led by Peter Vario, that the lieutenant identified as under "great influence from the Luchese crime family."[40]

The International Brotherhood of Teamsters Union local at Shoreham, Local 242 headed by John Cody—who is presently in jail after being convicted in 1982 of seven counts of an eight-count racketeering indictment—is "controlled by the Gambino crime family," said the lieutenant.

Further, he said, organized crime has been involved in deciding where building materials for Shoreham came from.

Correspondent Ed Bradley asked the lieutenant: "Is there any doubt in your mind but that organized crime had their hands in the construction of that [Shoreham] plant and took money out of it?"

"There's no doubt in my mind," he replied. He described Shoreham as a "perfect pork barrel for organized crime to reap money out of . . . on no-show jobs, on kickbacks, on being able to get rid of stolen merchandise."

Other principal unions at Shoreham identified by law enforcement authorities as linked to organized crime are the Boilermakers Union Local 5 and Operating Engineers Union Local 138, both under the influence of the Gambino family.

Even the security guards' union at Shoreham is connected to organized crime. Kenneth McCallion, a former special prosecutor with the Organized Crime Unit of the U.S. Department of Justice, noted on the 60 Minutes broadcast that "it is a matter of public record that Daniel Cunningham purchased" the Allied International Union of Security Guards and Special Police "and that the union has been controlled by organized crime from the time of its inception in the late 1960s."

The Columbo family dominates this union. Then Cunningham went on to create an affiliate, Local 1, Power Plant Police & Security Officers, that covers the security personnel at Shoreham and other nuclear plants.[41] In 1982, Cunningham was convicted of thirteen counts of a forty-two count indictment charging crimes ranging from racketeering to bribery to embezzlement, and he is now in jail. The union was then turned over, according to law enforcement officials, to Michael Franzese, son of Long Island organized crime leader John (Sonny) Franzese. The younger Franzese was arrested in late 1985 by the FBI on a twenty-eight count racketeering indictment.

"LILCO should have posted a sign outside the plant saying, 'Hail, hail the gang's all here,' " commented County Legislator Wayne Prospect, a Dix Hills Democrat.[42] After the 60 Minutes program, he introduced a resolution in the Suffolk Legislature, which passed, calling on the New York State Public Service Commission to "determine the extent to which the infiltration of organized crime at Shoreham contributed to the exorbitant cost overruns of the Shoreham facility."

The Suffolk County and New York State governments, following the *60 Minutes* broadcast, called on the NRC to investigate the "serious allegations concerning the presence and influence of organized crime at the Shoreham nuclear power plant site. . . . The implications of these allegations on the safety and security of the Shoreham plant are self-evident." Their brief added, "The state and county further move that these matters be given first priority, and that the NRC hold in abeyance any consideration of issues relating to the licensing or operation of Shoreham pending the completion and public scrutiny of the NRC's investigation."[43]

The NRC did not give the matter even last priority. This was despite the point made by correspondent Bradley on *60 Minutes* that at Cody's trial "it was revealed that, in general, if he didn't get a kickback from contractors, they wouldn't be able to deliver concrete. And who did get the concrete job at Shoreham? In some cases, the same contractors who had earlier supplied defective concrete for the county sewer system."

I assisted the *60 Minutes* team in helping to pin down the sources for the story on the Shoreham concrete scandal.

One angle concerned two inspectors from the Suffolk Department of Public Works who disclosed anonymously that their jobs involved being stationed at the plant where much of the concrete for Shoreham came from. They were there to inspect concrete being prepared by the same company for the county for use on roads and sidewalks. Whenever they rejected concrete as being below standard for the county, they said, the load was shifted to inspectors from the Shoreham project, also posted at the concrete plant, who invariably would approve it and send it on for use in the nuclear plant. One of the inspectors agreed to go on *60 Minutes* and repeat this. Preparations were made for him to be filmed, in disguise with his voice altered. But, at the last minute, he declined to do so out of fear of retaliation.

LILCO steadfastly has refused any independent inspection of Shoreham. In 1981, the newly elected Suffolk County administration of Peter F. Cohalan said it would drastically curtail most of the county's intervention on Shoreham in NRC proceedings if LILCO would agree to a physical inspection of the plant. But LILCO would agree only to an inspection of two of the plant's systems—"a representative electrical system and a representative mechanical system." If the inspection of these systems identified "serious deficiencies," then LILCO would "take appropriate action . . . including further inspection and testing of other systems." Said Elaine Adler Robinson, who had been a Suffolk legislator and after an election defeat was hired by LILCO as associate director of public affairs, a complete inspection "simply is not feasible if the company is to put the plant into operation in 1983."[44]

The Suffolk legislature subsequently moved to place a referendum on the ballot demanding a full Shoreham inspection. The resolution read: "Shall Suffolk County actively oppose the issuance of an operating license for the Shoreham nuclear power plant until the Shoreham plant has been subjected to a complete physical inspection and design review by Suffolk County?"

However, a group of Shoreham supporters largely composed of scientists from Brookhaven National Laboratory challenged the referendum in court and had it thrown off the ballot.

Then there is the question of where the nuclear plant was constructed: directly over an artesian or free-flowing well and on water-saturated land especially sensitive to earth movements.

Former Shoreham worker McCrystal located the relevant documents in the collection at the Shoreham-Wading River Public Library. He subsequently told the NRC "that LILCO delayed notifying the NRC just long enough to keep anyone—particularly the NRC and the EPA [U.S. Environmental Protection Agency]—from being able to obtain any further information" about the "well that is directly in the ground under the reactor building."[45] Meanwhile, he said, the papers showed that LILCO rushed to "lay down the reactor mat," a concrete platform base for the plant, to cover the well and prevent any further examinations of it.

McCrystal pointed to LILCO's "Final Safety Analysis Report," submitted to the government in 1977, in which in a section entitled "Appendix 25: Summary Report of Geotechnical Studies of Reactor Building Foundation," LILCO stated: "It is concluded that no artesian condition exists in the soils underlying the reactor building."

However, this was "in direct contradiction" of a 1970 report from the American Drilling & Boring Company of East Providence, Rhode Island, done for LILCO and found at the library by McCrystal, entitled "Report on Grouting of Artesian Flow" at the Shoreham site.

McCrystal noted it was also contradicted by a 1977 Stone & Webster report, "Capping of Flowing Well, Shoreham Nuclear Power Station." The Stone & Webster report provided details of a meeting between its engineers, representatives of LILCO, and other contractors on the project, at which, said the report, "the surficial [sic] geology was reviewed in an effort to determine the source of the artesian water." It went on: "The following scheme was developed to permanently seal the well. The sand pile would be encircled with a dike linked with an impervious membrane. No attempt would be made to seal the well until the general level of the backfill surrounding the well had been brought to elevation minus-five. The reason for this was to reduce the possibility of more blowouts occurring nearby as a result of probing and destroying the well's impervious wall.

Steven Englebright, curator of geology at the State University of New York at Stony Brook as well as a Suffolk County legislator, said when he heard Stanchfield testify about the 1981 earthquake and his resignation from the Shoreham project because of LILCO's "lie" concerning its impact, he began reexamining the geology of the Shoreham site. Englebright, a specialist in sedimentology, said he was long suspicious about the plant's location, and this suspicion increased when, in 1984, he and other county legislators were given a tour of Shoreham. ". . . When I asked about the possibility of an earthquake, boy, did I get a strong reaction." Englebright, the founder and director of the Museum of Long Island Natural Sciences at the university, said that LILCO then sent him reports on the site's geology and they "confirmed to me that something was amiss."[46]

He was assisted by Stanchfield, who also had been looking into the stability of the Shoreham site, collecting geological information on seismic activities in the region, because he felt he had "hit a raw nerve" when he quit the project citing the earthquake.

In 1985, Englebright charged that his reexamination showed that the Shoreham plant "is sited in groundwater," built on top of an artesian well on water-saturated land highly vulnerable to earthquakes. He said he saw "all hell breaking loose in the nuclear plant" in the event of an earthquake. Further, he said the plant "may lie immediately above a deep fault" in the earth. He charged that "there has been a coverup from the beginning by LILCO" in terms of geological problems at the site.

Englebright presented a 1981 "Safety Evaluation Report"[47] on Shoreham done by the NRC that stated that during the course of construction there was a "flowing well disturbance" and "some local foundation disturbance due to the development of the flowing well condition." The report continued: "This well does not appear to have caused an adverse effect on the gross seismic stability of the reactor foundation," an assurance Englebright did not accept.

It said that bedrock at the site "is estimated to be at a depth of 1,000 feet" and the site's "subsurface materials . . . consist of glacial outwash materials underlain by interbedded sands, clays and silts." These "loose surficial [sic] sands which extend down to elevation minus-twelve feet mean low water were removed and replaced with compacted granular backfill. . . . The reactor building mat foundation is at elevation minus two feet mean low water." This showed, said Englebright, "the plant is sited in water-saturated land below the water table."

The NRC report also identified a north-south fault line "twenty miles nearly due north across the Long Island Sound" from Shoreham in an area called the Triassic Valley Basin and "formed by the Connecticut Valley border fault." There has been no analysis of whether that fault continues south, said Englebright, but he regarded it as "possible, in fact, likely" that this fault continues from Connecticut twenty miles south under the Long Island Sound to Long Island, and "that Shoreham is right on top of a fault." He asked why the Triassic Valley Basin fault would "turn suddenly right or left" and not "continue heading south, under the Long Island Sound, directly to Shoreham." Also, a second fault has been identified by the NRC, called "New Shoreham," that is 40 miles long and is southeast of Long Island, 65 miles from the Shoreham plant site.

Englebright said that LILCO selected the Shoreham site "on the basis of flawed assumptions" and coming upon the artesian well on the site as construction proceeded was a surprise to LILCO. This geological situation coupled with prospects of earthquakes caused a "coverup by LILCO."

He compared the effects of earthquake shock waves on a nuclear plant built in such a location with what occurs when one stands at the edge of ocean surf, in water-saturated sand.

"If you jostle your body," he explained, "you move the sand grains. By weighting and unweighting, you place the sand in suspension, and you fall through the sand into the water." At Shoreham, he said, "you have a monstrously heavy plant" in water-saturated sand. "Earthquake waves will lift and drop land, weight and unweight what is on the surface of the land. During an earthquake, what would happen to the plant? Would it list to one side? Would it begin falling through the sand? Would pipes be sheared off, control rods jammed?" Also, he noted, "you don't need an earthquake to see sudden settling. Major land shifts have regularly taken place along Long Island's North Shore."

"A-Fuel Is Slipped in at Shoreham," was the headline in the New York *Daily News*[48] after, in the dark of night, a convoy of nineteen flatbed trucks brought in 112 tons of uranium fuel to Shoreham on July 25, 1982. LILCO officials said they kept the delivery secret and made it in the post-midnight hours because they feared a demonstration by Shoreham opponents. The fuel, packed in 34,720 fuel rods each thirty to forty feet long, came from the General Electric plant in Wilmington, North Carolina.

LILCO was accused by State Senator Franz Leichter and Suffolk Legislator Prospect of violating the law with its shipment.[49] Among other things, they pointed out that the trucks were unmarked, in violation of state law requiring vehicles transporting hazardous material to be marked, and that the convoy followed a route through New York City not prescribed for the shipment of hazardous materials, and without notifying the city, both in violation of city health code regulations. There was, however, no prosecution.

In 1984, LILCO loaded fuel into the plant, but its attempts to have Shoreham begin operation with tests at what the NRC describes as low power—up to 5 percent of a nuclear plant's full power—were held up because of chronic problems with the plant's backup diesels. The first test of one of the backup diesels, the 1983 test that George Henry witnessed and that resulted in the diesel's crankshaft cracking in two, was the first of a long string of breakdowns of the diesels. Cracks were found throughout all three diesels, including cracks in crankshafts and cylinder heads.

The diesels were manufactured by Transamerica Delaval of Oakland, California. An NRC-commissioned study of the diesels in 1983 concluded that a major design error by the manufacturer was responsible for the cracks. So serious was the design error—underestimating the stress on the crankshafts—that the NRC ordered testing of similar diesels at other U.S. nuclear power plants.

Plants with the same Delaval diesels already in place were listed by the NRC as Southern California Edison's San Onofre 1 and Mississippi Power & Light's Grand Gulf 1 plants. The same diesels, said the

NRC, were to be installed at thirteen nuclear plants under construction besides Shoreham. Other models of Delaval diesels are in thirty other nuclear plants.

During the uproar over the Shoreham diesels, it was disclosed that Transamerica Delaval had been cited 59 times by the NRC for violation of federal codes in the fabrication of diesel engines. The violations, some of which concerned flaws in crankshafts, included Delaval's using unqualified welders, having improperly calibrated instruments, and failing in "material control."[50]

The NRC report also criticized LILCO, declaring that an inspection of Shoreham maintenance records showed that LILCO had not been maintaining the diesels properly by not adequately lubricating them.

LILCO tried feverishly to prove that the diesels that it had purchased for $2.1 million in 1974 were adequate. "We're basically satisfied with Delaval," said LILCO public relations person Hickman. "But we are unhappy with the recent problems."[51] LILCO went as far as to send two engineers to Rahfa, a settlement in the An Nafud desert in Saudi Arabia near the Iraqi border, where the same model Delaval diesels were being used to provide electricity and power a pumping station for an oil pipeline.

In February 1984, an NRC licensing board ruled that it had no confidence in the diesels and refused to give LILCO permission to conduct the low-power tests without further hearings. Then the NRC itself—amid intense pressure being applied by LILCO in Washington—set up a special licensing board to consider the matter further, with orders that it expedite its schedule. With it clear that an NRC majority was attempting to get Shoreham into low-power operation fast—with working backup diesels or without them—Suffolk County and New York State went to the U.S. District Court in Washington and charged that the NRC, particularly its chairman, Nunzio Palladino, had been violating the principles of due process and the NRC's ostensible role as a regulatory agency. Judge Norma Holloway Johnson imposed a restraining order on the NRC.

That had a short-lived effect on the NRC. In May 1984, it ruled that because of the problems with the diesels, LILCO would have to apply for an exemption from the NRC rule that mandates that approved backup electric power be available for low-power testing of a nuclear plant. Then, in November 1984, the NRC approved loading of fuel into Shoreham and tests at "sub-criticality," short of a chain reaction. And, in February 1985, by a vote of four to one, the NRC granted LILCO an exemption from the bâckup power requirement and gave it a license for tests at up to 5 percent of Shoreham's rated 820 megawatts of full power.

NRC Commissioner James Asselstine dissented strongly in this vote, as he has on many Shoreham votes. "LILCO has not met its burden in this case, and should not be given an exemption to the requirement," he declared. The rule "that a plant have a fully qualified on-site source of emergency AC power is not an insignificant safety requirement; it should not, therefore, be modified without compelling reasons for doing so. The essential question presented by LILCO's exemption request becomes then: should the commission waive one of its safety requirements so that a licensee with financial problems can 'send a signal' to Wall Street? I believe not. The commission should not be in the business of relaxing its licensing requirements merely because a particular licensee is having financial difficulties."

The other four members of the NRC reacted angrily to the charge by Asselstine that they were letting Shoreham test at low-power merely because of LILCO's financial problems. The utility was, as it has been for years, at the brink of bankruptcy because of Shoreham, and seeking further loans to pay for the project. It had been pushing for the NRC to give it permission to begin low-power tests to assure prospective lenders that there was a likelihood of Shoreham going into operation. The NRC majority protested, in an addendum, that Asselstine "impugns" their "motives" by claiming this was the purpose for their decision.

The majority also noted that although the troubles with the Delaval diesels meant that there was no NRC-approved backup electrical system at Shoreham, LILCO had provided an "alternative system" of diesels that, although involving equipment not certified for nuclear plant functions, had "sufficient capacity" to provide electricity "in the event of a concurrent loss-of-coolant accident" during low-power operation "given the low accident probability involved." Thus, said the NRC majority, LILCO had made "good faith efforts" to establish alternative backup power.

Henry described the alternative system as "a mess." The additional diesels brought in by LILCO to supplement the Delavals also "can't be counted on in the event of an emergency." Four of these diesels, he said, "are secondhand army-surplus General Motors diesels LILCO bought from New England Utilities. They're thirty-five years old. They're sitting on wooden skids outside with no enclosure, no shelter, exposed to the elements. They are to be run through an old Allis Chalmers switch gear. The control cable has been laid on top of the ground, a few inches of dirt put on top of it. And the kicker is that these diesels don't have their own fuel tanks. LILCO plans to pull a fuel tanker truck alongside and siphon the fuel out of the truck. When the truck runs down, it is supposed to leave, go down the hill and be refueled at a pumping station." Then there were three smaller diesels, manufactured by Colt Industries of Beloit, Wisconsin, to back up the General Motors diesels, also not certified for nuclear plant use and with spare parts "not available."

Henry added, "It's a shabby setup, but this is the way Shoreham was built from the outset and it's continuing now. . . . The NRC has stretched its neck so far out on the backup diesels for Shoreham, it has set a precedent for every other nuclear plant in the U.S. I've never seen anything so bogus. What is involved is against all the NRC regulations, against all the industry regulatory guidelines. LILCO has rewritten the book, and the NRC won't stop them."[52]

Also, the NRC majority, in letting LILCO go ahead with the low-power testing, stipulated that the Delaval diesels be run at lower capacity than at what they were rated, although the NRC, just a year before, had fined LILCO $40,000 for conducting tests of the diesels at low capacity in order to have them pass and not break down in the process.

Suffolk County and New York State went to court to try to prevent the low-power testing. They charged the NRC was "refusing to do its statutory duty . . . abandoning its impartiality and advocating the interests of LILCO . . . and abusing its hearing process to prevent petitioners from fairly making a case" in a "veritable burlesque of due process." The problems of the backup diesels were reviewed. It was emphasized that because Shoreham had no approved evacuation plan, it was unlikely that the plant would ever go into commercial operation. (Low-power tests do not, under NRC rules, require evacuation plans to be in place.) By subjecting Shoreham to low-power testing, the county and state also stressed, the plant would become contaminated with radioactivity and there would be an additional $150 million cost to decontaminate it, if it never was allowed to operate commercially.

Later, in February 1985, an NRC appeals board revoked LILCO's low-power license on the grounds that the additional backup diesels had inadequate security to safeguard them from sabotage. In June, the NRC reversed its earlier decision on that basis. But then, a week later, the NRC rereversed itself and said that it was satisfied that security requirements needed to be met only on the Delaval diesels, and had been.

Of the tortuous NRC process on Shoreham, Lawrence Coe Lanpher of the Washington, D.C., office of the law firm of Kirkpatrick & Lockhart, which has been representing Suffolk County, said: "There's been nothing like it. It has been an all-out effort to get Shoreham licensed, to—at all costs—get it on line for our friends LILCO. It's a terrible example of the regulatory process at work."[53]

Finally, in July, the U.S. Court of Appeals ruled on the county and state court challenge to the low-power testing. But, by that time, Suffolk County Executive Cohalan, under heavy pressure from LILCO, had just changed his position and said he was now for a test of an evacuation plan LILCO had drawn up for Shoreham.

In a decision handed down on July 3, the court ruled that "the accuracy of petitioners' contention that no full-power license will ever be granted due to the lack of an emergency evacuation plan is far from indisputable. We note, in this regard, the recent actions of the Suffolk County executive suggesting the possibility of county cooperation in an emergency plan."

"LILCO has for years been gambling with ratepayers' money and losing," said Governor Cuomo. "They are doing it again with this decision. One would hope they would learn from their mistakes."[54]

The day of the court ruling, NRC officials handed LILCO executives their low-power license for Shoreham.

In the middle of the night on July 7, 1985, a chain reaction was begun at the nuclear plant. Control rods were pulled at 2:35 A.M. and, at 5:48 A.M., Shoreham "went critical," LILCO public relations person Carol Clawson proudly announced.[55]

What followed were several months of low-power operation of the plant accompanied, throughout, by mishaps—some of which could have been quite serious if the plant were operating at full power.[56]

Indeed, LILCO had to twice declare emergency alerts—advising the NRC and local police each time that an "unusual event" had occurred. One alert involved problems with critical water level indicators in the plant, another the failure of a valve in the emergency core cooling system.

The mishaps began during the first week of operation, four days after the chain reaction began. LILCO technicians opened the wrong valve, causing venting of the air from the reactor building into the atmosphere outside. The valve was opened at 4:15 A.M. and the mistake discovered by a supervisor at 6:30 A.M., said the NRC. Karl Abraham, public relations person for the NRC's Region I, said it was a "deviation" from NRC rules, "a minor development" because there was no radiation in the reactor building.

Said Governor Mario Cuomo, "In less than a week, they've had an accident. Nobody's hurt, it's not tragic, it's not dramatic. I'm not saying it is. But what it reveals is their incapacity to create a level of confidence in the people and their performance. They are not good at this, they never have been and they have proved it over and over again."

By the weekend, there was a bigger mishap: A malfunction of a valve controlling the flow of water—which is what cools a nuclear plant like Shoreham—caused the water level above the reactor's core to fall. A pipe began to vibrate, LILCO officials said afterwards, and then the pipe broke causing the valve to fail. The water level above the reactor core fell 12.5 inches before the plant—operating at 1.8 percent full power—went through what LILCO described as a "hot shutdown."

There must be constant flow of water in a nuclear plant so water is covering the reactor core at all times. A stoppage of water leading to an uncovering of the core—a stoppage of just 15 to 30 seconds—can result in a loss-of-coolant accident and a core meltdown. Unless the emergency core cooling system in the plant begins functioning within that time, the core becomes molten hot and can no longer be cooled. It begins melting through the bottom of the nuclear plant—why such an accident has been called the "China Syndrome" accident.

"Test Run for Shoreham Bringing Out Problems," was the headline in the July 16th issue of The New York Times.

Of LILCO's operation of Shoreham, Richard Kessel, executive director of the New York State Consumer Board, said: "It's like putting a loaded gun in the hands of a baby."

On July 26, a valve was improperly opened again. This time, what the NRC estimated was 7,000 gallons of radioactive water—LILCO claimed it was 3,000 gallons—spilled to the reactor's suppression pool and the vital water level above the reactor core dropped 50 inches.

Said Legislator Prospect: "This and the earlier accidents at Shoreham make it quite obvious that the Shoreham plant is a nuclear lemon. The responsible thing now would be for the NRC to revoke the license it gave LILCO to operate Shoreham at low power."[57]

"We have known," said Southampton Town Supervisor Martin Lang, "that LILCO could not build Shoreham properly. Now, it's clear, there's no way LILCO can operate it safely."[58]

On August 6, the manual control rod drive sequencer at the plant failed.

On August 21, the coolant system at Shoreham automatically stopped with the plant operating at 4 percent of full power.

On August 28, instruments indicated that a key cooling system valve was closed, but an inspection showed it was not.

On August 31, the plant was shut down when an alarm indicated a problem with the compressed air system that runs some plant instruments.

On September 6, the plant was shut down again when gauges reported low pressure in the coolant system.

And, on September 8, the first "unusual event" was declared. NRC rules call for an "unusual event" to be declared when "there is a potential degradation in the level of plant safety." This one was sounded when gauges at Shoreham monitoring the water level went completely off the scale. Later, inexplicably, they returned to normal, LILCO reported. The plant had been operating at 1.25 percent of full power at the time the gauges went awry, said LILCO Vice President Freilicher, and shutdown procedures were begun, but because the gauges returned to normal as the shutdown proceeded, it was stopped and the plant was kept running at .7 percent of full power. John Leonard, LILCO's vice president for nuclear operations, said it was kept operating because LILCO felt the source of the problems with the gauges could be best determined while the plant was running.

Then, on September 12, a technician gripped a valve, checking to see whether it was closed. The valve was closed, but the pressure of his grip somehow caused the gauges reporting the water level to go haywire again. This time the plant was shut down for a week. "Gauge Problems Plague Shoreham," declared the *Newsday* headline.

Jack Strosnider of the NRC said of the gauge difficulties: "They seem to be having more trouble with this at Shoreham than we have seen at other nuclear plants." But he was not concerned about the overall record of the low-power tests. Neither was General Electric public relations person, David J. Crowley: "What's happening at Shoreham is not unusual for a nuclear plant. You could liken it to sea trials for a ship. The whole purpose is to shake out the system."[59] And LILCO, through it all, was unconcerned. Out of its public relations office came press release after press release, most beginning with:

"Hicksville, N.Y.—The Long Island Lighting Company reports that the low-power testing program at the Shoreham Nuclear Power Station is progressing in a routine manner."

On September 24, a LILCO statement said that the reason for the gauges not operating properly was some "mildly radioactive" water in a "dip" in the piping system leading to them. "We have found the problem and corrected it," said LILCO public relations person Carol Clawson.

The next day, another "unusual event" was declared when a motor-operated valve in the emergency core cooling system failed. LILCO officials said the valve became inoperable when the four mounting bolts of the motor that was running it all broke at once.

There was, meanwhile, a slight change in LILCO's PR approach to the low-power testing. In a press release, Leonard was now quoted as characterizing the testing as "a series of shut-downs interspersed with short periods of operation."

So it went until October, when LILCO announced that "the testing program at Shoreham has now been successfully completed." In January 1986, however, Jane Alcorn, coordinator of the Citizens Lobby Opposing Shoreham (CLOSE), reviewing Shoreham papers at the document room at the Shoreham-Wading River Public Library, found papers stating the testing was not over.

The first clue came in an NRC report from October that said, "Shoreham weathered the passage of Hurricane Gloria across Long Island with no damage. The plant remained in cold shutdown during the entire event." The report added: "All low-power testing has been suspended indefinitely while LILCO employees from Shoreham are assisting with the restoration of power elsewhere on Long Island." Then, in a December NRC report, Alcorn noticed a passage about how "four systems will require retesting"—including water-level controls and the emergency core cooling system—and this "will proceed following outage."[60]

John Berry, an NRC inspector at Shoreham, subsequently confirmed that the reactor would be restarted and low-power testing resumed.

Berry said that LILCO would be "bringing the plant back up and rerunning some of the tests. They completed all the tests that are required by the NRC, but the testing program indicated that some things had to be repaired. It wasn't that any system completely flunked, but there were little things that didn't pass in a couple of systems."[61]

Among elements of the plant needing work, he said, was "a control rod that had excessive friction on it. That control rod didn't pass, it was replaced and will be retested when they come back up." Work also needed to be done, he said, on water-level controls—"because of the problems with the erroneous water-level readings"—and on the emergency core cooling system.

Berry also revealed that at one point during the low-power testing there was a "power spike"—Shoreham's level of power went to beyond the 5 percent of full power LILCO had been given a license to run it up to by the NRC. "On August 15 there was a period of time, about three to five seconds, when they went to 5.8 to 6.3 percent power during a start-up evolution. The feedback linkage, a mechanical linkage which tells the control system what position the feedwater valves are in, became disconnected." There was a sudden influx of "cold water and that has the effect of increasing the power of the core."

Berry said that Shoreham would be returned to criticality and more low-power testing conducted in a few months. He anticipated that LILCO would have the plant running again "probably for two or three weeks at a minimum. I honestly couldn't tell you the number of weeks. It depends on how many other things they want to do. They're free to do it under the 5 percent license."

Few were surprised with the news that more low-power tests had to be run—after LILCO said the testing was completed. It followed "the pattern of LILCO trying to get away with whatever it can," Jane Alcorn said. "They don't always like us to know what the truth of the situation is at that plant. While LILCO may publicly say one thing, the actuality is not always what they told us."

Alcorn's family—her husband and four children—lives less than two miles from the plant. She fears for their lives if the plant is ever allowed to operate. "Shoreham has been shown time and time again to be one of the gravest dangers to ever face Long Island."

NOTES

1. George Henry in an interview with the author, January 1985.
2. Dale Bridenbaugh in an interview with the author, May 1979.
3. James H. Conran's comments were made in testimony before an NRC board in Riverhead, April 6, 1983, at which the author was present.
4. Warren Liebold and Matthew Chachere conducted the investigation and issued their report on April 13, 1982.

5. Steven Englebright's comment was made in an interview with the author, March 1985.
6. The following comments by George and Vickiann Henry were made in an interview with the author, January 1985.
7. The following comments by Ronald Stanchfield were made in an interview with the author, January 1985.
8. George Henry and Ronald Stanchfield testified at a special meeting of the Suffolk Legislature on January 30, 1985, at which the author was present.
9. Comments by this unnamed former inspector were made in interview with the author, February 1985.
10. John Everett testified at a trial in December 1979—"The People of the State of New York vs. Matthew J. Chachere"—at which the author was present.
11. The warning by John Everett's father to his son was reported in *The New York Times*, December 7, 1979.
12. This and the following comments by John Everett were made in interviews with the author, December 1979.
13. Jock McCrystal's testimony was given at the Chachere trial, and before an NRC board in April 1982 in Hauppauge, at which the author was present. Additional comments were made in interviews with the author, and also in *The Sun*, a Bridgehampton newspaper, July 29, 1982, and *Newsday*, February 17, 1985.
14. John Huber's charges were made before the NRC board sitting in Hauppauge in April 1982, in interviews with the author, April 1982, and in statement to the NRC at the agency's regional office in King of Prussia, July 13, 1983. Record of that interview was entitled: "Transcription, Statement of John Huber."
15. Hugh L. Thompson's statement was contained in memorandum dated September 6, 1985, to the commissioners of the NRC. It was entitled: "Board Notification No. 85–074, Allegations Concerning the Shoreham Nuclear Power Station."
16. Jack Strosnider's statement was contained in a letter to Stanchfield, dated February 19, 1985.
17. Ronald Stanchfield in an interview with the author, November 1986.
18. James Morgo in an interview with the author, November 1986.
19. James Conran's testimony came at an NRC hearing in Riverhead April 6, 1983, and in an affidavit filed with the Atomic Safety and Licensing Board conducting that hearing, entitled "In the Matter of LONG ISLAND LIGHTING COMPANY (Shoreham Nuclear Power Station, Unit 1), Affidavit of James H. Conran."
20. The affidavit of NRC higher-ups was filed with the NRC board the week of March 10, 1983; *Newsday*, March 17, 1983: "5 NRC Aides Back LILCO on Safety."
21. *Newsday*, March 17, 1985.
22. *Newsday*, March 17, 1985.
23. Comments by Judy Ahrens and William Morris were made in an interview with the author, May 1979.
24. Martin Reynolds' comments were made in an interview with the author, May 1979.
25. June Bruce in an interview with the author, May 1979.
26. Concerning the technical terms in the reports, Gregory Minor of MHB explains: "Stiffeners" are steel designed to aid in withstanding earth movement;

"LDT's" are linear displacement transducers, which measure the change in a material after thermal expansion; "embedment supporters" are steel plates embedded in concrete for bracing; "quenchers" are designed to diffuse the jets of steam that would be injected into the suppression pool in the event of a mishap; "refueling bellows" are seals between the containment and reactor to aid in refueling; "Farr filter" is a filter made by the Farr Manufacturing Co.; an "RCIC pump" is a reactor core isolation cooling pump, part of the emergency core cooling system.

27. Michio Kaku's comments were made in an interview with the author, May 1979.
28. This LILCO statement was issued May 16, 1979.
29. Michio Kaku and the author appeared before the New York City Council's Environmental Protection Committee, June 15, 1979.
30. Albert Toth's comments were made in an interview with the author, May 1979.
31. Ira Freilicher in an interview with the author, 1979.
32. Paul Giardina letter to NRC, dated June 1, 1979.
33. Suffolk County filing with the NRC was dated May 17, 1979.
34. Statement of Robert T. Carlson, Chief, Reactor Construction and Engineering Support Branch, NRC Region 1, in a letter to the author, dated July 10, 1979.
35. *Seven Days*, October 26, 1979.
36. Warren Liebold and Matthew Chachere report, April 13, 1982. Problems with Shoreham dome were contained in 1974 Atomic Energy Commission inspection reports. Problems with anchor bolts were discussed in an August 24, 1975, report from LILCO consultant Gerald F. Kubo, and 1975 Nuclear Regulatory Commission reports. Problems with blueprints were examined in 1978 NRC reports including those entitled: "CONTRACTORS DOCUMENTS DO NOT REFLECT LATEST REVISIONS" and "TORN ENGINEERING DRAWINGS IN FILES OF SAFETY-RELATED PIPING."
37. From letter from Patricia Bower to the NRC, January 3, 1983.
38. These and the following comments were made by Bower in interviews with the author, March 1983 and December 1985.
39. Van Howell in an interview with the author, December 1985.
40. Remo Franceschini's comments about Shoreham and organized crime-linked unions were made on *60 Minutes*, which aired on March 24, 1985. He specifically cited Local 66 of the Laborer's Union and Local 242 of the International Brotherhood of Teamsters Union on that broadcast. Kenneth McCallion cited the Allied International Union of Security Guards and Special Police on that broadcast. In a subsequent interview with the author, Franceschini stressed that these unions as well as two other principal unions at Shoreham—Boilermakers Union Local 5 and Operating Engineers Union Local 138—were organized crime connected. "They've long been infiltrated," said Franceschini. In another interview with the author, Raymond Jermyn, deputy chief of the Rackets Bureau in the Suffolk County district attorney's office and the specialist for that office in the prosecution of organized crime, confirmed what Franceschini said. "There's no question these five unions are all connected to organized crime. This has been demonstrated time and time again," he said. McCallion and Jermyn also stressed that the unions have been identified in government legal documents as organized crime connected. In an interview in *Insight* magazine, January 20, 1986,

Franceschini further spoke on the issue, describing Shoreham as "a pork barrel for organized crime. They controlled the place. There was featherbedding, duplication of work, and millions skimmed off that job."

41. An article detailing the links of the Allied International Union of Security Guards and Special Police and its Local 1, Power Plant Police & Security Officers to organized crime was featured in *Forbes* magazine, February 14, 1983. The article, "Brother Cunningham and the Guards," noted that in 1980 this union

> began organizing nuclear plants all over the East Coast. From Indian Point to Shoreham, from Connecticut Yankee to Peach Bottom, Cunningham signed up both guards employed by utilities and guards working for such professional agencies as Burns and Pinkerton, Purolator and Wackenhut.

42. Wayne Prospect's comments were made in an interview with the author, March 1985.

43. The Suffolk County and New York State motion was filed before the NRC on March 27, 1985, and was entitled: "MOTION OF NEW YORK STATE AND SUFFOLK COUNTY FOR IMMEDIATE INVESTIGATION OF ALLE-GATIONS CONTAINED IN '60 MINUTES' BROADCAST."

44. Suffolk County negotiations with LILCO on a Shoreham inspection were covered by the author in 1981. LILCO's insistence on agreeing initially to an inspection of only two systems was reported in numerous news articles. Adler Robinson's comment was made in an interview with the author, September 1981.

45. Jock McCrystal testified before the NRC board meeting in Hauppauge, April 1982.

46. Comments by Steven Englebright were made in interviews with the author, March 1985.

47. NRC report cited by Englebright was entitled "Safety Evaluation Report related to the Operation of Shoreham Nuclear Power Station, Unit No. 1" (NURED-0420), which was issued April 1981.

48. New York *Daily News*, July 26, 1982.

49. Charges by Franz Leichter, a Democrat from Manhattan, and Wayne Prospect were contained in "Violations Charged in N-Fuel Transport," *Newsday*, July 30, 1982.

50. Articles on faults with Delaval diesels included an article in *Newsday*, August 15, 1983, headlined: "Report Faults Manufacturer, Tests of N-Plant Generator." It said:

> A report prepared for the U.S. Nuclear Regulatory Commission has pinpointed numerous problems in both manufacture and testing of the emergency diesel generators at the Shoreham atomic plant, most dating back more than a year. The study, a copy of which was obtained by *Newsday* yesterday, criticizes both the generators' manufacturer and Long Island Lighting Co. It describes equipment that arrived with wrong or missing parts, improper manufacture and other defects. Once at Shoreham, maintenance records indicate incorrect procedures—including improper lubrication—or incomplete verification that correct tests were done on the diesels, the study said.

Other *Newsday* stories included: "N-Plant Flaw Feared Widespread," September 3, 1983; "Shoreham Diesels' Troubled History," September 4, 1983; "N-Plant Diesels Stir New Probe," October 25, 1983; "N-Plant Flaws Laid to

Design Error," November 4, 1983. There were also many stories on the issue in the weekly press.

51. Jan Hickman's comments were made in *Newsday*, August 24, 1983.
52. George Henry's comments were made in an interview with the author, June 1985.
53. Lawrence Lanpher in an interview with the author, 1985.
54. Gov. Mario Cuomo's statement, *Newsday*, July 5, 1985.
55. Carol Clawson's comment, *Newsday*, July 8, 1985.
56. Problems during low-power testing at Shoreham were chronicled in numerous news accounts including: "Wrong Valve Opened During Shoreham Test," *Newsday*, July 12, 1985; "N-Plant Shutdown Cause Is in Doubt," " 'Hot Shutdown' at Shoreham," *Newsday*, July 14, 1985; *Newsday*, July 15, 1985; " 'Operator error,' malfunction: Problems Plague Shoreham Tests," *Suffolk Life*, July 17, 1985; "On Again, Off Again for LILCO," *The Suffolk Times*, July 25, 1985; "S'ham Shuts Down Twice in 3 Days," *Suffolk Life*, September 11, 1985; "Gauge Problems Plague Shoreham," *Newsday*, September 15, 1985; "Shoreham Is Shut Down Because of Faulty Gauges," *The New York Times*, September 17, 1985; "Low-Level Alert at Shoreham," *Newsday*, September 19, 1985; "Shoreham Motor Fails," *Newsday*, September 26, 1985; "Valve Fails During Testing at Shoreham Nuke Plant," *Suffolk Life*, October 2, 1985; and many others.
57. Wayne Prospect in an interview with the author, July 1985.
58. Martin Lang in an interview with the author, July 1985.
59. Jack Strosnider's and David J. Crowley's comments were made in *The New York Times*, September 17, 1985.
60. Jane Alcorn's information was given in an interview with the author, January 1986.
61. John Berry's comments were made in an interview with the author, January 1986.

3

POWER BROKER
OF
THE NORTHEAST?

The demise of a plan to build a nuclear power plant right in the middle of New York City catapulted the Long Island Lighting Company into nuclear power—with Shoreham conceived as one part of a string of many LILCO nuclear plants.

As crazy as it seems today, the Consolidated Edison Company of New York planned in the early 1960s to build a nuclear plant in Ravenswood, Queens, along the East River directly across from Manhattan just north of the Queensborough Bridge.

"Nuclear power was considered safe by many people," said Martin Gitten, public information manager of Con Ed, of how Con Ed perceived attitudes then. Now, "in the real post-TMI world," said Gitten, "we would probably not propose to build a nuclear unit because of the unclear market and regulatory conditions."[1]

Con Ed applied to the U.S. Atomic Energy Commission (AEC) in December 1962 for a construction license for the Ravenswood project. The AEC had been created in 1946 specifically to promote—and regulate—commercial nuclear technology. (In 1975 the AEC's regulatory responsibilities were given to a new Nuclear Regulatory Commission [NRC], composed of five members appointed by the President with the advice and consent of the U.S. Senate. Its nuclear promotion activities and involvement in the military side of nuclear technology went to the U.S. Department of Energy.)

The Con Ed reactor was to be manufactured by the Westinghouse Electric Corporation. (Westinghouse and General Electric, the manufacturer of Shoreham, are the Coca-Cola and Pepsi of nuclear power: Over 80 percent of nuclear power plants in the world are of Westinghouse or GE design.) The project, Con Ed said, would cost $175 million.

The same year, Con Ed had completed its first nuclear plant, Indian Point 1, a 275-megawatt facility twenty-eight miles north of the city line. It went into commercial operation in January 1963. (Built without an emergency core cooling system, Indian Point 1 was permanently shut down in 1974 after Con Ed decided that it would be too expensive to add one.)

One New York City newspaper, the *Journal American* (June 17, 1963), declared that even if the Ravenswood nuclear plant wasn't built, that shouldn't stop a nuclear plant from going up elsewhere in the city. "We can understand the fears held by many people that construction of a nuclear power plant in Queens would constitute a constant threat to health and safety," said the 1963 editorial. "But we do not believe that these fears should be permitted to panic the City Council into banning all nuclear reactors. . . . The City Council will be turning its back on the inevitable wave of the future if it succumbs to ill-advised demands for a ban on all nuclear reactors within the five boroughs."

There was tremendous opposition to the Ravenswood plant among city residents. Opponents of the project packed a City Council hearing at which a bill to prevent its construction was considered.

Even a former chairman of the AEC was critical of the plan. David E. Lilienthal said: "I would not dream of living in the Borough of Queens if there were a large atomic power plant in that region."[2]

More than five million people, it was estimated, lived within five miles of the site where the 1,000 megawatt plant was to be located.

In 1963, the *Long Island Press* quoted from an AEC document that stated "that a reactor such as Consolidated Edison plans should be '13.7 miles from the nearest boundary of a densely populated place.' Considering that the Ravenswood site is almost smack in the geographic center of New York City with its teeming millions, and that the 13.7-mile zone overlaps even Mineola [in Nassau County on Long Island] on one side and Newark [New Jersey] on the other, opposition to it is understandable, to say the least."[3]

Con Ed canceled its Ravenswood project in January 1964. "No atoms for peace in Queens," was the lead of a January 7, 1964, story in the *New York Herald Tribune* by its science editor, Earl Ubell. "The Consolidated Edison Co.," he went on, "cancelled its plans yesterday to set a huge atomic-power plant in the backyards of New Yorkers."

But Con Ed said it wasn't giving up on building nuclear plants in the city. Con Ed Chairman Harland C. Forbes asserted: "Our faith in the future of nuclear power in the New York City area remains undiminished."[4] (And, in 1970, Con Ed announced it would build two nuclear plants on man-made islands in Jamaica Bay off Queens—but that plan was stymied as well.)

Despite the AEC report urging that reactors not be sited close to "a densely populated place," the news accounts of the Ravenswood cancellation reported that AEC officials did not believe it meant the end of the notion of nuclear plants within city boundaries.

Just as the Con Ed announcement came, according to the *Herald Tribune*, three officials of the AEC were presenting their views on problems of placing reactors in cities. At "a session of the Nuclear Energy Writers Association . . . they had just finished saying that the AEC was undecided on the entire problem of nuclear reactors in cities" and "although the ordinary rules for the location of reactors could not be met in New York, engineered safeguards could overcome the restrictions."[5]

A *New York Times* story quoted one of the AEC officials, Joseph A. Lieberman, assistant director of nuclear safety in its Division of Reactor Development, as saying "he believed some manufacturers now possessed the ability to build safe reactors within city limits 'because they have already proposed to do it.' "[6]

The nuclear industry was disappointed by cancellation of the nuclear plant at Ravenswood (where there had been two conventional Con Ed power plants and, in 1965, a third was completed). The *Herald Tribune* story said the industry "was looking toward its construction as a test case for other cities."[7] Andrew R. Jones, manager of the preliminary plant engineering section of the atomic power division of Westinghouse, said to *The Times* of the Ravenswood reactor: "We are firmly convinced that it would be a very safe device."

Meanwhile, eagerly looking to fill the vacuum its officials regarded as being created by Con Ed's cancellation of Ravenswood was the Long Island Lighting Company.

With Con Ed deciding not to go with this nuclear plant in New York City, and the federal government becoming somewhat concerned about letting nuclear plants be located in cities, LILCO officials figured it was time for their company to move aggressively into the picture.

LILCO's service area, although having a far denser population than most areas in the United States, was still less highly populated than New York City. Importantly, nuclear plants need massive amounts of coolant water—a plant of 1,000 megawatts requires a million gallons a minute to operate. (Shoreham, at 820 megawatts, would need 600,000 gallons a minute.) LILCO officials saw the island on which their company was located as being perfectly situated to provide massive amounts of coolant water for many nuclear plants. Water from the Long Island Sound, separating Long Island and Connecticut, could be utilized for nuclear plants along the North Shore. On the South Shore, at several sheltered points along the Atlantic, nuclear plants could be constructed that would use ocean waters as coolant.

The LILCO officials envisioned the collection of nuclear plants the company would construct as providing electricity to New York City and throughout the Northeast.

In terms of getting abundant cooling water, the best place to site nuclear plants in the Northeast, LILCO knew, would be along the coast. But the Atlantic Coast from Boston down through New Jersey was—and is—one of the most thickly populated coastlines in the world. From Long Island, off this coast, LILCO executives dreamed, they would have a base to provide the entire region with electricity. LILCO would become the power broker of the Northeast. Shoreham would be the first of many nuclear plants.

The company whose executives were spinning such heady schemes had, meanwhile, a record of dismal management.

Indeed, well before the years of being on the brink of bankruptcy because of Shoreham, LILCO for years had been on the brink of bankruptcy for more conventional reasons.

In the 1930s and through the 1940s, LILCO was regularly on the ropes. "You heard about LILCO being in tremendous difficulty, ready to go belly up," recounted Anne Mead, a Long Island lawyer and judge who, since 1978, has been a member of the New York State Public Service Commission.[8]

The PSC, in its 1947 Annual Report, devoted pages to a plan by LILCO for "consolidation and recapitalization." To rescue itself financially, LILCO at the time wanted to merge with three LILCO subsidiaries and recapitalize its debt.

The PSC report cited an "extensive investigation and study" directed by PSC Chairman Milos Maltbie into the financial structure of LILCO and its subsidiaries. This investigation's conclusion was critical of the LILCO plan and reviewed the events that brought the companies to their state of near-bankruptcy. "[The plan] listed investments by the parent, Long Island Lighting Company, and by its subsidiaries, in the stocks of each other and of associated companies, transactions which have turned out badly; and intercompany loans upon which the Long Island Lighting Company has slim chances of recovering anything."

LILCO's plan "would result in a capital setup top-heavy with funded debt," said the PSC report and, again citing the investigation into LILCO, declared, "When a public body is reconstituting a system to put it on a secure and sound basis, it would be most careless or indifferent to experience if it voluntarily approved a ratio of debt to net assets of over 60 percent, not to mention 70 percent."

The arrogance LILCO has become known for in recent years was also noted then. The PSC report spoke of how "pressure has been brought to bear upon the commission, not only by company officials but by others, to give its approval to the company plan," but the PSC "will not permit itself to be high-pressured."

The 1948 PSC Annual Report said the common stocks of LILCO and its subsidiaries "have no value" and "are not backed by assets." LILCO had, meanwhile, put together an amended version of its consolidation and reorganization plan. The PSC was upset over the new plan as well. "Apparently, the originators of this scheme aim to evade or avoid the laws of the State of New York."

This report also noted that in September 1948 Con Ed announced it had taken first steps to acquire control of LILCO and had filed a petition with the PSC for its planned takeover of the troubled Long Island utility.

Con Ed, in a September 21, 1948, statement released at its Manhattan headquarters, said that its "acquisition of the Long Island Lighting properties is in the public interest because the service areas involved are side by side and because it would be possible to effect operating economies through the joint use of certain facilities and to improve the service rendered to the public. . . . The reconstituted Long Island [Lighting] would be operated by responsible local management . . . and the acquisition would result in an improvement in Long Island's credit and facilitate not only the refunding of its long term debt, but also the financing of its construction program."

In testimony before the PSC that December, a Con Ed executive elaborated on how LILCO's credit standing would be aided by a Con Edison takeover because of the lower percentage of Con Ed debt compared with the high percentage of LILCO debt in relation to assets.[9]

In 1950, Con Edison decided not to take over LILCO.[10] Meanwhile, another New York City-based institution, Citibank, then called First National City Bank, was coming to the utility's aid.

The tie between Citibank and LILCO was to become central in LILCO's future. In large part, LILCO came under the financial oversight of this extremely powerful American bank.

In a 1973 *Newsday* series on "Corporate Closeness," reporter Kenneth Crowe stressed the Citibank-LILCO link in an installment entitled "LILCO's Ties That Bind."[11] "When LILCO was going through a corporate reorganization in the late 1940s and was considered a questionable financial risk, First National City Bank was the only bank that would lend it substantial sums of money," Crowe noted. "First National City Bank continues to extend an important line of credit to LILCO." Further, the bank's trust department held then (and still does) one of the largest blocks of LILCO common stock "and performs such financial services for the utility as serving as transfer agent for LILCO's stock." In the 1950s, a senior vice president of the bank, Eben W. Pyne, was placed on LILCO's board of directors. (Pyne remains a LILCO board member thirty years after, the only LILCO director with such tenure. He belongs to a three-member committee overseeing LILCO's nuclear program.)

Pyne also was a connection, the article pointed out, between LILCO and Stone & Webster, the Boston-headquartered company chosen to be the architect-engineer and construction manager of the Shoreham project—picked even though its price was $2 million higher than that of the lowest bidder. Noted Crowe, "There are a number of business-director-financial links between LILCO and Stone & Webster. . . . The thread of these ties can be traced through LILCO Director Eben Pyne."

Crowe cited a study that for nearly two decades has been a handbook for journalists, investigators and others examining how the nuclear industry is structured and how it works.

It is a report entitled "Competition in the Nuclear Power Supply Industry" and was prepared for the AEC and the U. S. Department of Justice in 1968 by Arthur D. Little, Inc., a Cambridge, Massachusetts-based management consulting firm.

The analysis found a lack of competition in the nuclear industry and a situation in which the same companies dominating nuclear power also dominated non-nuclear energy. Further, it discovered a pattern of the companies composing the nuclear industry being tied together with interlocking directorates, an officer or board member of one company sitting on the board of another.

"Competition between nuclear and fossil as a factor of significance in the energy market is dependent upon the existence of separate companies in the two fields," said the report. "If the companies serving the two markets were to become the same by evolving into nuclear/fossil energy companies, the nature of competition between them would change significantly. The development of firms diversified in the energy field would pose a threat to inter-modal energy competition." In other words, if nuclear power were to be offered as a substitute for oil or coal—or in later years solar energy—and the different forms of energy were not provided by different companies, companies controlling all the forms might manipulate the situation, eliminating alternatives.

The Arthur D. Little, Inc., study provided a list of "major oil companies . . . entering other energy-producing industries," especially the nuclear industry through uranium exploration and mining.

The report determined there was a "concentration in the building of nuclear plants." Then, as now, the field was dominated by Westinghouse and GE. And, it said, "interlocking directorates were found to be widespread" in the entire nuclear industry. Such interlocks are "sometimes considered beneficial from a managerial point of view but sometimes thought to be potentially injurious to competition," said the analysis.

The analysis featured a large pullout flow chart—a diagram entitled "Corporate Relationships through Director Affiliations"—that showed the connections through interlocking directorates between First National City Bank, Chase Manhattan and other banks to companies in the nuclear industry and then to utilities involved in nuclear power, including LILCO.

Eben Pyne's name was on the top line of the flow chart, with his LILCO position noted. The chart then connected him to First National City Bank and then connected the bank, through interlocking directorates, to elements of the nuclear industry. It linked Pyne to Stone & Webster through his membership on the board of W. R. Grace & Company, a conglomerate heavily involved in producing chemicals, whose chairman, J. Peter Grace of Long Island, was a Stone & Webster director. Also, the chart noted that Whitney Stone, chairman of Stone & Webster, was a W. R. Grace director, too. Further, the chart showed that Transcontinental Gas Pipe Line Corp. is owned partly by Stone & Webster. Transcontinental has supplied LILCO with most of its natural gas. The chart also noted Stone's membership on the board of directors of Chase Manhattan Bank, whose trust department along with the trust department of First National City Bank, have been major holders of LILCO stock.

Out of all this, Crowe crafted his article, including interviews with LILCO executives on the interlocks. Crowe confronted John J. Tuohy, then the chairman of LILCO. He wrote that Tuohy was asked in an interview, " 'Are you aware of any financial or corporate interlocks between LILCO, the banks that service it, or any of its directors—and Stone & Webster?' He replied, 'None.' LILCO's chairman was shown a chart [the Arthur D. Little, Inc. report's flow chart] depicting in graphic form the interconnections laid out between Pyne, the director, First National City Bank, W. R. Grace, Stone & Webster, Transcontinental, Chase Manhattan, and LILCO. Tuohy's response was, 'You astonish me. All that is of great interest. It really has nothing to do with anything.' "

The article continued that Tuohy and LILCO President Edward C. Duffy "said the contract was awarded to Stone & Webster by LILCO's board of directors on the recommendation of LILCO's management."

There was another link between LILCO and Stone & Webster—not revealed in any report at the time, not disclosed by Duffy and not known until years later, when the New York State Public Service Commission embarked on a major investigation of LILCO's management of Shoreham's construction. Duffy's son-in-law, Richard L. Forrester, was marketing engineer at Stone & Webster when it got its contract with LILCO. He was deeply involved in his company getting the LILCO work, the state investigation found, with Duffy, then LILCO's executive vice president, pivotal in recommending his son-in-law's company to LILCO's management and board of directors.[12]

The U.S. Federal Trade Commission in the 1970s conducted a study on interlocking directorates between banks and energy companies.[13] It said that it was trying to determine whether "interlocked energy companies use their position to deny or limit credit available to their competitors or to a segment of the industry to which they are antagonistic," and whether such companies "influence bank credit policies to encourage or inhibit various alternative energy sources and industry structures." That investigation got nowhere because, said the FTC, the banks would not cooperate, claiming it did not have jurisdiction and that its demands for information would require them to produce millions of pages of material and, thus, were unreasonable.

An issue surfacing but not analyzed in the Arthur D. Little, Inc. report, but since examined in detail elsewhere, was the involvement of the interests of the Rockefeller family in nuclear energy—an aspect of nuclear energy that, like so many others, is demonstrated in the extreme by the story of LILCO.

High on the list in the Arthur D. Little, Inc. report of the "major oil companies" going into the nuclear industry were components of what had been the Standard Oil Trust. The Standard Oil Trust was a monopoly created by John D. Rockefeller that dominated the American oil business—from the wellhead to the pump—until the U.S. Supreme Court in 1911 ordered a "trust-bust" of the empire, breaking it into thirty-eight components. The Supreme Court's action followed years of disclosures by the investigative reporters, the muckrakers, of the early years of the twentieth century in America. They pointed to the Standard Oil Trust as a glaring example of an octopus-like monopoly grabbing control of all competition, engaging in corrupt practices, manipulating governments, and going worldwide with its domination of a resource. The court declared that the Standard Oil Trust was a monopoly functioning "to drive others from the field and exclude them from their right to trade."

Although the trust was supposedly broken up by the Supreme Court decision, there has been documentation over the decades, including government analyses, showing that most of the companies that were spun off—Standard Oil of New Jersey (Exxon), Standard Oil of New York (Mobil), Standard Oil of Indiana (Amoco), Standard Oil of California (Chevron), and so on—still function closely together.[14]

Besides dominating the oil business, the Rockefellers soon became leaders of American and global finance. John D. Rockefeller had fought with bankers when he began to build his empire, and in the end, his family wound up in command of several banks—including First National City Bank or Citibank and Chase Manhattan. Citibank has become the biggest bank in the U.S.; Chase Manhattan, the third largest.[15] (Bank of America is second.)

Important to the development of nuclear power, both banks made major investments in the new technology. Further, both gained interlocking relations at the directorial level with many companies in the nuclear field, including Westinghouse and GE, and through their trust departments, the banks acquired much Westinghouse and GE stock.

The involvement of the Rockefeller family interests in nuclear power, through the components of the old Standard Oil Trust, the family's banking interests and activities of family members in government, has been detailed in a number of books both on nuclear energy and on the Rockefellers.

In *NUCLEAR INC., The Men and Money behind Nuclear Energy*, Mark Hertsgaard described how "Rockefeller family interests have supported nuclear power from the very beginning. The Rockefellers got their start in nuclear in 1950, when they hired Lewis Strauss, recently resigned AEC member, as their investment adviser." In 1954, Laurence and David Rockefeller, two of John D.'s grandsons, founded the United Nuclear uranium company, and Chase Manhattan, of which David was chairman, became the first bank to establish a nuclear power division. In 1955, Nelson Rockefeller, a third grandson, who was then serving in the White House as President Eisenhower's special assistant, "persuaded Eisenhower to reinvigorate and expand the Atoms for Peace program to include more training for foreigners and increased funding for exporting U.S.-manufactured research reactors." As governor of New York between 1959 and 1973, "Nelson worked hard and successfully to stimulate, through state subsidies, the private development of nuclear power in New York." And in 1975, as vice president of the United States, "he pushed for creation of a federal Energy Independence Authority, a $100 billion program of government subsidies and loan guarantees intended to stimulate U.S. domestic energy production. Most of the money was targeted on such nuclear-related projects as breeder reactors, uranium enrichment and fuel reprocessing."

Nuclear power was a highly questionable economic risk in the 1950s—as it is now. But the Rockefeller offspring tackled it the way their grandfather tackled the oil business, and they brought to nuclear energy many of the traditions laid down by John D. As to the dangers of nuclear power, one former Nelson Rockefeller associate (who requested anonymity) once told me his attitude was: "You have to live dangerously."

Thus LILCO, a regional utility with a shabby record, found itself in the 1950s involved with some of the most powerful forces in the U.S. It did have one thing in common with them: LILCO, too, had spent years eliminating competition.

The first electric company on Long Island was not LILCO. It was the Babylon Electric Light Company, founded in 1886—just four years after Thomas Edison opened the world's first central station for electricity on Pearl Street in Manhattan. The company, in western Suffolk, made use of a natural Long Island energy source to generate electricity: hydropower. Its source was the waterfall on Sumpwams Creek at the eastern edge of Babylon Village. Hydropower was also used to generate electricity by the first power company in eastern Long Island: the Riverhead Electric Light Company. Its founder, J. Henry Perkins, utilized the waters of the Peconic River, which flows through Riverhead, to create electricity.

The first electric company in Nassau was in the Village of Oyster Bay. The Oyster Bay Electric Light Company was formed in 1891, producing electricity with hydropower from the waters of Mill Pond.

As the new century arrived, other utilities providing electricity, principally with coal-fired power generators, formed on Long Island: Roslyn Light and Power Company, North Hempstead Light, Heat & Power Company, Port Washington Electric Light, Heat & Power, Town of Hempstead Gas & Electric Company, and so on.

LILCO was formed in 1910. Relates the utility in its official history:[16] "On New Year's Eve in 1910, incorporation papers were filed in the office of the Secretary of State in Albany signifying the birth of the Long Island Lighting Company." It was created by the merger of four small electric companies: Amityville Electric Lighting Company, Northport Electric Light Company, Sayville Electric Company and Islip Electric Light Company—all in Suffolk County. "The act was a simple one with no public fanfare, yet it was significant in that it marked the beginning of the shift in the gas and electric business on Long Island from individual, local concerns to a county-wide and eventually an island-wide organization. The principal originator of the new company was a mechanical and electrical engineer, Ellis L. Phillips." Phillips, an 1895 Cornell University graduate, had come to Long Island to advise trolley owners in Huntington and Northport on new equipment.

For many years, LILCO's main office was not on Long Island, but at 50 Church Street in Manhattan, now the site of the World Trade Center. On June 19, 1911, LILCO officially began as a utility with

1,048 electric meters and forty-two employees. LILCO revenue that first year totalled $70,000. Phillips moved fast to expand LILCO.

By 1915, the history recounts, LILCO had bought the first electricity company on Long Island, the Babylon Electric Light Company, along with electric companies in Port Jefferson, Bay Shore, Southampton and Huntington. By 1920, LILCO had acquired the Riverhead Electric Light Company.

LILCO, its history says, had trouble acquiring gas companies on Long Island.

> The entry of the Long Island Lighting Company into Nassau in 1923, through the merger of the Nassau Light and Power Company and the purchase of Queens Borough Gas and Electric, was not without incident. Rather, it was marked by the beginning of an intense struggle with the area's gas people. Headed by Nassau and Suffolk Lighting, the gas companies stubbornly resisted the intrusion of new electric service to various parts of the county. The dispute was only resolved, some years later [in 1927], when the Nassau and Suffolk management decided to sell to Long Island Lighting.

In 1925, the history continues, "the purchase of the East Hampton Electric Light Company stretched the company's area from the city line to the easternmost point on the island, Montauk Point."

LILCO kept its general offices in Manhattan until 1939, when it moved to Mineola. Acquisitions continued until 1964, when LILCO bought the Patchogue Electric Light Company. By then, there were no utilities left for LILCO to take over other than the three public utilities in Freeport, Rockville Centre and Greenport—which would not sell out.

"Utility service on Long Island has grown," LILCO's history—prepared in the 1960s—concludes, to "finally, one gas and electric company serving over one million electric and gas customers. Coal and rosin have given way to natural gas, and the waterfall-driven generator to modern steam turbines, which in turn will be replaced by atomic reactors."

LILCO made plans to have the first of these LILCO atomic reactors at Shoreham.

The State of New York under Governor Rockefeller, meanwhile, preceded LILCO in announcing what originally was supposed to be the first nuclear power plant on Long Island—a government-built facility operated partly by government and partly by private companies, including LILCO. Advanced in 1962 by the Rockefeller administration in cooperation with the AEC, it was named SURFSIDE—an acronym for Small Unified Reactor Facility with Systems for Isotopes, Desalting and Electricity. It was to produce radioisotopes for industry, turn salt water into fresh and generate electricity, all at the same time. Rockefeller created a New York State Atomic Research and Development Authority that he put in charge of the project's development. It was to be built with state and federal funds on land fronting the Long Island Sound in Jamesport on Long Island's North Shore and run by the state authority, the AEC, the U.S. Department of the Interior, any private water companies interested and LILCO.[17]

SURFSIDE was abandoned when the national administration, which was Democratic, decided not to provide matching federal funds for the scheme of the Republican governor. New York State Senate Democrats also became critical of the state nuclear power program Rockefeller was proposing, of which SURFSIDE was a part. (Another part, subsequently, was Shoreham—state funds were to be channelled through the state atomic authority to LILCO for the reactor.[18]) A *Newsday* story related that the Democrats "charged that the program was another Teapot Dome scandal, larcenous and a sell-out to private utilities."[19]

On April 12, 1966, with a press conference, LILCO announced its Shoreham project. The estimated cost was "in the $65–75 million range," said the press release that company officials distributed at LILCO headquarters in Mineola.

MINEOLA, L.I.—The use of atomic energy to produce electricity for Long Island was moved a big step forward as Long Island Lighting Company announced that it had initiated proceedings with local authorities to rezone a portion of a site on the north shore of Suffolk County for the Company's first nuclear electric generating plant.

LILCO President John J. Tuohy disclosed that the proposed atomic plant is to be built on a 455 acre site that the Company has contracted to purchase in the Town of Brookhaven, located between the villages of Shoreham and Wading River, and overlooking the Long Island Sound. . . .

Total cost of the atomic unit, Mr. Tuohy indicated, is estimated to be in the $65–$75 million range. Present plans, he said, call for major construction to begin by about late 1969. Operation of the plant is figured for 1973 when its power output of 500,000 kilowatts or more is scheduled to begin flowing into the LILCO system. . . .

. . . an atomic power plant allows us to maintain . . . high standards of service with a minimum impact on the environment, since nuclear energy facilities produce no smoke or combustion by-products to affect the atmosphere.

Given out at the press conference, too, in a folder on which "LILCO Shoreham Atomic Power Project Information and Press Kit" was embossed in gold, were two slick booklets prepared by LILCO. One was entitled *The Shoreham Project* and opened with a statement by Tuohy with a description of the proposed site and plant, the timetable and how LILCO would conduct a public information program including setting up a "permanent public information center at the plant site with exhibits, films and other features of interest and educational value." (It never did.) In conclusion, Tuohy stated: "When completed, the Shoreham Project will represent the culmination of preparatory effort by LILCO in the atomic power field."

The booklet then featured photographs of a "sampling of U.S. atomic power plants" and closed with "Questions and Answers on the Shoreham Project."

Among them:

"**Q:** Why build an atomic power plant?

"**A:** Because we believe atomic power is the way of the future and the economics are favorable for Long Island today."

There was to be wide distribution to people on Long Island, LILCO executives said, of the second booklet, *Atomic Power on Long Island.* That would be "part of," *Newsday* later reported, "LILCO's campaign to familiarize the public with the use of nuclear energy for generating electricity" to avoid the sort of "adverse reaction from Long Islanders to the proposed construction similar to the experience of the Consolidated Edison Company. . . . Con Ed decided last year to withdraw its application for a nuclear power plant in the Ravenswood section of Queens after two years of opposition from residents who feared it would be a hazard."

Atomic Power on Long Island described nuclear power as safe and economical. It said that any nuclear plant constructed must be approved by the AEC. "The licensing procedure involves a detailed re-

NEWS from

AN INVESTOR OWNED, TAXPAYING COMPANY

250 OLD COUNTRY ROAD
MINEOLA, LONG ISLAND, N.Y.
•
JACK STRANDFELDT
(516) PI 7-1000, EXT. 508

FOR RELEASE: Wednesday P.M.
April 13, 1966

Mineola, L. I.; - The use of atomic energy to produce electricity for Long
Island was moved a big step forward as Long Island Lighting Company today
announced that it had initiated proceedings with local authorities to rezone a portion of a site on the north shore of Suffolk County for the
Company's first nuclear electric generating plant.

LILCO President John J. Tuohy disclosed that the proposed atomic plant
is to be built on a 455 acre site that the Company has contracted to purchase
in the Town of Brookhaven, located between the villages of Shoreham and
Wading River, and overlooking Long Island Sound. Permission from the Town
is being sought by the Company to use about one-half of the property for
electric generating plant use. The balance would remain in a residential
status.

Total cost of the atomic unit, Mr. Tuohy indicated, is estimated to be
in the $65-75 million range. Present plans, he said, call for major construc-
tion to begin by about late 1969. Operation of the plant is figured for 1973
when its power output of 500,000 kilowatts or more is scheduled to begin
flowing into the LILCO system. At that time, the plant's contribution to town
property tax revenues, based on current rates, is expected to exceed $1,500,000
annually.

President Tuohy said that the specific reactor design for the new LILCO
plant had not, as yet, been chosen. He did say, though, that it would likely
be of the so-called light-water type. Plants of this nuclear design are now
in operation at Indian Point, New York, and in New England; and are under

M O R E

First page of LILCO press release announcing Shoreham.

view of the plant's safety not only by the AEC's own highly competent regulatory staff but also by a panel of independent experts. And once the plant has been placed in service, its operation is monitored by the AEC." Of radioactivity routinely released during the operation of a nuclear plant, "an exceedingly small quantity indeed, is released to the environment—air or water—on a controlled basis and in compliance with rigorous regulations established by the U.S. Atomic Energy Commission." And as for radioactivity, "It is sometimes forgotten that our environment is naturally mildly radioactive and that, strictly speaking, we ourselves are radioactive due to the presence in our bodies of trace amounts of naturally radioactive substances. Radioactivity is thus a matter of degree."

Of costs, the booklet said that "since the first developmental plants were built, the cost of atomic power has been halved and halved again. In large sizes, atomic plants either now are or soon will be economically competitive with the best fossil-fuel-fired plants in many parts of the country."

The "present expectation," said the LILCO booklet, "is that atomic plants will account for between 10 and 15 percent of new power plant construction as we enter the seventies, and perhaps 30 to 40 percent in the eighties. At this rate atomic power may well account for half of all the electricity produced by the United States by the turn of the century." (As of 1985, atomic power provided 15 percent of electricity in the country.) The booklet struck a note that LILCO would repeat over the years: that nuclear power was needed to meet a growing need for electricity. "LILCO's power load . . . grows each year."

Assisting in the preparation of *Atomic Power for Long Island* was June Bruce, formerly with the AEC, whom LILCO hired for its public relations staff as it positioned itself to move heavily into nuclear power.

The federal government's nuclear "establishment" was another key element in LILCO's emergence into nuclear power.

Inspiration, encouragement and support were provided to LILCO by government scientists at Brookhaven National Laboratory, a facility established by the federal government on Long Island in 1947 for researching "the peaceful aspects of nuclear science." It was set up by the AEC basically to be a taxpayer-supported research and development facility for nuclear technology and has close ties with the nuclear technology bureaucracy in Washington, D.C., to the nuclear industry and to other government nuclear laboratories. LILCO, the utility close at hand, would become, for large numbers of personnel at the laboratory, their "pet" utility. From its beginning, there would be an intimate connection between LILCO and its nuclear program and Brookhaven National Laboratory.

Atomic Power for Long Island noted a part of the Brookhaven National Laboratory/LILCO link under a section headed "LILCO Participation in Atomic Power Development."

The LILCO booklet related:

One winter day in 1953, two LILCO engineers drove out to Brookhaven National Laboratory to attend the first of what turned out to be a year-long series of weekly lectures on reactor design principles and related topics. The lectures were held on Wednesdays and it was not long before the attendees became known around the Laboratory as the "Wednesday Boys." The association with the Brookhaven staff proved to be of mutual advantage. There was much to learn and the atmosphere at the Laboratory was a stimulating one. In return, the LILCO engineers brought a fresh point of view to bear on many difficult engineering problems with which the Laboratory was then dealing in the reactor field. On completion of the lecture course, we sent a man to work full-time at Brookhaven—an arrangement that we maintained for five years—and over the years have continued to keep in close touch with the Laboratory's reactor activities.

A month after the Shoreham announcement, it was noticed that on a chart in *Atomic Power for Long Island* summarizing LILCO's power plant construction program, a second nuclear plant was listed, to go into operation three years after Shoreham. The LILCO public relations staff confirmed it. "LILCO Weighs 2nd A-Plant for LI," was the headline in *Newsday* (May 27, 1965). LILCO officials subsequently said the second plant also would be going up in Shoreham, would be a "twin" of the first and called Shoreham 2.

The following year, Governor Rockefeller was back announcing another new state-initiated nuclear plant project for Long Island—or rather off Long Island. In March 1967, Rockefeller said his State Atomic and Space Development Authority was now "considering the development of an offshore nuclear power plant, possibly beneath the sea"—as the *Newsday* story reported it.[20] "He said that the nuclear reactor could be underwater with the turbine placed on stilts." But this project, like SURFSIDE, got nowhere.

Meanwhile, LILCO was developing its plans.

In 1967, LILCO announced what would be its third nuclear plant, to be built at Lloyd Neck in the Village of Lloyd Harbor in Huntington Town, twenty miles west of Shoreham on Long Island's North Shore (thirty miles from New York City). A *Newsday* story on the project in Lloyd Harbor quoted a LILCO public relations person as saying LILCO was moving ahead with several nuclear projects because "nuclear plants are cleaner and do not pollute the air and water as the conventional plants do."[21]

LILCO soon purchased the site in Jamesport where Governor Rockefeller wanted to put SURFSIDE and began planning to build four nuclear plants on it—Jamesport 1, 2, 3, and 4. The LILCO nuclear family was blossoming, or so it seemed: The utility disclosed that there would be more than twins at Shoreham—it would be nuclear triplets, three nuclear plants at Shoreham.

It commissioned Eco Systems, a subsidiary of the Grumman Corporation, to evaluate eleven nuclear plant sites: in Shoreham, Jamesport, Cutchoque, Baiting Hollow, Mattituck, Roanoke Point, East Marion and Sagaponack.[22]

A report by the State Public Service Commission listed nineteen "suitable" sites for nuclear plants on eastern Long Island—in addition to Jamesport. These included two sites in Riverhead and an eleven-mile strip of land along the Long Island Sound from northeast of Riverhead to Mattituck that could be a site for seventeen more nuclear plants.[23]

The Suffolk Times editorialized that LILCO was aiming "to become the largest energy supplier in the Northeast grid."[24]

Newsday reported in 1976 that LILCO "foresees a total of eleven nuclear power plants on Long Island by the turn of the century."[25]

LILCO public relations people, then worried about public reaction, said—as June Bruce phrased it—the additional plants were "not definitely planned."[26]

But in July 1976 at a State Public Service Commission hearing on LILCO's application to run thirty-seven miles of 345,000-volt, double-circuit transmission lines down the spine of eastern Long Island, Howard Tarler, a PSC engineer, gave testimony to the contrary. While under cross-examination by Tom Twomey, attorney for the Long Island Farm Bureau, Tarler testified that the lines were designed with extra capacity to service three nuclear plants at Shoreham and four at Jamesport, at least. Adam Madsen, LILCO's planning director, then confirmed this to reporters.[27]

Eastern Long Island was "being set up to become a nuclear power park to satisfy the electrical needs of the Northeast," declared Two-mey.[28] The headline of a full-page advertisement of Eastern Suffolk for Safe Energy declared that "LILCO Plans to Exploit the East End by Converting It into a Nuclear Power Plant Zone for the Northeastern States."

LILCO, meanwhile, also began a study of the "feasibility" of placing a "floating nuclear station" in the Long Island Sound.[29] This facility would be built by Offshore Power Systems, which Westinghouse set up as a subsidiary in Jacksonville, Florida, to build "floating" nuclear plants.

Electricity would be *the* form of energy, LILCO executives were saying, and nuclear energy *the* way it would be generated. LILCO reported to the PSC that it planned to "rely exclusively on nuclear baseload generation"—to become an all-nuclear utility. Wilfred O. Uhl, who, as LILCO manager of engineering, executive vice president and as LILCO president, would be instrumental in these plans, told me once that by the year 2,000 there would be "no more oil, no more gas" and all the energy to heat houses, to run (electric) cars, to move everything and anything would come from nuclear power plants.[30]

LILCO heavily promoted the consumption of electricity. Until 1956, it sold electric appliances out of its main office. It pushed all-electric homes. In 1965 it introduced a special rate for homes heated with electricity. Later, it launched "The New Good Life Program" through which, according to the booklet describing it, LILCO would present "The Good Life Award" to employees who "help us sell an Electric Heat conversion." Cash incentives were given, the amount depending on whether the sale was for electricity or commercial electric heat. "Lucky keys" were also distributed to employees helping to sell electricity, with those holding "100 of these keys . . . automatically becoming a member of The Key Club," winning further "special" awards including, for the "grand prize winner selected from all the Lucky Keys . . . a two week vacation in Europe."

In a speech on April 24, 1973, before the American Society of Mechanical Engineers on "Electric Heat and the Environment," Charles Pierce, a LILCO senior vice president who would go on to become chairman of the LILCO's board of directors, said that "electric heat is not merely unobjectionable, but is the more desirable of the heating sources which can be used," the "ideal method for heating." And, Pierce emphasized, "the introduction into the LILCO system of nuclear energy will further advance the overall advantages of electric heat."

LILCO saw itself as a leader in nuclear powered generation—on the verge of enormous power.

But the first order of the big nuclear business ahead would be clearing the way for Shoreham, a procedure which the company presumed would be only *pro forma*. After all, the AEC had never denied a construction or operating license to any nuclear plant project anytime, anywhere in the U.S. (This record continued up to the AEC's demise in 1975, and the NRC has continued it through the present day.)

But the AEC construction permit hearings for Shoreham turned out to be something that neither LILCO, nor the nuclear industry, nor the government nuclear "establishment" ever expected—a landmark trial for nuclear power in America. They are viewed by some as the origin of the anti-nuclear movement in the U.S. "Even though a lot of people woke up after Three Mile Island," said Richard Pollack, former head of the Ralph Nader-created anti-nuclear group Critical Mass, "we regard Shoreham as the real beginning."[31]

NOTES

1. Martin Gitten's comments were made in a letter to the author, December 4, 1985.
2. Reported in *The New York Times*, January 7, 1964.
3. *Long Island Press*, June 15, 1963.
4. Reported in *Journal American*, January 6, 1964.
5. *Herald Tribune*, January 7, 1964.
6. *The New York Times* January 7, 1964.
7. *Herald Tribune*, January 7, 1964.
8. Ann Mead's comments were made in an interview with the author, December 1985.
9. A December 10, 1948, press release from Con Ed identified Charles B. Delafield, assistant to Con Ed President Ralph H. Tapscott, as telling the PSC on that day that

   the acquisition of the Long Island system by Consolidated Edison will enable the Long Island company to secure the funds required for plant expansion at a better interest rate than would be possible if the Long Island system continued as an independent company. This improvement in credit would stem from the lower percentage of debt in the Consolidated Edison system, compared with the high percentage in the Long Island company.

10. Con Ed issued a press release on February 28, 1950, which said: "Consolidated Edison Company of New York, Inc., announced this morning that its Board of Trustees has decided to withdraw its request for approval to acquire control of the Long Island Lighting Company. . . ."

11. The segment, "LILCO's Ties That Bind," was published on March 22, 1973.

12. The Duffy-Forrester-Shoreham connection, uncovered in the New York PSC's investigation of Shoreham, is contained in a February 1984 PSC document entitled, "Investigation of the Shoreham Nuclear Power Station, Project Management and Owner Oversight Testimony, Testimony of Ted K. Osborn, Bijoy K. Misra and Phillip S. Teumim." According to a PSC source, PSC investigators became aware of the link when Edward Duffy died and the name of his son-in-law, Richard L. Forrester, appeared in his obituary. Further details on this connection are provided in Chapter 5.

13. The Federal Trade Commission study was reported in *The Wall Street Journal*, August 27, 1976.

14. As a report entitled "The Structure of the U.S. Petroleum Industry" issued by the Special Subcommittee on Integrated Oil Operations of the Senate Committee on Interior and Insular Affairs concluded: "The pattern of leading companies in gasoline marketing resembles the marketing territories of the antecedent Standard Oil Trust Companies of 1911."

15. The Rockefeller interests in Citibank and Chase Manhattan have been detailed in many works including a study entitled *Our Masters' House: Economic, Political, and Ideological Control of the U.S. by the New York Financial Groups* by Jimm Dann and Daniel Stern (1979).

16. The title of LILCO's official history is "LILCO and the Community."

17. "A-Power Water Plant for LI Called Feasible," *Newsday*, October 16, 1963.

18. "State May Use Cash Aid in Drive for LI A-Plant," *Newsday*, June 16, 1966.

19. *Newsday*, March 17, 1967.

20. "Gov Asks Offshore LI Atom Plant," *Newsday*, March 27, 1967.

21. *Newsday*, October 10, 1967.

22. *The Long Island Traveler-Watchman*, February 3, 1977: "One such report, prepared for LILCO in 1973 by Eco Systems, a subsidiary of Grumman, identifies 11 possible plant sites."

23. Reported in *The Long Island Traveler-Watchman*, February 3, 1977.

24. *The Suffolk Times*, May 20, 1976.

25. *Newsday*, July 14, 1976.

26. June Bruce's comment appeared in *The Suffolk Times*, July 22, 1976.

27. Reported in *The Suffolk Times*, July 22, 1976.

28. *The Long Island Traveler-Watchman* noted in its February 3, 1977, account by its then managing editor, John Rather:

The Long Island Farm Bureau wants to know how many nuclear power plants could appear on the east end before this century is over, and is demanding a copy of a 2000 page federal study on nuclear power "parks" the bureau thinks may show possible sites here for as many as 20 power reactors. Farm Bureau attorney Tom Twomey has written the Nuclear Regulatory Commission in Washington asking for a copy of the January 1976 report under the Freedom of Information Act. In his letter, he says the report "indicated that huge nuclear centers, each containing about 20 atomic reactors, can be 'feasible, practical and even desirable' power options for many locations around the country."

The story continued with an interview with an NRC public relations person, Karl Abraham, who said there was a reference

in a part of the report discussing possible sites for nuclear power parks or single reactors within 75 miles of the urbanized corridor running from New York to Boston. The report, said Abraham, notes that sea water sites within 75 miles of the corridor exist on the coast of New Jersey and on the eastern part of Long Island, but "selection of these sites would arouse considerable public opposition."

The report, the story went on,

did conclude, however, that consideration should be given to establishing nuclear power parks in which as many 20 plants would operate, with nuclear fuel reprocessing facilities located on the same site. . . . The report, prepared by NRC staffers at the request of Congress, falls short of recommending the establishment of the parks, saying only that "the national interest would be served best by the appropriate state or federal energy authority taking careful account of the nature and social characteristics of each potential site to locate the number and kind of facilities best suited to that location."

29. Reported in "Next: A Floating Nuke?" *The East Hampton Star*, September 7, 1978. LILCO commissioned a $17,250 study on the plan in 1977, according to the annual report it filed with the U.S. Federal Energy Regulatory Commission. The first floating nuclear plant had been targeted for placement 100 miles south of Long Island—eight miles northeast of Atlantic City—as a project of Public Service Electric & Gas of New Jersey. According to publicity material provided by PSE & G, the idea originated with a company president, Richard Eckert, who, while taking a shower, got the idea that siting nuclear plants at sea would be a way to provide them with the massive amounts of coolant water they need. The utility then proposed the notion of floating nuclear plants to Westinghouse, which set up a subsidiary to build them. The NRC, in 1984, gave the subsidiary, Offshore Power Systems, a license to manufacture eight such plants. But PSE & G then decided it didn't want any, and no other utilities have placed orders.

30. Wilfred Uhl's comments were made in an interview with the author, August 1977.

31. Richard Pollack's comment was reported in *Newsday*, November 15, 1981.

4

THE BATTLE
AND THE
DISCLOSURES BEGIN

It wasn't Shoreham 1 or even Shoreham 2 that initially caused difficulties for LILCO. It was the announcement of the nuclear plant in
Lloyd Harbor that led to trouble—big trouble—for the ambitious
utility.

Shoreham was (and is) the residence of many Brookhaven National Laboratory scientists. The village is less than five miles north of
the main center of the laboratory. It was assumed that the nuclear
scientists would be solidly behind the nuclear plant project. Indeed,
Brookhaven National Laboratory scientists led the drive for nuclear
power in Shoreham, even formed a group that they called Suffolk
Scientists for Cleaner Power and Safer Environment to participate—
in support of LILCO—at the AEC hearings on a Shoreham construction permit. Individually and in a string of groups succeeding Suffolk
Scientists, they were (and still are) leaders in the fight for Shoreham
and LILCO's nuclear power program.

LILCO anticipated no problem from the administrator of Suffolk
County government. County Executive H. Lee Dennison was an engineer who had a reputation for loving construction projects. His terms
in office were marked by frequent announcements of new bridges,
canals and buildings he wanted to see constructed. He would fondly
recall being on a C-47 flying to Alaska during World War II and with
an Army general drawing up a plan with pencils on a piece of scrap
lumber for a new military town.

"I've known this was in the works. I'm very happy about such a
tremendous project coming into our area," said Dennison on the day

of the LILCO Shoreham announcement in 1966. "It will bring desirable employment to the county. . . . This is fine industry."[1]

Dennison had once wanted to preserve as a park the land LILCO had contracted to buy at Shoreham, a beautiful combination of forest, wetlands and beaches with a panoramic view of the Long Island Sound, and Connecticut off in the distance. There had also been a proposal put forward by several Shoreham residents to have the land become a park.

An archaeological exploration between 1967 and 1969 by the Nassau County Museum of Natural History determined that the land had been home for some of Long Island's early Native American inhabitants.[2] The research concluded that there had been four Indian settlements on the site 4,000 years before. Found were hundreds of artifacts: numerous quartz spearpoints and stones used for scalping hides, cutting, and holding down fish nets. The Indians dug soft clams, the researchers explained, noting evidence of pits on the site in which the clams were baked, and also ate deer, turtles and hickory nuts. The Indians of the area lived in grass-covered huts and used dugout canoes to travel to Connecticut, its coast just eighteen miles away. The "undisturbed" nature of the tract had been a major attraction for the museum's researchers, said Ronald Wyatt, curator of archaeology at the Nassau County museum.

Shoreham is a village in the Town of Brookhaven and the town supervisor, Charles R. Dominy, was anxious to see his town get tax revenues from the plant. He said on the day LILCO announced its plans for Shoreham he had already scheduled a town board hearing for the next week on rezoning to industrial use for half of the 450 acres LILCO planned to buy from the Steers Sand and Gravel Corp. "It will be a good, clean operation, with no smoke, soot or dirt, and it will add another piece of highly assessed property to the town tax rolls," said Dominy.[3] LILCO officials said the plant would provide more than $1.5 million a year in town property taxes.

Mayor George Beatty of Shoreham, where the village and school district stood to profit enormously from tax revenues from the nuclear plant (some 80 percent of village and school district revenues would come from LILCO), said Shoreham residents would favor the construction. The plant, he said, "would do no harm to anybody."[4]

There was an obvious conflict involving the Shoreham site from the outset.

Contiguous to it was an active U.S. Army Nike missile base. The base was wedged into the nuclear plant site—bounded on its northern, eastern and western borders by the LILCO site. A battery of guided missiles was just several thousand feet from where a nuclear power plant was supposed to be built.

But this didn't bother anyone at the time.

Newsday, in an editorial on "LI's Nuclear Future" (May 7, 1966), noted that LILCO "plans to build one and possibly two nuclear power plants on Long Island; the state is building a $2.3 million nuclear research center on the Stony Brook campus of the State University of New York, and Rockefeller is fighting to have $3.5 million restored to his budget to make possible the world's first nuclear-powered water desalinization plant. . . . The nuclear age is a time of excitement." The dominant daily newspaper in Nassau and Suffolk went on to urge that a bridge from Long Island to New England "must be built" and an eastern Long Island jetport, too. "Long Island is growing and change is inevitable," said the paper, which has long been a proponent of Long Island development.

The *Newsday* account of the Shoreham rezoning hearing said those present "demonstrated . . . that they had learned to love the atom. . . . The relaxed attitude of the Shoreham area residents to nuclear energy was generally attributed to the proximity of Brookhaven National Laboratory whose atomic facilities are only five miles away and to the fact that many of the residents are employed there."[5]

Then, the following year, 1967, LILCO announced its nuclear plant project in Lloyd Harbor—and it was another story.

LILCO did not have the kind of inside track in Lloyd Harbor it had in Shoreham, although LILCO secretary Edward M. Barrett lived there and presented LILCO's case at village meetings, and LILCO senior vice president Charles Pierce was also a resident. There was no other LILCO connection, no domination by, no presence of, Brookhaven National Laboratory scientists. Also, the lure of tax revenues meant nothing to most of the residents of Lloyd Harbor, a wealthy community.

And most importantly, two of the residents of the village were highly informed about nuclear power—and communicated their information to other residents.

They were Ann and William Carl. Ann Carl is a woman of many talents and accomplishments: a biologist, a military pilot, indeed the first woman test pilot and the first woman to solo in a jet, and a writer on environmental issues. "She was most knowledgeable," said Irving Like, attorney for the Lloyd Harbor Study Group, formed by the Carls and other Lloyd Harbor residents to fight the nuclear plant project. "She taught the rest of us."[6] Her husband was an engineer at the Grumman Corp.

Nearly all 100 people crowding a Lloyd Harbor Village Board meeting soon after the LILCO announcement were against the undertaking.[7] Barrett told the board that LILCO was under contract to buy 45 acres and was negotiating to purchase 2 more parcels, one 50 and the other 85 acres. In total there would be 180 acres along the Long Island Sound for the plant's site.

A letter from Ferdinand Eberstadt, who owned the 85 acres, was read by the mayor. Eberstadt wrote that he had not yet sold any land to LILCO, had serious reservations about the safety of the nuclear plant project and its impact on the environment, and was concerned about it causing a "serious depreciation in village real estate." Some village officials cited an increased village tax base with the plant, which LILCO estimated would cost $150 million. That wasn't accepted by most people at the meeting as a good enough reason for having a nuclear plant in their village.

Barrett said "if we find the village does not want us to build," LILCO would go to other locations on Long Island to construct nuclear plants. "They have to be built."

In response to the demands from those at the meeting for a study of the effects of a nuclear power plant on Lloyd Harbor, the village board said it would consider having a study done by a private engineering firm. Later, the village conducted a mail survey of property owners and found most were against the nuclear plant project. Then the Lloyd Harbor Study Group issued an analysis of the plant's impacts. LILCO quietly let the project drop and focused its attention back on Shoreham.

But the Lloyd Harbor Study Group decided not to drop its fight despite the LILCO pullout—and to challenge Shoreham. For its members, "it was not just a 'not in my backyard' issue," attorney Like recounted. The Lloyd Harbor Study Group ultimately expanded into a coalition of environmental and civic groups from all over Long Island opposed to the Shoreham project.

However, the forum in which the fight to prevent Shoreham from getting a construction permit was to be fought—an AEC licensing proceeding—was loaded in favor of the other side. "My first reaction was that I was dealing with a kangaroo court," said Like.

The AEC had devised a licensing process to give the impression of due process. In fact, the system was quite the opposite. (The NRC has continued exactly the same system.) On one side would be the entity applying for a license to construct or operate a nuclear plant. Then there would be "staff"—members of the AEC technical staff and AEC lawyers. Then there would be public participation—"intervenors," parties permitted by the government to make statements, present witnesses, file briefs and question the applicant's witnesses.

Within the context of AEC rules, and later those of the NRC, a hearing board would consider the case and make a decision. Its members would be two "technical members" and a lawyer, the lawyer being the chairman. For many years, the three would be called just licensing board members, but in the 1970s—to better project an image of an objective judicial proceeding—the NRC began calling them "judges." They have never been selected as judges normally are. They are not elected like many state and local judges. There is no peer review such as the bar association screening most judges undergo. There is no congressional involvement as required for federal judges. There is no legislative oversight.

The "judges" would be, as Like phrased it during the Shoreham hearings, "hardly impartial." He brought numerous motions to have the hearing board panel disqualified because its "members have a vested interest in the development of atomic power. . . . There is no way we can win at this hearing."

Selected by the AEC and then the NRC, the "judges" in deciding whether a nuclear plant should be built or should be allowed to operate would come from either the staff of the agency, the national nuclear laboratories, corporations involved in nuclear contract work for the government, or academic institutions receiving government funding for nuclear research, or be individuals otherwise connected to the nuclear field.

The hearing board would be assisted by "staff"—the AEC and then NRC technical people and lawyers who would make their own recommendations, nearly always in favor of a nuclear plant proposal. (The AEC staff was early and strongly in favor of Shoreham.) The staff would then work in support of the applicant during the licensing proceeding.

The initial hearing board for the Shoreham construction permit hearings included Dr. Hugh Paxton of the staff of Los Alamos Scientific Laboratory, funded by the AEC to develop military nuclear technology, and Dr. A. Dixie Callahan, a physicist with the Union Carbide Corporation, contracted by the government to run Oak Ridge National Laboratory, another government center for nuclear technology. The chairman was Jack Campbell, a Sante Fe lawyer and former governor of New Mexico.

"Here you had," said Like, "the former governor of New Mexico—known as the playground of the AEC and nuclear industry for its extensive uranium mining and milling, Los Alamos Laboratory, other nuclear facilities and an overall close relationship with nuclear technology—and two technical members connected to the national nuclear laboratories."

Like's strategy in countering LILCO and the AEC under these circumstances was, "If you can't beat them, you can at least expose them" and, meanwhile, turn the hearings into a public learning experience, a forum on nuclear power. It would be a strategy, after the Shoreham hearings, followed by "intervenors" in nuclear plant construction and operating license hearings all over the U.S.

Like had a clear notion of the need to combine public exposure and political action with legal initiatives in a fight against an extremely powerful adversary.

Like had become well known as a specialist in environmental law, for his work on the Fire Island National Seashore. He subsequently was a lawyer for opponents of Con Ed's Storm King power plant, represented Suffolk County in its opposition to oil drilling off Long Island's shores, and wrote the New York State Conservation Bill of Rights, which became a part of the State Constitution in 1970. Ann Carl, who came to know Like when she was a member of the Citizens Committee for a Fire Island National Seashore, asked him to represent the Lloyd Harbor Study Group.

Like detailed his Shoreham strategy in a paper delivered before the American Bar Association and American Legal Institute during the hearings.[8] In it, he spoke of the "allegedly impartial mediators between those who would spoil the environment and those who would save it." The AEC, he said, "is a classic example of the military-industrial research and development complex. . . . The litigant with limited resources enters a David-and-Goliath confrontation, pitting himself against the utility, the AEC technical staff, and the titans of American industry. Arrayed on their side, as well, are the huge complex of dependent trade associations, economic interest groups, public relations media, the scientific, engineering and technical resources of the AEC, the AEC national laboratories and sponsored research and the AEC's Congressional protectors."

Further, the AEC "has gained powerful allies among the major corporations, the military services, utilities, universities and research institutes in the United States and abroad. Thus, the citizen who challenges an AEC license project is met not only by the applicant and the technical staff of the commission which has recommended the issuance of the license, but also the well-orchestrated chorus of the nuclear power technologists.

"The question naturally arises—why should the concerned conservationist litigate a 'no-win' contest . . . where defeat is probable?" asked Like. "What is to be gained in such a contest?"

He declared, "The administrative arena must be used as an educational forum to alert the public to the project's adverse effect on environmental quality. The environmental stakes must be vividly dramatized as a prelude to organizing political action to block the project or correct its deficiencies. . . . Viewed in this perspective, a losing environmental cause is worth fighting for because it adds to the ecological enlightment of the public. It is even possible that a prospective polluter may be induced to abandon its plans or at least improve upon them if it knows that its project will provoke environmental challenge.

"As a basic strategy," he continued, "an agency proceeding should be treated as a multi-media confrontation in which the agency proceeding itself is both the medium and the message, transmitting to the public the truth about the abuse of the environment." The public, he noted, "does not attend long, drawn-out agency hearings devoted to technical details, no matter how relevant they are . . . but intelligent reporters, assigned by newspapers, magazines, radio or television networks to cover controversial hearings, can make a serious attempt to grasp the essence of scientific and technical points brought out by testimony," and "thus the improvement points raised in the proceedings can be passed on to the public. . . . Comprehensive press coverage also insures that the agency's transgressions will not go unnoticed. The intervenor must therefore strive to make the hearings as interesting and informative as possible in order to sustain the interest of the media in covering them as a source of daily news items.

"A new lawyer-client relationship must be developed," Like said, "which reflects the nature of the struggle as a part legal, part political campaign. The lawyer and his client, the environmental organization, must create a team composed of the lawyer, technical consultants, layman interrogators, evidence gatherers and political activists. The team must carefully utilize its expert resources and non-legal members to achieve a 'no win' success.

"The environmental issues must be simultaneously tried on multiple levels—the agency, the media and the arena of public opinion," he declared. "In a major 'no win' environmental case, the intervenor must combine its trial tactics with mastery of the theories and practices of the communications art and media if it is to inform the public of the nature of the environmental degradation and the deficiencies of the applicable regulatory process. . . . Success in winning the ultimate environmental objective requires maximum use of the media and arts of communication in dramatizing the confrontation between the citizen and his corporate and agency adversaries."

Issues about nuclear power that would soon concern all of America were raised by the Lloyd Harbor Study Group in the 70 sessions of the Shoreham hearings, which lasted from 1970 into 1972 and were chiefly held in the ballroom of a Holiday Inn in Centereach, Long Island.

There was comprehensive testimony—on the connections between radioactivity and illness and death, on routine emissions from nuclear facilities and their health consequences, on how the concentration of radioactivity increases tremendously as it moves up the food chain, on how radioactivity is released at all stages in the nuclear "fuel cycle," on the dangers of transporting and storing nuclear waste, on an aircraft crashing into a nuclear plant, on sabotage, on the operating records of nuclear plants, on quality control, on "engineered" yet untested nuclear plant components, on LILCO violating construction standards—even when the plant was in the planning stages.

The issue of nuclear plant accidents and their consequences was fully probed, including the loss-of-coolant "China syndrome" core meltdown, explosions that could occur during it, and the nuclear runaway and its potential for an instantaneous, massive steam explosion. Well before the Three Mile Island accident and its supposedly "mysterious" hydrogen bubble, there were many hours of testimony at the Shoreham hearings on the probability of an explosive hydrogen bubble forming during a loss-of-coolant accident.

Also, the issue of insurance in the event of a nuclear plant accident was examined; the question of evacuation on crowded Long Island was explored, and so were the issues of economics of nuclear power and alternatives to it.

Experts in all these areas were called to testify, largely by the Lloyd Harbor Study Group. And, as the hearings progressed, Ralph Nader's Center for the Study of Responsive Law, Connecticut Action Now, and Fairfield County Citizens for Environmental Control were admitted as intervenors—reluctantly by the AEC—and also called some witnesses.

Midway through the hearings, a federal court ruled that the AEC had to abide by the National Environmental Policy Act (NEPA), passed in 1970 and requiring government agencies to consider all environmental aspects, and alternatives to a project, before approving a project. Like, at the outset of the Shoreham hearings, had insisted that the AEC abide by NEPA. The AEC refused. However, in a strongly worded decision, the U.S. Second District Court of Appeals, in a case involving the proposal to build the Calvert Cliffs nuclear plant in Maryland, ruled that the AEC had to abide by NEPA. The court ruled: "We believe that the Commission's crabbed interpretation of NEPA makes a mockery of the act."[9] The Shoreham hearings began the first forum on nuclear power under the act.

They were the first nuclear plant hearings after Earth Day of 1970, an event that focused national attention on environmental degradation and raised awareness about the issues of nuclear power.

Like declared at the hearings as they began on September 21, 1970, that "our purpose is . . . to encourage the nation's scientific community to come in and testify, to make this a landmark case."[10]

Among the Study Group's first witnesses was Dr. James D. Watson, winner of the Nobel Prize for co-discovering the DNA molecule, as well as a Harvard University professor and director of the Cold Spring Harbor Laboratory on Long Island.

"The amount of research now being done on the connection between cancer and radiation is totally inconsistent with proposals for widespread introduction of nuclear plants into highly populated areas," he testified.

"The idea that the atom is safe is just a public relations trick," Watson continued. "What you want to do is to decrease man's exposure to radiation."

Of cancer, he said, "You have to pay a great deal of attention to the prevention of it." He was pessimistic about a "cure" for cancer because, he explained, the mechanisms that cause cancer appear to be "integral components" of the body's system that can later in life become activated—by agents that include radiation.

He spoke about how doses of radiation cause cancer after an "incubation" period of a number of years. "We must assume a linear connection between dose and probability of causation," he said. Of estimating what would be a low level of radiation, "You are gambling with the future of not only individuals, but of our society as it exists." And, he added: "I don't think one has the right to say a single life necessarily need be expended."

Said the Nobel Laureate about the nuclear industry: "Remarkably powerful and big companies have ruined themselves and everyone else by faulty technology."

Dr. Alice Stewart, credited with pioneering research on the dangers of what were long considered "acceptable" doses of radiation, came from England, where she was director of social medicine at Oxford University, to testify. Research by Stewart in the 1950s showed that children whose mothers received very small amounts of radiation through X rays during pregnancy—amounts not thought to be dangerous—had twice the risk of developing leukemia before the age of ten than those whose mothers had not. Her work, ultimately, revolutionized attitudes towards routine use of X rays.

Stewart detailed her research at the Shoreham hearings, noted that the earlier an embryo is exposed to radiation the more severe the cancer risk, and countered what had been the AEC and nuclear industry claim that there was a "threshold dose" below which radiation would not cause cancer. She said research had proved that any amount of radiation could cause cancer. "The risk is dose dependent and admits of no threshold."

Dr. Ernest Sternglass, professor of radiation physics at the University of Pittsburgh School of Medicine, testified about his findings that routine emissions of radiation from nuclear power plants, other nuclear facilities and atomic bomb tests—regarded by the AEC and the nuclear industry as "acceptable"—were already causing patterns of illnesses and deaths in the United States.

He explained that because cancer in adults from exposure to radio-activity took longer to appear, due to an "incubation" period, then impacts on fetuses and children, the latter groups were the first major victims of radioactivity.

He said his analyses of rates of infant mortality near seven nuclear facilities showed rates higher in areas which were downwind—in terms of prevailing air currents—from the installations than in the areas upwind and not regularly affected by the radioactivity given off. Nuclear plants he cited were: Dresden I in Illinois, Humboldt Bay Power Plant in California, Big Rock Point in Michigan, Shippingport and Peach Bottom in Pennsylvania; and nuclear facilities at West Valley in upstate New York, a nuclear waste dump and proposed nuclear reprocessing center; and the federal government's Hanford multi-reactor Hanford Nuclear Reservation in Washington, which also includes a nuclear waste dump.

He displayed graphs showing increased levels of infant mortality downwind (to the east) of Dresden I after it went into operation, and then graphs reflecting stable levels of infant mortality in Illinois counties upwind, to the west of the nuclear plant. The statistics appeared "to pinpoint the source" of the infant mortality. He spoke of his research involving increases of infant mortality in Suffolk County downwind (to the east) of a nuclear research reactor at Brookhaven National Laboratory. He said his analysis of health department statistics showed sharp rises in infant mortality in 1955 and again in 1961 and 1962 following sharp increases in gaseous radiation and radioactive liquid effluents generated by the laboratory's reactor in 1954 and 1955 and then in 1960 and 1961. The Brookhaven releases are "highly likely to be responsible for the increase" in infant mortality.

"The detailed breakdown of how the effluent gets into the diet and into the air and into the bones of the pregnant mother and into the fetus needs to be studied in detail," Sternglass said. "It is a study beyond my limited means, and I would urge the citizens of Suffolk County to insist that such a detailed study be carried out."

(After this connection was made, the Lloyd Harbor Study Group said that the government, in considering Shoreham, had "not factored into the total release picture . . . the emissions from Brookhaven National Laboratory whose property borders on the Shoreham Nuclear Power Station property." The northern edge of the laboratory then came up to the Shoreham site. Under cross-examination by Like, a

LILCO witness, Maynard E. Smith, a meteorologist, said that radio-activity from Brookhaven National Laboratory had been detected 120 miles from it. A participant at the hearings, Andrew Hull, secretary of Suffolk Scientists for Cleaner Power & Safer Environment, and a health physicist at the laboratory—in charge of monitoring its release of radioactivity—then took the stand and argued that the releases were within government limits.)

Sternglass connected an increase in congenital deaths in children in Nevada, downwind from where the AEC tested atomic bombs in Nevada—with "peaks" in the testing. Sternglass found a similar pattern in leukemia levels in Utah, also downwind from the bomb tests.

Dr. Charles Huver, professor of zoology at the University of Minnesota, stressed the toxicity of the radioisotopes created in the process of atom-splitting or fission—known as "fission products." He read from scientific literature stating that radioisotopes "are anywhere from a million to a billion times more toxic than most of the toxic chemicals . . . such as cyanide."

There was much testimony on how, when radioactivity moves up the food chain in nature, its concentrations increase enormously. Radioactivity, it was noted, is increased many thousandfold in plants and plankton that draw on radioactive water, and many thousandfold again in fish that have eaten the plants and plankton, and then increases many thousandfold again in humans when they eat the fish. And radioactivity on pasture land is increased many thousandfold when the grass becomes part of cow's milk, and again many thousandfold when people drink the milk.

Dr. Irving Lyon, professor of biology at Bennington College, testified for the Lloyd Harbor Study group that government radiation standards did not take into account "the whole question of biological concentration of radioactive nuclides." He said that food chains in the location of a proposed nuclear plant should be studied "to know specifically what meanings these could have for potential danger to living systems, including human beings."

Lyon spoke of cesium-137—one of the 200 fission products created in a nuclear power plant—and how it "substitutes for potassium in the soft tissues and muscles of bony fishes," concentrating in fish with a "factor of 6,500." Because cesium-137 does not pass through the body, it builds up as an organism consumes smaller organisms with traces of the fission product in their bodies. Eating just one pound of fish with that level of cesium-137 concentration would give a human an amount of cesium-137 equal to what the AEC considered the "total body burden" for the radioisotope, he testified.

LILCO had not considered concentrations of radioactivity in the food chain as "pathways to man," ways people could receive radioactivity from Shoreham, the Lloyd Harbor Study Group held.

Dr. Clarence Carlson, biology professor at Cornell University and a Study Group witness, asked a LILCO consultant, Dr. Alfred Perlmutter, a biology professor at New York University, about the effect of radioactivity on sealife in the Long Island Sound, a major source of sea food. Perlmutter replied: "How are you going to measure the effects?" Carlson declared: "We cannot do it, and the question should be whether we should be discharging."

The 600,000 gallons of water used each minute by the Shoreham plant, drawn from the Long Island Sound, would be returning to the sound slightly irradiated after going through the nuclear plant, it was established, and it would also be twenty degrees warmer.

LILCO witnesses conceded that radioactivity in minute concentrations would spread through the Long Island Sound in this way.

Dr. Matthew Cordaro, manager of LILCO's environmental engineering department, added that fish would be attracted to the "warm plume" of liquid discharge from the plant and these fish would get larger doses of radioactivity.

At the same time that radioactivity would be released through Shoreham's liquid effluent, there would be gaseous radioactivity emitted from the plant, witnesses testified. There was much discussion on meteorology and if a weather inversion, stagnant air, would make the gaseous radioactivity worse for the surrounding area.

It was conceded that as part of the fission process in the Shoreham plant, 450 to 500 pounds of plutonium—regarded as the most toxic substance in the universe—would be produced each year. (Studies have shown that a millionth of a gram of plutonium will cause fatal lung cancer, meaning that a pound of plutonium, if evenly distributed, could theoretically cause fatal lung cancer in more than twice the world's population—nine billion people. An ounce, only a tablespoon because plutonium is very heavy, could kill 200 million people. Once created in a nuclear plant, the manmade element remains radioactive for 500,000 years.)

Meanwhile, it was stressed by witnesses that radioactivity is released not only at a nuclear plant but at every step in the "nuclear fuel cycle"—when uranium is mined, in the extensive process through which it is made into fuel, when it goes through fission in a reactor and, finally, when the nuclear waste is shipped to be put into storage isolated from living things. Some radioactive waste emits radiation for hundreds of thousands or millions of years, it was established, while some stays hot with radiation for billions of years.

Lyon testified that a single nuclear power plant "cannot be considered alone" in terms of assessing its radioactive impact. It must be assessed with all the nuclear power plants in a region as well as other elements of this cycle.

Huver said: "You cannot separate the on-site pollution problem from the pollution problems of reprocessing and storage and actually getting the fuel in the first place."

Sternglass said: "The tragedy is that the effluent standards are set isolatedly [sic] for each and every separate facility so that they never exceed their own concentration. Unfortunately, the population as a whole is exposed to this sum total of all the various radioactive sources from all the various releases."

On the waste transport issue, LILCO's Shoreham project manager, Andrew W. Wofford, said the nuclear plant would produce 1.16 million pounds of solid radioactive waste a year. "The amount of material that has some activity that we plan to ship will be that figure," he testified. This nuclear waste—three truckloads every two weeks—would be taken down to the Long Island Expressway, then west on the expressway to New York City and then through New York City before heading to a nuclear dump site. Wofford conceded under questioning that he didn't know of any nuclear plant in the U.S. that shipped its waste through such a heavily-populated area. LILCO also admitted that it had made no study of the possibility of accidents involving the transport of the radioactive waste.

Dr. Benjamin Post, a Polytechnic Institute of New York physics professor, spoke of the likelihood of such accidents. "I think it is worse than dangerous," he said of nuclear waste transport. "It is almost criminally negligent for us to proceed with a plant of this sort."

As for the storage of nuclear waste, Dr. Jerold Lowenstein, an M.D. involved in nuclear medicine, said, "I don't think there's really any safe way of disposing of high-level radioactive waste. . . . [T]here will be accidents."

Witnesses also stressed that radioactivity is cumulative: Amounts absorbed from an X ray, from atomic bomb fallout, from discharges from a nuclear facility, from radioactive waste leaking into water—from all sources—build up in a person's body. Further, they emphasized that radioactivity in the environment is irreversible. It cannot be detoxified. Once let out into the air, water or earth, it is here for the "hazardous lifetime" of the radioactive material involved, up to billions of years.

Drs. John Gofman and Arthur Tamplin gave crucial testimony at the Shoreham hearings. Gofman, co-discoverer of four radioactive isotopes including uranium-232 and -233, was, with Tamplin, involved in starting the AEC's Lawrence Radiation Laboratory at Livermore, California. In the 1960s, they were assigned by the AEC to determine what would be "permissible" radiation exposure standards. A year before the Shoreham hearings, they had concluded that radiation was a far more serious hazard than previously suspected, that twenty times more deaths would occur from radiation-induced cancer and leukemia than had been previously believed, and that genetic damage had been underestimated even more seriously. The AEC and the nuclear industry were upset by the findings and applied pressure that forced Gofman and Tamplin out of their positions at the laboratory.

Their testimony was elaborated on in their book, *Poisoned Power*, published during the Shoreham hearings, which declared: "About a year ago, we began to perceive the dimensions of the massive hoax being perpetrated upon the public. It was very difficult for us to believe that what we observed to be occurring could truly be real. Indeed, up to that time we, deeply immersed in atomic energy research, had been lulled into the belief that nuclear electricity was the one atomic energy program which posed very little threat to society. How wrong we were. There is a real potential disaster ahead. . . . The public has been and *is being* deceived by a clever, well-financed propaganda campaign of delusions concerning 'clean, cheap, safe nuclear power.' . . . Concealment of truth from the public was regarded as essential.

"Radioactivity," they stated, "represents one of the worst, maybe the worst of all poisons. And it is manufactured as an inevitable byproduct of nuclear electricity generation. One year of operation of a single, large nuclear power plant generates as much long-persisting radioactive poisons as *one thousand* Hiroshima-type atomic bombs. There is no way the electric power can be generated in nuclear plants without generating the radioactive poisons. Once any of these radioactive poisons are released to the environment, and this we believe is likely to occur, the pollution of our environment is irreversible. . . . It is important that people learn *how* they are likely to be exposed to such poisons and *how* death-dealing injury is thereby produced in the individual and in all future generations."

The "top leadership" of the "nuclear juggernaut," they continued, "has displayed a total lack of comprehension of radioactive poison and its effect" and a "total lack of understanding of the basic principles of *sound* public health practices which must be applied to new, hazardous technologies. Worst of all, this same top leadership has demonstrated a lack of responsibility in meeting the moral obligation to provide the public with honest information concerning the real hazards which must be faced. We are not speaking of usual 'individual accidents.' Rather, we are concerned over the hazard of major calamities to human health and life, unparalleled in human history."

Tamplin declared at the Shoreham hearings: "I can see no reason for the construction of nuclear power plants anywhere."

There was considerable testimony on the proposed plant's location.

The Army Nike base was of much concern. The possibility of a Nike booster or warhead accidentally hitting the plant was raised. A retired Air Force colonel, Steven Gadler, testified that "electromagnetic fields" from the plant could trigger circuits and relays at the missile base. LILCO, it turned out, had not even mentioned the Nike base in its construction application to the AEC in a section covering what existed on adjacent land. "A more incompatible pair of land uses—atomic plant and Nike site—is difficult to imagine," charged Like.

The Nike base was closed after the construction permit was issued.

But of equal concern at the Shoreham hearings is a major U.S. Navy-owned facility—still in operation—five miles away. The base includes a large airfield from which the Grumman Corporation, one of the major manufacturers of military aircraft in the U.S., conducts flight tests of completed aircraft and flies experimental tests of new models. Also at the facility in Calverton is a plant at which the final assembly is done of many of Grumman's planes, including Grumman's F-14 Tomcat fighter.

Shoreham would be built four and a half miles from the end of the main runway of this military facility, a half mile to the west of the "extended centerline of the runway," the Lloyd Harbor Study Group noted. Documents were submitted in which the area of the plant's projected location was listed as a "high hazard area" by U.S. Air Force airport planners.

Although Shoreham's containment structure would be topped with a steel dome and have walls of concrete four and a half feet thick, the roof of the rest of the Shoreham plant was to be only light sheet metal over a thin layering of concrete, two inches in depth in some places, four in others. The Lloyd Harbor Study Group presented an analysis by the Public Service Company of New Hampshire concluding that 15 feet of concrete is required to resist the thrust of a "high performance military jet."

Documents were also submitted showing that as part of the licensing process for construction of the Davis Besse nuclear plant in Ohio, the Department of Defense assured the AEC that "military aircraft en route to or from this area will not be routed closer than ten miles from the site."

As to LILCO's claim that it was a low probability that an airplane would crash into Shoreham, the Study Group declared, "Accidents of a very low probability such as the sinking of the Titanic and two planes colliding over the Grand Canyon do occur."

And, the Study Group—with former test pilot Mrs. Carl doing much of the research on this issue—maintained that such a crash might not be such a low probability. Mrs. Carl presented analyses concluding that the "mortality risks" of flight tests of new and experimental aircraft, and military flights in general, were greater than those for commercial air carriers. Also, AEC staff members admitted under cross-examination that Shoreham was not designed to withstand the impact of an aircraft crashing into it.

Further, the plant was to be built on the instrument landing system approach to Long Island MacArthur Airport in Ronkonkoma, a regional airport, and adjacent to the holding pattern for the airport that serves New Haven, Connecticut. It would be, said Mrs. Carl, "beneath an area of high density air traffic."

Sabotage was raised as an issue—years before terrrorist attacks would become commonplace throughout the world. AEC witnesses conceded that they did not analyze the design or the operation of the plant in terms of sabotage—indeed, they dealt with the issue in a cavalier fashion.

One AEC witness, Roger Boyd, asked by Like if he was an expert in sabotage, replied, "Naturally not."

"Do you have any background in it?"

"I have never sabotaged anything, to my knowledge, in my life," Boyd said.

Like asked Richard Ireland of the AEC: "Do you have people who are knowledgeable in the sabotage area?"

"I suppose we have some form of spies working back there who know all about it," Ireland answered.

Like presented an article from a recent copy of *Nuclear Safety Magazine* that declared that "serious consequences to the public are possible" from sabotage of nuclear facilities, and he also showed a story from the *London Sunday Telegraph* about a threat of sabotage at a nuclear plant in England.

"In view of this activity," demanded Like, "do you think you should direct the applicant to provide design features as well as operational requirements to account for the possibility of sabotage?"

Ireland replied: "I don't think the situation is clear enough with respect to the potential for sabotage to make any decisions about it."

Like, in the context of sabotage, asked Ireland whether he knew "of any nuclear plant with a combination of defense airport, an atomic laboratory and a live Nike base as close to the plant as in this case?"

"No," Ireland said.

The operating record of nuclear plants was brought up. William Carl provided details on a number of early nuclear plants: Bonus in Puerto Rico, which never went to full power and was shut down four years after it went critical in 1964; Elk River in Minnesota, shut down four years after it went to full power in 1964; LaCrosse in Wisconsin, which went to full power in 1967 and "has had many operating problems"; Pathfinder in South Dakota, which went to full power in 1967 and was shut down the same year; Big Rock Point in Michigan, which went to full power in 1968 and "has had five major shutdowns"; Humboldt Bay in California, which went to full power in 1963 and "has been running at half power most of the time since, because of high radioactive emissions."

He said: "It is obvious that the first-generation experience, all less than 100 megawatts, was a miserable failure."

He reviewed larger reactors operating or then in the process of being built: Dresden 1, Oyster Creek in New Jersey, Nine Mile Point 1 in upstate New York, Browns Ferry 1 and 2 in Alabama, Monticello in Minnesota—and chronicled the problems they had.

The construction problems he cited at Oyster Creek were similar to the kind that would plague Shoreham. Numerous defects were found in the plant, including cracks in pipes and a series of valves that had "been traced to a surplus valve dealer." Meanwhile, the project's cost was rapidly escalating, and its owner, General Public Utilities, "while waiting" for the plant to go into operation "must buy substantial amounts of power at twice the cost of producing it itself."

Such a record, said Carl, "is enough to strike terror into the heart of any stockholder of a company 'going nuclear.' One would think that it might even give pause to a board of directors."

Working with Carl on the issue of quality control was an engineering associate of his at Grumman, Roger Langevin, a quality-control expert in the company's space program involved in setting standards and testing parts for Grumman's lunar module. Langevin also was professor of quality engineering at the State University of New York Agricultural and Technical College at Farmingdale.

Information Langevin elicited from witnesses included the admission that the engineer in charge of quality control on the Shoreham project had no experience in the field of quality control, that LILCO was not using the most recent construction codes in parts of the plant, and the company was not making use of "reoccurrence control"— project manager Wofford said that he didn't know what that term meant. Langevin explained that it was the study of failures in similar operating systems to prevent such failures in new and proposed systems and was a vital element in the concept of quality control.

The Lloyd Harbor Study Group charged that quality control quality assurance in commercial nuclear power was "significantly less definitive" than in the nuclear division of the U.S. Navy or the aerospace industry, indeed was "not comparable with that of a "typical aerospace program contractor."

The description of certain components of the plant as "engineered" was challenged. Said Carl: "It is inaccurate to call a safeguard an 'engineered safeguard' if it hasn't been tested." The correct term would be a "designed" safeguard, he said, because "engineered implies that a system has been designed, built, tested under the conditions under which it will have to operate, the failures of the components noted, redesigned, rebuilt and retested. Beyond this it should be tested for reliability. A catapult for an aircraft carrier is operated with a load 10,000 times before it is qualified."

LILCO was charged with violating standards while the plant was in the planning stage, well before the Shoreham inspectors and workers blew the whistle on violations of standards.

The Study Group alleged that LILCO had given false information to the AEC in connection with a nuclear steam supply system that came under a 1968 government requirement that such a system be "essentially 100 percent" accessible for inspection. LILCO, the Study Group said, falsely claimed that it had ordered the system a year before the standard took effect when, in fact, the equipment was ordered two months after the requirement came into being. Then, LILCO reported to the AEC that the system would not be fully accessible. The AEC staff approved of the system anyway on the basis that it would be 50 percent accessible. The Study Group declared that "50 percent is a long way from 'essentially 100 percent' " and that the AEC staff was deceiving the hearing board and the public.

The issue of a nuclear plant accident—a happening in which huge amounts of radioactivity could be released from a nuclear plant all at once—was a central issue.

When project manager Wofford was first questioned, he insisted that it was "impossible" for the Shoreham plant to have an accident that would result in a large-scale release of radioactivity into the environment. Later under questioning, he said that it was "conceivable, but not possible." He then said he wanted to elaborate: "It's conceivable that the sun won't come up tomorrow morning, but it's credible that it will."

Like pressed him on whether a major disaster at Shoreham was a possibility "as remote as the sun not coming up tomorrow." Wofford then changed his language to such an accident being "improbable."

Hearing board Chairman Campbell commented: "We started out talking about the impossible. Now it's improbable."

A large amount of government documentation was presented on the possibilities and consequences of a nuclear plant accident. Also, Dr. Richard Webb became involved in the Shoreham hearings as a witness, and thus first began to explore the types of accidents that he would become well-known for investigating: nuclear plant accidents in which explosions can occur.

Irving Like made heavy use of the first (and still relevant) major U.S. government study of nuclear plant accidents and their effects. Entitled *Theoretical Possibilities and Consequences of Major Accidents in Large Nuclear Power Plants*, it was issued in 1957, done by Brookhaven National Laboratory for the AEC and given the serial number "WASH-740" by the AEC.

"It must be clearly recognized," declared the report's opening pages, "that major releases of fission products from a nuclear power reactor conceivably could occur and that a serious threat to the health and safety of people over large areas could ensue."

Like pointed to these projections in WASH-740 of the consequences of a serious accident at a 200-megawatt plant:

For the three types of assumed accidents, the theoretical estimates indicated that personal damage might range from a lower limit of none injured or killed to an upper limit, in the worst case, of about 3,400 killed and about 43,000 injured.

Theoretical property damages ranged from a lower limit of about one half million dollars to an upper limit in the worst case of about seven billion dollars. This latter figure is largely due to assumed contamination of land with fission products.

Under adverse combinations of the conditions considered, it was estimated that people could be killed at distances up to 15 miles, and injured at distances of about 45 miles. Land contamination could extend for greater distances.

But the consequences of a serious accident at Shoreham, said Like, could be far more serious than WASH-740's estimate of up to "3,400 killed and about 43,000 injured," property damages of up to $7 billion and people being killed "at distances up to 15 miles, and injured at distances of about 45 miles."

This is because Shoreham, at 820 megawatts, would be four times the size of the 200-megawatt plant analyzed, he noted, and thus an accident at Shoreham could release far more radioactivity into the environment and be far more lethal.

Further, Like noted that WASH-740's figures were based on a plant being "about 30 miles from a major city" and population averaging "500 people per square mile" between the city and the plant. But population in a 30-mile radius of Shoreham, on Long Island and in Connecticut, was far higher than that.

WASH-740 specified why many things could go wrong in a nuclear plant:

1. Many power reactors systems will operate under high pressures. High pressure systems are subject to failure. 2. The cumulative effect of radiation on physical and chemical

Government and industry are investing heavily in studies to learn more about the principles of safe reactor design and operation.

Framing even hypothetical circumstances under which harm and damage could occur and arriving at estimations of the theoretical extent of the consequences proved a complex task.

To make the study we enlisted the services of a group of scientists and engineers of the Brookhaven National Laboratory and of another group of experts to serve as a steering committee. Through recent months these men have met with many additional expert advisors to test out judgments on the estimates arrived at.

We are not aware of such a study having been undertaken for any other industry. We venture to say that if a similar study were to be made for certain other industries, with the same free rein to the imagination, we might be startled to learn what the consequences of conceivable major catastrophic accidents in those other industries could be in contrast with the actual experience in those industries.

Remembering that this study analyzes theoretical possibilities and consequences of reactor accidents, we might note here the judgments presented on (1) possible consequences of major accidents and (2) the likelihood of occurrence of such major reactor accidents.

The portion of the study dealing with consequences of theoretical accidents started with the assumption of a typical power reactor, of 500,000 kilowatts thermal power, in a characteristic power reactor location. Accidents were postulated to occur after 180 days of operation, when essentially full fission product inventories had been built up.

Three types of accidents which could cause serious public damages were assumed. Pessimistic (higher hazard) values were chosen for numerical estimates of many of the uncertain factors influencing the final magnitude of the estimated damages. It is believed that these theoretical estimates are greater than the damage which would actually occur even in the unlikely event of such accidents.

For the three types of assumed accidents, the theoretical estimates indicated that personal damage might range from a lower limit of none injured or killed to an upper limit, in the worst case, of about 3400 killed and about 43,000 injured.

Theoretical property damages ranged from a lower limit of about one half million dollars to an upper limit in the worst case of about seven billion dollars. This latter figure is largely due to assumed contamination of land with fission products.

Under adverse combinations of the conditions considered, it was estimated that people could be killed at distances up to 15 miles, and injured at distances of about 45 miles. Land contamination could extend for greater distances.

In the large majority of theoretical reactor accidents considered, the total assumed losses would not exceed a few hundred million dollars.

As to the probabilities of major reactor accidents, some experts held that numerical estimates of a quantity so vague and uncertain as the likelihood of occurrence of major reactor accidents have no meaning. They declined to express their feeling about this probability in numbers. Others, though admitting similar uncertainty, nevertheless ventured to express their opinions in numerical terms. Estimations so expressed of the probability of reactor accidents having major effects on the public ranged from a chance of one in 100,000 to one in a billion per year for each large reactor. However, whether numerically expressed or not, there was no disagreement in the opinion that the probability of major reactor accidents is exceedingly low.

Passage from WASH-740 report.

properties of materials, after long periods of time, is largely unknown. Eventual serious failures may occur. 3. Various metals used in reactors such as uranium, aluminum, zirconium, sodium and beryllium, under certain conditions not at present clearly understood, may react explosively with water, also present in many reactors. During incidents of abnormal operations resulting perhaps in melting of some of the metals in contact with water and under the influence of radiation, chemical reactions of enough violence to rupture the containment vessels, with release of the fission products could occur. 4. After initial operation, many of the vital components become inaccessible for inspections. In non-nuclear plants, serious accidents are often averted through detection of incipient failure. 5. Much remains to be learned about the characteristics and behavior of nuclear systems.

Like attempted to obtain the revised version of the WASH-740, done at Brookhaven National Laboratory in the 1960s and taking into account the larger-size nuclear plants (such as Shoreham) planned and being built in the 1960s. But the AEC refused to release the report called the "WASH-740-update."

Although he was unable to get hold of the "WASH-740-update," Like did obtain a 1965 letter about it written by then AEC Chairman Glenn Seaborg to the Joint Congressional Committee on Atomic Energy, and entered it into the Shoreham record. The letter stated that the new report showed that the effects of a "catastrophe" at a nuclear plant "would be substantially more than the consequences reported in the earlier [WASH 740] study." (In 1973, the year after the Shoreham construction permit hearings ended, the AEC was forced to release the WASH-740-update by a challenge brought under the newly strengthened Freedom of Information Act. This report said potential consequences from a nuclear plant accident would be even worse with the larger reactors: up to 100,000 injured, 45,000 dead, property damage to between $17 billion to $280 billion. It declared that "the possible size of the area of such a disaster might be equal to that of the State of Pennsylvania.")

The loss-of-coolant accident was described in the WASH-740 as resulting "from a break in the primary coolant circulating system or from a rupture of the reactor vessel itself. Loss of coolant would permit the radioactive decay heat to melt the uncooled fuel, even though the nuclear reaction had stopped, and thereby permit release of volatile fission products." It warned: "The consequences of a loss-of-coolant could be serious."

A loss-of-coolant accident had been barely averted just a few years before, in 1966, at the Fermi nuclear plant near Detroit (the subject of John G. Fuller's 1975 book *We Almost Lost Detroit*).

The Lloyd Harbor Study Group obtained an AEC report done in the wake of that mishap, *Emergency Core Cooling, Report of Advisory Task Force*. "Reliable and practical methods of containing the large molten masses of fuel that would probably result from . . . a meltdown do not exist today," the task force wrote. "Accordingly, it is not considered possible to assure the integrity of the containment if meltdown of large portions of the core were to occur."

The Study Group pointed to expectations in government reports that explosions could occur during a loss-of-coolant accident. A prime cause, said the reports, was a highly volatile metal called zirconium used as the "cladding" on the rods into which the uranium fuel in a nuclear plant is encased. Zirconium was selected because it allows the neutrons from the fuel to pass freely between the rods so a chain reaction can be sustained. But zirconium, when hot, will explode spontaneously upon contact with air, water or steam. (Its main use other than in nuclear plants is in flashbulbs; there is a speck of zirconium in a flashbulb, twenty tons of it in a typical nuclear plant.) Pound for pound, zirconium has the explosive power of nitroglycerine. It has the potential to explode at 2,000°F—well below the 5,000°F temperature of a meltdown.

The government reports said that before exploding, zirconium reacts to heat by drawing oxygen from water or steam and letting off hydrogen, which itself can explode. (The hydrogen bubble that developed during the Three Mile Island accident and was of such great concern formed in this way.)

The reports described both zirconium forming a hydrogen bubble that can explode, and the zirconium itself exploding as among the "metal-water reactions" that could occur in a loss-of-coolant accident. WASH-740 said that "experiments performed at Westinghouse, Aerojet General and North American Aviation indicate that the zirconium-water reaction can be either a rapid oxidation or a violent explosion, depending on whether the zirconium is in massive form or finely dispersed." In experiments with "dispersed zirconium and water . . . the zirconium present reacted more or less completely with explosive violence." Further, noted WASH-740, "in the course of a water-metal reaction, hydrogen gas would be evolved. . . . If the hydrogen exceeds a certain critical concentration, an explosion is possible."

A report entitled *Potential Metal-Water Reactions in Light Water Cooled Power Reactors*, done by Oak Ridge National Laboratory in 1966 (the conclusions of which are still judged accurate), said that in a loss-of-coolant accident "significant quantities of core debris could accumulate at the bottom of the pressure vessel in about 10 to 60 minutes, and would probably melt through this vessel in about another 20 to 60 minutes. . . . The control rod materials themselves could possibly react with the surrounding steam. In addition, hydrogen formed by the metal-water reaction in the lower part of the core could possibly be absorbed in the upper part of the core."

Yet a third type of explosion during a loss-of-coolant accident was regarded as possible in the government reports the Study Group presented: a steam explosion caused by the molten fuel interacting with water in the reactor vessel.

Said the Oak Ridge report: "The effect of dropping masses of molten or partially molten metal in limited quantities of water is not well understood. This could happen in a loss-of-coolant accident with a simultaneous failure of the emergency core cooling system in which the melted core would drop into the water remaining in the bottom of the pressure vessel. There has been some experience with this in other industries, such as the steel and aluminum industries, to indicate the possibility of steam explosions if the molten metal encapsulates some of the water."

Ireland, of the AEC staff, admitted on the stand: "If you had a massive dropping of molten material to water, there is the possibility of a steam explosion."

Licensing board member Dr. Hugh Paxton, from the Los Alamos Scientific Laboratory, conceded: "Of course, steam explosions can occur."

Any of these explosions, the Study Group emphasized, has the potential to cause a "breach" in containment—because the containment is not designed to withstand a severe steam explosion—and out of this break, radioactive poisons could be released inside a nuclear plant. This would be before the core itself bores through the reactor pressure vessel and the concrete base of the plant as part of the "China syndrome"—allowing a radioactive cloud to billow out to poison surrounding areas.

Substantial documentation was presented on the nuclear runaway and its massive instantaneous steam explosion potential.

WASH-740, in listing nuclear plant accident types, described the loss-of-coolant accident as "a second major type of accident." The first accident type listed "The Nuclear Runaway."

It stated: "A nuclear runaway would result if the reactor were made supercritical and all safety instrumentation failed to function. . . . A possible consequence of an unchecked runaway could be the meltdown or vaporization of fuel elements and the possible release of fission products."

WASH-740 cited the "Borax experiment." At the National Reactor Testing Station in the Idaho desert, a miniaturized reactor, one five-hundredth the size of some recently built nuclear plants, was built. In 1954, the government tested what would happen if the reactor went to supercritical. The result was a steam explosion that ripped the reactor apart.

WASH-740 said the Borax experiment showed that "an inherently stable reactor is not always completely immune to destructive runaways by deliberate introduction of a large amount of reactivity at a rapid rate."

The nuclear runaway is also called a power excursion or reactivity accident because it creates a sudden, intense jump in the rate of nuclear reaction. When this happens, fission erupts in "exponential" growth instead of being controlled. Fission or atom splitting normally occurs in a nuclear plant a a rate of 30 millionths of a second. With this rate increasing exponentially in a nuclear runaway, it takes a fraction of a second for a section of the core to become white-hot, melt, and set off a steam explosion with the potential of blowing apart the containment of a nuclear plant. Research by nuclear engineer Dr. Richard E. Webb has shown that a nuclear runaway could happen in a number of ways, including control rods going out of control, a malfunctioning main steam valve, or displacement of the core by mechanical failure or earth movement.

The Study Group pressed AEC witnesses on the Borax experiment. Like noted in a question to Ireland that the Borax experiment caused a "violent transient, produced pressures estimated as high as 6,000 pounds per square inch. . . . Doesn't it suggest that there could be an accident of this order of magnitude?"

"I think it was deliberate that the reactor got hot—steam explosion, parts flew in the air," the AEC staff member replied. "I think probability is so remote you can forget about it."

Miniature reactor exploding in "BORAX-I" test. The blurred object in the right foreground weighs one ton. According to the government report: "Portions of the reactor tank, control rod mechanism, and reactor core have been hurled 80 feet into the air."

Photo: Argonne National Laboratory

But the Study Group then cited a nuclear runaway that was no experiment and in which people were killed. The accident occurred in 1961, in Idaho, on the type of small nuclear plant (an SL-1) the military then thought could be shipped to remote areas to provide power. The nuclear runaway at the reactor left a gory scene: one worker was found impaled on the ceiling one story above the reactor floor, a reactor control rod through his groin and out his shoulder pinning him to the ceiling. The bodies of all three men were hot with radioactivity.

"It was concluded," said Ireland, explaining the SL-1 accident at the Shoreham hearings, "that during the manual hookup of control rods, somehow or other because of manipulation of tools or whatever, one of the men or a pair of the men must have raised one of the control rods in some way to the point where the system became critical."

Webb's involvement at the hearings placed a trained nuclear engineer in a head-on confrontation with nuclear engineers supporting Shoreham. As with other witnesses it invited, the Lloyd Harbor Study Group asked him to join in the questioning.

On the SL-1 accident, he sharply questioned witnesses on the observation in government documents that the reactor "jumped nine feet during its excursion" and ruptured the piping going into the reactor pressure vessel. The Study Group subsequently charged that if a nuclear runaway occurred at Shoreham, "every pipe going into the reactor pressure vessel would be severed and the emergency core cooling system would be effectively disconnected."

On December 4, 1970, *The New York Post* described the scene as Webb conducted his questioning:

> Webb put LILCO and General Electric experts through a ringer of questions that at times seemed to stump and baffle the men who are committed to build the utility's 820,000 kilowatt nuclear generating facility. . . . In his questioning of LILCO and GE engineers, Webb posed some of the most technical queries about nuclear reactor plants since the hearings began in September. And the experts didn't always have the answer.

In recalling the Shoreham hearings, Webb emphasized recently that he did not go to the Shoreham hearings with a position against nuclear power. "I was still pro-nuke, but I thought we needed to ask questions," he said.[11]

He had served under Admiral Hyman Rickover in the Navy for four years, with primary responsibility for the nuclear reactor portion of the first commercial nuclear plant in the U.S., Shippingport near Pittsburgh. It was built by the government under the supervision of Rickover and opened in 1957. Webb said severe nuclear plant accidents were not discussed or considered by the Rickover group. He had thought an accident at a nuclear plant would be confined to inside the plant. A "Hazards Summary Report" that Rickover's staff used "assumed containment," he said. It assumed that the reactor containment "would contain" radioactivity released in an accident. "My recollection is that we weren't told about the WASH-740 report." Only in "the last months with Rickover," he said, by pressing questions, "did I learn that reactors pose a risk to the public."

After the Navy, he became an engineer at the Big Rock Point nuclear plant in Michigan. Here, "safety meant eyeglasses and helmets." He became especially concerned how Strategic Air Command B-52 bombers were using the plant as a practice target in low-level simulated bombing runs. He told the Study Group about this practice and a subsequent crash of a B-52 near the plant, and this became part of the Study Group's arguments on air crash dangers at the Shoreham hearings.

While at Big Rock Point in 1967, Webb wrote a letter published in the newsletter of the Consumers Power Company noting that the flights were occurring "sometimes six times per day at sometimes ear-shattering closeness. I think it is wrong to use a nuclear plant for such practice because of the horrible consequences of radioactive release if one of these planes crashed into the plant." The company replied that it had lodged a complaint with the Defense Department. In 1971, a B-52 on a practice bombing run crashed two miles from the plant— "in a line" with it, said the *Detroit News*, with the bomber hitting "the water like a skipping stone" and erupting, the paper quoted a witness as saying, with "one hell of an explosion."

Ireland's explanation at the Shoreham hearings: "I think some of these SAC bombers and other aircraft presumably use the Big Rock plant as a navigational aid for some strange reason I don't understand."

Webb had left the utility before the B-52 crash near Big Rock Point. He read an article by Dr. Edward Teller in the American Nuclear Society's *Nuclear News* on the "great hazard" on the use of plutonium in the breeder reactor. "Teller was worried about an explosion at a breeder reactor." Webb then believed—as many nuclear physicists and engineers still do—that the breeder reactor, a nuclear plant fueled with plutonium, would be the reactor of the future. The thinking was that "without the breeder we would start running out of fuel in thirty years at the rate they were projecting nuclear energy, because of the natural scarcity of fissionable uranium." Only uranium-235, which is 0.7 percent of the uranium found in nature, undergoes fission. The remainder is uranium-238. When uranium-238 is bombarded with neutrons, rather than splitting, it absorbs a neutron and becomes the supertoxic manmade element plutonium, which is also fissionable. The theory of the breeder reactor is to use plutonium as fuel surrounded by a "blanket" of uranium-238. As the plutonium undergoes fission, the uranium-238 absorbs neutrons and thus "breeds" more plutonium fuel.

Webb said he decided that he "would study for a doctorate in nuclear engineering with an emphasis on the theory of reactor physics so I could independently evaluate the accident hazards of nuclear power plants, especially the breeder."

On a graduate fellowship, he enrolled at Ohio State University in Columbus and was just finishing his dissertation when Ann and Bill Carl called and asked him about reactors. "I mentioned that I was studying the breeder and finding serious explosion potentials, but I had not yet undertaken a serious investigation of light water reactors," uranium-fueled reactors like the Shoreham plant cooled by ordinary or "light" water.

The Carls asked him to come to Long Island to participate in the Shoreham hearings. "Before I went out there," said Webb, "I placed a call to Battelle." Battelle Memorial Institute is a laboratory in Columbus which had done considerable work on reactor hazards for the AEC (and in recent years has done much for the NRC). "I knew that they were doing studies on light water reactors. I figured I'd call them to see what I could learn about their investigations of light waters. Wayne Carbiener, the manager of the contract for light water reactor hazards evaluation, talked to me. I was a member of the nuclear establishment, and he was very free to discuss details of their work. I asked questions about what kinds of studies Battelle was doing in the area of core meltdowns and asked him what they had found.

"He said, 'We're looking at steam explosions.'"

"I asked, 'How serious is this?' I had then no feel for the explosion potential of light water reactors. 'Numerically, how strong are these explosions?'

"He said that the melting of just 3 percent of the core could cause enough of an explosion to rupture the reactor containment. I was very alarmed to hear that—only 3 percent! It was looking like these things were really dangerous. I asked if this was written up in a document that I could have a copy of and study.

"He said, 'No, we're not at liberty to give it out.' After I pursued the matter explaining that the public was entitled to the document, he started to talk very guardedly. He said the report was the property of the AEC and he had no authority to distribute it."

A few days later, Webb was at the Shoreham hearings. They were the first nuclear plant licensing proceedings he had attended. "I appreciated this hearing," said Webb. "I thought it would be an opportunity to ask questions and get answers, a good way to get at the truth, better than informal private discussions. Irving [Like] gave me advice on how to conduct questioning in such a way as to establish facts. I had a lot of questions I wanted to ask, but before I could raise any of them, a lawyer LILCO had brought up from Virginia read from what looked like a treatise about why I was not qualified to ask questions, basically because I hadn't received my doctorate yet." (The lawyer was from the firm of Hunton & Williams of Richmond, Virginia, which specializes in representing utilities in nuclear power plant cases.)

Webb was finally allowed to ask questions, and one of the first he asked of an AEC witness was whether he was aware of a study that established that a heat-up of 3 percent of the core can cause a steam explosion. What followed was "a long conference" involving the AEC staff. The witness then said he was aware of no such report, and other AEC witnesses—and then LILCO witnesses—said the same.

Webb said as he continued to ask questions on accident issues, he was surprised by the resistance he encountered. "It was a big shock to me to find fellow nuclear engineers being tight-lipped, not wanting to cooperate in answering questions, not forthcoming, treating me like an adversary."

Then, "As soon as I got back to Columbus, I called Wayne Carbiener and asked him for the citation of that document. This time he refused to talk. This time he was uncooperative. He refused to discuss the matter. He abruptly ended the conversation, but before he hung up he said three words: *Nuclear Safety Journal*."

Webb looked up the journal, published by Oak Ridge National Laboratory in Tennessee. "I went into the library and, sure enough, there were volumes of *Nuclear Safety Journal*. I started with Volume 1 and studied each volume page by page. Finally, about three hours later, I found a small paragraph buried in one of the volumes. It said a draft report of a 'core meltdown evaluation' had been done by Battelle for the AEC. That might be it, I thought. So I telephoned Ann and Bill Carl and Like and recommended they subpoena that report."

When he was next at the Shoreham hearings, in April 1971, "Irving Like had the document. He had obtained it from the AEC." It was entitled *Core Meltdown Evaluation* and was written by Carbiener and six other scientists at Battelle.

"Sure enough, there were graphs plotting the percent of the core which, if molten, could cause a steam explosion and rupture the reactor vessel," said Dr. Webb.

The report said, "The percent of core dispersed into water needed to get a steam explosion that would cause vessel failure is only in the range of perhaps 2 to around 8 to 9 percent." Thus, an explosion could possibly occur at even less than 3 percent.

"I studied it," Webb said, "and at that point I realized that there was a real problem with these light water reactors, an explosion potential for blowing the containment building apart." Subsequent research into the Battelle calculations, Webb explained, showed that the most serious explosion would have power "the equivalent of 150- to 200-thousand pound TNT bombs—150 to 200 World War II blockbuster bombs going off all at once."

He noted, too, that when the Battelle report was formally issued three months later, designated by the AEC as BMI-1910, "I checked the published version with the draft we obtained. I found it was exactly the same except for one paragraph, which was expunged. The deleted paragraph contained Battelle's recommendation about what to do with the implications of their calculations: serious consideration, they said, should be given to placing nuclear plants deeply underground."

With the realization of the gravity of the accidents that could occur at light water reactors such as Shoreham, Webb, on his second visit to the hearings, probed widely into the range of nuclear plant accident hazards—from core meltdowns to the nuclear runaway.

Back in Ohio he felt the results of that inquiry. Like, in his paper on Shoreham strategy, had noted the

> fear or reluctance of qualified scientists and technicians to testify against a project recommended by the AEC. Various factors have dissuaded scientists and engineers—even those with strong concerns about the environmental effects of nuclear power projects—from testifying on behalf of citizens in such litigation. These include loss of employment or consultant contracts with the AEC, the utilities and the nuclear power industry, curtailment of research grants to universities with whom the prospective expert witness is affiliated, and other forms of economic and professional harassment.

Following his involvement at the Shoreham proceedings and a one-day appearance at AEC hearings in Toledo on a construction license for the Davis-Besse plant, Richard Webb received a letter terminating his fellowship and expelling him from the nuclear engineering program at Ohio State. However, he appealed to the graduate school, was reinstated, and went on to receive his doctorate.

In the years since the Shoreham hearing, he has continued investigating nuclear plant accident hazards. He has served as a consultant on nuclear accident issues in the U.S. and Europe. His 1976 book *Accident Hazards of Nuclear Power Plants* is considered a landmark work on the subject.[12] He has done extensive analyses and a large amount of other writing in recent years working towards a "full analysis of nuclear hazards to help resolve the issue."

Another issue raised at the Shoreham hearings was the absence of insurance to cover people in the event of any kind of nuclear plant accident.

Like argued that because of the unparalleled scale of a nuclear plant disaster, it was "understandable that all the insurance companies in the U.S. . . . . cannot see their way clear" to insuring against a nuclear plant accident. He pointed to the Price-Anderson Act, first passed in 1957 by Congress, under pressure from the AEC and the first segments of the nuclear industry, to get utilities involved in nuclear power. Utilities were resisting because of the liability—insurance companies would not assume responsibility for a nuclear power plant accident. The act declares that in order "to encourage the development of the atomic energy industry" the federal government would "limit the liability of those persons liable for such loss . . . from nuclear incidents."

Like noted that the Price-Anderson Act set an absolute ceiling of $560 million on the damages that could be recovered by victims of a nuclear accident—despite the estimates of possibly thousands injured and dead and the projection of property damage as high as $7 billion in the WASH-740, issued the same year. The federal government would pay $500 million of the $560 million.

"In summary," the Lloyd Harbor Study Group said, "before selecting a site for a nuclear plant, it should be clearly understood that it is a fearsome machine that can cause so much damage that for practical purposes, it can be said to be uninsurable."

The Price-Anderson Act is still in effect with a slightly higher limited liability, $640 million. That is an even smaller fraction of the consequences projected in the WASH-740-update and in the latest U.S. government analysis of a major accident at a nuclear plant. Insurance companies still refuse to provide coverage for any nuclear plant accident. All homeowners insurance policies in the U.S. contain a "nuclear clause" declaring: "This policy does not cover loss or damage caused by nuclear reaction or nuclear radiation or radioactive contamination."

The matter of evacuation in the wake of a nuclear plant accident was also raised at the Shoreham hearings—particularly how evacuation could be handled on Long Island with its large numbers of people and limited access.

Like asked Irwin Spickler of the AEC: "Have you documented in any way the feasibility of evacuating people?"

Spickler: "No."

Like: "Did you make a study of the road patterns in the area?"

Spickler: "Only in a general way."

Like: "Did you make a study of the traffic volume?"

Spickler: "No."

Like: "Are you aware of fact that Suffolk County is 'dead end'?"

Spickler: "No."

Like: "Do you know what that means?"

Spickler: "No."

Like: "If you were going to evacuate large numbers, how would you do it and which direction would they move?"

Spickler: "I am not responsible for evaluation of emergency plans. And emergency plans are evaluated at operating license stage."

"You are the site evaluator. Isn't ease of evacuation a site-related problem?" Like went on, asking Spickler if he agreed with a statement in a deposition from the Nassau County Planning Commission that Long Island's transportation system is one of "bottlenecks and accidents, delays, cancellations on the railroad, infrequent and inaccessible buses," that auto "traffic exceeds capacity," that it is "stop-and-go every rush hour," and that "more traffic will mean virtual paralysis."

Like asked, "Is that an accurate description?"

"Yes," said the government witness.

Among the most incredible statements made at the Shoreham hearings came from Shoreham project manager Wofford about how people on the Long Island Sound beaches adjacent to the plant site would be warned of an accident and what they should do.

"I am sure in the event such happened," said Wofford, "we would send a messenger down and we would suggest they leave. They could swim away if they wished."

The Study Group argued that "if an accident occurred at Shoreham, appropriate and effective arrangements could not be made . . . to protect the public health and safety and to permit ready removal and evacuation of people from the project area and nearby population centers."

But Governor Campbell, the chairman of the AEC hearing board, ruled that the hearing board had no authority to decide on the evacuation issue, that it would be up to the board that decided on an operating license for Shoreham to consider the matter. The Study Group took strong exception, stressing that the important question of whether any effective emergency plan could be developed for Long Island would only be dealt with after large amounts of time and money were invested in building the nuclear plant.

The economics of nuclear power were brought up at the Shoreham hearings. The Study Group brought in Dr. Alexander Kusko, a consulting engineer from Massachusetts and a specialist in power plants.

He testified that there was more potential energy in known reserves of oil than fissionable uranium that could be used in a nuclear power plant. He cited several estimates that there was only a "thirty-year supply" of recoverable uranium-235 in the world.

Kusko spoke of the poor operating record of nuclear plants. They do not have a capacity factor or operating record, like conventional power plants, the electrical engineer stressed. (Nuclear plants, because of their complexity and vulnerability to breakdown, have established a capacity of about 55 percent compared to 90 percent for conventional power plants.)

He testified that conventional power plants had "environmental effects which are predictable and whose costs to control are predictable as well. In the case of nuclear plants, there are environmental effects that have not been resolved and costs that not yet may have been included for the lifetime of the plant. Such extra costs include decommissioning, handling and transportation of fuel elements and waste, insurance and modifications to meet existing or new government standards. . . . The uncertainties of the nuclear plant costs must not be neglected." (Because of the toll of radiation, nuclear plants cannot be used after thirty years and must be "decommissioned," unlike conventional power plants, some of which have remained in service for over a century.)

Using LILCO's figures, Kusko compared the company building a new conventional power plant to a nuclear plant and said, from an economic view, the former was preferable—in fact, it would save LILCO money.

The Study Group maintained that if LILCO "had made an objective and logical comparison" of building a conventional plant rather than a nuclear facility, it "would have seen that the savings to the customers would have been in the area of a half a million dollars annually."

Alternative sources of power—solar and wind power—were brought up in the last days of the Shoreham hearings.

Nuclear power is simply unnecessary, Everett Barber of the Yale University School of Architecture testified. "Solar energy can be and is now being used in this country for domestic water heating, space heating and cooling." Solar energy has been shown "in many cases . . . to be more attractive than conventional systems."

For the same cost as Shoreham (at that point in 1972, LILCO had increased Shoreham's estimated cost to $300 million), a system of wind generators propelled by the strong breezes blowing over Long Island could be constructed—and produce as much electricity, testified William E. Heronemus, a civil engineering professor at the University of Massachusetts. Further, he said, the network of windmills he proposed would be compatible with the environment; they would produce "no radiation, no nuclear waste."

Wilson Clark, a staff member of the Environmental Policy Center in Washington, D.C., which in 1975 published his book *Energy for Survival: The Alternative to Extinction*, stressed energy efficiency. He said Shoreham would not be necessary if LILCO assisted the public in maintaining the same standard of living using less energy.

There were many other issues raised at the Shoreham hearings. The Lloyd Harbor Study Group charged that the AEC had "not made a reliability study of the diesels" that were to provide back up electricity to the plant. It raised the issue of nuclear plant workers being "allowed ten times as much radiation as the public, and when they reach the limit they are said to be 'burned out.' It is known that radiation has genetic effects on the offspring and can cause mutations. No study or analyses have been made as to the genetic effects on the offspring and public gene bank of this radiation." (This standard for workers still exists.) It argued that many of the components for Shoreham were "built to the 1965 and 1966 technology," which it held was becoming obsolete in the early 1970s. (Those components would now be 20 years old.)

Various instances of impropriety by LILCO were alleged, including the company's claim on the construction permit application that the adjacent land "is largely undeveloped." The Study Group presented a list of existing and planned housing developments and stressed that Shoreham was in what was described by demographers as "the fastest growing county in the U.S."

There had been "no analysis of the danger to our water table," pointed out the Study Group, "from radioactivity that might leak" from the plant into the underground water table—which is Long Island's sole source of water. Indeed, Stone & Webster was "not aware" that Long Island is one of several areas in the U.S. that depends solely on its underground water table for potable water, it charged.

Not only did experts testify, but average people did, too. Arthur McComb, a hardware store owner from Ronkonkoma and a former Brookhaven town clerk, came to almost every session of the Shoreham hearings and finally was given three minutes to take the stand. He testified that Shoreham would result in "rotten fish, contaminated groundwater and air, an irradiated food chain, an increasing hazard of the transport of spent nuclear fuel over highways and through communities, and for who knows how long after decommissioning, a monstrous, contaminated monument to our children on a thousand unusable acres after forty years."

At the Shoreham hearings, everything about nuclear power was put on the table.

LILCO still calls them the "most contested proceedings in the history of nuclear power."[13] And perhaps, if they were held before an impartial tribunal, there might be a different result.

But the AEC had no intention of breaking its record of granting a construction or operating license for a nuclear plant, after hearings, to every utility seeking one.

The Shoreham hearings, too, had a role in ending the AEC. Congressman Lester Wolff from Kensington, in Nassau County, and the only federal legislator from Long Island then against Shoreham, went to the hearings and testified that the plant "would be a colossal gamble with the health of future generations." In the process, he got a clear view of the AEC in action. Wolff, who served as a Democrat in Congress from 1964 to 1980, said recently that his experience at the Shoreham hearings convinced him that the AEC was in conflict of interest, serving as both promoter and regulator of nuclear power. "It was clear that the culprit and the cop were the same person," Wolff recounted.[14]

Back in Washington, he worked on a bill to break up the AEC. "These people just treated the whole question of radiation in such a cavalier fashion that this could no longer continue." He got a number of people involved, including then U.S. Senator Robert Kennedy.

During the Shoreham hearings, the Study Group and many of the witnesses it presented challenged the AEC. Mrs. Gene Schrader, of the Center for the Study of Democratic Institutions in California, charged the AEC hearing board on Shoreham with having "a proprietary air about the entire nuclear industry."

Marvin Kalkstein, a professor of political science at the State University of New York at Stony Brook, accused the AEC of being an

example of an "amoral" government agency. It was given "monopolis-
tic powers 20 years ago under which it developed its own sense of
mission without ever checking back to see if that mission was reasonable."

During the hearings, the Study Group joined with five other organizations—the Conservation Society of Southern Vermont, the Chesa-
peake Bay Foundation, Businessmen for the Public Interest of
Chicago, the Colorado Student Lobby and the Cortland Conservation Association of New York State—in a lawsuit filed in District
Court in Washington demanding that the AEC give up one of its two
conflicting functions.

At a press conference the groups held in Washington, Like said:
"The AEC's conflicting roles of promoter and regulator of atomic
power, its enormous financial and vested interest in the promotion and
development of nuclear fission power, and the manner in which it has
interpreted its statuatory responsibilities disqualify it from judging
whether the benefits of atomic power outweigh its risks."[15]

In 1975, four years after the Shoreham hearings ended, the AEC
was disbanded, with the NRC continuing its regulatory function—
but not, supposedly, its nuclear promotion role.

"Approval is virtually a certainty," noted a *Newsday* story on April
12, 1973, the day the AEC had scheduled making a decision on a
construction permit for Shoreham. The paper noted that all the other
nuclear plant projects that had come before the AEC and "had been
subjected to a full set of hearings . . . have been approved," and thus
it was assumed Shoreham would also be—after 70 days of hearings,
116 witnesses and a transcript record of 15,000 pages.

LILCO had no doubts about the outcome. On the day the Shoreham construction permit was granted, it had already spent $77 mil-
lion on building the nuclear plant—more than it originally said
Shoreham would cost in total to build.[16] There was a photo on the
front page of *Newsday* on that day showing the massive steel frame of
the plant's containment building—already built to a height of 75 feet.
The Study Group had tried to stop the construction work, but LILCO
claimed it was just "site preparation," and the federal government
agreed.

That $77 million would be the first of the many millions and then
billions of dollars spent on Shoreham.

NOTES

1. H. Lee Dennison's comment was reported in *Newsday*, April 13, 1966.
2. Reported in *Newsday*, May 20, 1970.
3. Charles Dominy's comments were reported in *Newsday*, April 13, 1966.
4. Mayor George Beatty's comment was reported in *Newsday*, April 2, 1966.
5. *Newsday*, June 3, 1966.
6. Irving Like's comments, here and following, were made in an interview with the author, October 1985.
7. Reported in *Newsday*, July 17, 1967.
8. Irving Like's paper was given during the American Legal Institute-American Bar Association Course of Study on Environmental Law, held in Washington, D.C., January 28–30, 1971. From that address Like also adapted an article entitled "Multi-Media Confrontation—The Environmentalists' Strategy for a 'No-Win' Agency Proceeding," and published it in *Ecology Law Quarterly*, Vol. 1:495.
9. The court also declared in the Calvert Cliffs case:
   The Atomic Energy Commission, abdicating entirely to the other agencies' certifications, neglects the mandated balancing analyses. Concerned members of the public are thereby precluded from raising a wide range of environmental issues in order to affect particular Commission decisions. And the special purpose of NEPA is subverted.
10. This and the following testimony is from the record of the AEC construction permit hearings on Shoreham.
11. Dr. Richard Webb's comments, here and following, were made in interviews with the author, 1985–1986.
12. Richard Webb, *Accident Hazards of Nuclear Power Plants*, Amherst, Mass.: University of Massachusetts Press, 1976.
13. *Newsday*, November 15, 1981.
14. Lester Wolff's comments were made in an interview with the author, December 1985.
15. *Long Island Press*, January 7, 1972.
16. Reported in *Newsday*, November 15, 1981.

5

THE WORLD'S
MOST EXPENSIVE
NUCLEAR PLANT

The nuclear plant that LILCO originally said would cost "in the $65–$75 million range" would, LILCO projected in 1985, cost $4.55 billion. Then LILCO announced that it would have to spend another $1.167 billion on "post-operational capital costs"—changes in the plant after it opened. That brought the price of Shoreham to $5.7 billion[1]—a 7,600 percent cost overrun.

However, LILCO also said in 1985 that for each month Shoreham did not operate, it had to pay "carrying charges" on its debt for the plant "of $45 to $55 million each month."[2]

Thus, expectations are that the final cost of Shoreham could be in the $6.5 billion to $7.5 billion range—a 10,000 percent cost overrun.

Shoreham is, by far, the most expensive nuclear plant per proposed kilowatt of electricity ever built in the world.

Perhaps the best way to visualize the cost of this nuclear project is by looking at the people now in the process of paying LILCO's gargantuan bill, as LILCO shifts its Shoreham costs into its rate base.

Christmas Day, 1985. William Shaw is working—for the first time on a Christmas Day—in his Pine Neck Country Store, "working for LILCO."[3]

"This is our first Christmas open," says Shaw at the register. "I'm forced into it. I'm going to be forced to work New Year's Day, too. For the first time, we were opened on Thanksgiving Day. I have no choice. The LILCO bills are enormous! We have to stay open today to pay the LILCO bill. It's getting impossible to survive because of LILCO," he says to the sounds of Christmas music in the relatively small (4,500 square feet) market in Noyac.

"Who wants to work on Christmas Day?" he says, totaling a customer's bill for a six-pack of beer. "It's a horror. When I told my wife we'd have to stay open Thanksgiving and Christmas this year, we had a violent argument. I reexplained the perilous situation we're in with LILCO, and she understood."

In the spring, summer and early fall when tourism expands the population on Long Island's East End and the store is the busiest, the LILCO bill is between $3,300 and $3,800 a month, says Shaw. He goes to his office and comes back with a bill from the past summer. In the off-season, to save on electricity, to try to cut down the LILCO bill, "we shut down two walk-in coolers, three coolers for soda and turn off half the lights in the store." That leaves only three coolers operating. Still, the LILCO bill off-season, even with the conservation measures, averages $1,800 a month cutting severely into the profits from the store.

LILCO rates are "rising out of sight," says Shaw. Just two years ago, a LILCO bill for a month during the busy part of the year would total $2,000, for the off-season $1,400.

What would happen if LILCO bills double, the expected result if LILCO is allowed to put its Shoreham plant into operation and pass on to ratepayers most of its costs?

"Out of business! That's what would happen. We'd be out of business," says Shaw. "Look at the way it is now. Since September I've not been able to take a salary out of here. If it weren't for some investments, we could not live. If LILCO rates double, I'd have to shut the building down. That's the truth."

Of Shoreham, "It's a boondoggle," says Shaw.

"Although I don't like the bureaucracy of government, with LILCO I think it [a public takeover] would be the only way to go." LILCO, Shaw says, "is a company out of control. They don't know what they're doing. It's very badly managed."

Shaw notes that he "came from big business." Before operating the Pine Neck Country Store in recent years, he was the chief executive officer of EBS Manufacturing in Hauppauge, Long Island, which produces equipment for the aircraft industry. When he began his corporate job, he says, "it was made very clear that I would be held personally liable for any mismanagement. I can't understand how

LILCO can be operated by people who have mismanaged funds, who don't know what they're doing, who waste millions of dollars on public relations companies. Look what happened when they got rid of Charlie Pierce [the former LILCO chairman]. They rehire him at $152,000 a year as a consultant. That's slapping the public in the face. The top management of LILCO should all resign."

It is January 1986. The New York State Public Service Commission (PSC) has just granted LILCO a new rate increase, agreed to let it collect an additional $68.7 million a year—all LILCO asked for, and all to go towards Shoreham. And Charlotte Giel in Charlotte's Gift Cottage in Cold Spring Harbor, Long Island, is telling of how she has been "threatened and harassed" by LILCO and is afraid of being forced out of business because of skyrocketing LILCO bills for her little store.[4]

"We began having problems in 1982 when the LILCO bills started to really jump," she is saying. "We tried to resolve it by paying LILCO one lump sum—$823.03—which brought us up to date, and then we entered into a contract to be on a budget plan and pay $375 a month. We completed our part of the deal. We paid them the $375 each month. Until 1982 our bills were running between $200 and $300, and $375 should have covered anything. Then we received an estimated bill of $1,200—for one month! Our bills shouldn't run anything like that. We don't use much electricity. The store is only 1,500 square feet. It's a mom-and-pop store. We sell gifts, baby things, China cups and saucers. We don't have any machines, other than a cash register. We're only open five and a half days a week."

She protested that bill to the company as well as a series of subsequent, also inordinately high, LILCO bills with estimated amounts. Meanwhile, she held to the budget plan agreed to, and LILCO dealt with her "with such arrogance, such belligerence." Its representatives have "actually threatened—several times—that they are going to smash down my door and take the meters." One billing supervisor, she says, told her he "would take pleasure in putting me out of business."

At one point, a LILCO representative came and "stood in the middle of the store demanding $1,300 or, he said, he would turn off the electricity," she recounts. "I had to give the man the money, even though I just paid them $375 for the month. As he left, he took a Hummel figurine and said, 'I'm going to take this for the aggravation.' " Mrs. Giel reported the taking of the figurine to LILCO, and "They didn't want to know."

At the PSC hearing on her conflict with LILCO, a utility representative insisted that "nobody entered into a contract putting us on the budget plan—even though I have a letter from the woman who did." The PSC hearing officer decided that the wording of the LILCO letter was vague, and ruled in LILCO's favor.

LILCO now claims she owes $7,200. After owning the gift shop for twelve years, Charlotte Giel fears that because of LILCO, she may lose it. "I am scared to death. They are trying to put me out of business."

Her husband, Anthony Giel, speaks of LILCO having an attitude "that is not only arrogant, it is a Gestapo attitude. It smacks of Nazism." He tells of being at the store when LILCO workers cut the electricity and a representative announced: "That's what's going to happen unless you cooperate with LILCO." Giel says: "What they have done to us is a terrible thing. At one point, I thought we should pull up stakes—and let them have Long Island." But the Giels are trying to hold on and keep their business despite LILCO.

Because of Shoreham, LILCO's rates have been soaring, and the attitude of LILCO officials amid the utility's financial plight has been desperate. The figures in LILCO's most recently released financial report tell the dismal story: Funds invested in "nuclear construction" at Shoreham are nearly $4 billion and rising, and "total assets" of the company other than Shoreham amount to $2.8 billion. LILCO has been trying to build a nuclear plant with funds that far exceed the utility's worth.

Why the astronomical Shoreham cost overrun?

In 1979, the State Public Service Commission ordered an investigation of Shoreham construction costs at the urging of Joel Blau, a PSC staff counsel. Blau had become suspicious about what was happening on the project. LILCO's estimated price for Shoreham had gone beyond $1 billion (to $1.22 billion) in 1977. In 1976 and 1978, LILCO had asked the PSC to let it immediately charge ratepayers for a portion of Shoreham costs as "construction work in progress." The PSC agreed, saying in both instances that it was an "extraordinary remedy." Normally, the PSC would not shift construction costs into the rate base of a utility until the construction was completed. But, because of LILCO's financial condition, said the PSC, it would allow the utility to pass on some Shoreham costs to ratepayers at once. The two rate cases totaled $255 million. In its actions, the PSC made an exception to its policy of basing rates on the "used and useful principle." This holds that a utility cannot charge ratepayers for a project that is not "used and useful" in providing service. It stems from an 1898 U.S. Supreme Court decision. Also, a 1978 report on Shoreham, commissioned and supervised by the PSC and done by the management consulting firm of Booz-Allen Hamilton of New York City, found extremely low efficiency on the Shoreham job. Blau thought the pattern of cost escalation and poor performance on the project raised questions about the prudency of LILCO's management.

The New York PSC has the power to bar a utility from passing on to ratepayers costs that have not been "prudently incurred," although the New York PSC and agencies elsewhere in the U.S. that regulate utilities have not made much use of this authority until recently. Usually, regulatory agencies have let utilities pass on to ratepayers the full cost of any capital project undertaken plus a "rate of return" or profit when the project is completed. The notion behind this has been to make utility projects attractive to investors. The effect, in the years of nuclear plant projects, has been that there has been no regulatory obstacle, indeed there has been an incentive for utilities to build expensive nuclear plants, as detailed in Ron Lanoue's 1976 book, *Nuclear Power Plants: The More They Build, the More You Pay*.

The PSC May 1979 order on the Shoreham inquiry stated that its purpose would be

> to investigate and determine: 1. whether the costs of the Shoreham facility were prudently incurred by Long Island Lighting Company; 2. whether the steep escalation in Shoreham's costs was attributable to factors within the control of LILCO's management; and 3. to what extent, if any, the incurred cost of the Shoreham facility exceeds the reasonable and prudent cost of such a facility because of LILCO's imprudence, mismanagement and gross inefficiency.

Two months later, after LILCO announced a new delay in its anticipated completion of the project, the PSC split the investigation into Phase I, to look into the "total remaining costs" of Shoreham, and Phase II, a "retrospective investigation into the total project's costs."

Phase II began in 1981. To conduct it, the PSC assigned only one person full-time—attorney Blau. He was assisted by a technical expert, a valuation engineer, working part-time. A consultant was hired on a limited budget. Blau asked LILCO for numerous records.

LILCO stonewalled, providing records at an extremely slow pace and refusing to provide some information.

"There is no justification for LILCO's slow responses to staff's interrogatories, especially when one considers the nature of staff's requests," declared Blau in a 1982 brief filed with William C. Levy, the PSC administrative law judge assigned to the case.[5] He declared that there was a "pattern of untimely responses." As an example of LILCO refusing to provide information, Blau's brief noted that the probe sought to "evaluate costs by tracking systematically the cost increases for specific physical elements of the project. This, in our view, was the most logical approach to this investigation." LILCO, in reply, advised Blau "that it could not provide cost information in the format outlined. . . . The company stated that it was 'unwilling to perform the work of staff's consultant by re-analyzing Shoreham's budget in the peculiar manner staff's consultant desires.' " Another Blau brief complained that LILCO was refusing to physically part with some documents, insisting that they be reviewed at LILCO facilities.

Stone & Webster, meanwhile, was refusing to provide some documents claiming they were "proprietary." The brief declared that "if those documents are not forthcoming, staff will seek *subpeona ducus tecum* to obtain them."

When what information LILCO was willing to release came dribbling in, it became clear to Blau that the documents totally contradicted assurances that LILCO executives had given the PSC through the years about the Shoreham project.

A critical document in this regard was titled *Shoreham Nuclear Power Station Schedule and Construction Management Evaluation*, prepared in 1977 by a group of five high LILCO executives. This report charged:

> The inaccuracy of the monitoring and controlling systems on site, a vital element in management awareness and control, serves as a striking example of Stone & Webster's lack of concern for the physical progress of the job. Evidence of critical design problems has been suppressed by Stone & Webster in several instances in favor of not having to address them urgently and thereby highlighting engineering difficulties. . . . We do not believe that the Stone & Webster excuses of LILCO interference, contractor ineptitude, and poor craft productivity, can shift the central respo..sibility that LILCO should seri-

ously consider the replacement of Stone & Webster with a more competent Construction Manager.

The report said that the "disadvantages" of continuing with Stone & Webster as construction manager at Shoreham would include

continued reliance by construction management on complex, expensive and inaccurate management information systems and planning techniques which have proven to be invalid in the past, a continued reluctance to accept responsibility for construction progress and a finger-pointing attitude toward problem identification and resolution, continued shielding of engineering problems due to the same corporation having both the engineering and construction management responsibility

and leaving Shoreham construction in the hands of a firm that had been responsible for "poor performance to date for four years of construction, management resulting in numerous schedule delays and budget increases."

The document, which became known as the "Gang of Five Memo," led to LILCO in 1977 talking over construction management at Shoreham with an entity that it called Unified Construction Organization, UNICO.

"The information provided showed that there were serious problems with LILCO's management of the project," noted the 1984 PSC staff report of the Shoreham investigation.[6] "This was inconsistent with earlier information provided by LILCO, and with its filed testimony" to the PSC. "At this point, staff determined that there was evidence of serious management problems which to assess properly would require an increased effort by both staff and its consultant."

A "full-blown retrospective investigation of LILCO's management of the Shoreham project" was then begun, related the staff report.

A multi-disciplined group of professionals, including lawyers, engineers and accountants, along with computer and clerical support was assembled as the Shoreham Task Force. This group consisted of eighteen full-time individuals selected from various divisions within the Department of Public Service; fifteen additional employees of the DPS were used on a part-time basis for tasks related to the investigation.

We launched an unprecedented examination of LILCO's books and records pursuant to the commission's authority under the Public Service Law. The Shoreham Task Force conducted a thorough on-site investigation of LILCO at its various offices in Hicksville, Mineola and at the Shoreham site. The files of 66 departments and offices were reviewed for Shoreham-related information. The task force also examined personal files of 58 managers, including the chairman of the board and president of LILCO. . . . We obtained approximately 10,000 documents. In addition, we obtained the company's computerized accounting information system for Shoreham and developed our own computer capability to analyze this data.

The PSC investigators also went through the files of contractors, and finally got access to all of Stone & Webster's records.

The "Findings and Conclusions" of the PSC staff investigation declared:

LILCO's management has failed to address adequately the management responsibilities entrusted by its shareholders, ratepayers, and regulators. LILCO's management actions in aggregate have been deficient and unreasonable. The project management organization, inconsistently supported by top management and the board of directors, has afforded inadequate leadership to the project team. This deficiency not only allowed, but caused significant inadequacies in the performance of engineering and construction of the Shoreham project. The contributions of Stone & Webster as architect/engineer and construction manager were deficient both within the scope of the work under its internal control, and as a result of improper management by LILCO.

LILCO had every opportunity to have a successful project. The plant is now unfinished ten years after the initially targeted commercial operating date [and its cost will make it] the most expensive plant per kilowatt of rated capacity to date [in the U.S.].

LILCO effectively lost management control of the project immediately following commencement. It failed to undertake the important initial planning activities needed to establish an overall project organizational strategy for implementing required production, management and oversight activities and the respective assignments of roles and responsibilities. Similarly, LILCO failed to undertake the need for, and, therefore, did not initiate the foundation for basic project control systems. These are the management tools that help management to measure progress, to detect problems, and to take required corrective action. LILCO has failed to establish responsible guidelines and policies, and has not properly identified and analyzed viable options when corrective action was necessary. LILCO has been deficient in the manner in which it has directed the resources available, by diminishing the capacity of experienced team members through role confusion and interference, and by placing inexperienced persons in key positions. This lack of guidelines, ground rules, and competent leadership has kept the project organization from being an effective project team.

LILCO's management of Stone & Webster as architect/engineer and as construction manager until 1977 has been similarly deficient. In light of LILCO's inexperience with the complexities of nuclear plant design and construction and its ineptitude in overseeing the process as owner/client, an exemplary performance would have been required by Stone & Webster to compensate for LILCO's inadequacies. Stone & Webster's performance was not exemplary, but quite the contrary. It continually failed to provide adequate engineering support to construction, and its tenure as construction manager was marked by chaos and lack of management direction at the construction site.

LILCO was not adequately attentive to engineering management. By failing to monitor progress and problems closely, LILCO did not keep itself properly informed of engineering status and problems of interface with construction. Thus, it was inadequately prepared to determine the root causes of problems, or to analyze the validity of crucial Stone & Webster recommendations.

[LILCO's] unstudied takeover of construction manager in 1977 placed inexperienced personnel in lead positions. LILCO's management of the Shoreham project was flawed in the initial stages and, although realigned several times during the course of the project, has seen little or no improvement. Capabilities have not evolved. The confusion of roles and inability to effectively align resources has persisted throughout. The deficiencies have remained. LILCO's overall management of the Shoreham project, and the ineffectual performance of Stone & Webster as primary production contractor, have been deficient and unreasonable.

The report's conclusion continued that "the substantial final delay caused by the diesel generator failures in 1983 represents a telling culmination of the management inadequacies identified throughout the project."

The PSC report examined various areas in detail and gave determinations of where disallowances for imprudent costs should be made. Under "Diesel Generators," it said:

> The participation by LILCO and Stone & Webster in the procurement, fabrication, testing and installation of the diesel generator sets for Shoreham represents a prime example of the combined effects of inept and deficient oversight by management. Within this overall deficient performance on the diesels, two flaws, one in action and the other in inaction, emerge as the most unreasonable.
>
> First, reliability of the diesel engines was the single most important performance criterion. [Yet, when LILCO ordered the diesels from Transamerica Delaval, Delaval had] . . . no experience in producing diesel engines for nuclear power plants. LILCO's selection of an unproven engine represents a needless risk. Other manufacturers offered LILCO proven engines, and two vendors even had experience fabricating emergency diesel generators for nuclear plants. Under the circumstances, LILCO management took an unreasonable and unwarranted risk in selecting Delaval's prototype engine for Shoreham.
>
> Second, certain tests were required by Stone & Webster to establish the integrity of the crankshaft. Stone & Webster failed to complete its professional responsibility to obtain the information needed for a proper analysis of the test results. Since LILCO was not overseeing the resolution of this problem as it should have done, LILCO was not aware of Stone & Webster's omission. If the test results had been analyzed properly, the presence of the underdesigned crankshaft suspected by Stone & Webster and LILCO would have been known in 1976.

Not seven years later one crankshaft broke during testing (the scene George Henry witnessed), and cracks were found in the others.

The PSC staff urged "adjustments" totaling at least $1.55 billion in what LILCO should be barred from charging its ratepayers for Shoreham. Of the $3.84 billion that LILCO in 1984 was estimating Shoreham would cost, the PSC staff recommended that $2.29 billion be the "allowable cost to rate base." Any additional Shoreham cost increase because of delays resulting from the diesels should be fully absorbed by LILCO, it said.

The staff report also took up which LILCO arguments as the claim that additional NRC regulations in the 1970s played a major part in the cost overrun. "Shoreham was not unique in facing the regulatory change and impact of the 1970s," said the report. "The multitude of regulatory changes and the ensuing management tasks were not unique to Shoreham. That some of the plants with a regulatory history similar to Shoreham have been completed and are now operating argues that the management task is achievable."

Many shelves in the PSC file room in Albany are devoted to the documents, transcripts of interviews and other information on which the PSC staff based its report.

There are records concerning how Stone & Webster was chosen by LILCO.[7] A report by investigators—employees of a Los Angeles-based consulting organization, Theodore Barry & Associates, contracted by the PSC to assist in the inquiry—tells of how "the process for reviewing and selecting the architect/engineer and construction manager was not rigorous." LILCO executive vice president Edward Duffy "submitted a memorandum to the board of directors recommending the hiring of Stone & Webster as both architect/engineer and construction manager. . . . On the basis of this memorandum, on May 31, 1967, the board authorized Duffy and other officers of the company to hire Stone & Webster." The investigators related that "we were surprised to discover that Mr. Richard L. Forrester, a Stone & Webster marketing engineer at the time those activities took place, was the son-in-law" of Duffy. "Mr. Forrester was partly responsible for Stone & Webster's obtaining the architect/engineer-construction manager and preliminary work contracts for the Shoreham project."

They said that, in 1966, Forrester "hosted" LILCO executives, including William J. Burns, LILCO's manager of mechanical and civil engineering, "at Stone & Webster's facilities in Boston," and seven months later, Burns "requested a proposal from Stone & Webster for engineering services. . . . That request was placed through Mr. Forrester." Also, it was noted that Forrester's resumé "states that he '. . . participated in four major proposals which resulted in awards to Stone & Webster including . . . the Shoreham Nuclear Station for Long Island Lighting.' "

Duffy, the investigators pointed out, "approved the hiring of Stone & Webster. The Duffy-Forrester relationship presented an obvious conflict of interest. Mr. Duffy should not have participated in the process and should not have made recommendations to the board."

Stone & Webster had been one of five firms seeking the Shoreham job. It estimated its services would cost $16.6 million, lower than the $16.75 million estimate of Bechtel, but higher than the estimates of Burns & Roe, $14.5 million; United Engineers and Constructors, also $14.5 million; and Ebasco, $15.75 million.

However, the original estimate turned out to be a fraction of Stone & Webster's fee because LILCO's contract with the company and indeed with other Shoreham contractors, too, was for "cost-plus." LILCO agreed not only to a fixed amount but also to pay them for any extra costs they encountered during construction. That resulted in Stone & Webster making way over its original $16.6 million cost estimate for the Shoreham project; eventually, they received over $350 million from LILCO.

The PSC staff considered this LILCO's failure "to exercise its responsibilities to protect its interests at Shoreham contractually, both at project inception and through later revisions to the Stone & Webster contract."

After the staff report was completed, Levy and a second PSC administrative law judge, Thomas R. Mattias, were given the task of examining the evidence in the Shoreham case, conducting hearings and suggesting a course of action to the seven-member PSC. They considered not only the staff report but filings by LILCO and Suffolk County, the New York State Consumer Protection Board and a group called Long Island Citizens in Action, and testimony given and documents presented at hearings. At the hearings, which took place through 1984, 79 witnesses were presented—51 of them LILCO witnesses. "The resulting record," the PSC staff noted in their 137-page "Recommended Decision," issued in March 1985, "consists of some 11,654 pages of transcript and approximately 2,775 exhibits, many of which consist of voluminous reports and multi-document exhibits."[8]

The judges declared: "After hearing the many weeks of testimony in this proceeding and after careful review of the record and briefs, we conclude, for all the reasons hereinafter set forth, that LILCO mismanaged the Shoreham project. The record demonstrates that the company, almost from the outset of construction in 1969, lost effective control over project costs and schedule and did not regain control until at least early 1984, when its chairman, president and senior officials resigned. This continuing failure, and the steep escalation in project cost estimates and schedule delays are reflected in the increase in cost estimates from $70 million in 1965 to a current estimate of $4.2 billion and a commercial operating date slippage of about 10 years." (In 1984, Catacosinos, who had been a member of the LILCO board since 1978, took over as president, chairman of the board and chief executive officer of LILCO.)

The PSC administrative law judges reviewed "the details of LILCO's continuing mismanagement of the Shoreham project" in "seven major areas or categories"—Project Planning and Management, Construction Management, Engineering and Design, Quality Control Programs, License Proceedings and Regulations, Diesel Generators, and Quantification.

Project Planning and Management. "We conclude," they said, "that LILCO failed to develop a project plan adequate to oversee Stone & Webster management of the project, to identify roles and responsibilities, to develop accurate and timely reporting systems which would enable it to monitor, measure and control costs and scheduling, to adequately staff monitoring groups or to adequately prepare for its critical owner oversight role."

They noted how, "in 1968, Arthur Sugden, then LILCO vice president of engineering, advised senior management that there were differences between nuclear and fossil construction in terms of manhours required, the effects of regulatory requirements on design, licensing delays, potential for retrofitting because of AEC requirements, schedule slippages at other nuclear plants, premium pay demands by craft [experienced craftspeople] at other nuclear projects, public relations problems with conservation groups, rigid quality control requirements, and a sharp increase in Shoreham's costs of almost 300 percent in a three-year period. LILCO ignored Sugden's advice to defer Shoreham until those differences could be studied further, and the company proceeded, without adequate planning, or any overall project plan."

Construction Management. "We conclude that, throughout Shoreham's construction, LILCO failed to staff adequately its prime area of responsibility as owner of the plant—cost and schedule control," they said. "The record shows that construction labor productivity was low due to inadequate supervision, poor planning and lack of management support. From the outset of the project, productivity rates failed to meet the rates projected in estimates and schedules. This failure to meet projected goals was consistent and continuing. A mid-1974 field audit acknowledged the decline in worker productivity and noted that many workers were inactive. An absence of supervision around the site was noted. Aware of the problem, LILCO also acknowledged at this time that poor productivity was a factor in the increase in Shoreham's estimated cost. Nevertheless, LILCO failed to address the problem and its causes. Reports throughout the mid-1970s continued to indicate inadequate productivity at Shoreham."

They said, citing a LILCO internal report, that in 1977 "productivity had deteriorated to the point where LILCO observed that 'the project was running at half speed' and 'that the site resembled a government job.' " In 1977, LILCO "work sampling studies confirmed [that] crafts were utilized for direct work only 21 percent of the time at Shoreham."

In November 1980, "Paul Sowa, a LILCO consultant, reported that he saw little supervision . . . and that craftpersons did not appear to be kept busy. Low productivity dogged the Shoreham project from start to finish, and virtually every group or individual who investigated the problem reported that one of its primary causes was inadequate supervision of the labor force, an area entirely within LILCO's control. . . .

"LILCO attempts to excuse low craft productivity by stating that it emphasized safety and reliability, and that it had to contend with new NRC safety-related regulations. But every other nuclear plant constructed in the time period had to contend with these same regulatory requirements; and the majority met this challenge by maintaining much higher levels of productivity than Shoreham."

Further, the administrative law judges said, "planning and scheduling deficiencies contributed significantly to construction delays and low labor productivity. . . . For example, contractors' meeting minutes for March 1976 contain the following comments: 'LILCO stated that two months ago they had instructed Courter to throw caution to the winds and jam all available pipe into the buildings. Now they are running out of material.' "

Engineering and Design. "LILCO mismanagement of the engineering effort required at Shoreham added unnecessary costs and contributed to schedule delays. LILCO argues that Shoreham's engineering difficulties were due entirely to regulatory changes beyond its control. While regulatory imposed changes were a factor, for which we have adjusted, the schedule slippage and the increases in engineering and construction manhours were due in large measure to LILCO mismanagement. This conclusion is supported by published industry data regarding total engineering manhours, cost, and design changes for a number of comparable nuclear projects. It is also supported by reviewing specific Shoreham engineering and design decisions.

"For example, increasing the size of Shoreham's reactor from 540 megawatts to 820 megawatts without changing the size of the reactor building created a concern that space limitations within the building would increase the likelihood of interferences and lead to overly congested working areas." Trying to put the larger-size reactor into a building designed for the smaller one became even more problematic, they said, with new industry and government safety requirements established in the early 1970s.

"The design of the reactor building was not set until concrete was poured in 1973. . . . The record shows, however, that management did not reassess the soundness of the original decision not to modify the reactor building size before the first concrete for that building was poured, a failure with substantial cost consequences.

"The company argues that the crowded conditions in Shoreham's secondary containment were not foreseeable before concrete was poured." But the administrative law judges said, "The record shows that projects contemporaneous with Shoreham were designed with substantially larger reactor buildings. LILCO and Stone & Webster do not appear to have considered the new regulations in the context of their implications for the reactor building size. . . . Reasonable management would have assessed the impact of the new regulations on the 1969 decision not to increase the size of the reactor building before the concrete pour began. LILCO's failure to do so was imprudent."

They cited LILCO's selection of GE's Mark II reactor containment design. GE's existing design in the 1960s was called Mark I and featured considerable air space to absorb steam pressure in the event of an accident. But the large volume was costly because it required a good deal of steel and concrete, so GE developed the Mark II, a smaller containment utilizing a pool of water under the reactor. In this design, pipes lead from the reactor and from the air around it into the pool. The theory is that pressure built up during an accident will channel itself through the pipes and down into the water in the pool that would absorb it. LILCO was the first utility to order the Mark II design. LILCO, GE and Stone & Webster ballyhooed the order by announcing it in a paper at the American Power Conference in 1967. (Dale Bridenbaugh, with GE at the time, recalled, "They tooted their horn pretty loudly. It seemed strange to me that a utility with no nuclear experience took the first order of an entirely new design. . . . It was just another chance that LILCO took along the way."[9])

Serious design problems were later found in the Mark II (despite the AEC having approved it). The water pool did not, it turned out, adequately absorb pressure. Millions of dollars had to be spent to make changes in the Mark II containment at each of the plants built with it. The administrative judges noted that "the Mark II containment had not been designed to accommodate forces to which the containment structure would be subjected during certain accidents that might occur," but LILCO was unaware of the problem because it "failed to schedule" tests of the untried design "at the time of its selection. Had these tests been properly and timely conducted, the hydrodynamic load problem would have been discovered much earlier." LILCO learned about the defect in 1973, when GE discovered it, and then LILCO "failed to adopt a systematic approach" to making modifications. The Mark II problem and LILCO's handling of it "resulted in additional costs"—$25 million, they said—and delayed Shoreham "approximately two years."

Quality Control Programs. "We conclude that LILCO failed to develop or to staff adequate Shoreham quality control programs," the administrative law judges declared. LILCO "failed to anticipate staffing needs for the quality assurance program, or support construction adequately. There were not enough qualified persons for QA inspections of construction work. LILCO's quality control program was ineffective in correcting problems or preventing their recurrence."

Licensing Proceedings and Regulations. "We conclude that LILCO mismanaged its response to the changing regulatory environment and requirements." They spoke of new industry codes for piping that LILCO waited much longer than it should have to implement. They cited government codes on the separation of electric cables that LILCO had agreed to abide by in its final safety report on Shoreham filed with the government, but then LILCO went ahead and made "21,000 electrical installations violating the criteria. The NRC demanded prompt correction of violations. Resolution of electrical separation violations impacted Shoreham's construction schedule and required rework."

Diesel Generators. The administrative law judges noted that Delaval "had never previously qualified and installed its engines in nuclear service, a fact that was known to Stone & Webster and LILCO and should have alerted them to the importance of careful monitoring and supervising testing."

Also, "The Shoreham specifications . . . were 36 percent above the power levels at which this engine had been operated. At the power levels required by Shoreham, the Delaval engine was an unproven prototype and represented an untested risk."

Delaval, at Stone & Webster's request, did a "torsiograph" test on the diesels in 1975 to confirm or disprove the stress problems. But the test report did not discuss the measured stress levels, and Stone & Webster "never sought the information pertaining to measured stresses; the problem was dropped and not resolved until the crankshaft failed in 1983. The actual stress values derived from the 1975 torsiograph test indicated that the crankshaft was undersized. Reasonable review by Stone & Webster would have uncovered this design flaw no later than early 1976, seven years before the crankshaft failed."

Said the administrative law judges: "The diesel generator failure, repairs, replacements and delay which began in 1983, and continue to the present are due to inadequate management oversight for which LILCO is responsible as owner and licensee of the Shoreham project. Stone & Webster acted as LILCO's agent for the monitoring of Delaval's performance under the contract between LILCO and Delaval. LILCO, as principal, is responsible for Stone & Webster's essentially negligent failure to ensure the diesels satisfied contract requirements and specifications."

They added that if Stone & Webster was not aware of the design error in 1976, it became aware in 1977 that Delaval had begun putting a thicker crankshaft in the same model diesel engine. Delaval supplied these to "at least twelve U.S. utilities . . . for service in nuclear plants," with Shoreham left as the only domestic nuclear plant with the Delaval diesels with the undersized crankshafts.

Quantification. The term refers to how costs resulting from imprudency should be broken down. The administrative law judges made an "engineering adjustment," a "construction adjustment," a "schedule delay adjustment" and a "diesel generator adjustment" and set dollar amounts for imprudency in each category. The total came to $1.2 billion that they recommended "the commission exclude from rate base" because these costs had "been imprudently incurred. The amount will require further adjustment, if Shoreham's cost and schedule are further revised." The main difference between their determination and the $1.55 billion figure arrived at by the PSC staff was that they did not disallow LILCO the full costs resulting from the delay in the plant being able to open because of the diesel problems. The administrative law judges disallowed half of the delay cost, maintaining the remainder was due "to Shoreham's unique licensing history and not to factors within the control of LILCO."

They also rejected LILCO's definition of prudency. The "standards proposed by" LILCO and witnesses it presented on the subject "are inconsistent with and go beyond" the PSC's view. "A theory which suggests that large scale complex projects are inherently unmanageable has no place in public utility regulation," they said. "The public is entitled to expect that such undertakings by public utilities are controllable. LILCO's proposed standards would insulate its management."

They continued: "It is important to emphasize that the commission's prudence standard—whether the conduct was reasonable at the time under all the specific circumstances—is based upon sound public policy. It serves to deter the inclusion in a rate base of excessive and unjustified costs and thereby acts as an incentive to improve the quality of utility management. If a public utility—a monopoly—can saddle its captive ratepayers with excessive and imprudent costs, it has little or no incentive for efficiency and cost savings. The prudence rule is a regulatory substitute for the discipline that would be imposed by a free, competitive, market economy where the penalty for mismanagement and imprudent costs is a loss of jobs, profits or business failure."

Interestingly, among LILCO witnesses testifying in the prudency case, and mentioned in the decision, was one Roger Boyd, who had figured as a major witness at the 1970–71 AEC Shoreham construction permit hearings involving the Lloyd Harbor Study Group. Then he was on the AEC staff. Boyd testified at the 1984 PSC hearings as vice president of KMC, Inc., a company based in Washington, D.C., and described in the PSC-recommended decision as "formed to provide a consulting service to the utility industry principally on nuclear power plant licensing issues before the NRC." Boyd, it was noted, "testified that the most significant event to have an impact on licensing for Shoreham was the intervention of third parties in the federal proceedings."

He did not conceal his prior role as a government regulator of Shoreham. He testified: "In my capacity as assistant director for reactor projects in the AEC's Division of Reactor licensing and later as director of the Division of Project Management, I was the individual ultimately responsible for Shoreham's construction permit and operating license review. This responsibility continued throughout my career with the AEC and the NRC."

Eben Pyne, the Citibank senior vice president and LILCO board member, testified with LILCO President Wilfred Uhl in the PSC case about the role of the board of directors in major decisions concerning Shoreham. They said that involvement of the board in the decisions was extensive.

In a 130-page *Opinion and Order Determining Prudent Costs* issued in December 1985, the seven-member PSC agreed with its two administrative law judges. "We conclude that the record as a whole amply supports the judges' findings," they declared.[10]

They also commented: "Our investigation of Shoreham's costs is well grounded in our statutory responsibilities and the traditional rules relating to utility regulation. The case itself, however, is far from typical, for we have never before been called upon to review a utility's management of a project so complex, costly and lengthy."

A majority on the commission voted to disallow $1.395 billion of Shoreham costs from going into LILCO's rate base—the biggest penalty, by far, ever meted out by a regulatory agency in the U.S. to a utility for mismanagement.

Three members of the commission, including Anne Mead, dissented and said more should be disallowed. They set $1.875 billion as the proper figure, maintaining that the judges and the commission majority "erred" in attributing half rather than all the delay costs resulting from the diesel problems to LILCO. They said that even if there had not been the challenge to Shoreham going into operation led by Suffolk County and New York State because of evacuation planning, "LILCO could not have proceeded" and operated the plant, and this was "entirely due to the failure of the diesel generators." LILCO should be penalized "the entire diesel-related adjustment recommended by staff of $893 million," they said.

Also, the dissenters complained that the majority, in "fixing the amount of costs disallowed as a result of imprudence . . . has effectively precluded the possibility that additional imprudent expenditures will have been made by LILCO after the record in this proceeding was closed. We believe this is a disservice to both the ratepayers and LILCO."

Throughout the prudency case, the position of LILCO was one of denial. Declared LILCO in a press release after the PSC administrative law judges' decision: "The costs of Shoreham were prudently incurred. LILCO believes that changes in federal regulations, especially those after the Three Mile Island accident, and other factors beyond the company's control caused the cost overruns at Shoreham."[11]

After the commission action, LILCO public relations person Carol Clawson said: "High costs associated with Shoreham were the result of regulatory changes, high construction costs in the New York metropolitan area, delays caused by opposition to the plant and refusal of local government to support emergency planning."[12] LILCO announced it would challenge the PSC decision in court. It complained that the penalty could bankrupt the utility. In its 1985 annual report, LILCO said the disallowance could "jeopardize the company's ability to meet its financial obligations" and it then "might be required to file a petition for relief under the Federal Bankruptcy Code."

The New York PSC action was seen as having influence on other regulatory agencies in the U.S. Michael D. Foley, director of financial analysis for the National Association of Regulatory Utility Commissioners, said: "This may stiffen the back of other commissions in making these decisions. Other regulators often look to New York."[13] Earlier, he said, "When one thinks of troubled nuclear plants, Shoreham is at the top of the list. This should certainly be a bellwether case."

Georgia regulators looking into the Alvin W. Vogtle, Jr., nuclear project, and California regulators investigating the Diablo Canyon project, had sought advice and information from New York, as had utility regulators from other states, New York PSC officials said. "Our advice was sought because the New York Commission was the first out of the starting gate with a large-scale prudence audit of a nuclear project," said Robert Simpson, assistant PSC counsel.[14]

Peter A. Bradford, chairman of the Maine Public Utilities Commission, said: "This ought to send a pretty clear message to shareholders that there are adverse consequences in playing a passive role while major construction projects get out of hand."

Paul L. Gioia, who began in New York State government as assistant counsel to Governor Rockefeller and was named by Governor Hugh Carey in 1981 to be chairman of the PSC, was in that position when the Shoreham penalty was imposed. He said: "This is a very substantial offset. It's going to hurt the company."[15]

One element in how Shoreham became the world's most expensive nuclear plant—and not considered by the PSC—was imprudency by the PSC itself.

Noting how "the PSC congratulated itself for protecting ratepayers and for being tough on LILCO," Thomas Ellis, who monitors the PSC as an economist with the Albany-based Safe Energy Coalition of New York State, said after the PSC Shoreham prudency action: "The penalty is offset by the fact that no utility has been bailed out as often or for as long or for as much as LILCO. Customers have paid $1 billion for Shoreham. It is my opinion that the PSC's regulation (under several chairmen) of LILCO and Shoreham will go down as one of the greatest regulatory disasters of all time."[16]

The PSC's "desire to bring Shoreham on line," he said, "has been so overwhelming that it will not let rational judgment get in its way." The New York PSC is "like other regulatory agencies, a captive of the industry it is supposed to regulate." It has "continually ignored the views of the public made at PSC hearing after hearing that Shoreham is an economic nightmare, that its costs are outrageous and that LILCO is incompetent. Shoreham is the worst example of mismanagement in the history of nuclear power, a textbook case of how not to build a nuclear plant, and the regulation of LILCO has been a disgrace.

"The PSC," continued Ellis, "could have made them stop at any time, and it would have saved everybody money. In addition to the money lost because of the extensive mismanagement in the construction of the plant, because the plant is so poorly built, it will lose money if it is allowed to operate." Ellis described the current PSC chairman, Gioia, as "very much pro-utility, and a tyrant to boot."

On December 24, 1985, *Village Voice* senior editor Jack Newfield wrote an unusual "Open Letter on Shoreham" to Gioia. "You are responsible for keeping alive LILCO's dream of putting this lemon on line," asserted Newfield. "You have *never* rejected a LILCO petition to increase utility rates."

The "fundamental purpose of" the PSC "is to protect ratepayers from wasteful and exploitive practices by utility companies," Newfield wrote. "Since your appointment to a six-year term in 1981, you instead have protected LILCO's management and investors by granting almost all of LILCO's rate increases in the amounts sought, condoning its imprudent expenditures, and even endorsing its absurd claim that Long Island residents should pay for the damage caused by Hurricane Gloria this September. All these decisions have inverted the PSC's legal mandate—the protection of consumers from abuses by a monopoly regulated by the state."

Newfield was particularly concerned—as were LILCO ratepayers—about LILCO's $68.7 million rate increase plan being considered then by the PSC. This "is really a bridge loan to LILCO, involuntarily paid by its own victimized ratepayers," he wrote. "You are supposed to be a regulator—not a banker. If you give LILCO this unjustified rate increase, you will allow this mismanaged monopoly to prolong its fight to open Shoreham for another year. You will be winking at Wall Street, and Wall Street will then let LILCO roll over its debt and collect more loans. These loans would allow the Shoreham fiasco to continue."

Two weeks later, the PSC approved that rate increase, with Gioia declaring that it was "clearly warranted."[17]

The PSC's handling of LILCO and Shoreham has been, said Ann Mead, a continuing case of "regulatory neglect."[18]

She dissented on the $68.7 million rate hike request, as did Rosemary S. Pooler and Gail Garfield Schwartz, the same minority (all Democrats) that dissented on the prudency disallowance and wanted a higher penalty. In the rate case, Mead proposed, with the backing of Pooler and Schwartz, an eight-point LILCO cost-cutting program including a 10 percent salary reduction for LILCO management, a reduction in LILCO's advertising program and an end to further Shoreham expenditures. The PSC majority (three Republicans and Gioia, who says he is a political independent) rejected that.

Mead, in an interview, noted that she has been "filing dissents on a lot of LILCO issues since 1978," when she was appointed to the PSC. "When I filed my first dissent in 1978, in a rate case, we weren't getting a straight story from LILCO." But most of the PSC staff and the commissioners "believed what LILCO told them. LILCO kept saying we will be on line next year—each year they said that. Meanwhile, they built a house of cards.

"It got to the point that two years ago I tried by memo to get the chairman to become very involved in LILCO and its financial dealings. LILCO then had a negative cash flow—not no cash flow, but a negative cash flow. It seemed to me that the house of cards was going to fall."

Blau was "one of the guys who worked very had to try to do something about LILCO, and he was really not supported, for instance, when he started the prudency case. Blau should have been given a great deal of assistance immediately, she said. "We should have been into that with both feet." (Blau ultimately left the PSC and is now director of utility intervention of the State Consumer Protection Board.)

Mead spoke of her protests against allowing LILCO to raise its rates for "construction work in progress, CWIP. I have objected consistently to allowing CWIP into the rate base. If the project is a good one, the marketplace ought to be willing to finance it. Putting CWIP into the rate base allows a company to go ahead and do things without taking a good look at what they're doing. The members of the commission majority, however, agree with staff that CWIP is an inexpensive way to provide funds to the company so it can proceed with its construction."

The PSC's conduct concerning one element of the Shoreham project—a mine in New Mexico from which the uranium to fuel Shoreham was supposed to be supplied—was looked into by an investigatory body. "Bokum and LILCO—it was a disaster, a pure and simple disaster," said Ann Mead about LILCO's venture into uranium mining.

A Suffolk County grand jury agreed and, in a 1981 report, placed much blame on the PSC for not monitoring LILCO and thus contributing to the disaster.

"It is clear," said the grand jury report, "that the public interest cannot be served when those regulated dictate to the regulators and when the regulators acquiesce in such dictation."[19]

The mine is in a patch of desert 65 miles west of Albuquerque. LILCO got involved with the mine after its executives made connections with Richard Bokum. Bokum, a geologist, had been president of United Nuclear Corporation, the uranium mining company founded by Laurence and David Rockefeller. He subsequently left United Nuclear, which was one of the nation's major uranium mining firms, and founded his own, Bokum Resources.

LILCO approached him in 1975 after Westinghouse canceled its contracts to supply uranium to LILCO and other utilities at $10 a pound. Uranium prices were jumping sharply—to $40 a pound by late 1975, and there were predictions of $100 per pound of uranium. LILCO had estimated using 11.5 million pounds of uranium for Shoreham over its thirty-year life. They thought that would result, at $10 a pound, in a $100 million fuel cost. At $100 a pound, Shoreham fuel costs would rise to $1 billion.

LILCO officials were impressed by Bokum. "Mr. Bokum is one of the last classic entrepreneurs in this country," said LILCO's financial vice president, Thomas O'Brien, who came to LILCO in 1975 after twenty years as a Citibank vice president.[20]

Bokum said he had found a likely spot for mining uranium in what is called the Grants Mineral Belt in New Mexico, which has produced nearly half of the U.S. uranium supply. LILCO signed a contract with him in 1976 for 5 million pounds of uranium from the mine he would dig. The price of the uranium was to be $25.55 a pound in 1978 and rise to $40.40 per pound in 1985. LILCO advanced Bokum a $15 million "security deposit" so he could get started digging. But Bokum decided his mine needed to be more than twice as deep as most uranium mines—2,100 feet. By 1978, the shaft was at 1,760 feet, the ore being found was low-grade, and Bokum encountered severe flooding.

He couldn't clear up the flooding because his water pumps broke. Work on the mine was delayed for several months while the pumps were repaired. Meanwhile, LILCO decided to buy another one million pounds of uranium from Bokum to be delivered in 1986 and 1987 for $62.50 a pound. They also gave him an additional advance of $5 million. Bokum then signed a contract to build a mill that would refine the uranium, but because he said he had no funds for the purchase, LILCO lent him $46.1 million in 1978. It also agreed to buy another four million pounds of uranium.

The mine continued to flood. All along, the PSC had let LILCO advance the tens of millions of dollars to Bokum, but in 1980, with LILCO in financial difficulty because of Shoreham, the PSC staff was getting worried. It recommended another $1 million advance from LILCO to Bokum to keep the water pumps in the mine running, but, the staff advised the PSC, LILCO was "throwing good money after bad" in the Bokum venture.

Bokum, meanwhile, was doing well personally with the money LILCO had lent him. He drew a $60,000-a-year salary; paid off the $2 million investment in the property; used $1.5 million to explore other uranium properties in which LILCO had no claim; spent $2.7 million in stock deals; and gave political friends shares of Bokum stock. The FBI investigated his giving Bokum stock to New Mexico state legislators.

In 1981, Bokum announced he was unable to continue with the mine. LILCO went to court to foreclose on the mine. Bokum counter-sued LILCO for $720 million, charging that LILCO, all along, had financial control over Bokum and had engaged in "fraud" and "breach of fiduciary duty" that caused Bokum's problems. There were also suits by LILCO stockholders against the utility, charging it failed to disclose details of its Bokum venture and through it engaged in "gross negligence and breach of fiduciary duty."

The mine now lies flooded and abandoned. LILCO has lost $120 million on the deal. It has returned to Westinghouse to get its uranium for Shoreham.

The Wall Street Journal in a 1981 story on the venture told of how LILCO counted on "a small financially troubled company" to supply it with uranium for Shoreham, how the mine was flooded and how the Bokum company never produced "any uranium in its nine-year history. . . . In fact, Bokum's most successful mining venture to date has been in the treasury of the Long Island Lighting Company."[21]

The Suffolk grand jury, noted *The Journal*, in investigating the matter was "trying to determine whether any LILCO officials profited from the Bokum deal and whether the uranium outfit has any ties to organized crime."

Along with LILCO's top executives, a key witness in the grand jury investigation was another party who invested in Bokum while LILCO was bankrolling the company: Aladena "Jimmy the Weasel" Frattiano, a Los Angeles organized crime hitman turned government informer. The day Frattiano came to Riverhead, Long Island, to testify before the grand jury, helicopters flew overhead with heavily armed federal agents and police inside, and a small army of police was posted on the ground.

"The grand jury considered," said its report, "allegations of bribery and kickbacks, the financial involvement of organized crime, misuse and diversion of funds, misconduct, nonfeasance or neglect in public office by public servants."

It issued no indictment only because, said a source in the district attorney's office recently, in 1970 a provision of the New York Public Service Law that had made failure to obey that law or orders of the PSC a felony was repealed.

The grand jury scathingly criticized the PSC. It said the commissioners "do not have their own individual research staffs," and with "few exceptions" they "have had little or no experience in utility regulation prior to their appointment by the government." They "are expected to deal with an extremely large volume of petitions (as many as 80 at one meeting)," face "severe time constraints (sometimes having one day to review hundreds of documents)" and "in fact, in many instances, the commissioners do not even read the actual petitions and supporting paper submitted and only examine the relevant staff report for each petition." The "consistent practice, with few exceptions" of the staff, meanwhile, is "blind reliance on utility representations."

The grand jury said that in the LILCO/Bokum affair, there were: "1. No inspections of the [Bokum] corporation's books and records; 2. No inspection of the corporation's properties; 3. No interviews of corporation personnel; 4. No interviews of utility personnel; 5. No independent geological examinations conducted or commissioned; 6. No analyses of the corporation's technical and managerial ability . . . ; 7. No requests to industry sources for data either as to the status of the corporation or the current nuclear fuel market conditions; 8. No requests to government authorities in New York or elsewhere for intelligence concerning the corporation and its principals. Despite the glaring lack of independent verifications . . . the commissioners approved the agreement and authorized the advance of $15 million," the initial "security deposit."

The grand jury went on that it "was unable to discover any monitoring whatsoever by the commissioners or staff of the operations" of Bokum and its continuing relationship with LILCO. Meanwhile, LILCO sometimes didn't ask permission from the PSC for its further advances and additional contracts with Bokum and simply sent notices announcing them, and on other occasions asked for PSC permission. The PSC "based upon the representations of the utility and with little, if any, independent verification and examination of the facts and circumstances," approved the advance.

"The mine shaft has never been completed and is now flooded," said the grand jury. "Not a single unit of the fuel product has been produced or delivered," and LILCO "is on public record as seeking to pass along to its consumers any loss incurred."

Because of what it learned about how the PSC operated through the Bokum case, the grand jury called for "the popular election of PSC commissioners," an end to having no transcripts of PSC meetings and "full and true" records kept, and giving PSC commissioners "their own personal research staff." It also called for a "monetary forfeiture for each offense of $100,000" for a "utility, corporation or person" who violates the Public Service Law or a PSC order—and a return to the law of the provision making failure to obey the law or a PSC order a felony. Elimination of the criminal penalty and in its place the setting of a civil fine of $10,000 involved an "insignificant" sum to a "multi-million dollar public utility corporation," said the grand jury.

In September 1985, a PSC majority—with Mead and Pooler dissenting—granted LILCO approval to continue spending on the Bokum mine through 1985, but said it "would not approve expenditures by LILCO to preserve" the "mine past the end of 1985, unless the utility can provide a detailed justification for doing so."

Another factor in the high cost of Shoreham involves the two principal manufacturers of nuclear plants in the world—General Electric and Westinghouse—which convinced utilities that nuclear power was economically feasible.

In the middle 1960s, the manufacturers built a string of nuclear plants themselves at artificially low guaranteed prices. These were called "turnkey" plants because utilities would be sold the finished product and need only turn a figurative key and start it up.

In the 1950s and early 1960s, most utility executives did not believe that nuclear power was economical. The cost of building a coal-fired power plant in 1958 was $150 per kilowatt of capacity. In contrast, the cost to the federal government of building Shippingport, the first commercial nuclear plant in the U.S., was $950 per kilowatt of capacity.

Up until 1963, only 19 nuclear plants had been ordered in the U.S. and these were relatively small plants, most less than 100 megawatts, most not completed.

Then, in December 1963, GE signed a contract for its first turnkey plant: a 650-megawatt power plant to be built for the Jersey Central Power & Light Company. GE guaranteed it would construct the plant, called Oyster Creek, for $65 million—$100 per proposed kilo-watt of capacity. Other GE and Westinghouse turnkeys followed.

"The turnkeys made the light water reactor a viable product," said GE nuclear vice president Bertram Wolfe. "They got enough volume in the business."[22] Oyster Creek led to a flood of nuclear plant orders in the '60s and was a major factor in LILCO's decision to begin its ambitious nuclear power plant program.

The fact, however, was that Oyster Creek was underpriced by GE to attract new business. In 1968, GE admitted that Oyster Creek cost nearly double the original estimate of $100 per kilowatt to build.[23] Some of the 13 early plants were sold at losses of more than $100 million each. The turnkeys were a "financial disaster," Wolfe admitted. The Arthur D. Little *Competition in the Nuclear Power Supply Industry* report said that GE and Westinghouse had been "under severe pressure to obtain business for their sizeable engineering organizations," and spoke of "skepticism . . . on how long prices representative of Oyster Creek could be maintained."

On January 1, 1967, GE and Westinghouse abandoned turnkey nuclear projects. LILCO, in announcing Shoreham in 1966, estimated a cost that approximated Oyster Creek's $65 million. But the nuclear loss-leaders were soon to be no more. And LILCO would be building one of the first nuclear plants in the United States constructed without a guaranteed price, and like many utilities, it would be involved in a project costing far more than it thought.

As *Fortune* magazine said in an article in 1969, the year the plant opened, Oyster Creek's $65 million fixed price showed GE was "more interested in developing a market for nuclear power plants than in making immediate profits."

Importantly, all through this period the AEC was endorsing the industry's claims of competitively priced nuclear plants and proclaiming the profitability of nuclear power.

In their 1979 book *Light Water: How the Nuclear Dream Dissolved*, Harvard economics professor Irvin Bupp and French nuclear expert Jean-Claude Derian wrote, "On the average, the cost of all light water plants ordered in the mid- and late 1960s was underestimated by more than a factor of two in constant dollars." Larger and larger cost overruns soon became the rule in the nuclear industry.

In LILCO's hands, however, the sharply rising costs of building a nuclear power plant, like other things involving the utility, has gone to the extreme.

Forbes magazine (February 11, 1985) ran a cover story on nuclear power economics. "The failure of the U.S. nuclear program ranks as the largest managerial disaster in business history, a disaster on a monumental scale," it stated. "The utility industry has already invested $125 billion in nuclear power, with an additional $140 billion to come before the decade is out, and only the blind, or the biased, can now think that most of the money has been well spent. It is a defeat for the U.S. consumer, and for the competitiveness of U.S. industry, for the utilities that undertook the program and for the private enterprise system that made it possible. Without even recognizing the risks, the U.S. electric power industry undertook a commitment bigger than the space program ($100 billion) or the Vietnam War ($111 billion)."

Accompanying its cover story, *Forbes* featured an article examining Shoreham economics. Under a headline, "Something Rotten in Suffolk?" *Forbes* began its account of how, "if it ever gets into operation, Long Island Lighting Company's Shoreham nuclear power station will probably produce the highest-cost commercial nuclear power in the world."

The phony picture projected by the nuclear plant manufacturers, backed by the AEC, of the economics of nuclear power was a factor sending LILCO into its nuclear program.

A critical economic element allowing LILCO to continue, as the costs of building just one nuclear plant far outstripped its total assets, was LILCO's tie-in with America's biggest bank, Citibank, and through it, involvement with some of the most powerful economic forces in the U.S.

The year LILCO announced Shoreham, its stock sold for as high as $32. In recent years, with the dollar worth less than half as much, its stock has been selling in a range of from $6 to $11—10 to 15 percent of its original value considering inflation.

LILCO now has the lowest Standard & Poor's bond rating of any major utility in the U.S.[24]

But Citibank has come to the rescue with major loans, and has served as "lead bank" in arranging for it and other major banks to economically assist LILCO with mammoth influxes of cash, thus allowing LILCO to go on with Shoreham, to continue on the road of making it the world's most expensive nuclear plant.

In a report that it was required to file with the U.S. Security and Exchange Commission in 1985, LILCO stated that "due primarily to the problems relating to Shoreham, the company has for several years experienced severe financial problems," but "nevertheless, as a result of an interim financing program . . . the company believes that it is able to maintain its financial viability."[25]

The continual bank bailouts of LILCO have been a target of an effort called LILCOBUSTERS organized by the Shoreham Opponents Coalition, an umbrella group of environmental and civic organizations against Shoreham.

LILCOBUSTERS took form in 1985 as LILCO was negotiating an extension of a $150 million loan it had received from a group of fourteen banks in September of the year before.

A demonstration was held at which a brochure was distributed noting, "LILCO's huge investment in the $4.3 billion Shoreham nuclear plant has brought the company to the brink of bankruptcy. To save its skin, LILCO begged another $150 million loan from fourteen major banks last September. Without that money, LILCO would have been forced to abandon Shoreham and end its fight against the ratepayers of Long Island. With the loan, however, LILCO has been able to persist in its efforts to open Shoreham and so pass the buck onto ratepayers. If LILCO and the banks have their way, Shoreham will increase Long Islanders' rates by 100–130 percent. And that's not all; LILCO needs still more money. The company is presently negotiating with those same fourteen banks for an extension of its $150 million line of credit. If the banks agree, LILCO will be able to pour more money into the bottomless Shoreham pit."

There was a list in the brochure of the banks and the amounts of their loans, a list topped by Citibank. It then included: Chemical Bank, Chase Manhattan Bank, Morgan Guaranty Trust, Manufacturers Hanover Trust, Bankers Trust Company, Irving Trust Co., First National Bank of Chicago, Toronto Dominion, Marine Midland Bank, European American, First National Bank of Boston, Security Pacific National Bank and Bank of New York.

LILCOBUSTERS called for people to withdraw their money from banks propping up LILCO. "Join with friends and neighbors to remove your money from any of the fourteen banks lending to LILCO," said the brochure. "Together we will act to give LILCO and its backers a financial message of our own."

LILCO got even more help in early 1986 from banks. A group of 42 banks led by Citibank allowed LILCO to refinance $1 billion in debt—with a provision that it need make no payments for three years.

"Wall Street has been closely watching LILCO's negotiations with its banks," reported *The Wall Street Journal*, "because if a refinancing package hadn't been agreed upon, the utility would have had $657 million in debt payments this year, which might have forced it to file for bankruptcy-law protection. In addition to the $1 billion of bank debt, LILCO has about $2.1 billion in public debt."[26]

Banks in that deal included the fourteen banks in the earlier $150 million loan and, according to the New York PSC, the following domestic banks:[27] Mellon Bank, Continental Illinois National, National Westminister Bank Group, Provident National Bank, Connecticut National Bank, Lincoln First Bank, Extebank and Norstar. Also involved, according to the PSC records, were these foreign banks: Barclays Bank, Bank of Tokyo, Gulf International Bank Grand Cayman Branch, Midland Bank, Toronto Dominion United Kingdom, The Industrial Bank of Japan Trust Co., The Daiwa Bank, The Mitsubishi Bank, The Sanwa Bank, County Bank, Algemene Bank Nederland Cayman Islands Branch, Bayerische Landesbank Girozentrale Cayman Islands Branch, Canadian Imperiale Bank of Commerce Trust Company, Credit Lyonnais Cayman Islands Branch, J. Henry Schroder Wagg & Co., Société Financière Européenne Finance Company, Svenska Handelshanken, The Dai-Ichi Kangyo Bank, The Somitomo Trust & Banking Company and Den norska Creditbank Luxembourg.

Also included was the Long Island Trust Company, which has had a special relationship with LILCO. Before leaving to head the CIA, William Casey was on the board of both the Long Island Trust Company and LILCO. Besides providing loans to LILCO, Long Island Trust has run numerous newspaper advertisements boosting Shoreham.

Citibank has also done more than provide money and oversight to LILCO. It has been a financial backer of an organization started by LILCO in 1985 to promote LILCO, called Citizens to Open Shoreham, which changed its name in 1986 to Citizens for Shoreham Electricity.

Although LILCO has been on the brink of bankruptcy for years because of Shoreham, its executives still receive handsome salaries, topped by the $275,000-a-year salary currently received by Catacosinos. Catacosinos also arranged, when he took over as LILCO's chief in 1984, a contractual agreement that he receive $600,000 if and when he leaves the company—referred to by the press at the time as a "golden parachute." He also has a limousine and driver.

LILCO's executive vice president has been netting $143,500 and other senior vice presidents between $90,000 and $100,000.

Charles Pierce was given a $152,000-a-year package for "consulting and supplemental pension benefits" when Catacosinos replaced him as chairman. That was in addition to Pierce's $98,000 a year in LILCO retirement benefits, according to documents obtained by the State Consumer Protection Board. Wilfred Uhl was given a consulting contract of up to $70,000 a year when Catacosinos replaced him as president. That was in addition to $44,000 a year in retirement benefits.

"This is an absolute insult and a slap in the face to every ratepayer who is being asked to pay the rate increases . . . shareholders who have had to go without dividends, and . . . those LILCO employees who were laid off," said Richard Kessel of the Consumer Protection Board.[28]

Soon after taking over as LILCO chief, Catacosinos fired nearly 1,000 of LILCO's workers, mostly maintenance workers, to save $100 million a year. He then insisted on "givebacks" in workers' wages, pension, medical and dental benefits and, in return, offered workers LILCO stock.

"LILCO management hasn't done anything right in a long time," said Richard Thompson, business manager of Local 1049 of the International Brotherhood of Electrical Workers, during the bitter, eight-week strike that followed. "The corporate decisions have been wrong. The only thing they had going for them was their employees, and now they've got nobody."

After the strike, the Consumer Protection Board discovered, LILCO distributed to managers who had replaced striking workers $35,000 worth of air conditioners, clothes washers, dryers, videocassette recorders, baseball gloves, fishing rods and televisions. The merchandise was given to 200 managers, including two vice presidents and an assistant vice president, in what was termed an executive raffle. "It was like a TV game show," said Kessel. "But this company ought to be in the business of giving public service, not giving away fishing rods and TVs."[29]

After Catacosinos took over, dividends from LILCO stock were suspended.

But with the constant rate support of the PSC and loans from banks led by Citibank, LILCO still kept showing a profit in recent years of from 13 to 15.5 percent.

As a January 9, 1986, memo marked "FOR INTERNAL USE ONLY" prepared by the New York City financial consulting firm of

Morgan Stanley declared: "With the continued support of the New York Public Service Commission and LILCO's lending banks, the company will be able to survive with or without Shoreham being placed in commercial operation."

The Morgan Stanley memo noted that the $68.7 million rate hike—"LILCO's entire request"—the PSC granted LILCO that month, "further demonstrates the commission's willingness to grant rate relief to LILCO despite the controversy surrounding Shoreham."

The $1 billion bank refinancing "allows LILCO some breathing room and alleviates a cash crisis that would have taken place in June if their bank debt came due," said Morgan Stanley.

Meanwhile, as the PSC and the banks have kept LILCO going, all along the price of Shoreham has gone up . . . and up . . . and up . . . and up. And LILCO has continued to insist that whether Shoreham goes into operation or not, the public would pay.

Shoreham, said Charles Komanoff, a nationally known consultant and author on nuclear power, "is now not only the most expensive nuclear power plant per kilowatt ever built, it is the most expensive commercial power plant of any kind per kilowatt ever constructed."[30]

A key reason for Shoreham's astronomical price, he said, is that the project got lost amid LILCO's grand design for nuclear power on Long Island. "Basically, LILCO got mesmerized that Long Island was going to be a nuclear energy model, a nuclear energy laboratory for the rest of the country. It's as if the minute they received the permit to build Shoreham, they forgot about it and focused their attention on the dozen or more additional nuclear plants they planned to build of which the plants at Jamesport would be the prototype. Shoreham was like a first child for people planning a family of a dozen or more."

Also, said Komanoff, at 820 megawatts Shoreham was "going to be an anomaly, relatively small" compared to the series of 1,150 megawatt plants of Westinghouse design and other very large nuclear plants. So, LILCO "lost control of what was going on" at Shoreham.

The project's cost zoomed through "a combination of changing safety requirements, a changing design approach, out-of-control unions, out-of-control contractors, and especially an out-of-control Stone & Webster."

Komanoff has been consultant on nuclear power economics to the Office of Technology Assessment of the U.S. Congress, the U.S. Department of Energy and the states of California, Illinois, Pennsylvania, Florida and ten other states, including New York on Shoreham. He has been a consultant to the New York State Consumer Protection

Board and Suffolk County on Shoreham. He was a witness in the PSC Shoreham prudency hearings.

He said LILCO's obsession with its "nuclear power dream, a fantasy which disappeared years ago, is particularly sad because it diverted LILCO from steps that other utilities have taken to protect the environment and at the same time keep energy costs down. These other utilities didn't have their money and management tied up in chasing nuclear power, and they pursued energy stabilization rather than energy expansion." Two key things these utilities have done, said Komanoff, has been "converting from oil-fire to coal with proper pollution controls, and instituting financial incentives for customer efficiency. They provided zero or low-interest loans to promote conservation, which has been in their own and their customers' long-term interest." But LILCO, hooked on nuclear technology and "desperate for short-term cash," has gone in another direction.

Komanoff said that if Shoreham ends up with a price of $5 billion, that will mean it will cost $6,000 per kilowatt of electricity.

But, further, the capacity factor—the actual output of the plant "as a percentage of design"—has to be considered, he noted, in arriving at what Shoreham electricity would cost. If Shoreham is able to match the 55 to 60 percent capacity factor of most existing nuclear plants, that will mean that over its 30-year life, he said, its electricity will run 20 to 25 cents per kilowatt hour. "That would be four to five times the current 5 cents a kilowatt hour cost of LILCO's oil-fired electricity. It would be three times the 8 cents per kilowatt hour cost of plants fired by coal but fitted with full pollution controls making them cleaner than oil."

Another element was deeply involved—and still is—in getting LILCO hooked and keeping it hooked on nuclear power: the federal government's nuclear "establishment."

From the beginning, government scientists at Brookhaven National Laboratory were providing inspiration and backing for LILCO's nuclear program. From the outset, they led the promotion of LILCO's nuclear program. They have continued in the front line with LILCO ever since. And, indeed, as LILCO's top managers came under a dark cloud as evidence of massive LILCO mismanagement of the plant mounted in the PSC investigation of Shoreham, and LILCO's top executives were forced to resign in 1984, LILCO was actually taken over by a former top official at the national laboratory set up after World War II to devise nonmilitary applications of nuclear technology.

NOTES

1. The $5.7 billion eventual price of Shoreham was reported in *Newsday*, September 15, 1985.
2. LILCO's declaration about carrying charges was made in its December 1985 "Notice of Special Meetings and Proxy Statement."
3. Comments by members of the William Shaw family were made during interviews with the author, December 1985.
4. Comments by Charlotte and Anthony Giel were made during interviews with the author, January 1986.
5. From "Staff's Motion to Defer Cross-Examination and Filing of Staff Testimony," March 29, 1982.
6. The PSC staff report was entitled "Investigation of the Shoreham Nuclear Power Station" and issued February 1984.
7. From the investigation's "Project Management and Owner Oversight Testimony," February 1984.
8. From "Recommended Decision by Administrative Law Judges William C. Levy and Thomas R. Mattias," March 12, 1985.
9. *Newsday*, November 15, 1981.
10. From PSC "Opinion and Order Determining Prudent Costs," December 16, 1985.
11. *Newsday*, March 14, 1985.
12. *The New York Times*, June 27, 1985.
13. *The New York Times*, June 29, 1985.
14. Robert Simpson's comment was reported in *The New York Times*, June 27, 1985.
15. Paul Gioia's comment was reported in *The New York Times*, June 27, 1985.
16. The comments by Thomas Ellis are from *Newsday*, August 7, 1985, and from an interview with the author, February 1986.
17. *Newsday*, January 9, 1986.
18. Ann Mead's comments, here and following, were made in an interview with the author, December 1985.
19. From "Grand Jury Report" of "Suffolk County December Grand Jury III, Term 13," dated July 9, 1981.
20. The quotes from Thomas O'Brien and Richard Bokum, here and following, are from *Newsday*, November 19, 1981, part of series "Shoreham: What Went Wrong," by Stuart Diamond.
21. *The Wall Street Journal*, June 19, 1981.
22. *Newsday*, November 15, 1981.
23. From *Newsday*, November 15, 1981.
24. From *The New York Times*, October 20, 1985.
25. From a document entitled "Quarterly Report under Section 13 or 15 (d) of the Securities Exchange Act of 1934, for the Quarter Ended September 30, 1985."
26. *The Wall Street Journal*, January 8, 1986.
27. PSC documents on which banks with the loans to LILCO are listed are entitled: "Long Island Lighting Company Domestic Bank Commitments," dated September 30, 1985, and "Long Island Lighting Company Eurodollar Credit Agreement," dated January 7, 1986.
28. Richard Kessel's comments were reported in *Newsday*, June 15, 1984.
29. *Newsday*, May 3, 1985.
30. Charles Komanoff's comments were made in interviews with the author, January and February 1986.

6

THE LILCO-U.S. ENERGY ESTABLISHMENT LINK

"The classic picture of the scientist as a creative *individual*, a man obsessed, working alone through the night, a man in a laboratory pushing an idea—this has changed," wrote David Lilienthal, the first chairman of the U.S. Atomic Energy Commission.

"Now scientists are ranked in platoons. They are organization men," Lilienthal observed in 1963 in his book *Change, Hope, and the Bomb*. "In many cases the independent and humble search for new truths about nature has been confused with the bureaucratic impulse to justify expenditure and see that next year's budget is bigger than last's."

He wrote about the "elaborate and even luxurious laboratories that have grown up at Oak Ridge, Argonne, Brookhaven" and the headlong rush to use nuclear devices for "blowing out harbors, making explosions underground to produce steam, and so on," which show "how far scientists and administrators will go to try to establish a nonmilitary use" for nuclear technology.

Nuclear power is an extension of the effort to develop atomic bombs for World War II. Its origins go back to the Manhattan Project, the wartime crash program to build atomic bombs, and the scramble at the end of the war as many of the scientists, government bureaucrats and corporations involved in bomb building moved to somehow continue in nuclear technology.

Of all utilities in the U.S., none has had closer ties with this establishment than LILCO. It was in the middle of the area where

LILCO is located that the U.S. government, after the war, set up a key facility to develop nonmilitary uses of nuclear technology: Brookhaven National Laboratory.

Scientists at the federal government laboratory have provided pivotal encouragement and support to LILCO and its nuclear program from its beginning to the present day. The Manhattan Project created a huge technological empire: 600,000 people were involved in an undertaking on which $2 billion, in 1940s' dollars, was spent.

Establish a government office for anything, give a corporation a government contract for anything—even a wartime exigency—and a vested interest is created. The Manhattan Project created an extraordinarily far-ranging complex of vested interests, a technological empire of historic proportions.

It began with a letter from Albert Einstein—written from his summer home in Peconic, Long Island, just fifteen miles east of Shoreham—to President Franklin D. Roosevelt in 1939. Fission through the splitting of the uranium atom had recently been conducted for the first time in Berlin. Physicist Leo Szilard, a refugee from the Nazis, like Einstein, feared that Hitler might be developing a bomb based on the energy unleashed during fission.

He persuaded Einstein to write the letter to Roosevelt that noted, "Some recent work by E. Fermi [an Italian refugee from Mussolini's fascism] and L. Szilard, which has been communicated to me by manuscript, leads me to expect that the element uranium may be turned into a new and important source of energy in the immediate future. Certain aspects of the situation which has arisen seem to call for watchfulness and, if necessary, quick action on the part of the Administration." The letter spoke of how "it may be possible to set up a nuclear chain reaction in a large mass of uranium" and how "this new phenomenon would also lead to the construction of bombs, and it is conceivable—though much less certain—that extremely powerful bombs of a new type may thus be constructed."[1]

To develop an atomic bomb, an entity code-named the Manhattan Engineering District, which became known as the Manhattan Project, was established under the auspices of the U.S. Army. Scientists and engineers were gathered and put to work at facilities quickly and secretly built at locations scattered across the U.S.

Among the biggest were laboratories and manufacturing plants at Los Alamos, New Mexico; Hanford, Washington; Argonne, Illinois; and Oak Ridge, Tennessee. Large corporations and universities managed the facilities and the engineering and production at them. It was the "basic wartime policy of General Leslie Groves [a major general in the Army Corps of Engineers and head of the Manhattan Project] and the Manhattan Project that contracting with a few of the nation's largest and best qualified companies and universities was the most expeditious and effective way to develop, design and produce atomic bombs," explained a 1967 Brookings Institution study, *Contracting for Atoms*.

GE and Westinghouse got their start in nuclear technology in the Manhattan Project. Stone & Webster did, too, engineering the facility where the first successful nuclear chain reaction took place, under Dr. Fermi's direction, hidden under the west stands of the University of Chicago's Stagg Field. Stone & Webster also served as principal contractor of the massive construction at Oak Ridge.

By 1945, four atomic bombs had been made, one of which was used for the first test of an atomic explosion at the Alamogordo bombing range in New Mexico in July 1945, and two that were dropped the following month on Hiroshima and Nagasaki, Japan.

Meanwhile, with so many people and large companies and big contracts involved, the Manhattan Project had become a major part of the U.S. economy.

As the war ended, there was anxiety among many of those involved over what the war's finish and presumably the end of the Manhattan Project would mean for them. Many of the scientists and government officials didn't want to see the endeavor and their jobs over; corporations didn't want to see their contracts ended.

James Kunetka in his book *City of Fire* on Los Alamos Laboratory, wrote how, with the war over, there were now the problems of "job placement, work continuity . . . more free time than work." There was "hardly enough to keep everyone busy. . . . Without a crash program underway the Laboratory found itself for the first time discouraging overtime, and staff members and their families were encouraged to take accumulated leaves."

Some of the people and corporations could continue building atomic bombs, and they did. Atomic bombs, however, are not items that lend themselves to commercial spinoff. Of course, many were manufactured and stockpiled.

But what else could be done with nuclear technology to perpetuate the Manhattan Project establishment?

There had been studies made within the Manhattan Project as the war ended of how its activities could be extended. At the project's laboratory in Argonne, Illinois—designated as the Metallurgical Laboratory—two committees were established, one headed by Zay Jeffries, a GE executive, to look into the future of the government's Manhattan Project laboratories, and the other headed by Richard C. Tolman, science advisor to General Groves. Both committees urged research into and development of scientific and industrial applications of nuclear technology.

In the first nuclear reactors lay a clue for an industrial use of fission. They had been built at Hanford to turn nonfissionable uranium-238 into a manmade element called plutonium-239, which like relatively rare uranium-235 could fission. (The Hiroshima atomic bomb was fueled with uranium-235, the Alamogordo and Nagasaki bombs—and most nuclear weapons made since—fueled with plutonium-239.)

The theory: modify the design of these reactors to use the heat of fission to boil water to make steam turn a turbine to make electricity.

However, there were objections to this notion.

The Committee on Post-War Policy, headed by Tolman, concluded: "The development of fission piles solely for the production of power for ordinary commercial use does not appear economically sound or advisable from the point of view of preserving national resources."[2]

Meanwhile, the political vehicle to permit the establishment created by the Manhattan Project to go on, the Atomic Energy Act of 1946, was passed. It set up a five-member Atomic Energy Commission, its members appointed by the president with the advice and consent of the Senate. On December 31, 1946, the AEC took over from the Manhattan Project; the project's facilities and personnel were put under control of the AEC.

The Atomic Energy Act opened with a "Declaration of Policy" stating: "Research and experimentation in the field of nuclear chain reaction have attained the stage at which the release of atomic energy on a large scale is practical. The significance of the atomic bomb for military purposes is evident. The effect of the use of atomic energy for civilian purposes upon the social, economic, and political structures of today cannot now be determined. It is a field in which unknown factors are involved."

Under the AEC, Los Alamos Laboratory became the Los Alamos National Laboratory. The laboratory was destined to remain committed to the design and development of nuclear weapons. The Hanford Engineering Works became the Hanford Nuclear Reservation, where plutonium fuel for nuclear weapons would continue to be produced and where a nuclear waste dump—now the largest nuclear dump in the U.S., and probably the world—would be maintained.

Three major AEC "multiprogram national laboratories" were established. One was Argonne National Laboratory, what had been the Manhattan Project's Metallurgical Laboratory in Argonne, Illinois. The second was Oak Ridge National Laboratory, what had been the Manhattan Project's Clinton Laboratory in Oak Ridge, Tennessee. And the third, built at what had been a U.S. Army base called Camp Upton on Long Island east of New York City, was Brookhaven National Laboratory (BNL).

"At the end of World War II, the need was seen to continue the teamwork of Government and scientific institutions that had proven effective in wartime work in order to ensure the continued progress of nuclear science in peacetime," a BNL annual environmental report recounted. "The wartime programs under the Manhattan District had given rise to centers of research and nuclear science that continue to be active at Los Alamos, New Mexico . . . the Clinton Laboratory in Oak Ridge, Tennessee, and Argonne Laboratory . . . but no similar center had developed in the Northeast where many of the nation's scientists, as well as industries, were concentrated. The establishment of a new laboratory near New York City was therefore proposed. As a result, Brookhaven National Laboratory was founded." It was, as *Newsday* associate editor William Sexton has written, "manned in good part by alumni of the Manhattan Project."[3]

In the 1940s and 1950s, numerous schemes came out of the U.S. government's nuclear establishment to promote nuclear technology and sustain the army of scientists and government officials and corporations that got its start in the Manhattan Project.

A major effort was put into the use of nuclear explosives to blast a new canal through the isthmus of Panama, what was dubbed the "Panatomic Canal." The AEC, although planning on using as many as 250 nuclear devices with a total yield of 120 megatons—which would rain radioactive debris on a large section of Central America—insisted that "potential external radiation doses will be far below the lethal levels and well below levels known to produce obvious clinical symptoms in man." Finally, the AEC's Division of Peaceful Nuclear Explosives canceled the project because of "prospective host country opposition to nuclear-canal excavation."

Many other government plans were advanced to utilize nuclear explosives to alter the surface of the planet. "Nuclear explosives are, among other things, large-scale low-cost excavation devices. In this respect, with the proper pre-detonation study and engineering, they are ideally suited for massive earth-moving and 'geological engineering' projects, including the construction of harbors and canals," noted the AEC publication, *The Atom and the Ocean*. "The use of nuclear explosives in this manner may one day change the very shape of the world ocean."[4]

Nuclear technology would be used to fix up a "slightly flawed planet," asserted Glenn Seaborg, a nuclear scientist and co-discoverer of plutonium in 1941. As an advisor to the AEC from its inception, presidential science advisor in the 1950s, and AEC chairman between 1961 and 1971, he figured strongly in the promotion of these schemes. Dr. Seaborg described himself as nuclear technology's number one "salesman."[5]

There was an AEC scheme to close the Straits of Gibraltar. The Mediterranean would then rise and desalinate so its waters could be used to irrigate the Sahara Desert. Seaborg observed that "of course, the advances of a verdant Sahara would have to be weighed against the loss of Venice and other sea level cities."[6]

There was a scheme to build nuclear-powered airplanes. Over $1 billion was spent on the project called "Nuclear Energy Propulsion for Aircraft."[7] It was canceled in 1961 by the Kennedy administration because of concerns about the nuclear-powered airplanes leaving trails of radioactivity in their wake and the consequences if one of them crashed. No nuclear-powered airplane ever flew.

Some $2 billion was spent to develop nuclear-powered rockets, including an effort called "Nuclear Engine for Rocket Vehicle Application" (NERVA) and a succession of programs called Project Pluto, Project Rover and Project Poodle.[8] There were also concerns about the nuclear-powered rockets leaving trails of radioactivity, and the consequences if one of them crashed. Finally, this venture was canceled, too. No nuclear-powered rocket ever got off the ground.

Indeed, most of what can only be called mad scientist schemes of the government's post-Manhattan Project nuclear establishment were getting nowhere.

The strongest effort centered on the use of the heat of fission or atom-splitting to boil water and thus generate electricity. However, first the U.S. utility industry—traditionally conservative—had to somehow be convinced to accept this notion.

The 1946 Atomic Energy Act was altered to allow private industry to build nuclear-powered electric generating plants. The original act forbade private ownership of nuclear materials and established an absolute government monopoly on nuclear technology.

A new Atomic Energy Act, passed in 1954, provided for the AEC to issue licenses to private companies to build and operate commercial nuclear power plants. It also gave the AEC the dual functions of promoting and regulating this private nuclear industry. From the start, the government made it easy for companies to get licenses to build and operate nuclear plants. "The authors of the Atomic Energy Act of 1954 copied their provisions for reactor licensing almost word for word from the Federal Communications Act of 1934, which established procedures for the federal licensing of radio stations," noted Daniel Ford in *The Cult of the Atom: The Secret Papers of the Atomic Energy Commission* (1982).

AEC Chairman Lewis Straus claimed in 1954 that nuclear power would produce "electrical energy too cheap to meter."[9] Throughout the 1950s and 1960s, the AEC would publicly insist nuclear power was economical, but in fact it knew otherwise.

In 1982, U.S. Representative Ronald Dellums of California, a Democrat, was able to declassify a 1952 AEC document in which the AEC admitted that the use of nuclear power for electricity alone could not be made economical. Only if reactors combined the generating of electricity with the production of plutonium fuel for atomic bombs could there be any financial sense to the undertaking, said an editorial in the AEC publication, *Reactor Science and Technology*. These nuclear power plants were called "dual-purpose reactors."

"All groups agree that no reactor could be constructed in the very near future which would be economic on the basis of power generation alone," said the editorial.

But the journal pointed to a recommendation to the AEC from Dr. Charles A. Thomas, executive vice president of Monsanto Chemical Co., "on ways of bringing industry into the atomic energy picture on a more realistic basis," *Reactor Science and Technology* stated,

On June 20, 1950, Dr. Thomas sent the Commission a letter, stating that he believed the time was ripe for industry, with its own capital, to design, construct, and operate reactors for the production of plutonium and power. This suggestion was based on the following assumptions: that the long-term military requirements for plutonium exceeded the then existing and planned production facilities; that it would be desirable to reduce the cost of this metal [plutonium] to the government; that it would likewise be desirable to make use of the large quantities of heat attending the production of plutonium and not being utilized under existing conditions; and, finally, that the most practicable use of such heat would be for the generation of useful quantities of electric power.[10]

So, said the AEC, "all parties concur in the belief that dual-purpose reactors are technically feasible and could be operated in such a fashion that the power credit would reduce the cost of plutonium by a considerable amount."

In the years that followed, the U.S. government would claim a separation between atomic power for war and the "peaceful atom." In fact, the government's rationale for commercial nuclear power from its inception was for it to combine electric production with the production of plutonium for use in nuclear weapons. Now, in the 1980s under the Reagan administration, the claimed division has faded as the federal government actively pursues a program to extract plutonium from commercial nuclear plants for nuclear weapons.

Meanwhile, in the 1950s the utility industry still resisted getting involved with nuclear power.

This was despite the AEC's Power Reactor Demonstration Program begun in 1955 through which the AEC offered subsidies, including free nuclear fuel for up to seven years. It also arranged government financial assistance for companies involved in nuclear plant manufacturing. And the AEC announced that its national laboratories would do research and development on reactor design and other aspects of commercial nuclear power and pass on the technology to industry.

The key year for commercial nuclear power development in the U.S. was 1957. That was the year the liability obstacle was dealt with.

Herbert Yount, vice president of Liberty Mutual Insurance Company, told the Joint Congressional Committee on Atomic Energy in 1956 why the insurance industry wanted to stay clear of nuclear power. "The hazard is new. It differs from anything which our industry has previously been called upon to insure," he testified. "The catastrophe hazard is apparently many times as great as anything previously known in industry and therefore poses a major challenge to insurance companies. . . . We have heard estimates of catastrophe potential under the worst possible circumstances running not merely into millions or tens of millions but into hundreds of millions and billions of dollars. It is a reasonable question of public policy as to whether a hazard of this magnitude should be permitted. . . . Obviously, there is no principle of insurance that can be applied to a single location where the potential loss approaches such astronomical proportions. Even if insurance could be found, there is a serious question whether the amount of damage to persons and property would be worth the possible benefit accruing from atomic development."[11]

The Price-Anderson Act, through which the federal government limited all liability in the event of a nuclear plant accident to $560 million with the government paying the first $500 million, met that major concern.

"The power development program was bogged down," Representative Melvin Price of Illinois, a cosponsor of the act, later recounted. Utilities "wouldn't risk going into this unchartered area without some type of indemnification protection."

The Price-Anderson Act was passed in 1957 despite the issuance in the same year of WASH-740, the government's first major study of nuclear plant accidents, which said the consequences of a single accident could be as many as 3,400 killed, 43,000 injured and $7 billion in property damage.

The year 1957 also saw the opening of the Shippingport nuclear plant in Pennsylvania, built by the federal government under the direction of Admiral Hyman Rickover. (Stone & Webster was contract engineer on the project in which a Westinghouse reactor was used.)

And, critically in 1957, the reluctant utilities were told in no uncertain terms by the government: We'll build nuclear plants if you won't.

"It is the commission's policy," declared AEC Chairman Straus, "to give industry the first opportunity to undertake the construction of power reactors. However, if industry does not, within a reasonable time, undertake to build types of reactors which are considered promising, the commission will take steps to build the reactors on its own initiative."

So an intimidated U.S. utility industry was forced into nuclear power by U.S. government policy.

A center for AEC research into commercial nuclear power from the outset was the AEC's Brookhaven National Laboratory on Long Island. Besides doing research that the AEC and the nuclear scientists at BNL hoped would further the development of commercial nuclear power, the laboratory began presentations for utilities and the nuclear industry on reactor design and other nuclear power topics. These were the Wednesday lectures that LILCO referred to in tracing its first connections with nuclear power in its booklet *Atomic Power for Long Island* that it distributed when it announced Shoreham.

Dr. Herbert Kouts was among the government nuclear scientists deeply involved in the early BNL research into and presentations on commercial nuclear power. He has remained highly active, for the more than thirty years since, promoting commercial nuclear power both in and outside the national laboratory.

Reflecting the semireligious belief he and many other nuclear scientists at BNL have in nuclear technology, Kouts declared in an interview: "I have faith in nuclear power. It's a tremendous thing."[12]

It's also what Kouts has depended on since 1950 for his living. He arrived at BNL that year to head its group working on reactor shielding design. Speaking of the 1950s and the beginning of the emphasis at BNL on obtaining and sharing information about commercial nuclear power, Kouts recalled: "The AEC had established a policy of trying to transfer technology to the industrial sector. Those were the days when none of the industrial know-how existed, when people from all kinds of industries were trying to find out what was going on."

From 1952 to 1968, Kouts headed the Experimental Reactor Physics Group at the laboratory, and between 1968 to 1973 led its Technical Support Organization.

In 1973, like other BNL scientists before and since, he joined the federal government's nuclear technology bureaucracy in Washington, D.C. Kouts became director of the AEC's Division of Reactor Safety Research until the AEC was disbanded in 1975, when he became director of the Office of Nuclear Regulatory Research at its successor agency, the NRC. He thereafter returned to BNL where, since 1977, he has been chairman of its Department of Nuclear Energy. In 1984, Kouts was described in the nuclear industry trade press as a "leading prospect" for a seat on the NRC.

Kouts, in a recent interview, said he is "still mystified by nuclear power becoming so controversial. I think it's because some people want a simpler life. They want to go back to the agrarian concept. They don't like big business. Utilities are big business. They would generate electricity by burning oil in their backyards. Also, some people attack nuclear power because they associate it with nuclear weapons. Also, some people feel that nuclear power is mysterious, that there is something horrible about it."

Nuclear power produces toxic substances, the nuclear scientist conceded, "but its toxicity doesn't bother me. Gasoline is a pretty toxic material. You're not going to drink the stuff. Yet we pass it around all the time."

Kouts, besides promoting nuclear technology in his official capacity, has, like many other BNL nuclear scientists, been busy through the years promoting it privately, especially the nuclear program of the local utility—LILCO.

In his private function, he has defended the government's nuclear establishment. In testimony, for example, before a New York PSC board considering LILCO's twin-nuclear plant Jamesport project, Kouts noted that it has been "implied that the [Nuclear Regulatory] Commission played politics and did not put safety first. That is a distortion that must be commented on. . . . I don't mean to imply that only the narrowest matter of nuclear safety is considered in these circles. The Commission has always regarded its function as requiring some need for balance. They have been constantly reminded that safety reviews should not take forever to complete, because the nation needs the energy."

In 1983, Kouts joined with two other nuclear scientists in preparing *A Report on the Shoreham Nuclear Power Plant,*[13] made at the request of Suffolk County Legislator Gregory Blass. Their report concluded "that the engineering and construction at Shoreham seem to reflect careful attention to final safety of the plant. We are now convinced that LILCO has tried to build a safe plant at Shoreham." (Blass said recently, "The report was extremely limited and of minor scope.")

Also in 1983, Kouts was named a member of the New York State Fact-Finding Panel on the Shoreham Nuclear Power Facility[14] after pressure for his appointment was brought by Citizens for an Orderly Energy Policy, a group of Brookhaven National Laboratory scientists that admitted to receiving much of its funding from the United States Committee for Energy Awareness, a Washington-based organization financed by utilities.

Conclusions by a majority on the panel, which was chaired by John H. Marburger, president of the State University of New York at Stony Brook, included the determinations that: Suffolk County adopted its position that there could be no successful evacuation in the event of a serious Shoreham accident "after commissioning studies of reasonable quality"; the "Shoreham plant will probably prove to have been a mistake in the sense that everyone might have been better off if the plant had never been built"; its location "would not be acceptable as a licensable site under current siting practices"; LILCO "did not prepare itself adequately for its foray into the technology of nuclear power, and still lacks credibility as the operator of a nuclear power plant"; the "NRC practice of deferring consideration of off-site emergency response planning feasibility until after completion of construction does not make sense"; the "projections for Long Island's future electrical energy needs on which the Shoreham construction schedule was originally based were obviously overestimated."

Kouts dissented: "Refusal to operate Shoreham would go a long way toward ending the nuclear power alternative for both New York State and the county. This would injure the strength of the nation as it requires energy independence."

He also wrote his own addendum to the report in which he maintained: "There is a widespread view that nuclear power is dangerous. We believe that this is not true. Public fear of nuclear power is encouraged by some people for ideological reasons. These people believe that they can bring about economic and social change by attacking high technology." As to the question, "Is nuclear power safe in light of possible accidents?" Kouts replied: "The question does not make sense in an absolute way, because nothing is absolutely safe."

In 1984, Kouts' department at BNL almost got a federal contract to analyze the problems with the diesel generators at Shoreham—leading to strong protests from Suffolk County. "The gentleman the NRC wants to put in charge of this inquiry has a strong personal bias for nuclear power," said Chief Deputy County Executive John Gallagher, who also questioned BNL's "expertise" in the field of "diesel mechanics."[15]

Suffolk County's attorney on Shoreham, Herbert Brown of the Washington, D.C., office of Kirkpatrick and Lockhart, in a letter to the NRC declared: "These individuals have a blatant conflict of interest."[16]

Kouts defended his department's getting the contract to consider the critical issue. "We are also a laboratory that assists the Nuclear Regulatory Commission in many areas and in many ways," he maintained.[17] But in view of the county complaints, the NRC did not go through with the arrangement.

Among other scientists at BNL (which had 3,200 employees and a budget of $193 million in 1985), Andrew Hull is also promoting nuclear power.

Hull has admitted that there is a "vested interest" by some of the government nuclear scientists at BNL in nuclear technology. Some approach nuclear power "emotionally, in the sense that this is a useful technology and ought to be employed. You take pride in what you are doing," he said in an interview.[18]

Hull was a metereologist for the airlines before going back to school, undergoing training at Oak Ridge National Laboratory in health physics, and beginning his second career at BNL. He has been active in successor groups to Suffolk Scientists for Cleaner Power & Safer Environment—also composed of BNL scientists promoting LILCO's nuclear program, including Citizens for an Orderly Energy Policy. He has been a regular speaker at all hearings on LILCO nuclear projects. He testified at the New York PSC's hearings on LILCO's Jamesport project that "hard data" shows that nuclear power has "a tenth the occupational mortality and injury rate of conventional cycles" and "the amount of fuel stored at a large oil-fired electrical station, more probably poses a catastrophic risk than that of a major nuclear accident."

Through the 1960s and 1970s, Hull was in charge of monitoring radioactive effluents from BNL. During that period, the laboratory was found to have been polluting the Long Island environment with radioactivity.

On April 13, 1973, the *Long Island Press* ran a front page banner headline reporting that the day before AEC approved a construction permit for Shoreham. That article was connected to another front page story: "RADIOACTIVITY," it was headlined, "Discovery of Isotope Threatens Scout Campout." The piece spoke about how the discovery of radioactive tritium found in the Peconic River—a major and scenic Long Island river that begins on laboratory grounds—was causing "state and county officials to be wary about a possible Boy Scout camporee in the county's Peconic River Park."

The story continued: "The tritium comes from Brookhaven National Laboratory's high flux beam reactor. . . . A representative of the lab said the discharges really were insignificant." (The laboratory's research reactor was constructed by Stone & Webster.)

The New York State Department of Conservation found during the 1970s that radiation levels in the Peconic River were the second highest in waters near any nuclear-related facility in New York State. Only in Cattaraugus Creek near the former Nuclear Fuel Services Inc. nuclear fuel reprocessing facility and waste dump in upstate West Valley, which was closed because of radioactive leaks, were there higher readings. "Water samples from the Peconic River continue to show an influence from operations at Brookhaven National Laboratory," said one typical state report.

The situation remains to this day. There are deposits in the Peconic of tritium, which has a half-life of 12.5 years making it hazardous to human health for more than a century, and cesium-137 and strontium-90, with hazardous lifetimes twice as long as tritium. Radiation has been found in fish and clams in the river, the banks of which are often dotted with people, most frequently poor black residents of Riverhead, fishing for food.

Also in the 1970s, the U.S. Environmental Protection Agency reported that concentrations of strontium-90 in milk at dairies near BNL were "among the highest reported anywhere in New York State."

In a 1975 "Environmental Statement," the preparation of which Hull directed, the laboratory declared: "Unavoidable adverse environmental effects from the operation of BNL arise from radioactive, chemical, or thermal components in waste effluents being released to the atmosphere, the Peconic River, or the ground as well as from the preemption of land and other resources. Adverse effects may be both on site, such as limiting the use of certain areas for other purposes, and off site, such as the radiation dose to man incurred as the result of the operation of BNL." The report said that 20 acres at the laboratory "may need to be committed to long-term control because of radioactive contamination." It said that levels of cancer and genetic defects may rise in the surrounding area as the results of BNL's activities, but claimed that any increase would be negligible.

In a 1978 *Annual Environmental Report*, BNL said that levels of strontium-90 twenty-two times higher than the EPA limit were found in a well on laboratory grounds. The report also said that homes "immediately east of the laboratory site" had amounts of strontium-90 in their wells that were "25 percent of the EPA standard."

Hull, during his years as supervisor of environmental monitoring at BNL, stressed that its discharges of radioactivity were "within acceptable limits." He said that "without question it's safe to fish in the Peconic. A diligent fisherman might pick up an extra milli-roentgen or two." Of strontium-90 in the milk at nearby dairies, he claimed this was solely the result of atmospheric nuclear tests in the 1950s and 1960s.

Of the high level of strontium-90 found in the well on laboratory grounds and BNL's estimate that this contamination will move with the groundwater beyond its boundaries and into adjacent residential areas in 60 years, Hull said he expects there will be "dilution at work" cutting down the concentration by then. "I don't expect to be around here sixty years from now to make the measurements," he said, "but I don't think they'll be too high." As to strontium-90 from the laboratory already in the wells of nearby homes, he said, "There's plenty of strontium-90 in the milk everybody drinks already," caused, he claimed, from atmospheric nuclear weapons testing.

Hull, after participating in the federal government's response to the accident at the Three Mile Island nuclear plant, was promoted from being in charge of environmental monitoring at BNL to being a full-time member of the government's "radiological emergency response team" then set up at the laboratory. It has the responsibility of going to the scene of accidents involving the release of radioactivity and determining their seriousness.

In the same way he has downplayed the radioactive discharges from BNL, he did not take very seriously the impact of the accident at Three Mile Island—and is not worried about the effects of nuclear plant accidents in general.

In a lecture at BNL entitled "Three Mile Island as Seen from the Mainland: An Environmental Perspective," given six months after the Three Mile Island accident, Hull declared: "In terms of the amounts and kinds of radioactivity released and the resultant radiation dose to the surrounding population, from an environmental perspective the incident at the Three Mile Island Nuclear Power Station . . . has to be ranked as a relatively minor event."[19]

Recently, Hull described the Three Mile Island accident as a "big media event. It showed that a meltdown is not a catastrophe in terms of the public. It showed that defense in depth worked." He insisted that no one's health was affected, despite the findings by Ernest Sternglass of the University of Pittsburgh School of Medicine that radioactivity released in the accident has caused many thousands of cases of infant mortality. Hull said, "That's nonsense. These fluctuations could happen anyway." He is convinced that in a nuclear plant accident, "hellish releases of radioactivity are not possible."

Hull was treasurer of Suffolk Scientists for Cleaner Power & Safer Environment, which stood with LILCO in the original AEC construction permit hearings on Shoreham. He said that BNL scientists "formed Suffolk Scientists because of what seemed to be the lack of scientific validity of some of the people the Lloyd Harbor Study Group was bringing in to testify at the Shoreham hearings. We decided that to intervene ourselves, we needed—and I don't mean this in an invidious way—an organizational cover."

It was at those hearings that Hull first encountered Sternglass, who testified about releases of radioactivity from Brookhaven National Laboratory causing increases of infant mortality in Suffolk. That testimony led Hull to take the stand to insist Brookhaven's releases were within government limits.

Hull commented, "Considering that the laboratory's first role in terms of nuclear power was seeing it as a hopeful thing to develop, it has only been natural that many scientists at the laboratory support nuclear power." He added that the special interest by Brookhaven National Laboratory scientists in LILCO's nuclear program is appropriate "because it's in our backyard."

He saw no conflict of interest in his activities as an outspoken booster of nuclear technology in charge of monitoring radioactivity from a major nuclear facility (the national laboratory) and his now being responsible for alerting people about whether they are endangered by a nuclear accident.

"This is a viable technology," Hull declared. "It works well. The hard facts are that it is safer than any real alternative. The problem is that some people have linked it up with the continuum of the bomb, and think that anything that says nuclear is bad."

In a letter (on BNL stationery) to Dr. Helen Caldicott, author of *Nuclear Madness*, after they debated nuclear power on the *Today* show, Hull complained of "the irrational driving forces in the debate about nuclear power having already produced ridiculous misallocations of national resources for the reduction of trivial tasks." He told Caldicott that "to any informed professional who knows something about radiation medicine and/or nuclear technology," she hadn't done "much homework," although her arguments "may impress that portion of the credible public who wants to believe the worst about nuclear power for whatever reasons."

Hull was among sixteen BNL scientists who, in February 1986, issued a *Shoreham Safety Report*, financed and distributed by Citizens for Shoreham Electricity, a group set up by LILCO and funded by LILCO, Citibank, GE, Stone & Webster and other companies with an investment in Shoreham.

The report declared that "the Shoreham plant is well-constructed, safe, and ready to begin generating electricity." The report's foreword said: "We are a group of scientists who work at Brookhaven National Laboratory and live near Shoreham. Because of the location of Brookhaven—a major national research facility—Suffolk County is endowed with an unusually large concentration of scientists who are authorities in nuclear safety and energy analysis."

Through early 1986, the scientists appeared in a blitz of radio and TV commercials and print advertisements in the New York metropolitan area attesting to the safety of Shoreham. Jim Blew, the staff director of Citizens for Shoreham Electricity, said the budget of the advertising campaign would total $700,000, with much of that money coming from LILCO. "This is brazen," charged Richard Kessel, head of the State Consumer Protection Board, as the campaign began. "Less than a week after they get an increase from the Public Service Commission," he said of LILCO, "they turn around and spend a significant amount of money on something like this."[20]

At BNL, the dangers of radioactivity are minimized not just by individual nuclear scientists but on an institutional level. For example, a laboratory booklet, *The ABC's of Radiation*,[21] distributed to staff members to familiarize them with radioactivity, declares: "Is Radiation Dangerous to You? It can be; but it need not be. Danger from radiation depends upon the degree of exposure. How dangerous is fire, or exposure to the sun? How dangerous is electricity? It depends upon your exposure. We all use fire. We use electricity, but we do not take chances. We have learned to live with these agents, and we can learn to live with radiation too."

There has been personal tragedy as a result. Arthur Humm began working at the laboratory in 1949 and in 1968 was promoted to director of radiation protection at the laboratory's reactor. During the late 1970s, his brother-in-law, Simon Perchik, was an assistant Suffolk district attorney in charge of environmental prosecution and, on numerous occasions, accused BNL of contaminating Suffolk County's environment. As a result, Perchik had many arguments with Humm, who defended the laboratory and its practices—until they cost him his life.

One BNL practice was pumping out a pool into which irradiated water from the reactor flowed, and then having Humm, wearing only a face mask, attempt to scrub away radioactive residue on the walls of the pool with a brush. He developed lung cancer. In 1981, a terminally ill Humm brought a multi-million dollar lawsuit against the federal government charging that his lung cancer was a result of inhaling radioactive particles in this process. He subsequently died—a victim, said Perchik, of the irresponsible way the national laboratory deals with radiation.

"Artie, as he was dying, felt that the safeguards afforded him by the laboratory were inadequate," said Perchik. "The face mask was a very rudimentary face mask that could leak. It was the kind house-painters wear."[22]

Of BNL, Perchik said: "You have a bunch of mad scientists doing experiments in the cellar—and nobody is looking in."

Lorna Salzman, chairman of the New York branch of Friends of the Earth, and long an observer of BNL, has declared: "That an agency of the federal government, namely Brookhaven National Laboratory, has insisted on its inalienable right to irradiate people is, I believe, irresponsible and unethical and in defiance of common sense and good public health practice."[23]

The Suffolk Legislature in 1979, because of the radioactive pollution caused by the laboratory, considered a resolution asking the federal government that "all facilities at Brookhaven National Laboratory pertaining to nuclear energy be terminated and the handling of nuclear materials immediately cease."

While the dangers of nuclear technology and radioactivity are minimized at BNL, a science has been made out of maximizing the problems of all energy sources besides nuclear energy.

The National Center for Analysis of Energy Systems was set up at the laboratory in 1976.[24] Formation of the center was announced by Dr. Joseph Hendrie, a nuclear physicist at BNL, a staunch advocate of nuclear power, and then chairman of its Applied Science Department. The following year he left the laboratory to become chairman of the NRC and was chairman during the Three Mile Island accident. In the first hours of the accident, Hendrie admitted, "We are operating almost totally in the blind. His information is ambiguous, mine is nonexistent, and I don't know, it's like a couple of blind men staggering around making decisions."[25] He returned to BNL in 1981.

When announcing the center, he said it would fill "the need for detailed interdisciplinary studies of the relations between the technological, economic, social and environmental factors of energy system analysis."

The center has stressed that nuclear power is the preferable energy supplier. Its reports include *Health Costs of Substituting Coal-Electric as an Alternative to Nuclear Power in a Nuclear Moratorium*, which forecasts thousands of additional deaths yearly from air pollution in the event of a freeze in nuclear plant construction and the wider use of coal-fired power plants. Soon after the government-funded report was issued in 1977, one of its authors, Samuel Morris, testified "as an individual" at the New York PSC's hearings on LILCO's Jamesport project, presented the report to the panel and went on to dismiss the likelihood of catastrophic nuclear plant accidents. "The probability of such events is quite low," he said.

The report's other author, Leonard Hamilton, in a BNL lecture entitled "Power versus People: Cutting the Human Costs," stressed that "improvement in the public perceptions of the true health costs [of energy] will not necessarily reduce the attacks on power, but it might improve the quality of skepticism about such Nader statements on nuclear safety that: 'The Titanic was supposed to be unsinkable. It sank,' " and bring "a realization that, on many of these issues, the Friends of the Earth work out as support for Colonel Qaddafi."[26]

In the laboratory's weekly publication, the *Brookhaven Bulletin*, front-page stories are regularly featured, such as one headlined "Health Effects of Photovoltaic Cells."[27] It said that BNL scientists were finding that there are "toxic effects [ranging from] interference with nutrition to cancer" from the chemicals used in photovoltaic cells, which convert sunlight directly to electricity. Another story reported on how BNL scientists were finding that geothermal energy had pollution problems. "What could be cleaner and more natural than using Mother Earth's heat to produce energy? Well, natural but clean it's not," began this article. "What's the pollution problem? After geothermal steam has done its work, it's condensed into water, and non-condensable gases are released to the atmosphere. Hydrogen sulfide, H_2S is one of these gases. At low concentrations, H_2S has a rotten egg smell. At high concentrations, it can be toxic."[28]

In turn, there is a downplaying of problems with nuclear power. A front-page report on a speech by Victor Bond, the laboratory's associate director, before the College of Physicians of Philadelphia noted how he declared that "central to the problem of acceptance of nuclear power is the 'continuing misapprehension that radiation is somehow more harmful and lethal than are other physical or chemical agents.' " It quoted the associate director as dismissing the claim that plutonium is "the most toxic substance ever known to man. This is manifestly untrue . . . plutonium is a 'piker' compared to many other radioactive, chemical and biological toxins."[29]

The promotion by BNL scientists of LILCO and its nuclear program has long been an issue on Long Island.

In 1980, there was a demonstration in front of the main gate at the laboratory, where armed security guards are posted.[30] Protest leaders charged that there was a "priesthood of scientists" at Brookhaven National Laboratory pushing nuclear technology, and an "interlocking directorate between LILCO and Brookhaven" because Phyllis Vineyard, the wife of the laboratory's director, George Vineyard, was a member of the board of LILCO.

At a 1983 hearing before the New York State Fact-Finding Panel on the Shoreham Nuclear Facility there was an incident involving Dr. Anthony Fainberg, a nuclear scientist at the laboratory who had come, along with nine other BNL scientists, to testify in support of Shoreham.[31] The hearing had to be recessed when Fainberg angrily erupted over a charge by a professor of marine science that Fainberg and the other BNL scientists were advocating Shoreham because they were "in the pocket of the nuclear industry."

"No! We're not! That's a damn lie!" screamed Fainberg. "You're lying!" he continued, as one official of the panel rushed for the police and its chairman hurriedly called a recess.

Outside the hearing room, Fainberg continued to heatedly protest, while C. Douglas Hardy, professor of marine science at the Southampton Campus of Long Island University, continued his criticism. He told Fainberg: "Your group [Citizens for an Orderly Energy Policy] is supported by the nuclear industry. You're talking through your pocketbook. Your career is on the line and you're scared."

At the same hearing, before the recess, BNL nuclear engineer Peter Kroeger declared: "There's nothing in life without any risk." Also, BNL nuclear scientist Les Fishbone testified: "The likelihood of a terrible catastrophe has been calculated by experts in this field to be quite insignificant."

BNL nuclear physicist Edward R. Lessard claimed that U.S. government studies of the atomic bombings of Hiroshima and Nagasaki indicated that the effects of radioactivity were smaller than what was earlier presumed. He also gave a lengthy presentation—with charts—concerning the Three Mile Island accident and said there was only "one statistical death" as a result of that mishap. He also noted that he was a "captain" of the federal radiological emergency response team stationed at BNL.

Among those responding to the BNL nuclear scientists at that hearing was Steven Librot of Wading River, which is located just west of Shoreham. He testified that "a doctorate in physics should not give people the right to act as God. The scientists told us in the '40s that radiation was completely safe, in the '50s that X rays could be used to treat acne and see through feet in shoe stores, and now they tell us low-level radiation is safe to dump in our soil and rivers. They have forgotten the basic principle of science: There are no final answers, only the present state of knowledge. Let these people take their experiments back to the laboratory where they belong and stop poisoning our world and experimenting with earth's life."

Suffolk Legislator Wayne Prospect, in the conflict over the 1986 advertising blitz for Shoreham involving BNL scientists, charged: "Basically, Brookhaven Laboratory scientists have been a dial-a-lobby for LILCO. You're dealing with bright people, but they look at nuclear power not as a practical question that society has a right to handle in an appropriate way, but as a revelation from the atomic brotherhood of which they are members. They are so wrapped up in their own careers involving nuclear technology that they live and breathe it and can't see it objectively. They don't want to deal with the fact that maybe it's a stillborn technology. Every time LILCO needs a pro-nuclear point of view expressed, they dial a lobby and go to Brookhaven National Laboratory."

During most of Shoreham's construction, Dr. George Vineyard was director of BNL. He began at the laboratory in 1954, was named deputy director in 1967, and in 1973 became director—BNL's fourth director, all of whom were physicists.

In 1978, Vineyard was one of "100 top-echelon executives,"[32] as *Newsday* described it, who joined together in the Long Island Action Committee, a group initiated by *Newsday* in the wake of a series it ran in 1978 called "Long Island at the Crossroads." The two-week series urged a future of high-technology development for Long Island with energy provided by "safe" nuclear power. *Newsday* advocated creation of a "power structure" to work towards this goal, and the Long Island Action Committee was set up as that structure.

Its first chairman was LILCO board member William Casey. LILCO Chairman Charles Pierce was a founding member. At least one of the early meetings of the Long Island Action Committee was held in the board room at the headquarters of the Long Island Trust Co., the bank where Casey was a board member and that also has been a major financial supporter of LILCO. (Casey left the committee's chairmanship in 1979 to manage Ronald Reagan's presidential campaign, subsequently becoming CIA director, and was replaced by Evelyn Berezin, a physicist.)

Chosen to be executive director of the Long Island Action Committee was Ellis Laurimore Phillips, Jr., son of the founder and first president of LILCO.

Vineyard and J. Peter Grace, chairman of W. R. Grace & Company, were the featured speakers at one of the major activities organized by the Long Island Action Committee, a 1980 symposium on Long Island's Next Fifty Years.[33]

The Long Island Action Committee later merged with the Long Island Association of Commerce and Industry.

Meanwhile, Vineyard, according to Andrew Hull, was "supportive in an avuncular way" of Suffolk Scientists for Cleaner Power & Safer Environment and other efforts by BNL scientists on behalf of LILCO and its nuclear power program.

In 1974, a year after Vineyard became BNL's director, his wife, Phyllis, became a member of the board of LILCO. She remains on the board where she has, throughout her tenure, been a staunch advocate of nuclear power.

Vineyard resigned as BNL director in 1981 amid a major controversy involving the construction of a high energy accelerator or atom-smasher at the laboratory. The situation, in many ways, paralleled Shoreham. There were environmental conflicts, extensive construction delays, a huge cost overrun, and criticism of the undertaking. Rallying behind the project, named ISABELLE by BNL officials, were some of the same individuals and organizations who, at the same time, were rallying behind LILCO and Shoreham.

The ISA in ISABELLE was for "intersecting storage accelerator" and BELLE, French for beautiful, "tacked on," as Newsday explained it, "because scientists think the machine is beautiful."[34] The name also made the proposed project appear more attractive to government funding sources.

Through the early 1970s, BNL officials lobbied hard in Washington for ISABELLE. In 1977, Congress agreed to appropriate $5 million for what was to be a $275 million project.

At the outset, there was an environmental collision. The laboratory bulldozed 200 acres of protected freshwater wetlands at the headwaters of the Peconic River to prepare a site for the huge accelerator, to be a donut-shaped device with a circumference of 2.4 miles. Environmentalists were stunned by the devastation. The New York State Department of Environmental Conservation said BNL's denuding of the landscape could alter plant and fish life along and within what was described as the only river in the United States running through pine barrens.[35]

The lead of a *Newsday* story described the construction site this way: "From the air, it looks as if some crazed giant mole has been at work burrowing through 500 acres in the heart of Suffolk County's scrub pine."[36]

In operation, ISABELLE would have additional environmental effects, the Final Environmental Impact Statement prepared by BNL on the project conceded. It would generate radioactivity, with tritium a key radionuclide produced and "available for migration . . . to the water table." Still, BNL said, "ISABELLE will be designed and operated so as to have a minimal impact on the environment," and it "will be a much smaller inherent source of radiation and will produce much less environmental radioactivity" than the reactor at the laboratory.[37]

The statement continued: "The major unavoidable adverse effect due to the operation will be the consumption of electrical energy" although, it said, "both peak demand and sustained load can be met by the Long Island Lighting Company."

BNL has been the biggest single user of LILCO electricity—with a peak demand of 42 megawatts. ISABELLE would double that, said the statement, adding that, with ISABELLE, the laboratory would use "approximately 3 percent of the total amount [of electricity] presently generated by LILCO."

(BNL, for many years, was given a cut rate by LILCO for the electricity it used. That ended in 1980 after New York PSC Administrative Law Judge David Schechter, in a LILCO rate case, attacked the "underpriced" special contract rate.[38] Subsequently, the PSC declared that the rate LILCO was charging BNL for electricity "may not even recover the marginal running costs—with no allowance for earnings." It went on: "There is plainly no basis for [such] preferential treatment at the expense of the general body of ratepayers.")

ISABELLE, which was begun in 1978 to be completed in 1985, was already three years behind schedule in the early 1980s.

And its cost was rapidly rising. By 1981, BNL was admitting that the price of ISABELLE could reach $475 million. Later there were estimates that the cost could total $500 million—nearly twice BNL's original estimate.

William J. Broad, in a November 1980 *Science* magazine article, stated: "The future of the ISABELLE project is anything but promising. The project is teetering on the brink of a technological failure that would set the high energy physics program in the United States back by many years and might ultimately lead to closer supervision of the way in which projects such as ISABELLE are planned and carried out."

Science added: "In 1966, an observer said that the process whereby a federal agency asks groups of high energy physicists how to dispose of the public purse is like 'asking a hungry cat to make recommendations about the disposition of some cream.' In recent years, U.S. budgetary strictures have set a $300-million-a-year limit on the appetites of high energy physicists. Problems such as those with ISABELLE point out the necessity of keeping a close watch not only on how much money is spent but also on how it is spent, lest the hungry cats spill what little cream is left. Whether the current difficulties will lead to reform in the long-range planning of and research for particle accelerators remains to be seen."

Meanwhile, BNL launched a campaign to continue ISABELLE, described by *The New York Times* as "the most expensive single scientific project in the country, with the exception of the Space Shuttle."[39]

Vineyard's resignation coincided with the appearance of a report in *Science* headlined, "Limping Accelerator May Fall to Budget Axe." Dr. George A. Keyworth, President Reagan's science advisor, was quoted in the article as saying: "We still don't know the best way to build the accelerator, and the cost is rising very rapidly." Vineyard insisted—as he quit—that ISABELLE had "turned the corner by overcoming technical difficulties."[40]

He was replaced as BNL director by Dr. Nicholas Samios, who had been its deputy director and also, with ISABELLE project in trouble, had been assigned to head the project. Also a physicist, Samios came to BNL in 1959. Robert Hughes, president of Associated Universities, Inc., a group of nine eastern universities that describes itself as a consortium operating BNL for the government, said that in selecting Samios, "in a natural way, we turned to one of our key leaders."[41]

(Associated Universities, Inc. first was under contract to the AEC; since the AEC's disbandment, it is under contract to the U.S. Department of Energy. DOE provides on-site supervision of the laboratory with a twelve-member group, which in recent years has been headed by David Schweller, who before joining the federal government was a nuclear industry reactor engineer.)

For two years, the campaign staged both in and outside the BNL for ISABELLE continued. Laboratory personnel took to wearing ISABELLE T-shirts and distributing ISABELLE Frisbees. Congressional and other federal representatives were met by BNL-uniformed chauffeurs at New York area airports and driven in BNL cars to the laboratory for a day of tours, meals and persuasion.

The Long Island Committee for Jobs and Energy Independence (JEI), a group of business executives, union leaders and others making LILCO's nuclear program its principal campaign, widened its activities to push ISABELLE. Jack Kulka, a Long Island builder and co-chairman of the group, was quoted in a press release it issued as saying: "We must maintain the high quality of technology we have come to know here on Long Island."[42]

The press release continued: "The educational community on Long Island, knowing the importance of ISABELLE and Brookhaven Laboratory, summed it up best through Ann Marie Scheidt, Director of Public Affairs at the State University at Stonybrook [sic], at a recent planning meeting of JEI. She commented, 'The main reason for Stonybrook University on Long Island was the proximity to the Brookhaven Laboratory and its research facilities. We must successfully bring about the reinstating [of money for ISABELLE]. Stonybrook needs Brookhaven and we must work together for this project.' " Separately, Dr. John Marburger, the president of the State University of New York at Stony Brook, said: "ISABELLE is a Northeast United States question. Loss of a project like this and the resulting long-term decline of BNL is just another in a series of setbacks for the Northeast. . . . It would be morally devastating to the region if we were to lose this project."[43]

The Long Island Committee for Jobs and Energy Independence held a rally on behalf of ISABELLE at the headquarters of a major union booster of Shoreham, the International Brotherhood of Electrical Workers. The *Newsday* account of the rally featured a photograph of Samios, wearing a large button reading "ISABELLE means JOBS," at the rostrum giving an address, standing next to former U.S. Representative John Wydler of Long Island, a leading backer of LILCO's nuclear program during his tenure in Congress and since.[44]

"This is really grass roots," said Martin Blume, a BNL associate director, at the rally, for which a Dixieland band was hired to play. "It's nice for the people out at the lab to understand that the people of Long Island are behind them."[45]

Laboratory officials in 1982 quietly changed the name of ISABELLE to CBA for "colliding beam accelerator," to describe "a less costly and ambitious project that one federal official said is more fitting for the 'no-frills' reality in Washington," noted *Newsday*.[46]

But, by whatever name, the project was in big trouble. In 1983 the Department of Energy's High Energy Physics Advisory Panel voted to scrap the undertaking, on which $100 million had been spent. Representative William Carney, a leading LILCO supporter in Congress, in whose district Shoreham is located and where ISABELLE was supposed to be, complained: "I have serious concerns over the abandonment of the federal taxpayers' investment in favor of a new billion-dollar dream machine."[47]

When Vineyard resigned as BNL's director to return to its physics department as a senior scientist, Hughes, of Associated Universities, Inc., said in a letter to all laboratory employees that "under Dr. Vineyard's direction . . . strong ties have been maintained with academic and user communities."[48] The universities involved in Associated Universities, Inc. are Columbia, Cornell, Harvard, Johns Hopkins, Pennsylvania, Princeton, Rochester, Yale, and the Massachusetts Institute of Technology.

But the academic institution that, during Vineyard's directorship, BNL became particularly close with was the State University of New York at Stony Brook. LILCO, at the same time, established strong links with the state university.

Thus, at the school—which began in the 1960s as a small institution to train science teachers, but under a succession of three presidents, all physicists, became a sprawling university center with an emphasis on science and technology—another meeting ground was created for major forces promoting nuclear technology on Long Island.

The local governing board of the campus is the Stony Brook Council. In 1976, Dr. R. C. Anderson, an assistant director of the laboratory, became chairman of the Stony Brook Council, a position he still holds. The council is crucial in selecting the president of the university.

The entity that raises and manages funds for research projects at the university, not covered by tax monies, is the Stony Brook Foundation. In 1975, LILCO chairman Pierce became chairman of the Stony Brook Foundation. The vice chairman of the foundation from 1978 to 1985 was Anderson. Although Pierce resigned as LILCO chairman in 1984, he remains on the foundation board in his role as LILCO consultant. The new chairman of the Stony Brook Foundation is Santoz T. Abrilz, Jr., an industrialist who had been a leader in pushing Shoreham as co-chairman of the largely LILCO-financed Citizens to Open Shoreham, now Citizens for Shoreham Electricity, and as chairman of the energy committee of the Long Island Association of Commerce and Industry.

It was through his membership on the Stony Brook Foundation, beginning in 1975, that William Catacosinos, former BNL assistant director, got "tied into" LILCO, according to a former long-time associate who asked to remain anonymous.[49]

Through the connection he established with LILCO on the Stony Brook Foundation, the ex-associate said, Catacosinos became a member of LILCO's board in 1978. He also became a member of the board's "nuclear oversight" committee. (Also in 1978, Catacosinos donated $500,000 to the Stony Brook Foundation to fund awards for research into cancer. They are called the Catacosinos Fellowships.)

And, in 1984, Catacosinos took over the management of LILCO when the utility's executives were forced to resign because of problems involving Shoreham.

Although he is not a nuclear scientist, his years at BNL left Catacosinos with the kind of absolute faith in nuclear power that Kouts, Hull and many of its other nuclear scientists share. It was during his "experience" at BNL working "around" its reactor, Catacosinos has said, that he decided nuclear power was safe.

Catacosinos' former associate describes him as a driven, extremely ambitious, single-minded, uncompromising person—with a belief in nuclear power growing out of his years at BNL. "He's a person who will race his car down the highway full-speed, and if there's water ahead and no bridge—he'll drive right into the water," the ex-associate said. "Bill has tunnel vision. Once he has made a decision to do something, he will follow it through—regardless of the consequences. His way is to push ahead, no matter what happens until what he's pushing succeeds brilliantly or fails brilliantly."

The former associate said, "That's the way he did it," at a computer company in Hauppauge, Long Island, that Catacosinos founded in 1969 with several colleagues From BNL. "He took great risks, some would say he was reckless. He drove hard, and as a result suffered some brilliant disasters and achieved some brilliant successes. He's taking the same approach with Shoreham. There's no middle ground. He has to win or he has to lose completely. To negotiate is not in his nature."

The ex-associate said two elements motivate Catacosinos. One is his being "driven with personal ambition" from growing up in a working class immigrant family in Manhattan where his father ran a grocery store. "My theory is that what Bill would like to get personally out of LILCO is a national reputation which would allow him to become a U.S. ambassador." The second, he said, involves Catacosinos' background as an administrator at BNL.

Catacosinos came to BNL in 1956, just discharged from the Navy as a lieutenant junior grade. He was 26 and became an administrative officer, ultimately assigned to the laboratory's reactor. In 1961, he was appointed an assistant business manager, and in 1962, business manager.

In the same year he received a doctorate in business administration from New York University. The ex-associate said that Catacosinos sought the doctorate because he thought he wouldn't otherwise "be accepted" at the laboratory—where many employees have doctorates.

In 1964, Catacosinos was BNL's assistant director in charge of business management and business administration. He held that position until 1968, when he left to go into business. The former associate said that Catacosinos "was the businessman of the group of Brookhaven Lab people who started" Applied Digital Data Systems, which specialized in producing multi-user small business computer systems. The firm, with Catacosinos as its chairman and chief executive officer, had sharp ups and downs, according to the ex-associate. Some of the downs had to do with changes in market conditions, others had to do with risks taken by Catacosinos, he said.

The profits from the company allowed Catacosinos to move to a 57-acre estate in Mill Neck, on the North Shore "Gold Coast" of Nassau County.[50] The firm was a $50 million-a-year operation when it was sold in 1980 to National Cash Register. Catacosinos "stayed on after the purchase for nearly two years to make sure things went smoothly," said the ex-associate.

In the end, Catacosinos and National Cash Register wound up on bad terms. In 1984, Applied Digital Systems sued Catacosinos for $2 million in damages charging that shortly before the sale he had improperly increased his annual pension benefits by $178,000. He was entitled to $112,353 a year, claimed the suit, but he had arranged to get $290,947 a year—as of 1985. The suit said that Catacosinos altered the pension arrangement with a legal opinion from a lawyer with whom he had a "long personal and professional relationship" and whom he "believed that he could influence . . . to render an opinion which would enrich" him. Catacosinos has claimed the suit is "totally without merit."[51]

When he took over as chairman, chief executive officer and president of LILCO, Catacosinos arranged for a five-year contract with annual pay of $275,000. In addition, he arranged that "upon termination" of his employment, he would be retained as a LILCO consultant, according to the LILCO "Proxy Statement" of 1985, "for five years at $160,000 for each of the first two years, $120,000 for the next year, and $80,000 for each of the remaining two years"—the so-called $600,000 "golden parachute." Among other benefits, Catacosinos arranged to receive $10,000 a year "for maintenance of his personal security," according to the statement.

After taking over the utility, Catacosinos announced to the Long Island Association of Commerce and Industry that under him LILCO would conduct "guerrilla warfare" to put Shoreham into operation.[52] "Long Island needs Shoreham," he insisted. He told state legislators at a private meeting that if Shoreham didn't open, LILCO would be out of business. He said he wanted to see some form of "interim certification" from the U.S. Nuclear Regulatory Commission to allow Shoreham to open on a limited basis, "with major renovations later."[53]

He also said, "My job at the moment is to preserve LILCO. We have to do the things that are necessary to allow us to continue to operate with our own cash flow."[54] He ordered the "austerity program" that cut back the LILCO work force by 987, and then insisted on employee "givebacks" which led to LILCO's first strike. And he ordered the suspension of payment of dividends on LILCO stock—a situation which still exists at this time.

Governor Cuomo met with Catacosinos and offered state help to keep LILCO solvent in return for the abandonment of Shoreham. Catacosinos refused. "The plant is completed, the plant is a quality plant and the plant is deemed safe," he declared at a subsequent press conference.

It became quickly apparent that the commitment of Catacosinos to nuclear power was, if anything, even more deep-seated than it was for LILCO executives who had come before him.

Catacosinos, it became clear, was a nuclear zealot—straight out of the government's nuclear establishment. He would wax poetic about nuclear technology in the same terms those in the establishment had used, since the end of World War II, as they promoted nuclear technology to keep their establishment going.

"Nuclear is the cleanest, safest mode of electricity today," Catacosinos stated at an interview with several reporters.[55] He said that a person living near the Three Mile Island plant during the 1979 accident absorbed less radioactivity than he or she would taking a transcontinental flight.

But under questioning, he conceded that he had no knowledge of important studies concerning nuclear power. Asked about the WASH-740-update, the analysis done at Brookhaven National Laboratory—while he was there—that concluded that a single accident could devastate an area the size of Pennsylvania, Catacosinos said he was not familiar with this report. Asked about the 1982 study done at Sandia National Laboratories projecting the specific consequences of a core meltdown at nuclear plants in the U.S., including Shoreham, he said he was not familiar with this report.

As to what would happen in a nuclear plant accident, Catacosinos said that radioactivity released would simply go "up in the atmosphere."

In terms of Shoreham, he denied any problems. Of charges by workers at the plant of serious flaws in construction, he said "each" of these charges had been "investigated and found to be not true. . . . Nothing has been proven as far as I am concerned." Of demands by Suffolk County for an independent inspection of the plant, he said, "We've had three inspections already." Of the conclusion by the New York PSC that there had been pervasive mismanagement of Shoreham construction, he said there was "no significant mismanagement."

Nor was he concerned about Shoreham's economic impact. Of LILCO rates doubling to pay for Shoreham, Catacosinos declared: "Why should the cost of electricity stagnate?"

Catacosinos' viewpoint clearly has its roots in the historical approach of the nuclear establishment.

In 1977, Dr. Alvin Weinberg, a nuclear physicist and long-time director of Oak Ridge National Laboratory (noted for his declaration that "we nuclear people have made a Faustian bargain"[56]) spoke at BNL on "An Acceptable Nuclear Future."[57] Vineyard introduced him to the 400 laboratory personnel in the audience as "one of the fathers of energy policy."

Weinberg called for a "cadre that from now on can be counted upon to understand nuclear technology, to control it." He declared: "I don't think my friends in the utility business will like this very much, but we need a different institution for the generation of the electricity. The nuclear system is much more complex than fossil fuel systems, and places demands on the utility industry that is beyond its traditional role. Nuclear technology ought to be placed in the hands of a consortium, or the government should be in charge of generation. No utility president or vice president need lose their jobs. The utilities would continue to distribute electricity. There will have to be a sense of immortality in this institution because the nuclear enterprise, once started, will be hard to abandon."

Weinberg, who was involved in the Manhattan Project, said that there should be large nuclear "centers," with the kind of "security we had at nuclear plants during the war." He said, "In a sense we will buy order at the cost of freedom." Manned by members of the "nuclear cadre," each "place would become an extended family, like Brookhaven. If anything goes wrong, there would be strength in depth."

He also said that there would have to be a transition to breeder reactors fueled with plutonium because fissionable uranium was "running out." He also predicted that there would be a core meltdown at a nuclear plant "once every twenty years."

He bemoaned that the debate over nuclear power was "taking on the color of a religious war."

But, he said, "fears about fission energy will subside as the public acquires familiarity with radiation. The view will wane. There are still some among the elderly who think there is something spooky about electric light bulbs." (In an earlier magazine article, Weinberg had asserted: "If a cure for cancer is found, the problem of radiation standards disappear."[58])

With Catacosinos' takeover of LILCO management, a long-time member of the government's nuclear establishment took over LILCO—aiming to rescue its faltering nuclear dream.

Faced with widescale opposition at home, he would lead LILCO in looking for assistance where the government's nuclear establishment normally went to get aid: from the federal apparatus in Washington, D.C.

He would stress to a generally receptive audience there: It is not just LILCO at issue. In Washington, he would have LILCO argue, in the embattled Shoreham situation on Long Island the future of nuclear power in the United States is at stake.

TO: Thomas Dillon *DOE*

FROM: Donald P. Irwin *LILCO*

DRAFT AGENDA 4/6/84

DOE ⅛ 250 D.5DO M

I.   BACKGROUND

LOANS DUE OF 4/27

    A.   Urgency of Need for Federal Participation

NET WORTH ⁸8B
SHOREHAM 7.8B

END OF APRIL
KEY *BEGINNING OF MAY*

        1. Financial crisis at LILCO

HOSTILE

        2. Pending litigation with Suffolk County and
           New York State on LILCO legal authority to
           implement emergency planning; now in New
           York State Court; LILCO seeking to remove
           to federal court

BROOKHAVEN SCIENTISTS

URGENCY:
WOULD LIKE
FEDERAL RESPONSE
WITHIN 1-2 WEEKS
FROM LOCAL
ASPECTS.

        3. Pending litigation against Suffolk County
           in federal court: (a) COEP suit, (b) LILCO
           suit; hearing Monday on motions to intervene,
           to dismiss

    B.   DOE: Premises of Participation in Exercise

    C.   ....   —1600 people

II.   ISSUES TO BE DISCUSSED

        1. Scope and Nature of Federal Personnel in
           Exercise and Actual Response

           a.   Who's in charge for FEMA?

           b.   How will DOE be used? Other agencies?

           c.   What is Brookhaven's role?

        2. Substantive relationship between LILCO/LERO
           personnel and federal counterparts

           a.   Federal assumption of authority   *FEMA IS DIRECTOR OF LERO.*

           b.   Method of implementing federal authority: *"FEDERAL CAP"*
              (1) LERO recommendations to federal officers;
              (2) deputization of LERO employees

           c.   How relationship is to be memorialized --
              memorandum of understanding, policy statement
              by FEMA, etc.

Memo for a meeting between LILCO and the U.S. Department of Energy.

NOTES

1. The Albert Einstein letter is on exhibit at the Roosevelt Home in Hyde Park, New York.
2. Quoted in *The Cult of the Atom: The Secret Papers of the Atomic Energy Commission* by Daniel Ford, 1982.
3. *Newsday*, August 6, 1985. William Sexton's column began: "One doesn't have to go all the way to Japan to see a memorial to Hiroshima's victims."
4. From *The Atom and the Ocean*, which is described on the back of its cover as "one of a series" of publications issued by the AEC "on understanding the atom." It was published in 1967.
5. *The Cult of the Atom.* Other important books on the promotion of nuclear technology include *NUKESPEAK: The Selling of Nuclear Technology in America*, by Stephen Hilgartner, Richard C. Bell and Rory O'Connor, Sierra Club Books, 1982.
6. From *Man and Atom* by Glenn Seaborg and William R. Corliss, New York: E.P. Dutton and Co., 1971.
7. *Nucleonics*, vol. 19, no. 4, April 1961.
8. *The Nuclear Barons*, by Peter Pringle and James Spiegelman, New York: Holt, Rinehart and Winston, 1981.
9. Lewis Strauss made the comment at a Founders' Day Dinner, National Association of Science Writers, September 16, 1954. Speaking of "unlimited power," he said, "It is not too much to expect that our children will enjoy electrical energy too cheap to meter."
10. *Reactor Science and Technology*, vol. 2, no. 3, October 1952.
11. These statements by Herbert Yount, and the Melvin Price and Lewis Strauss statements following, are quoted from *Perils of the Peaceful Atom: The Myth of Safe Nuclear Power Plants* by Richard Curtis and Elizabeth Hogan, New York: Doubleday and Company, 1970.
12. Herbert Kouts' statements were made in an interview with the author, January 1986.
13. *A Report on the Shoreham Nuclear Power Plant* was issued on January 14, 1983.
14. The report by New York State Fact-Finding Panel on the Shoreham Nuclear Power Facility was released on December 13, 1983.
15. Reported in *The East Hampton Star*, February 24, 1984.
16. Herbert Brown's comment was made in *Newsday*, March 6, 1984.
17. From Herbert Kouts' letter to *Newsday*, February 18, 1984.
18. Andrew Hull's statements were made in interviews with the author, January and February 1986.
19. An article on the Hull lecture appeared in *Brookhaven Bulletin*, September 21, 1979.
20. *Newsday*, February 1, 1986.
21. Brookhaven National Laboratory publication 9–73–10M.
22. Simon Perchik in an interview with the author, February 1986.
23. Lorna Salzman in an interview with the author, October 1985.
24. Formation of the center was announced in a statement from Joseph Hendrie's office dated January 27, 1976. "I am pleased to announce the formation of the National Center for Analysis of Energy Systems here at the Laboratory," it began.
25. From a transcript of NRC deliberations, March 30, 1979.

26. From details of Leonard Hamiton's lecture in *Brookhaven Bulletin*, November 19, 1976.
27. "Health Effects of Photovoltaic Cells," *Brookhaven Bulletin*, August 17, 1979.
28. " 'Effluent' Mother Earth," *Brookhaven Bulletin*, December 5, 1980.
29. *Brookhaven Bulletin*, October 5, 1976.
30. The author witnessed the May 10, 1980, demonstration.
31. The author was present at the hearing August 14, 1983, observed the incident involving Fainberg, and witnessed the testimony.
32. *Newsday*, August 7, 1978.
33. It was held on February 8, 1980, at Adelphi University in Garden City.
34. *Newsday*, October 28, 1981.
35. "State: Brookhaven Project in Violation," *Newsday*, December 12, 1979.
36. *Newsday*, April 23, 1982.
37. From "Final Environmental Impact Statement, Proton-Proton Storage Accelerator Facility (ISABELLE)," dated August 1978.
38. Judge David Schechter made his determination on March 14, 1980.
39. *The New York Times*, September 14, 1981.
40. *The New York Times*, August 21, 1981.
41. Robert Hughes' statement was reported by Associated Press, December 22, 1981.
42. Long Island Committee for Jobs and Independence press release, dated March 30, 1982, entitled, "ISABELLE: The Northeast Crisis!"
43. John Marburger's comments were reported in *The New York Times*, September 13, 1981.
44. Reported in *Newsday*, April 24, 1982.
45. *Newsday*, April 24, 1982.
46. *Newsday*, October 19, 1982.
47. Reported in *Newsday*, October 20, 1983.
48. From a press release issued by Brookhaven National Laboratory, August 19, 1981, headed: "GEORGE H. VINEYARD TO RETURN TO FULL-TIME RESEARCH."
49. The former associate of William Catacosinos, who was interviewed by the author in December 1985, asked that his name not be published.
50. The estate Catacosinos purchased in Mill Neck was formerly owned by the Rockefeller family.
51. Details of the suit from "LILCO Chief's Ex-Firm Says He Padded Pension," *Newsday*, May 16, 1984.
52. William Catacosinos' comment about "guerrilla warfare" was reported in *The New York Times*, September 9, 1984.
53. Catacosinos' comments to state legislators were reported by Associated Press February 21, 1984.
54. Reported in *The Wall Street Journal*, March 8, 1984.
55. Catacosinos' comments were made in an interview with journalists, including the author, March 1985.
56. From *Science*, July 7, 1972.
57. The author was present at Weinberg lecture, given May 17, 1977.
58. *Science and Government Report*, February 15, 1972.

7

IN LILCO'S POCKET:
WASHINGTON, D.C.

"There's a scandal here," Herbert Brown, the attorney for Suffolk County on Shoreham, was saying from Washington in early 1984. "The question is whether the scandal will come out in time."[1]

"It's crass politics. LILCO has politicized the case completely." Dr. William Catacosinos, the new chief of LILCO, was involved in leading the utility, Brown said, in applying intense pressure in Washington—with the White House, the Department of Energy, the Nuclear Regulatory Commission and the Federal Emergency Management Agency. And the federal apparatus was moving in completely improper ways to come to LILCO's rescue.

"There have been some highly questionable things going on, a total abuse of rational procedure," Brown said.

Brown, who was experienced in nuclear power litigation—before Shoreham, his firm represented the State of California in its challenge to the Diablo Canyon nuclear project—described what was happening as a perversion of the regulatory process. LILCO was demanding a "rubber stamp" license for Shoreham, and "right now, considering the politicized status of Shoreham, anything is possible."

In the months that followed, the Reagan administration went to extraordinary lengths to assist LILCO in trying to get Shoreham running. It intervened directly in the process of regulation. It described the plant as a symbol of the future of nuclear power.

Secretary of Energy John Herrington declared in a major speech to a meeting of prominent figures in the nuclear industry in 1985 that Shoreham "has more than $4 billion in sunk costs. Yet it can't start because the local county has refused to test an emergency plan that nearly all experts have agreed is more than adequate to meet evacuation needs. The Shoreham plant must open! If it doesn't, the signals will be the low point in this industry's history. If it does, we are going to begin a brand new era."[2] (His claim that "all experts have agreed" that LILCO's evacuation plan was "more than adequate" was not true, but in the Reagan administration push for LILCO and Shoreham, the facts didn't matter at all.)

Why would one utility and one nuclear plant project on Long Island be regarded as so important by the federal government? Why would the Reagan administration go to the extreme lengths it did— and does—for LILCO and Shoreham?

One element to the answer lies in how LILCO "wired" itself to Washington. William Catacosinos, because of his background as a national laboratory administrator and also as a "management consultant" to the AEC during that period, had links to the federal apparatus. Backing LILCO was the nuclear industry's powerful lobbying machinery: the Edison Electric Institute, the American Nuclear Energy Council, the Atomic Industrial Forum. Helping, too, were Congressional figures routinely in favor of nuclear power, notably Senator Alan Simpson, a Republican of Wyoming, and two Long Island representatives, William Carney of Hauppauge and Norman Lent of East Rockaway, both Republicans and both long-time LILCO supporters and recipients of LILCO Political Action Committee campaign contributions.[3] Most importantly, Catacosinos was able to make rapid connections high in the Reagan administration by extensive use of two former federal officials with close ties to the administration.

Another element was the unbridled backing of nuclear power by an administration led by a president who for years had been the public representative for a principal company in the nuclear field, General Electric. Under him were other equally staunch advocates of nuclear power including several from the nuclear industry.

And a crucial element was timing. In January 1984, the month that Catacosinos took over LILCO, there were a series of severe setbacks for the nuclear industry that would lead it to call the month "Black January" and cause the Reagan administration to embark on an all-out program to save the industry. There, in the wake of "Black January" as the administration launched this program, appeared Catacosinos with others working on behalf of LILCO seeking massive and special help for the utility and saying, as the U.S. nuclear industry tottered, that its success depended on Shoreham. Their move for a federal bailout of LILCO was occurring at the right place at the right time.

Also, there had been uneasiness earlier in Washington about Shoreham setting a dangerous precedent for nuclear power on the evacuation issue. This developed immediately after Suffolk County officials concluded in 1983 that there could be no successful evacuation in the event of a Shoreham accident and began opposing Shoreham on that basis. Nuclear proponents feared that if this local opposition spread, other nuclear plants could also be held what they called "hostage" by local and state governments.

Catacosinos, soon after taking over LILCO, had put the chances of Shoreham going into operation bluntly: "The only possibility is for the federal government to step in."[4]

"LILCO Turns to Washington," was *Newsday*'s headline. "The final moves in the long chess game over the fate of the Shoreham nuclear power plant," the Washington-datelined article began, "are being played out here. Long Island Lighting Co., having lost its gambits to win the support of Suffolk County and New York State, is maneuvering in Congress and before federal agencies in a last-ditch effort to gain a license to operate Shoreham."[5]

Charles King Mallory III was one former federal official with close ties to the Reagan administration with whom Catacosinos worked—and who is still acting for LILCO in Washington. In February 1984, when Catacosinos met for the first time with then-Secretary of Energy Donald Hodel, he went with Mallory. Mallory was a member of the Department of Energy "transition team" formed after Reagan's election in 1980—the group that recommended those who received top positions at the DOE. Mallory, who works out of the Washington office of Hunton & Williams, LILCO's law firm on nuclear matters, also was formerly Hodel's boss. In the 1970s, both were in the Nixon administration, with Mallory as deputy assistant Interior secretary for energy and minerals, overseeing the operations of the Bonneville Power Administration, of which Hodel was administrator. (In that role, Hodel was central in creating the ill-fated Washington Public Power Supply System's five nuclear plants project.)

Lyn Nofziger, the chief political strategist for Ronald Reagan for two decades, was hired by LILCO at $20,000 a month as a consultant, and extensive use was also made of him.[6] Nofziger was a White House special assistant for political affairs in 1981 and 1982, then formed his own consulting firm while continuing to serve as an "informal consultant" to Reagan.

"They went to the top—the way if you wanted to buy oil from some prince in a shiekdom, you'd go to the top," Herbert Brown said in 1985. He was speaking in the Rayburn House Building in Washington during a break in a House subcommittee hearing on the Reagan administration's push for Shoreham. "You'd go to the top and figure you can pull strings from there. They did that because they became desperate, desperate because of their own blunders."[7]

Before Catacosinos took over, LILCO was an active presence in Washington through its own lobbying office. Among those helping LILCO smooth its way with Washington agencies was former U.S. Representative John Wydler. Wydler as a congressman had been an avidly pro-nuclear member of the Science and Technology Committee, and a recipient of campaign funds from the LILCO Political Action Committee. He was also chairman of the Long Island Congressional Caucus. Not along after the Garden City Republican retired from Congress in 1981, he went on LILCO's payroll. "I did consultation work for LILCO on problems with the nuclear regulatory board," said Wydler. He refused to discuss further what he did for LILCO and still does. He said he is still a LILCO consultant, though he would not say what he has been and is getting paid.[8]

With the election of Ronald Reagan as president in 1980, LILCO had an immensely supportive national administration to work with—although for over three decades every U.S. administration, Republican or Democrat, has supported the development of commercial nuclear power.

President Jimmy Carter, for instance, would claim to be a nuclear engineer on the basis of his military service under Admiral Hyman Rickover in the Navy, and declare that "nuclear power must play an important role."

But with Ronald Reagan, the U.S. got a president with deep and long ties to the nuclear industry. He was far more than host of *General Electric Theatre* on television. For eight years Reagan traveled the nation for GE—which with Westinghouse is one of the two global giants of nuclear power—in a capacity company officials described as GE's "general good will ambassador."

It was in that period, during the "downtime in his Hollywood acting career that the seeds of his political career were planted," a report on Reagan in *Broadcasting* (January 26, 1981) has noted. With movie work all but nonexistent for him, Reagan "drifted into television in the 1950s," connected with GE, and became host of its TV show and "spokesman for the company."

Reagan's strong point was being a skilled performer, an attractive up-front figure for GE.

Before GE hired him, he "was living from guest spot to guest spot on television, and he was nearly $18,000 in debt," according to Joseph Lewis' book *What Makes Reagan Run? A Political Profile* (McGraw-Hill, 1968). "He was so hard-pressed that he took a two-week job as an M.C. at the Last Frontier Hotel in Las Vegas, where he performed a routine kidding himself for not being able to sing, dance or tell jokes." Working for GE and "perhaps determined to atone for his past errors" as an "ultraliberal" in Hollywood, "Reagan became a full-time apostle for the conservative business viewpoint. GE rewarded him with an annual salary of $125,000, later raising it to $165,000."

In a 1960 GE internal newsletter, Reagan was quoted as saying: "When I go on tour for the company I make as many as 14 talks a day to various groups. One pretty high government official tried to have me shut up, but the president of GE told me to go ahead and say whatever I wanted to say."

That was often GE's sales pitch for nuclear power.

"Reagan's GE experience as a business spokesman crystallized his conservatism," observed Fred I. Greenstein's book, *The Reagan Presidency* (Johns Hopkins, 1983). "His GE years led in 1960 to his official transfer of loyalties to the Republican Party." Thereafter, "a group of conservative California businessmen" decided "to back his successful 1966 campaign for governor."

As a candidate for president, and as president, Reagan's positions on nuclear power have not deviated an iota from the positions of GE and the rest of the nuclear industry.

He said during his campaign: "Nuclear power is the cleanest, the most efficient, and the most economical energy source, with no environmental problems."[9]

Other statements about nuclear power by Reagan before he became president include:

• "The total radioactivity the people and the animals were exposed to in the immediate vicinity of the plant [Three Mile Island] was less than the difference between living in Dallas or living in the higher altitudes of Denver, Colorado."

• "To put things in focus, Dr. Alvin Weinberg of Oak Ridge [National Laboratory] brought a Geiger counter to a committee room of the U.S. Senate. It registered higher radiation than escaped at Three Mile Island."

• "All the waste in a year from a nuclear power plant could be stored under a desk."

Carl Walske, president of the Atomic Industrial Forum, a nuclear industry trade group, described industry emotions upon Reagan's election as mixed between "ecstasy, joy, pleasure and euphoria."[10]

"Nuclear-Power Industry Pins Hopes for Survival on Reagan Presidency," headlined *The Wall Street Journal* soon after the 1980 election. The story began:

> Like a drowning man, the commercial nuclear-power industry is grasping at the hope that Ronald Reagan can save it. . . . For the past several years, nuclear power advocates haven't had much to cheer about. Since 1975, only thirteen new nuclear power plants have been ordered in the U.S. while plans for 50 plants have been cancelled. No plants have been ordered in the past two years.

Utilities, said *The Journal*, had found themselves in a financial nightmare.

> Huge cost overruns engulf every nuclear project, forcing the utilities involved to raise billions of dollars more than originally planned. . . . Because the growth of demand for electricity has slowed, utilities have less capability to generate cash internally. And outside investors are becoming increasingly reluctant to provide the vast sums companies need to built plants.

The nuclear industry was hoping, said *The Journal*, that the Reagan administration would arrange for "less government involvement in safety regulation" and increased government support of nuclear power—greater financial aid and moving "to accelerate the licensing and building of nuclear plants."[11]

Reagan has tried to fulfill the nuclear industry's every wish. In 1981, as he announced steps by his administration to promote nuclear power, he declared:

> One of the best potential sources of new electrical energy supplies in the coming decades is nuclear power. The U.S. has developed a strong technological base in the production of electricity from nuclear energy. Unfortunately, the Federal Government has created a regulatory environment that is forcing many utilities to rule out nuclear power as a source of new generating capacity.

To "correct present government deficiencies and to enable nuclear power to make its essential contribution to our future needs," Reagan said he was ordering a "series of policy initiatives" including:

> directing the Secretary of Energy to give immediate priority attention to recommending improvements in the nuclear regulatory and licensing process. I anticipate that the Chairman of the Nuclear Regulatory Commission will take steps to facilitate the licensing of plants under construction and those awaiting licenses. . . . I am directing the Secretary of Energy and the director of the Office of Science and Technology Policy to meet with representatives from the universities, private industry and the utilities and requesting them to report to me on the obstacles which stand in the way of increased use of nuclear energy and the steps needed to overcome them in order to assure the continued availability of nuclear power.

Still, said Reagan, "eliminating the regulatory problems that have burdened nuclear power will be of little use if the utility sector cannot raise the capital necessary to fund construction of new generating facilities." He proposed "substantial incentives designed to attract new capital."[12]

The Reagan administration's nuclear push continued unabated during his first term. Simultaneous with it was a de-emphasis on the development of other energy forms. Nuclear power is "essential," Reagan maintained during his campaign, and the U.S. had "no choice." In office, he moved to ensure that there would be no choice. *The New York Times* noted on March 27, 1981, how the DOE was preparing "to eliminate or cut back severely nearly all its programs to encourage energy conservation and to develop renewable fuel sources." It reported,

> The long list of Federal programs affected . . . includes: solar energy research and development, wind energy and ocean thermal development . . . methane-fueled transport, residential energy efficiency, energy conservation for commercial buildings, consumer education on energy conservation, small-scale hydroelectric projects and energy audits by public utilities.

Among those with a nuclear industry background appointed by Reagan to high positions in his administration was Dr. Nunzio Palladino, who was named chairman of the Nuclear Regulatory Commission. For 20 years Palladino was a nuclear engineer at Westinghouse, one of the key engineers involved in developing nuclear technology for the company. His official NRC biography says that during this time he also was for "four years on loan to Oak Ridge and Argonne National Laboratory." It says that Palladino was "in charge of reactor core design" for the first nuclear submarine and the reactor used in "the Shippingport Atomic Power Station in Pennsylvania, the nation's first full-scale nuclear generating station." He was manager of Westinghouse's Pressurized Water Reactor Design Subdivision.

In line with his background, Palladino (who was supposed to lead a panel considering nuclear power objectively) as NRC chairman remained a nuclear power booster.

In a 1983 speech entitled, "Nuclear Power: It Has a Past, It Has a Present—and It Has a Future," Palladino said: "I believe that the nuclear power plant is an energy option that we need now and are going to need more of in the years ahead. . . . The U.S. nuclear industry is not dead."[13]

In another speech the same year, "Factors Affecting the Nuclear Future," Palladino stated: "For nuclear power, the challenge for the future that the industry as well as its regulators face is to do what is necessary to create a climate that will allow the utilities to add new plants when they are needed. I believe that the Nuclear Regulatory Commission and the nuclear industry working together can meet this challenge."[14]

The official NRC biography of Reagan appointee Thomas M. Roberts actually stresses his nuclear industry connection. Roberts "has firsthand experience in the manufacture of nuclear power plant components," it begins. He had been chief executive officer and president of Southern Boiler & Tank Works, Inc., of Memphis, Tennessee, a major producer of nuclear plant components.

In a 1982 speech, Roberts declared: "The burden is now on those who believe nuclear power to be efficient, safe, and necessary to make their case with a skeptical public. . . . Reassurance of the public is not only an important challenge for the industry. It is also an important aspect of political leadership." He added that "while the NRC is prohibited from promoting the program, other officials of the government are under no such constraint."[15]

Roberts has gone so far as to vote for a license for a nuclear plant "after saying he was sure his company had provided the reactor with the best containment liner in the country," *The New York Times* has reported. This occurred in the 1985 licensing of the Palo Verde 1 nuclear plant in Wintersburg, Arizona. *The Times* spotlighted Roberts in a story on "conflict of interest" in Washington, and the "revolving door" between government and industry.[16]

Leaving top executive positions at the Bechtel Corporation of California, the biggest contractor of nuclear plants, for appointments in the Reagan administration have been: Secretary of State George Shultz, who was Bechtel's president; Secretary of Defense Caspar Weinberger, who was a Bechtel vice president and general counsel; and Deputy Secretary of Energy W. Kenneth Davis, a Bechtel vice president and also former president of the Atomic Industrial Forum. Prior to his 22 years at Bechtel, Davis was the AEC's director of reactor development. He has declared that the nuclear industry's problems have been "distorted and inflated by critics."

Donald Hodel ran a consulting firm that primarily served utilities between the time he was forced out as chief of the Bonneville Power Administration and when he joined the Reagan administration. He left Bonneville following criticism for being—as U.S. Representative Jim Weaver of Oregon described it—"hellbent for energy growth at any cost."[17]

Hodel has made clear that he dislikes environmentalists with the same passion that he likes nuclear power. They "clamor for a return to a more primitive life,"[18] he has complained. As DOE secretary, he has emphasized that "this administration fully supports nuclear power as an imperative, not an option."

A former Oregon GOP chairman, Hodel was active in Reagan's 1980 campaign for president. His first appointment in the Reagan administration was as Interior Secretary James Watt's top assistant, an Interior undersecretary. Hodel had worked with Watt, along with Charles Mallory, at Interior in the Nixon administration. He then became DOE secretary, and would replace Watt as Interior secretary when Watt was forced to resign for making comments slurring religious and racial groups and the handicapped.

Reagan's first Treasury secretary, currently his chief of staff, Donald Regan, was chairman and chief executive of Merrill Lynch, Pierce, Fenner & Smith, which has been very active in brokering stock for the nuclear industry and utilities—including LILCO stock.

And heading the CIA has been former LILCO director and nuclear power booster William Casey.

But all the words and the actions by the Reagan administration in its first three years to promote nuclear power didn't avert "Black January." If the nuclear industry was "drowning" when Reagan took office, as *The Wall Street Journal* phrased it, it was sinking even faster in January of 1984. The Reagan administration reacted to the major setbacks with an even more intense drive to assist the industry—an effort that turned out to be pivotal for LILCO. Catacosinos began LILCO's lobbying blitzkrieg in Washington as that effort began.

The Reagan administration fully accepted the claim that Shoreham was critical to nuclear power's future. White House Science Advisor George Keyworth, a nuclear physicist who formerly headed the physics division at Los Alamos National Laboratory, declared after two meetings with William Catacosinos: "This may just be Shoreham in New York, but it clearly has national implications."[19]

Investigative reporter Ron Ridenhour looked into the Reagan administration's moves in early 1984 to aid nuclear power. The results of that investigation were published a year later in a New Orleans weekly, *Gambit* (March 30, 1985), in an extensive article entitled "THE RUSH TO LICENSE: MONEY VS. SAFETY."

"Black January—as that month in 1984 has become known within the industry—delivered body-blow after body-blow to the proponents of nuclear power, a pummeling for which even the most pessimistic analysts were not prepared," he wrote. "Spurred by a series of events . . . that the nuclear power industry, the utility industry and the financial community all saw as major calamities, the Reagan administration set in motion a series of steps early in 1984 that would eventually lead them into a concerted program to oversee the expediting of the licensing of more than twenty nuclear power plants"—including, importantly, Shoreham.

Ridenhour pointed out that "Reagan has long been an outspoken friend of nuclear power." But the program put into place then by Reagan administration officials "to expedite plant licensing has gone far beyond anything envisioned by even their most angry critics in Congress and the anti-nuclear lobby."

The Black January for nuclear power began with a January 11th U.S. Supreme Court decision refusing to set aside the $10.5 million judgment handed down in the Karen Silkwood case against the Kerr-McGee Corporation. Silkwood was killed on her way to show a reporter evidence she had compiled for her union on the Kerr-McGee plutonium plant in Oklahoma—safety violations, incidents of workers being contaminated, and radioactive releases. Previously, her home had been broken into and contaminated with plutonium, much of it put on food in her refrigerator. The Supreme Court's upholding of the Silkwood Oklahoma court jury verdict demolished the claim of the nuclear industry and the federal government that the regulation of "radiation hazards" was the exclusive domain of the federal government. Several state attorneys general joined the case, charging that position was an "uncharted expansion of federal pre-emption" intruding on "the historic powers of the states."

The following day, January 12, it was revealed that the Securities and Exchange Commission was investigating Hodel's former project, WPPSS, for defaulting on $2.25 billion in bonds. (Not long after, WPPSS collapsed financially.)

On January 13, an NRC licensing board did the unheard-of: It refused to issue a license for a nuclear plant, the nearly complete $3.35 billion Byron plant in Rockford, Illinois. It said it had "no confidence" that the plant was safe. (The NRC—holding to its record of never denying a license for a nuclear plant—subsequently overturned the board and let Byron go into operation.)

On January 16, Public Service Company of Indiana announced it was abandoning its half-completed Marble Hill nuclear plant on which it had already spent $2.5 billion. It said it was unable to raise the $5 billion estimated as needed to complete the project. This came amid evidence of poor construction.

On January 21, Cincinnati Gas and Electric announced it would convert its 97 percent complete Zimmer nuclear plant—a General Electric-made twin of Shoreham—to coal. Major construction defects were found at Zimmer: Construction documents had been falsified; steel beams were bought from a junkyard and labeled nuclear safety grade; college students were used to inspect critical reactor systems; thousands of welds were found to be defective. For years, NRC officials had dismissed complaints about Zimmer. Finally, a private investigator gathered evidence from workers, and then environmental groups and the Washington-based Government Accountability Project, which conducted its own investigation, were able to bring enough pressure to get the government to act. Commented Thomas Devine, legal director of the Accountability Project: "Zimmer is a look into the way the nuclear industry operates."

On January 24, the Philadelphia Electric Company suspended work on one of its Limerick nuclear plants because of financing problems compounded by the Pennsylvania Public Service Commission having ordered that the company raise the capital necessary without ratepayer assistance.

The New York Times, noted Ridenhour, meanwhile ran a story in which the nuclear industry was said to be "stunned," and another that said several nuclear projects (including Shoreham) "were threatening to bankrupt the utilities building them. Analysts from several of Wall Street's most powerful and influential stock brokerage and investment banking houses were quoted blaming 'regulatory delays' as the culprit for the industry's woes."

In response to Black January, there were meetings "between the White House, top Reagan administration officials and members of the financial community, the nuclear power industry and the utilities," reported Ridenhour. "A special White House-backed organization called the White House Cabinet Council on Economic Affairs working group on nuclear power" was formed "specifically to study ways to bail out a number of utility companies whose troubled nuclear construction programs were threatening to force them into bankruptcy." Out of that group came a

> Department of Energy Task Force on Nuclear Power Construction . . . overseen by Reagan's former chief advisor on energy matters, Danny Boggs [who had become the number two official, deputy secretary at DOE]. The DOE Task Force monitored a wide range of activities in the NRC, analyzed the information and then provided it to Boggs and then Secretary of Energy Donald Hodel, who in turn provided it to others in the government.

Ridenhour's *Gambit* report also said:

> While the administration publicly claimed that it would not involve itself in the licensing decisions of specific plants or in the decisions of local government regarding nuclear power, that claim was not true. Administration officials were in fact simultaneously mobilizing a wide range of elements of the federal government on behalf of specific utility companies, aggressively working behind the scenes to influence the decisions of the NRC, state public service commissions and other supposedly independent government bodies. . . . The ultimate goal

of all their activities was to force the licensing of more than twenty troubled, contested and unfinished nuclear plants. Once licensed, the administration next worked—and continues to work—to get the plants admitted into rate bases and onto utility bills.

The article noted Donald Hodel's major role, and a May 8, 1984, speech by Hodel in Washington to a nuclear industry group that revealed the Reagan's administration's "blueprint for saving the nuclear power industry." Ridenhour said that "the press generally played Hodel's remarks as just another speech." It was, however, a disclosure of "several major elements" of the Reagan nuclear plan "to expedite the licensing of the plants which were already under construction and preparing to apply for their operating licenses." Hodel emphasized Shoreham. He called for Governor Mario Cuomo's help in bringing Shoreham on line, and afterwards his office announced that Hodel had sent a letter to Cuomo asking for state support of a federally supervised Shoreham evacuation test. "Let's give safety a try," he wrote.

"Hodel," Ridenhour noted, "as part of the White House Cabinet Council on Economic Affairs working group's effort to save Shoreham, had been coordinating with the Federal Emergency Management Agency, the NRC and executives for the utility, LILCO, to try to find a way around Suffolk County's refusal to help draft an emergency evacuation plan."

During the spring of 1984, wrote Ridenhour, there were a series of meetings between LILCO officials and "top Reagan administration officials from the Departments of Treasury, Energy, Agriculture, Federal Emergency Management Agency, the Office of Management and Budget, the White House Office of Science and Technology, plus others." Both Hodel and Donald Regan were personally involved, said Ridenhour. There were other meetings of Reagan administration officials during this period with "members of the financial community and still other meetings with executives of the nuclear power industry—the architect/engineers, reactor manufacturers, etc." At the NRC, meanwhile, Nunzio Palladino was moving to have the Shoreham licensing proceeding expedited.

In April 1984, this author learned from a source in the federal government that "a deal" was arranged between the NRC, DOE and FEMA to allow the use of LILCO employees and DOE personnel—

from Brookhaven National Laboratory—in an evacuation plan, devised with FEMA, for Shoreham. This was seen as removing the principal stumbling block preventing Shoreham from going into operation, a federally required evacuation plan. The source said that the "main argument" Catacosinos was making in Washington "was that if Shoreham goes down, the entire nuclear industry would be in even more trouble than it already is."

The extraordinary assistance being provided LILCO by the Reagan administration was featured in *The Washington Post* the next month (May 6, 1984). The story was headlined: "U.S. Trying to Revive A-Plant That State, County Believe Is Dying." It said:

> Long Island's Shoreham nuclear power plant, one of the most imperiled in the country because of financial and technological problems, has become the focus of an unusual resuscitation effort by the Reagan administration. The intensive care takes on significance because the administration firmly opposes the notion of federal rescues for faltering private companies.

It pointed out that the Reagan administration "has not moved to save several other utilities facing bankruptcy because of troubled nuclear plants," and that the situation "pits an administration committed to state's rights against the state of New York and Suffolk County."

It said "the administration's efforts on LILCO's behalf follow a series of warnings from the LILCO chairman William J. Catacosinos that the utility will be forced to scrap Shoreham unless the government intervenes."

The Post highlighted the political oddness of the clash, quoting Deputy Suffolk County Executive Frank Jones as saying: "We're basically a conservative Republican community. We're not a bunch of left-wing pinkos. I've been a Republican committeeman for 20 years. . . . Shoreham for us is not a cause, it's a case."

Jones continued:

> It's not that we're unwilling to evacuate. It's that it simply can't be done. We spent one year and $600,000 studying this. The Long Island Expressway is jammed right this minute. If we had an accident, we'd have 1.5 million people on a five-road network fleeing into New York City. It'd be absolute total, complete chaos.

But Catacosinos was having no problem in the nation's capital getting the federal road cleared to enable Shoreham to run.

The day after *The Washington Post* story, *Newsday* carried a story headlined: "How LILCO Got U.S. to Listen." Catacosinos came to Washington, said *Newsday*, "at a time when many top officials in the Reagan administration were ready to listen." It related how in January 1984 there were "setbacks" for nuclear power, but

> with Hodel leading the charge, the administration has taken an unusual interest in Shoreham. There have been high-level meetings between the Department of Energy and the Federal Emergency Management Agency on the possibility of a federally supervised evacuation drill at Shoreham; officials of the White House science adviser's office have made a fact-finding trip to Long Island; the Shoreham difficulties have been mentioned in the deliberations of cabinet working groups.

After the events of January 1984, "the Reagan administration decided to make Shoreham a symbol of the whole licensing mess by doing everything they can to get Shoreham licensed—and whatever they cannot do legally, to do anyway," commented Michael Mariotte, editor of *Groundswell*, the publication of the Nuclear Information and Resource Service in Washington.[20]

Concern about Shoreham and the precedent it might set in emergency planning began surfacing a year before (in 1983) in Washington. Senator Alan Simpson had the Senate Environment and Public Works Committee's Subcommittee on Nuclear Regulation, which he chairs, hold a hearing after Suffolk declared its opposition to Shoreham on the grounds that evacuation was not feasible. Simpson is one of the most outspoken proponents of nuclear power in the Senate.

The April 15, 1983, hearing "was intended," noted the *Newsday* account, "to assess reactor emergency planning generally, but Shoreham became the center of attention. All sides agree that Suffolk's opposition, and New York State's pledge not to interfere, constitute a national test of the ability of local officials to stop reactors."[21]

Simpson charged at the hearing that Suffolk had a "death grip" on Shoreham as a result of the evacuation issue. Earlier, he had coauthored a provision, included in NRC authorization resolutions for funds, providing for the NRC to expand the regulations it established after the Three Mile Island accident requiring emergency plans as a condition for the operation of nuclear plants. Originally, the plans were to be developed by local or state governments, but with the addition the NRC could consider utility-created evacuation plans. (LILCO's would be the first, and so far only, one considered.) Simpson said at the Washington hearing that this provision should be further altered because of Shoreham to—as *Newsday* phrased it—"force U.S. authorities to act on substitute plans submitted by utilities."

Suffolk, he said, was being "crafty" in using evacuation as a device to try to block Shoreham. Simpson charged that if Shoreham was abandoned, it would be "throwing $3.2 billion down a rat hole."

Simpson got even deeper into the situation with the Catacosinos takeover. On February 21, 1984, he wrote to Senator George Mitchell, Democrat of Maine, that

the uncertainty over who will implement the emergency plan at Shoreham has tremendous adverse financial consequences for the company. . . . The resulting uncertainty over whether the plant will even operate has *contributed significantly* to the poor financial condition of LILCO. . . . But aside from Shoreham it is essential, in my judgment, that we act promptly to stem the rising tide of investor wariness over the emergency planning issue, so that we avoid any future problems of this magnitude.

Two days later, after a meeting with Catacosinos in Washington, Simpson told reporters: "LILCO can't continue very much longer because this company will . . . go broke." At the same time, he released a bill he had drafted that—as *Newsday* explained—"provides for a small cadre of federal officials to manage an emergency plan using many utility workers."[22]

A delegation of Suffolk County legislators met with Simpson in June 1984 to explain in person why they were against Shoreham going into operation. Legislator Gregory Blass said the impression he got was that Simpson "is one of the nuclear power fanatics. He sees nothing wrong with nuclear power, and he cannot accept the possibility of the experience we have had at Shoreham. We sat in a wide circle in his office, and he was extremely irate at the attitude of local citizenry against nuclear power."[23]

Three days after Simpson's subcommittee held its 1983 hearing, the House Committee on Interior and Insular Affairs Subcommittee on Oversight and Investigations, chaired by Representative Edward

Markey, a Massachusetts Democrat, held a hearing on Long Island on "emergency preparedness and the licensing process for commercial nuclear power reactors" as they applied to Shoreham.[24]

This all-day session well framed how evacuation had become the central issue in the Shoreham situation and the positions of all sides—prior to the 1984 federal Shoreham push.

Markey opened it by reading from the NRC report of its "own special inquiry" into the Three Mile Island accident, which said that "preparations for an emergency response to a nuclear accident . . . are incomplete, untried, haphazard or nonexistent." The 1980 report, prepared by an NRC Special Inquiry Group led by Mitchell Rogovin, continued, saying that

> the ability to carry out an evacuation plan in the area of a nuclear plant depends much more on the existence of adequate county and local emergency plans than on a FEMA-approved or NRC-approved plan. . . . The county and local levels are where the action is and where the specific details of the plan must be worked out.

Markey declared:

> Today, because of the enactment of a series of significant regulatory actions in this area, even the NRC defines emergency preparedness as "essential" to the operations of a nuclear plant. Emergency preparedness is a requirement. And, in part, it is a requirement because the events at Three Mile Island exploded the myth which claimed that serious nuclear accidents cannot occur. So now, even the perpetually optimistic nuclear industry and the bureaucratic NRC are confronted not with the question of whether we should plan for nuclear accidents, but how the plan should be formulated.
>
> The Shoreham controversy has raised the question of whether the development of adequate and acceptable emergency plans can in fact be accomplished at certain plants. Suffolk County government officials have reached the conclusion that Long Island cannot be successfully evacuated and have decided not to participate further in the planning process.
>
> Emergency planning is a problematic issue for the nuclear industry because unlike many of the technical safety issues, the resolution of this requirement demands public involvement.

The public must be involved. Ironically, the nuclear industry
has often found that public participation is not in their best
interest because the more the public learns about nuclear energy, the more opposed to it they become.

Markey added, "The U.S. Congress is going to be watching very
closely this plant and the ramifications that it has for the rest of the
nuclear industry."
Suffolk County Executive Peter Cohalan testified:

The point I wish to emphasize to you today is that a battle is
raging on Long Island. The question is whether the government of Suffolk County will be permitted to act as the government it was constitutionally created to be, and thus to protect
the well-being of its own citizens; or, instead the Long Island
Lighting Company is going to get its way and try to put this
local government aside by forcing the Shoreham nuclear power
plant into operation against the safety interests of this county's
citizens.

He said, "We are confident that we will prevail."
He noted how

in February of this year, the government of Suffolk County
determined that it would be impossible to protect the health,
safety and welfare of the public in the event of a serious nuclear
accident at the Shoreham nuclear power plant. We found that
given the particular constraints of Long Island's narrow elongated geography, its quickly shifting wind patterns, its limited
and confined road network, and other local conditions, neither
evacuation nor sheltering would protect the public from the
harmful effects of a serious Shoreham accident. Accordingly,
the county resolved that we will not adopt or implement a local
radiological emergency response plan.

Cohalan went on, "The county took this action after carefully
reviewing the draft county emergency response plan and various related analyses, studies and surveys which were prepared for us by a
consulting team of nationally recognized experts." Some $600,000
was spent for the work, he said. Then the legislature "held eight days

of comprehensive hearings to take expert and public testimony," and "traveled to the Three Mile Island area to discuss with local officials there the lessons which they had learned from the TMI accident."

The 18-member Suffolk Legislature, which as Cohalan noted had a Republican majority, and he, also a Republican, made the decision not to adopt the local emergency plan for Shoreham because it had no other acceptable choice.

We are elected officials whose oath of office is to protect the public's health, safety and welfare and to tell the public the truth. Had we taken other action and chosen to adopt an emergency plan, we would *in reality* have put into place a mere "paper plan" which would lull the public into believing that they were being protected when they in fact were not. This government has resolved to have no part in creating such an illusion. In reaching this decision, we have acted with our eyes wide open, because we recognize that the absence of local emergency preparedness means that the Shoreham plant cannot operate.

Put into the record were summaries of what the county's consultants had determined and the emergency plan they proposed. There was also a listing of the consultants: Dr. Edward P. Radford, who chaired the National Academy of Sciences Committee on Biological Effects of Ionizing Radiation; Dr. Kai Erickson, professor of sociology at Yale University; Dr. Robert Budnitz, who specializes in assessing risks of nuclear plant accidents; Dr. Fred Finlayson, a specialist in the consequences of radiological accidents; Dr. Stephen Cole, professor of sociology at the State University of New York at Stony Brook; Dr. James H. Johnson, assistant professor of geology at the University of California at Los Angeles; Dr. Donald J. Zeigler, assistant professor of geology at Old Dominion University; staff members of PRC Voorhees of Virginia, a firm which specializes in traffic planning; and Dr. Phillip B. Herr, principal in Phillip B. Herr & Associates, a Boston-based planning organization, and associate professor of planning at the Massachusetts Institute of Technology.

Herr's comments when he presented the 777-page proposed emergency plan and accompanying analyses to the Suffolk Legislature were included:

I am satisfied that the response plan is just about as good as could be devised for this circumstance, and that the consequence estimates are fully supportable by scientific analysis. . . . In the event of a severe plant accident, there are likely to be substantial public health consequences, not because of any emergency plan failure, but because *that* plant at *that* location makes those consequences essentially unavoidable.

The problems, according to the summaries provided to the House panel, included Suffolk County's having a population of 1.3 million residents, a figure that "swells in summer when visitors are attracted to the county's many recreational facilities." (Eastern Long Island is a major resort area for the New York metropolitan area.) Because of the large numbers of people involved, and based on surveys of county residents and data on the numbers of people who fled after the Three Mile Island accident, although they were not advised to evacuate, the consultants concluded that in the event of a serious Shoreham accident there could be more than a million people attempting to flee.

Then there was the "the unique configuration of Long Island, an elongated, narrow island" with Shoreham located near its center. Long Island's only direct links to the mainland are crowded tunnels and bridges at its western end. "A 360-degree dispersal of evacuating traffic is impossible."

Meanwhile, Long Island's "limited road network presents problems for any attempted evacuation." The island's main west-east road is the Long Island Expressway, which has three lanes going in each direction and is regularly jammed bumper to bumper. There are four smaller west-east routes. People living east of the plant and trying to escape radioactivity emitted during a Shoreham accident would have to travel in the direction of the source of that radioactivity. People on the island's East End would be trapped.

"Furthermore, the unique nature of radiation—being an invisible hazard undetectable by human senses—is likely to cause behavior that will hamper the effectiveness of any evacuation as people attempt to retreat from a danger they cannot see, hear, touch or smell."

The county's consultants projected that it would take from 14 to 30 hours for people to flee what the NRC calls the Emergency Planning Zone, or EPZ, around Shoreham. They recommended that this zone be 20 miles in diameter rather than the ten LILCO sought. Reasons they cited included "studies of human evacuation behavior" and "unpredictable wind patterns" on Long Island.

Long Island's positioning in the Atlantic causes it to be a place where winds are often brisk and quickly changing, which would allow the plume of radioactive particles that would be discharged in a major nuclear plant accident to move rapidly and shift direction without warning. Many projections were made of varying patterns of radioactive fallout after a serious Shoreham accident. "Nothing less than a 20-mile EPZ will offer adequate protection to the public."

The consultants found: "A nuclear accident at Shoreham that caused the release of significant radiation into the environment of Suffolk County would have a serious impact on the health, safety and welfare of Suffolk County residents." Computer projections showed that "even if the public were to take protective actions," in the event of a severe core meltdown there could be up to "577 early fatalities" and "1,270 early injuries" just in the EPZ around Shoreham. There could also be up to 1,700 cancer fatalities and 3,500 cases of nonfatal cancer within this zone. Outside of it, there could be up to 7,000 cancer deaths and 17,400 nonfatal cancers. In addition, the radiation released would lead to genetic diseases in future generations. And there would be "serious psychological distress" caused.

The projection of it taking up to 14 to 30 hours just to get out of the EPZ made evacuation in "most sectors" of the EPZ "not an acceptable protective action." People would be sitting in cars as traffic came to a virtual halt, unprotected if the radiocactive plume moved into the area where they were stuck. "On the other hand, sheltering (staying indoors), the only other available protective action, would expose the residents of Suffolk County within the EPZ to unacceptable doses of radiation, resulting in thousands of increased incidences of cancer and cancer fatalities." Sheltering would also not be acceptable because most residences in Suffolk County are wood frame houses "which do not provide as much protection from radiation as do brick or stone buildings."

And the 14- to 30-hour estimate also did not take into account vehicle breakdowns. "Running out of gas . . . will be commonplace." It was noted that the "average automobile" would run out of fuel in ten hours and the wide-scale abandonment of cars that would result would completely immobilize an evacuation effort. Nor did those times take into account "aberrant behavior. Drivers may not behave in an orderly fashion after several hours in what they believe to be a life-threatening queue."

Complicating things further would be an attempt by people living outside the EPZ to try to flee, further tying up movement. This was

called the "shadow phenomenon." Studies were quoted that found
that more than 144,000 people living as far as 15 miles from the Three
Mile Island plant evacuated after the 1979 accident, even though the
governor of Pennsylvania advised that only pregnant women and pre-
school-aged children within five miles of the plant should leave—an
estimated 2,500 persons. Surveys were made of what Long Island
residents would do in the event of a serious Shoreham accident in
which evacuation of an area of ten miles around the plant was ordered. "The survey discovered that 430,000 families—about half the
population of Long Island—intended to leave their homes in such a
case." That would be well over a million people. "A tendency to
evacuate voluntarily in such large numbers has obvious and severe
implications for emergency planning."

Yet further, there would be "role conflict" among emergency personnel who would be involved in an evacuation, it was found. Surveys
were made of volunteer firemen and school bus drivers. Of those
surveyed, in the first category, 68 percent, and in the second, 69
percent, said they would care for their families first.

The resolution passed by the Suffolk Legislature was included in
the record. The five-page, single-spaced bill approved by 17 of the 18
members of the legislature concluded:

> Since no local radiological emergency plan for a serious nuclear
> accident will protect the health, welfare and safety of Suffolk
> County residents, and since the preparation and implementa-
> tion of any such plan would be misleading to the public . . . no
> radiological emergency plan for response to an accident at the
> Shoreham plant shall be adopted or implemented.

Testifying for the county at the hearing were also Frank Jones,
Police Commissioner Donald Dilworth, and Professor Kai Erikson.

Speaking for LILCO was a panel including then President
Wilfred Uhl, LILCO Vice President for Public Affairs Ira Freilicher,
and Hunton & Williams lawyer W. Taylor Reveley III.

"Suffolk County is attempting to veto Shoreham using the NRC
emergency planning regulations," charged Uhl. "In an attempt to
stop the plant, it is misusing the process that was set up to encourage
state and local cooperation and participation in emergency planning."

Uhl asserted:

Suffolk County is saying that under NRC regulations, whenever a local government thinks that the radiological risk from
nuclear power is unacceptable or that the nuclear plant is unacceptable for any other reason, that it can shut down the plant
by simply refusing to participate in emergency planning. This
theory, which applies to plants already operating as well as
plants not yet licensed, would, if accepted, shift the debate over
nuclear safety from the NRC to local legislatures, city councils,
and boards of supervisors across the country. And the licensing
of nuclear reactors would then, in effect, be decided by the
short-range political pressures with the vote changing each
time the political winds shifted.

Asked by Rep. Edward Markey about LILCO itself preparing an
evacuation plan, Uhl said: "I think certainly the utility can put together such a plan. Yes."

Markey then inquired whether LILCO could "implement that
plan apart from cooperation with the county government?"

Uhl replied that if a serious Shoreham emergency actually occurred, it was "inconceivable" that the county would not get involved.
Further, "I think that the [NRC] licensing board would be able to
assume that in a real emergency, the governor would order the county,
if the county would not do it itself . . . to participate."

There were sharp comments from Representative Jim Weaver as
he questioned Uhl. Asked by Weaver whether, "with the benefit of
hindsight, would you today build Shoreham?" Uhl said there was "no
alternative . . . even in retrospect, I have to view it as a wise decision."

Weaver then recounted the economics of the plant, its huge cost
overrun, and asked what would happen if it "does not operate. . . .
Who pays for it?"

"The consumers will pay for it," said Uhl.

"In other words," said Weaver,

the stupid decisions you made, the stupid process, you are going to put on the consumer—is that it? I would say the shareholders should pay. The shareholders should swallow it or
management should be fired across the board. . . . And now
you are in here trying to foist a faulty emergency preparedness
plan on us, that the county will not support, the government
will not support. You do not give a damn, apparently, about

your people, their financial resources or their safety. I just find this intolerable.

Also testifying were leaders of two anti-Shoreham groups.

Nora Bredes, executive coordinator of the Shoreham Opponents Coalition, told of how the 5,000-member group "was formed in the summer of 1979, after the Three Mile Island accident, when the severity of that event, the confusion of the response, and the actual, required evacuation of pregnant women and children brought home to many of us here the threat posed by the Shoreham plant, nestled in our community's backyard." It was established to intervene in NRC hearings on Shoreham because

> we expected that the NRC's apparent chagrin and then resolve to improve after the Three Mile Island accident would make our legal intervention worth our time and resources. We believed then, as we still do, that Long Island is an unsuitable and dangerous site for a nuclear power plant. Our neighborhoods are too densely populated; the road network is too congested; and, with the Atlantic Ocean and Long Island Sound surrounding us on three sides with New York City on the fourth, we have no easy, expeditious way to escape the consequences of a large scale accident.

She also noted how in 1970, "the Lloyd Harbor Study Group, our figurative grandparent," raised the evacuation issue at the construction permit hearings for Shoreham, but LILCO and the federal government refused to consider the matter. She also said that "today Congress should recognize that its citizens have come of age. The patronizing attitude of the government is inappropriate and outmoded. We insist that if we had been given the right to vote for or against Shoreham, we, LILCO, the NRC, the courts and Congress, would not now be facing the uncertain, expensive and perhaps tragic outcome of the Shoreham licensing battle."

Leon Campo, chairman of the People's Action Coalition, spoke of how

> in Harrisburg, Pennsylvania, there stands a monument of steel and concrete filled with radioactivity. . . . As this monument is likely to stand as long as the one dedicated to George Washing-

ton and those in memory of Thomas Jefferson and Abraham Lincoln, it is imperative that its significance be appreciated. The Three Mile Island monument is a lasting reminder of our national government's indifference rather than its commitment to public safety, of Congress' determination to ensure the well-being of monopoly utilities to the detriment of the citizens, of the Nuclear Regulatory Commission's dedication to nuclear promotion at the expense of nuclear protection.

Campo criticized Alan Simpson and his plan to force federal government approval of utility evacuation plans.

Senator Simpson, who hails from Wyoming, the least populous state in the union, a state which has, in total, approximately one-third the residents of Suffolk County . . . does not appreciate that in the event of a malfunction at Shoreham, the number of automobiles on the roadways will exceed the entire population of Wyoming!

Campo charged that "Senator Simpson doesn't care about our safety . . . he is willing to set aside safety in behalf of LILCO and its monopoly friends." He further alleged that Simpson, "who represents more deer, jackrabbits and apparently jackasses than people, through blind loyalty may indeed keep his pledge to the utility monopolies." He also charged that Representative Carney, present for the hearing, was part of "the LILCO political network." However, Representative Thomas Downey asked that all these latter comments "be deleted from the record."

"Courtesy begets courtesy," agreed Representative Ron Marlenee of Montana, the ranking Republican on the committee, about Downey's motion. The official record of the hearing thus does not carry these charges.

Campo went on to argue that "no utility in the United States could or would submit what exists at Shoreham as a design for a nuclear power plant," and "LILCO's experiment with its first nuclear power project does not end when construction is terminated. Indeed, it only begins with the granting of a license."

Also testifying was a delegation of Brookhaven National Laboratory scientists, including Andrew Hull and Joseph Hendrie, the NRC chairman when the Three Mile Island accident happened.

Hull raised the

question [of] whether or not we have planned for other emergencies from other hazardous, obnoxious, toxic agents, fires,
floods, you name it, on anywhere in this level. And I somehow
am concerned as a health professional, which I am, as a health
physicist, that somehow we are not getting equal time in making a sensible assessment.

He noted a former emergency management director of Pennsylvania
said at a conference they attended in Sweden "that he had difficulty
seeing why we needed emergency plans for nuclear incidents that
were very far . . . outside the envelope for emergency planning in
general." Hull went on, "I somehow think we are selecting one particular thing when, as a health professional, I think that we ought to
take a look at where we are spending our money on emergency planning in general."

Hendrie spoke about "regulatory safety requirements that we imposed after Three Mile Island," which included the evacuation plan
regulation.

As we have thought about the Three Mile Island accident, and
the scientific studies have been done, it becomes more and more
clear that our previous estimates of the amount of radioactive
material that would come out of one of these plants even in the
worst accident was very much overestimated in those days. And
my best judgment now is that it is very unlikely that even the
worst reactor accident would produce any prompt fatalities.

Markey closed the Shoreham hearing by saying this "lays the
groundwork for further follow-up because this is not an isolated instance."

He declared: "It has come to this. It has come to Long Island. To
the most expensive nuclear power plant ever built. It has come to a
situation where after forty years, $40 billion in government subsidies,
one near meltdown, hundreds of near misses . . . now, Shoreham."

Representative Markey with the Subcommittee on Oversight and
Investigations and a second larger panel he was subsequently named
to chair, the Subcommittee on Energy Conservation and Power, indeed continued to follow up.

In July 1983, Markey wrote to Donald Hodel, noting that he had read a news article about a memorandum by Hodel "about events in New York State concerning emergency preparedness plans for serious nuclear reactor accidents." Markey asked for a copy of the memorandum reportedly sent to William A. Vaughan, the DOE assistant secretary for environmental protection, safety and emergency preparedness, "and his response to you on this subject. Additionally, I would like to receive copies of all documents concerning emergency preparedness for nuclear reactor accidents and the problems of implementing these plans written by, sent to, or routed through DOE since January 1983."

Hodel replied that "we would be pleased to make the Department's files on this subject available for your staff for review."

Members of Markey's committee staff then obtained copies of a 1983 memo from Hodel to Vaughan in which Hodel asserted:

The breakdown of Federal, state, local and private utility co-operation in developing and implementing a workable emergency evacuation plan in the event of a serious accident at a nuclear powerplant has become an issue of national significance. In two current cases in New York State involving the Shoreham and Indian Point reactors, either or both state and local authorities have declined to participate in establishing emergency evacuation procedures that are acceptable to the Federal Emergency Management Agency. Failure to resolve this deadlock will mean that these nuclear powerplants must remain idle, thereby penalizing economically their respective utility service areas. It also may establish a precedent that will complicate licensing power plants in other states. In view of these circumstances and the potential threat to the viability of the nuclear power industry, I would like for you to establish a DOE Working Group with yourself as chairman . . . to advise us of appropriate and necessary Federal Actions to remedy this situation. You should coordinate this activity with the FEMA, the NRC, and the National Security Council, and should keep appropriate Congressional staff advised.

Hodel's memorandum named this group the "DOE Working Group on Nuclear Emergency Evacuation Planning."

Vaughan's reply said:

There are two routes that the Working Group is pursuing: first, involving the short-term concerns, to determine what can be done to permit the Indian Point Plant to keep operating and to facilitate the Shoreham Plant's obtaining an operating license; second, to develop certain legislative and regulatory fixes to solve the generic problem and ensure that these situations do not recur elsewhere, including DOE nuclear facilities.

Markey and his staff stayed on the situation and later obtained papers from DOE files documenting the intense post-January 1984 Reagan administration push for Shoreham—papers pointing to the sort of "scandal" attorney Herbert Brown referred to.

They included a DOE summary, handwritten in block letters, of a meeting between DOE and FEMA officials on April 4, 1984, concerning the possibility of an "exercise" of a Shoreham evacuation plan.

It stated:

1. EXERCISE CAN BE SOMEWHAT CREDIBLE.

2. STATE IS VITAL.

3. NEXT STEP IS DEVELOPMENT OF EXERCISE PLAN—SITE SPECIFIC. . . .

4. FEMA WOULD BE WILLING TO PREPARE STRAW-MAN EXERCISE PLAN WITHIN A WEEK. THEN ASK FOR REVIEW BY DOE.

5. COULD HAVE NRC WRITE TO FEMA AND ASK THEM HOW FEMA WOULD DO SUCH AN EXERCISE. FEMA THEN SEND BACK THE PLAN, OR ALTERNA-TIVELY, FEMA MAKE AN ANNOUNCEMENT.

6. FEMA MUST BE NEUTRAL, NOT AN ADVOCATE.

The three-page summary went on to relate a meeting between Hodel and FEMA Director Louis O. Giuffrida: "HODEL/GIUF-FRIDA MTG TENTATIVELY SET FOR WEDNESDAY. IMPOR-TANT FOR LILCO TO KNOW THIS SO THEY DON'T THROW IN THE TOWEL. APRIL 27 LINE OF CREDIT DUE."

According to Richard Udell, a committee staff consultant to Markey, Charles Mallory's Hunton & Williams business card was stapled to the upper right-hand corner on at least a dozen of the items obtained from the DOE files.

STEPS TO IMPLEMENT A FEMA TEST CONCEPT

STEPS	RESPONSIBILITY
o Agreement on the General Concept of FEMA Implementation	DOE/Hodel
o FEMA-DOE Memorandum of Understanding on DOE Support Role	FEMA-DOE /OGC
o Directive to FEMA that they will test implementation of the plan (or alternatively, FEMA statement on their own authority)	White House (FEMA)
o Revised Radiological Emergency Response Plan submitted that addresses FEMA-identified deficiencies	LILCO (Support by FEMA, DOE-Emergency Operations, General Counsel, Nuclear Safety)
o Legal Issues Addressed by the "conceptual simulation approach". Can the exercise of "police powers" be simulated?	FEMA (DOE support by OGC)
o FEMA notifies State of New York and Suffolk County officials of intention to conduct a test of the Shoreham Plant.	FEMA
o FEMA consults with DOE and other agencies to determine necessary scope of the test. Determine generic elements of Shoreham Plan that do not require actual test because they have already been demonstrated (i.e., St. Lucie, etc).	FEMA (DOE support by Office of Nuclear Safety)
o Specific Test Plan developed (practical approach would be to use the St. Lucie Test Plan as a starting point) for the FEMA exercise.	FEMA, NRC (DOE support by Office of Nuclear Safety, Emergency Operations, Naval Reactors)
o FEMA, LILCO, DOE, and other agencies plan practical logistics for the test. Identify specific resources from DOE. Two or three meetings of a test management team.	FEMA (DOE support by Office of Nuclear Safety)
o Conduct Test.	LILCO, FEMA, DOE (Nuclear Safety) Other Fed. Agencies

Department of Energy memo concerning the necessary "steps to implement" a FEMA test of LILCO's Shoreham evacuation plan.

Among the documents was a "Draft Agenda" for a DOE meeting with LILCO representatives on April 6, an agenda prepared by Donald Irwin, another lawyer from Hunton & Williams, LILCO's law firm.

The Thomas E. Dillon to whom the "Draft Agenda" was directed is a senior DOE official. The handwritten notes on the document were there when it was obtained by Markey's staff, apparently written on the "Draft Agenda" by a DOE official.

Notice under "Urgency of Need for Federal Participation," the reference to "1. Financial crisis at LILCO" and, handwritten, "LOANS DUE 4/27 OF $250–$500 MILLION." Below that, also handwritten, is LILCO's financial dilemma cryptically outlined: "NET WORTH $8 B SHOREHAM $3.8 B."

The "LERO" referred to on the bottom of the page is the acronym for "Local Emergency Response Organization," created by LILCO in 1983. LILCO announced that LERO, made up of LILCO workers, would supervise evacuation of the public in the event of a serious Shoreham accident in the face of county and state government refusal to approve or implement a Shoreham evacuation plan.

The "Draft Agenda" went on in its following three pages to detail "Areas in which LILCO needs legal authority conferred by federal government." These included:

Exercise of command and control functions in making and implementing protective evacuation (shelter v. evacuate) recommendations for 10 and 50 mile EPZ, and for recovery/re-entry. . . . Traffic control, direction and facilitation by LERO traffic guides: implementation of traffic control strategies (blocking or rerouting traffic lanes, traffic direction. . . . Exercising law enforcement functions.

The agenda continued, "Specific relationships with which LILCO needs help" included with "School Boards" to formulate "plans for dismissal of children within the EPZ" and to make school "buses available for (a) evacuation of children from schools within EPZ (b) evacuation of general public from within EPZ," and in "developing plans for sheltering children."

A handwritten summary of that April 6 meeting declared:

1. WILL FEMA PARTICIPATE IN TEST IF NYS JOINS SUIT TO STOP THEM?

2. LILCO HAS TESTED EVERYTHING BUT TRAFFIC
CONTROL. THERE IS A LILCO PLAN TO DO THIS AND
USE COUNTY PEOPLE IF THEY ARE AVAILABLE.
3. FEMA EXERCISE PLAN AVAILABLE TO US NEXT
WEDNESDAY PER DILLON.
4. TESTING SCHEDULE:
TABLE TOP: 2 MONTHS (FEMA)
JUNE DATE—FEMA
LILCO CAN BE READY 5–6 WEEKS
5. NEXT WEEK: HODEL/GIUFFREDA/KEYWORTH
THURSDAY/FRIDAY (FRIDAY LIKELY)

NEED FOR FRIDAY:
1. PRESS RELEASE—FEMA STEVE & TOM
2. LETTERS TO COHALEN [sic], CUOMO, PALLA-
DINO
3. BASIS OF AUTHORITY—COULD BE IN PLAN—
STEVE WILL DO THIS (OR FEMA)
4. PHONE CALLS AND LETTERS . . .

A handwritten April 17, 1984, DOE memo entitled "Critical Issues," listed these "Presumptions":

1. Suffolk Co. will not participate in a real emergency.
Must represent real life.
2. Governor must not object.
3. NRC review & approval.
4. Resources—DOE, USDA, NNS, EPA, DOC, DOT . . .
5. Congressional review & approval.
6. Did not address . . . Brookhaven C & C [command and
control] role.
7. Accelerated contracting.

The emphasis throughout the DOE documents was that with the
Federal Emergency Management Agency assisting LILCO, the Shore-
ham evacuation issue could be overcome.
Said a May 4, 1984, DOE analysis:

The clear gap at this time is the need for a test of the LILCO
plan. Recently, FEMA informed NRC that it is "determining
the circumstances under which it might prepare a plan to exer-

cise the utility's off-site emergency plan." As part of that letter, FEMA stated that they had "authority to prepare a plan for comprehensive emergency response by the Federal Government at Shoreham in conjunction with the LILCO off-site emergency response plan" and that FEMA "may also undertake an exercise of such a plan under existing authority." If FEMA were to develop and test such a plan, there is a high probability that it would be a sufficient basis for licensing Shoreham. . . . We encourage FEMA to develop and test the plan. There is a good likelihood that such actions would provide a basis for resolving this Federal barrier to operation of the Shoreham plant.

Another undated DOE memo said:

It should be presumed that public officials will discharge the public duties and responsibilities conferred upon them, and will cooperate with federal authorities and private enterprises to take reasonable measures to protect public health and safety. It would appear that the current impasse regarding the Shoreham plant could be broken if an otherwise acceptable LILCO emergency plan were successfully tested on the basis of such a presumption. The purpose of the test would be to demonstrate that, notwithstanding the present lack of cooperation by state and local authorities, there is an adequate capability to respond to an emergency at the Shoreham plant, thus allowing LILCO to make the alternative showing required to obtain an operating license.

It continued: "In order to ensure that the test involves no violation of state or local law, the test should rely upon simulation of certain tasks expected to be performed by state or local authorities in an actual emergency." In early 1986, the Reagan administration, in fact, used federal personnel and people hired by a consultant to "simulate" the roles of Suffolk County and New York State officials in a drill of the LILCO Shoreham evacuation plan.

While obtaining the DOE papers, Markey also kept tabs on NRC actions on Shoreham—although he had more difficulty getting NRC documents and, at one point, had to threaten the NRC with use of Congressional subpoena power.

The Shoreham nuclear plant under construction, June 1977. *Photo credit: Karl Grossman*

On March 28, 1984, he wrote Nunzio Palladino about a March 20 memorandum he had come across from Palladino to the other NRC commissioners citing "LICENSING DELAYS" for nuclear plants. In it, under "steps," Palladino listed "For Shoreham, have the Commission consider a proposal from OGC [Office of General Counsel] for an expedited hearing on the diesel problem, or proposals for other possible actions so that at least a low power decision might be possible while awaiting resolution of the emergency planning issue."

Markey told Palladino:

I find your statement pertaining to the Shoreham case particularly disturbing. . . . Clearly this statement presents the reasonable inference that you have pre-judged the merits of this regulatory proceeding in three critical respects: (1) that the plant should receive a low power license regardless of its use of diesel generators that are known to be defective; (2) that there will be a "resolution of the emergency planning issue" and the plant will eventually receive a full power license; and (3) that the procedural rights and substantive comments of the intervenors do not have to be met and heard.

Markey said, "if you have made these pre-judgments, I believe it is imperative that you immediately recuse [excuse] yourself from voting on either the low power or full power license for Shoreham. If your intention was different, then I think you should clarify your views and reconsider your request for an 'expedited' process."

He also asked for "all documents leading to or resulting from your March 20, 1984 memorandum."

By April 12, his subcommittee still hadn't received any documents, and Markey asked for them "within five working days."

Further, he pressed Palladino about a meeting Palladino held on March 16, 1984, concerning Shoreham at which top NRC staff members were present, including the agency's executive director for operations, director of the Office of Nuclear Reactor Regulation, the executive legal director, and the NRC's chief administrative law judge, B. Paul "Tony" Cotter, Jr. Markey said that "apparently as an outgrowth of that meeting, and your subsequent memoranda, Judge Cotter appointed a new board to consider on an expedited basis" LILCO's application for a low-power license for Shoreham. A month before, on February 22, an NRC board had refused to grant LILCO a license because of chronic problems with Shoreham's back-up diesel generators. Among the subsequent memoranda Markey referred to was "a follow-up memorandum to the other Commissioners that included a proposed order drafted by Judge Cotter and a paper written by your own staff that would have set forth an expedited schedule in which the Shoreham low power licensing proceeding would be completed in thirty to sixty days."

Markey advised Palladino:

> In order that public confidence can be restored, if possible, to what has become an unseemly and confused process, I think that it is essential that you explain why you believe the Shoreham proceeding should be expedited as well as your reason for circulating the draft order prepared prior to hearing from and resolving the views of all parties.

Markey also again asked Palladino to remove himself from the Shoreham case.

Herbert Brown, through the Freedom of Information Act, subsequently obtained notes taken at the March 16 meeting by Cotter. At the chairman's meeting, wrote Cotter, it was warned that LILCO "will go bankrupt" if the earlier licensing board decision stood, and LILCO was now seeking to "get around diesel issue." Passages from the notes were included in a motion brought by Suffolk and New York State before the NRC for Palladino to either excuse himself from the Shoreham case or, if he refused, be disqualified.

The motion also reported that on February 24, 1984 (two days after the earlier licensing board decision), Catacosinos "had met with the NRC commissioners." Then, in a March 9 letter to LILCO stockholders, Catacosinos spoke of meeting with federal officials saying they now had a "greater understanding . . . of the crisis the company faces" and that "a timely resolution of the Shoreham situation and a resolution of the Company's critical cash shortage are essential to the continued viability of LILCO."

Charged the motion: "The 'greater understanding' of federal officials to which Dr. Catacosinos referred thus made itself felt in and through Chairman Palladino's office."

Palladino refused to excuse himself from the case. He insisted, "I see nothing in the filings of the parties, or in the underlying facts which demonstrates that I should take myself out of the proceeding."

Markey, meanwhile, found out about a closed-door NRC meeting on Shoreham and, in an April 24 letter to Palladino, asked that his subcommittee "be provided immediately with a copy of the transcript from yesterday's closed Commission meeting on the Shoreham proceeding."

He also asked, in an April 25 letter, for the other NRC documents he had been asking for:

> I am greatly alarmed and disappointed that the Commission has refused to keep Congress fully and currently informed. I believe that the Commission's refusal is unwarranted and at variance with the clear direction of the Atomic Energy Act. Because the Commission undoubtedly understands that it cannot lawfully withhold these documents, I am compelled to conclude that its refusal is designed to frustrate the oversight responsibilities of the Subcommittee. The unfortunate but inevitable inference created by this refusal is that the Commission is attempting to conceal information that would reveal it has acted improperly.

Markey warned that he would "present a motion authorizing the issuance of a subpoena *duces tecum* for the material. I would appreciate a written response either supplying the documents or providing your explanation for denial by the close of business today."

Palladino replied in an April 26 letter that the NRC "met to discuss your request," and a majority "voted against releasing the transcript in question. . . . In our view, no conceivable useful purpose could be served by breaching the confidentiality of that discussion." However, said Palladino, "we are at this time actively engaged in gathering documents which may fall within the categories requested in your letters."

Then the NRC began providing documents. And, on June 21, 1984, Palladino advised Markey that he had decided not "to participate in any further Shoreham proceedings." That was only temporary. In September, he was back, claiming, "It may be argued that to recuse myself would remove the shadow of doubt in some persons' minds about the propriety of the Shoreham proceeding," but "I believe firmly that the responsibilities of a commissioner are not optional."

Among the documents Markey finally obtained from the NRC were scrawled notes by Palladino—nearly indecipherable—of the

March 16 meeting. Under "Shoreham:" were "1. Applicant to file
proposal on diesel generation next week. 2. Staff Review—30 days. 3.
What level of risk is acceptable for this power. Is there a need for
emergency diesel generation at this power for this plant." The notes
also included the line: "Also look at reversing Bd. decision," referring
to the licensing board's decision the prior month denying LILCO a
low-power license.

Another NRC document obtained was a memorandum from Pal-
ladino to the other NRC commissioners dated April 17, 1984, titled
"MEETING WITH SECRETARY HODEL" and also marked "LIM-
ITED DISTRIBUTION." The memo told of

> my discussion with Secretary Hodel concerning the general
> malaise of the nuclear industry, and the confidence of investors
> in nuclear power. The point here was that even those plants not
> in trouble could be affected by loss of confidence. Two issues in
> particular were raised by the Secretary: (a) construction qual-
> ity assurance; and (2) emergency planning. . . . On emergency
> planning, the Secretary indicated that DOE was working with
> FEMA about specific ways the government may be able to
> provide police powers when state or local governments do not
> participate in emergency planning. The Executive Branch may
> have more to say on this general subject later.

Taking a critical stance on the NRC's actions on Shoreham—
indeed many of its actions—has been James Asselstine. Reagan appointed Asselstine as NRC commissioner in 1982. It would have
seemed that Asselstine would follow the administration's heavily pro-
nuclear line: He had been Alan Simpson's counsel on the Subcommittee on Nuclear Regulation from 1978 to 1981, for five years a staff
attorney with the NRC, and for two years assistant counsel to the pro-
nuclear Congressional Joint Committee on Atomic Energy.

But seeing firsthand the workings of the agency as an NRC commissioner, Asselstine became a voice and vote of dissent on the Reagan
NRC.

When the commissioners appeared before Markey's subcommittee
on May 17, 1984, for a hearing on the NRC's push for getting Shoreham licensed to operate, Asselstine said that Palladino had

> created the appearance of improper judicial conduct. . . . Any
> reasonable outside observer would conclude that by his actions,

the chairman had abandoned his role as the ultimate judge in this proceeding and had instead become an advocate for a particular outcome in the case—the issuance of a low-power decision within an unreasonably short time period.[25]

Palladino defended his actions at that hearing. They were also defended by Thomas M. Roberts and another Reagan appointee on the panel, Frederick M. Bernthal. Before being named an NRC commissioner, Bernthal, from Oak Ridge, Tennessee, was an aide to Senator Howard Baker and known as a principal promoter on Capitol Hill of the proposed Clinch River breeder reactor.

At a July 1985 National Science Foundation-supported workshop on nuclear power ("Know Nukes Institute") at the Antioch/New England Graduate School in New Hampshire, Asselstine said that he saw two Reagan administration strategies to get Shoreham into commercial operation. One involved the federal government saying, " 'We will step in,' and barracksing a group of federal people" at Shoreham to supervise an evacuation. The second involved going along with a nuclear industry claim that "source terms" for a nuclear accident should be changed, that an accident would not be as serious as had been thought, and so the evacuation zone could be reduced. He stressed there was no basis in fact for this.

Asselstine told the workshop, at which the author also spoke, that people can talk about risks in many of the ways energy is produced, but the "one big difference" about nuclear power is its "potential for highly catastrophic accidents." He also noted the involuntary quality of the nuclear risk. He cited a new NRC assessment that the chances of a core meltdown at a nuclear plant by the year 2005 were about 50-50. "In my personal judgment that level of risk is not acceptable," he said.

There was "complacency" toward nuclear plant safety at the NRC before Three Mile Island, he related. The attitude was that safety is "nice to have, but not like pumps and valves in a plant," not a vital component. A sort of denial held sway, wishful thinking that "severe accidents were remote, they were incredible." The Three Mile Island mishap showed the NRC that "severe accidents can happen." But soon "the shock of the accident had worn off" and "the kind of complacency that existed before Three Mile Island" returned.

Asselstine, a University of Virginia Law School-trained attorney, also expressed his concern for "fairness." He said he regarded it as "important" that government "adhere to procedural rules." But he said the NRC majority, in its rush to license nuclear plants, was not particularly concerned about this.

On evacuation, he said the NRC has "no authority over state and local government. We can't order state and local government to participate" in an evacuation plan. However, "emergency planning is not recognized as a very important factor by a majority of the commission now," he told the workshop.

The Union of Concerned Scientists, a group involved in nuclear plant safety, nuclear arms and national energy policy, strongly criticized the NRC's handling of Shoreham—particularly the 1984 attempt to expedite its licensing—in a report entitled, "SAFETY SECOND: A Critical Evaluation of the NRC's First Decade."[26] The 228-page report concluded, "The NRC, like its predecessor, the Atomic Energy Commission, too often behaves as a promoter of nuclear power rather than a tough regulator. As a result, the NRC is not living up to its primary responsibility: ensuring the public's health and safety."

The group criticized the NRC for, among other things, not enforcing "its own rules and regulations firmly and consistently," for having a "far too trusting and comfortable relationship" with the nuclear industry, for refusing to deal with general safety issues concerning nuclear plants, and for treating "as a nuisance . . . public participation in license proceedings, a right conveyed by federal law and protected time and again by federal courts."

According to the Union of Concerned Scientists, after ten years in existence, the NRC had a record that was "inadequate and disappointing." The scientists stated that "complacent and short-sighted attitudes of many NRC commissioners and high-level staff are at the root of the agency's poor performance."

Markey's view of the NRC: "There's this coziness with the nuclear industry, that's part of the problem. There's also an incompetence in the assumption that nuclear power is inherently safe. All these have combined to turn the commission into a lapdog rather than a watchdog."[27]

The new NRC licensing board that Nunzio Palladino had created in 1984 to expedite Shoreham getting a low-power license was led by the NRC's most senior administrative law judge, Marshall E. Miller. It also included Elizabeth Johnson, a nuclear physicist at Oak Ridge National Laboratory, and Glenn Bright, a nuclear physicist who for 20 years had worked for the Aerojet Nuclear Company.

"They couldn't have gotten more of a kangaroo court unless they went to Australia," said Suffolk County Deputy Executive Frank Jones.[28]

The board gave intervenors a record ten days (including Good Friday and Easter) for taking depositions from witnesses, hiring consultants and otherwise preparing for the new set of hearings. The NRC sent out a press release saying that the board would meet not only five days a week but on weekends "if necessary"—an unprecedented NRC licensing board schedule.

"The Reagan administration is friendlier to big business and big money than it is to families, communities and local government," said Nora Bredes. "In spite of our unified voice and actions, powerful federal bureaucracies guided by the Reagan White House, the DOE, the NRC and FEMA, are determined to ignore us and the law in order to license Shoreham. It is the kind of tyranical maneuver our government was formed to prevent."[29]

"Due process has died," said Herbert Brown.

Governor Mario Cuomo said the federal government was "going crazy running around avoiding all procedures and laws, hellbent on getting that plant into operation."

On April 24, 1984, the board's first day of hearings in Hauppauge, Betty Hoye of Shelter Island said: "The notoriety of this board has preceded it to this hearing room. It is no secret that the compelling circumstances motivating Miller and company is the impending financial demise of LILCO." She said that LILCO's financial situation was "not a proper concern of the NRC," and that public safety was.

As anti-Shoreham demonstrators marched outside, the board, under heavy police guard, convened again the following day. But by midday, Miller had to announce that hearings were suspended.

In U.S. District court in Washington, Judge Norma Holloway Johnson had just issued an injunction against the expedited Shoreham schedule. There was a possibility of serious constitutional violations of due process, ruled the judge, as she backed an appeal to the courts brought by Suffolk County and New York State. She ruled that "the plaintiffs have raised serious questions concerning the propriety of the decision to expedite the hearing . . . to such an extent that the interested parties cannot be fairly heard," and that "the expedited hearing schedule threatens to make the plaintiffs' participation . . . meaningless."

"The juggernaut's been stopped," said Frank Jones.

"There isn't any justice," complained William Museler, then the director of LILCO's nuclear office.

The following month, the Reagan administration would take a low profile on Shoreham—for a while.

The presidential election was coming up and the Reagan administration push on Shoreham was hurting the president on Long Island. As Harrison Raine wrote in the July 7, 1984, *New York Daily News*:

> President Reagan's political planners have passed the word to the White House and federal agencies that pro-nuclear power advocates in the Nuclear Regulatory Commission and the Energy Department are doing the President no favors by trying to clear the way for operation of the Shoreham reactor on Long Island. That's why efforts by NRC Chairman Nunzio Palladino and Energy Secretary Donald Hodel to help LILCO open the reactor have ceased. The suburbs of New York City, especially Long Island, are considered the key to a Reagan win in the state and its electoral votes. "Shoreham could have killed us," said one Reaganite.

Politics even caused Reagan to go further on Shoreham—to write, in order to rescue pro-Shoreham Representative William Carney, that he did not "favor the imposition of Federal Government authority over the objections of state and local governments" to a Shoreham evacuation plan.

Shoreham, long a hot political issue on Long Island, had become even hotter. It was *the* issue in the race in New York's First Congressional District, which includes Shoreham and where the incumbent was Carney, who has had extremely close ties with the Reagan administration. Now a Republican, Carney was earlier a Conservative, the first member of New York State's Conservative Party to be elected to the House of Representatives.

In April, George Hochbrueckner, a Democratic state assemblyman who had managed to get elected and reelected over a ten-year period in a largely Republican district, announced he would be seeking the Democratic nomination to run against Carney. Shoreham was Hochbrueckner's principal issue. "If William Carney had been part of the process in opposition to that plant, we might not have to see in this time in history the NRC doing an end run around the desires of the Suffolk County legislature, the county executive, as well as the governor of this state," Hochbrueckner said as he announced his candidacy.[30] Hochbrueckner's campaign advertisements included one featuring a Carney comment to a constituent opposed to Shoreham who had come to see him: "Look, if you're really concerned about the economics and safety of Shoreham, then move."

Also in April, Legislator Gregory Blass announced he was opposing Carney in the Republican primary. The heading of his initial press release stated: "CONGRESSIONAL 'CONNECTION' TO UTILITIES AND LOW POWER LICENSING FOR SHOREHAM." The connection was Carney. "Why are Florida Power and Light, Baltimore Gas and Electric, Boston Edison Co., Texas Utility Co., and San Diego Gas and Electric so interested in someone who is supposed to be *our* congressman, representing the people and not utilities throughout the nation?"[31] Blass' statement went on to list campaign contributions to Carney since his first election in 1978 from utility and nuclear industry PACs. Among other utility PACs listed as providing money to Carney were those of General Public Utilities, Georgia Power Company, Louisiana Power & Light, Consumers Power Company, Gulf States Utilities, Detroit Edison, Con Edison—and LILCO. There were campaign contributions from GE, Westinghouse and Stone & Webster PACs and the National Utility Contractors Association. Repeated contributions were made by the Construction Congress Committee of the Edison Electric Institute.

"Utility lobbyists have poured many thousands of dollars into the incumbent's campaign treasury over the past six years," said Blass, alleging a "connection" between these monies, Carney's voting record and his "silence on the latest railroading for Shoreham."

Meanwhile, as part of the Reagan administration publicly downplaying its Shoreham push, Donald Hodel gave an interview (*Newsday*, May 24, 1984) to say that the prospects for a drill involving LILCO's evacuation plan for Shoreham appeared "absolutely hopeless" because of the opposition of Governor Cuomo. "We are not going to seek to impose it over county and state objections," he said.

Catacosinos continued to fight for Shoreham, rejecting an offer by Cuomo for LILCO to abandon the nuclear project in return for the state agreeing to provide financial aid to keep LILCO without Shoreham solvent. Cuomo told Catacosinos that as a matter of public safety—to protect "the safety of our residents"—he was opposed to

Shoreham. He said he would have Shoreham put into a new, special PSC category—"nonlicensable" nuclear plant.

Catacosinos said no to the offer, even though the apparently the federal drive was over. "We haven't had any meetings with the Department of Energy on Shoreham in the last several weeks," said James Holton, a FEMA public relations person.

"The feds told him to hold on until after the election."

That, said Long Island environmentalist and builder Maurice Barbash, was the message he had gotten from high LILCO executives about what the Reagan administration was now telling Catacosinos. Barbash, former leader in the creation of the Fire Island National Seashore, was becoming active in the Shoreham situation due to his appointment to a Suffolk County "blue ribbon" committee formed to analyze the economics of Shoreham being abandoned.

Barbash told this author that LILCO executives he knew from community activities were telling him that the Reagan administration's message to Catacosinos in mid-1984 was that if LILCO could somehow hold on until a Reagan reelection, then a second-term Reagan administration would manage to put Shoreham in operation.[32]

In September, Blass received 48 percent of the primary vote, nearly winning over Carney—quite an accomplishment considering that Carney had organization support. Blass refused to support Carney "unless he reconsiders" his Shoreham stand.

Democrat Hochbrueckner continued to zero in on Carney over Shoreham. Carney, according to a source long close to him, then made a series of telephone calls to the White House. He asked, said the source, that the NRC take no action on Shoreham until after the election—a decision by the NRC on LILCO loading fuel into the plant and testing it at "sub-criticality" was scheduled—and also for a letter from Reagan that he could use to politically defuse the Shoreham issue. He also arranged for a letter from Hodel.

On October 18, 1984, two weeks before election, Carney held a press conference at which he displayed the letters.

The "Dear Bill" letter from Hodel, dated October 2, said:

> I want to take this opportunity to update you on our activities regarding the Shoreham nuclear power plant. As we assured you last spring and at other times when we discussed the concerns of the citizens of Long Island regarding Shoreham, the Department of Energy does not favor the imposition of

Federal Government authority over the objections of any state and local governments in matters regarding the adequacy of an emergency evacuation plan for a nuclear power plant such as Shoreham. Our position is clear. The Reagan Administration has always had faith in the ability of American citizens and local elected officials to handle the problems which confront them directly. As one of Long Island's most capable and vigorous elected officials, your advice and counsel regarding energy and economic policies which affect the future of your constituents have been extremely valuable to President Reagan and me. . . . You have been a vigorous advocate of the interests of Long Island, especially in behalf of Brookhaven National Laboratory and other Federal facilities. I look forward to your continued wise counsel on these and other issues in the years ahead.

The letter from Reagan read:

I want you to know of my appreciation for your continuing contributions to and support of my Administration. Your leadership and courage have been determining factors in the progress we have made in the last two years. On a matter of particular concern to you and the people of Eastern Long Island, I wish to repeat Secretary Hodel's assurance to you that this Administration does not favor the imposition of Federal Government authority over the objections of state and local governments in matters regarding an emergency evacuation plan for a nuclear power plant such as Shoreham. Your concern for the safety of the people of Long Island is paramount and shared by the Secretary and me. Thank you again for your support. I look forward to working with you in the years ahead.

Carney issued a press release headed: "CARNEY WINS WHITE HOUSE PLEDGE ON SHOREHAM." The press release quoted Carney as saying he was "delighted with the Administration's firm reaffirmation of its belief that this should be a local matter, decided by local officials. The President has done a great service for the people of Long Island by alleviating their concerns." At his press conference, he also said Reagan's letter "closes the door" on the opening of Shoreham.

Hochbrueckner turned up at that press conference and challenged Carney to a debate on Shoreham, noting that they had a radio debate scheduled for that morning that Carney canceled. Carney, saying he had an appointment with Reagan for later in the day in Washington, hastily left refusing to debate his challenger.

Hochbrueckner subsequently called the supposed federal commitment on Shoreham a "sham." He said, "The truth is that the federal government is already imposing the LILCO evacuation plan on Suffolk County. . . . The people have a right to an opportunity to separate truth from fiction and a right to a congressman who knows the difference."

Reagan, as he did virtually everywhere else in the U.S., won a landslide reelection victory on Long Island in 1984, and Carney was reelected, although he trailed the Reagan ticket substantially.

Later that November, the NRC voted to let LILCO load nuclear fuel at Shoreham and bring the reactor to "sub-criticality."

And, the Reagan administration continued trying to push Shoreham into operation—by imposing federal authority over the objections of state and local governments.

In January 1985, Reagan appointed a White House special assistant, John Herrington, to become the DOE secretary, replacing Hodel, who had to hurriedly replace Watt. Herrington was described by *The New York Times* on March 27, 1985, as a

> lawyer who was promoted from long-time volunteer work in political campaigns to become a troubleshooter in the White House. . . . As one of the most plain-spoken Reaganites at the White House, Mr. Herrington is credited by colleagues with improving the White House's job-filling process while also checking unabashedly on the Reagan loyalties of the hundreds of officeseekers filtered through his computers.

Brooks B. Yeager, Washington representative of the Sierra Club, said, "As far as we can find out, he doesn't have the remotest qualifications or background in energy management."

Herrington was confirmed by the Senate and sworn into office in February.

At first, Herrington claimed that under him the DOE was doing nothing about an evacuation plan for Shoreham. On March 13, 1985, appearing before the new committee Edward Markey was assigned to chair, the House Committee on Energy and Commerce's Subcommittee on Energy Conservation and Power, Herrington was asked by Markey: "What, if anything, is DOE doing with respect to Shoreham's emergency plans?"

Herrington, under oath, replied: "I don't think we are doing anything."

Markey asked him to provide documents concerning the DOE's involvement in the Shoreham evacuation plan if any were discovered. Herrington's response was that Markey's staff could look again in DOE files.

Among the documents Markey's investigators would find days later in those files was a Herrington letter dated March 8—five days before he claimed to the Congressional panel that his agency wasn't "doing anything" involving Shoreham evacuation plan—to FEMA Director Louis Giuffrida. It declared:

> Regarding the testing of the Shoreham Emergency Plan, it is my understanding that some progress has been made although we have yet to schedule an actual test. This matter is of vital importance if we are to avoid similar problems on other nuclear plants nearing completion. The Department of Energy will continue to support the testing of the Shoreham plan as soon as possible.

An undated DOE document included a draft of a proposed presidential executive order allowing for acceptance of the LILCO Shoreham evacuation plan. It gave the FEMA director power to work with "private sector organizations" to test and implement nuclear plant evacuation plans.

It began:

> LILCO is in serious financial trouble. A utility in the final stages of construction of a nuclear power plant has limited internally generated capital and thus is heavily reliant on raising outside capital. The investment community needs to see a clear path to final licensing to justify taking the risks of nuclear power. . . . Without access to the financial markets, the company will soon go past the point where it can continue to meet its obligations.

Under "The Solution," this memorandum recommended that the president "amend" the 1979 executive order that "consolidates the civil defense and emergency preparedness functions of the Civil Defense Act of 1950, the Defense Production Act of 1950, the Disaster Relief Acts and other authorities, into FEMA." A draft of that presidential order read:

> By the authority vested in me as President by the Constitution and the laws of the United States of America . . . and in order to protect the public health and safety in cases of incidents at nuclear facilities, it is hereby ordered as follows: Should state or local governments be unwilling, unable, or otherwise fail to participate in a timely manner in emergency planning adequate to meet federal requirements, the Director [of FEMA] is authorized and directed to work with private sector organizations to assure adequate civilian emergency planning, testing and implementation with respect to civilian nuclear facilities, and the Director shall utilize the resources of the Secretary of Energy in connection with such facilities.

Another DOE document, which was undated but from the events discussed was evidently prepared in late 1984, was headed "SHOREHAM LICENSING AND EMERGENCY PLANNING." It noted that the plant had been loaded with nuclear fuel and LILCO would soon be testing it at low power.

> Unfortunately, full power operation of Shoreham is not yet authorized, due principally to the refusal of Suffolk County, joined by New York State, to participate in the federally mandated off-site emergency preparedness planning process which is required by NRC before issuance of a full-power operating license. This "hostage plant" syndrome is a growing problem, with local governments raising the [evacuation] issue in other states, such as Pennsylvania, Texas and California.

But having both a state and a county oppose the operation of a nuclear plant based on evacuation issues, the situation on Shoreham "is both unprecedented and anomalous."

The document continued that "the current timetable for LILCO appears to be very tight. LILCO avoided bankruptcy by a matter of weeks in the summer of 1984." Banks, however, provided

> an additional $150 to $200 million; repayment of those funds (as well as the balance of the $4 billion investment in the plant) requires placing the plant into commercial operation. LILCO now projects commencing commercial operation of Shoreham in the fourth quarter of 1985, and indeed believes that it must do so within this time in order to avoid further financial problems. Commercial operation requires a full-power operating license, which cannot be issued until the Shoreham emergency plan has been successfully exercised.

It also suggested making the evacuation zone smaller.

> More recent evaluations of actual radioactive emissions data from Three Mile Island suggest . . . that accident-caused radioactive releases are much lower than had been expected in 1980. It thus appears that the public health and safety would be protected by a smaller zone for emergency planning than is now required.

This question of reducing "source terms"—what the NRC defines as "the quantity, timing, and characteristics of the release of radioactive material to the environment following a core melt accident"— was explored in another DOE memorandum. Written by DOE Assistant Secretary Vaughan and dated November 1, 1984, it stated: "Emergency Preparedness and Source Term are both important problem areas: —Emergency Preparedness is a technical/legal problem. —Source Term is a technical/emotional/political problem."

Under "Source Term Approach," the memorandum said: "Beyond the plants under construction, there will not likely be any new orders of nuclear powerplants unless and until the public becomes more comfortable and less emotional about the likelihood of being injured by nuclear powerplant accidents." However, "It is very likely that the NRC will not find sufficient support in the American Physical Society review due in December to reduce accident source terms as much as industry would like."

Indeed, the report by the American Physical Society's Study Group on Radionuclide Release from Severe Accidents at Nuclear Power Plants rejected the idea of a reduction in "source terms" determining that in a nuclear plant accident there would be less releases than once thought of some radioactive poisons, but greater releases of others.

The NRC staff itself would come to the same conclusion. "New source terms for many accident sequences were found to be lower than those in the Reactor Safety Study [a 1975 NRC report] but some were larger," it said in 1985.

Nuclear physicist Richard Webb found in his analysis of the source term issue that the federal government, in trying to reduce source terms, was making "arbitrary assumptions about the core meltdown process." For example, he said, only a small hole—seven feet square— in the containment dome is assumed to have been created. "Because the hole would be that small, it is then assumed that the release of radioactive fission products would be small—two percent. However, the fact is that the entire containment could be blown apart in a steam explosion." This could cause a "near full release of radiation."[33]

Webb also stressed that what occurred at Three Mile Island does not justify lowering source terms. Only through multiple strokes of luck, he said, was a catastrophe releasing massive amounts of radioactivity avoided. Further, "the conditions of the TMI accident were such as to favor fission product absorption inside the containment. . . . The government wants us to rely on a single experiment—a single data point—namely the Three Mile Island accident. It is not tenable."

Vaughan's memorandum said that a "reduction of two orders of magnitude" in source terms "would place the exposures in the same range as natural background. Many believe this magnitude of reduction is possible." He said if "source terms" could be reduced, "The public would relate more positively to these doses and [this would] improve the political climate for expansion of economically competitive nuclear power projects through less restrictive design requirements."

An accompanying document entitled "Preliminary Draft EVACUATION ZONE SIZE" asked: "Whether DOE should take an active role in the NRC reviews related to evacuation zone size or let the utilities carry the ball." It noted that "the NRC has been considering changing the plume exposure pathway Emergency Planning Zone from the present 10 miles to 2 or 3 miles. This change would greatly simplify emergency planning and reduce the potential for litigation and controversy concerning emergency planning." Under "Initiatives," it suggested: "Develop coordinated DOE source term position. Potential petition for rulemaking on reduced evacuation zone size."

Another undated DOE document found by Markey's staff declared:

The NRC Authorization Act of 1984 permits utility developed emergency response plans. In instances when a utility develops a plan and it is found to violate state and local law because certain police power functions are performed by other than the appropriate state and local officials, there are three basic approaches the utility may take to get NRC approval of the plan, and hence an operating license.

—PRESUMPTION: The NRC rulings and regulations should reflect the statutory requirement. For example, the NRC could adopt a presumption that in actual emergencies state and local officials will perform their "police power" duties and protect the public. Thus, portions of the plan which violate state and local law in non-emergency situations would not impede NRC approval of the plan because the appropriate state and local officials would be "presumed" to act in a real emergency.

—PREEMPTION: Pursuant to the Atomic Energy Act the field (or portions of the field) of "health and safety" around nuclear facilities is a federal one. Hence, state and local laws which conflict with an emergency response plan permitted by the NRC Authorization Act are preempted by the AEA [Atomic Energy Act] with respect to emergency plans.

—FEDERAL FIX: Under the Civil Defense Act of 1950, the President has the authority to plan and respond to man-made disasters. He delegated this authority to FEMA under EO [Executive Order] 1214B, and it may be redelegated. Thus, DOE may intercede and do emergency response planning in the areas which conflict with state and local laws.

Yet another undated DOE document pointed to a major legal setback for the LILCO evacuation plan: "On February 21, 1985 Judge William Geiler, New York State Supreme Court, held the

LERO plan illegal. LILCO plans to appeal the decision to a federal court on federal preemption grounds." This memorandum also said, "The broadest preemption argument is that the whole field of 'health and safety' is preempted by the federal government which permits utility response plans."

Geiler, on a challenge to the LILCO plan brought by Suffolk County, New York State and the Town of Southampton, said that LILCO

> intends to declare an emergency and advise citizens of the steps they should take to protect themselves. LILCO intends to manage a major, full-scale evacuation of a 160-square mile area. It intends to close public highways, re-route traffic and direct the flow of traffic. The utility intends to decide upon and oversee steps to secure public health within a fifty mile radius of the nuclear facilities. . . . It intends to decide when and in what fashion citizens may return to their homes in previously contaminated areas. LILCO maintains that these actions do not involve governmental functions and that its proposed "management" of the evacuation of the residents of Suffolk County would not involve an exercise of the state's police power.

LILCO's claims, said the judge, were

> without merit. . . . No amount of semantics can change the true meaning of the activities which LILCO proposes to perform in the event of a radiological accident at Shoreham. No amount of ink can cover up or blot out the fact that LILCO's "intended functions" are inherently governmental in nature and fall clearly within the ambit of the state's police power.

Justice Geiler said,

> The court has been unable to find any provision in the State Constitution or State statutes which authorize LILCO or any other private corporation to exercise any portion of the state's police power. In fact, any attempted delegation of police power to LILCO would amount to an unlawful delegation of governmental powers. A governmental unit cannot bargain away its police power to a private party or organization.

LILCO states that one of its corporate purposes is to create and sell electricity and thus it has the power to build or operate a power plant such as Shoreham. The operation of Shoreham, according to LILCO, is conditioned upon the existence of an adequate offsite emergency plan. Thus LILCO reasons that it has the implied power to implement the plan in furtherance of its corporate powers. LILCO's view of the scope of implied corporate power has no limit. . . . LILCO is mistaken in its view that the power to undertake actions necessary or convenient to effect its corporate purposes has no bounds. A corporation lacks power, express or implied, to engage in activities which are contrary to public policy. The implementation of the [LILCO evacuation] plan amounts to an exercise of the police power. The latter can only be exercised by the state and upon proper delegation, the municipalities. The exercise of such power by LILCO would accordingly violate the public policy of this state.

Geiler then explored "the philosophy of our founding fathers in creating our government," discussing "the political ideas behind the Declaration of Independence and the Constitution," before concluding: "LILCO has to realize that this is a government of law and not of men or private corporations."

Edward Markey, meanwhile, wrote in a letter to John Herrington that the new documents found in the DOE files were "at odds with President Reagan's and your own pronouncements on the [Shoreham] issue."

Governor Cuomo also protested to Herrington. A day after Suffolk adopted its position on Shoreham evacuation, the governor pledged he would "not be a party to any effort to impose an independently developed state plan upon Suffolk County." As LILCO and the Reagan administration pushed even harder to get Shoreham in operation and strong opposition on Long Island grew even greater, Cuomo became increasingly set against the plant. He pointed to Geiler's decision in a letter to Herrington and said that DOE's drive on behalf of the LILCO evacuation plan thus "amounts to advocating the achievement of an unlawful objective." Cuomo also told Herrington, "Your department's support of LILCO's plan is a direct contradiction" of Reagan's pledge given to Carney. And, he said, "The efforts of your department to promote LILCO's emergency plan over the constitutionally sound objections of the state and local governments is an affront to the sovereignty of New York State and an injury to the people of New York State."

In response, Herrington said that DOE's activities were "consistent with the president's policy."

Soon, Herrington's pronouncements on Shoreham became even more candid.

In what the DOE described as his first major policy speech, made in Chicago on April 23, 1985, at the American Power Conference, Herrington, calling nuclear power "one of the great energy strengths of this country," said the Shoreham plant must open. If it didn't, he asked, "What kind of signal are we sending for our future?"

In his speech the next month at the Nuclear Power Assembly in Washington, Herrington said that if Shoreham did not open it would be a "low point" for the nuclear industry and if it did, it would be the beginning of a "brand new era."

Also in May, Herrington came to Long Island and went on a tour of Shoreham conducted by Catacosinos. David Devane, a DOE public relations person, said that Herrington considered the opening of the plant a matter of national security, and that he "was impressed with the safety of the plant's construction."

Meanwhile, LILCO had suffered other sharp legal setbacks. On March 18, U.S. District Court Judge Frank X. Altimari ruled that Suffolk County had a legal right to refuse to participate in emergency planning for Shoreham.

The county's authority had been challenged by LILCO and Citizens for an Orderly Energy Policy, made up of Brookhaven National Laboratory scientists. "The county," said the judge, "through its elected legislators, has taken a position that a satisfactory evacuation plan cannot be fashioned, and that it can best provide for the health and safety of its residents by refusing to cooperate with LILCO. . . . This court cannot second-guess the wisdom of that decision."

Then, on April 23, 1985, an NRC licensing board that had been considering the LILCO evacuation plan—holding hearings for nine months at which 86 witnesses testified, amassing a record of 22,000 pages of testimony and exhibits—decided: "The activities it [LILCO] seeks to perform . . . are unlawful. We further find that because of the applicant's inability to perform these functions, the LILCO plan cannot and will not be implemented as required by regulation." The decision continued, "From a practical standpoint, the foregoing findings leave LILCO without an implementable, comprehensive, and effective emergency response plan for Shoreham."

Herbert Brown advised the Suffolk County Legislature in May: "In a normal case, we'd be telling you: you've won, because you've won everything." But, he said, LILCO had been engaged with the federal government in Washington in a "last ditch strategy to push the plant, to get it on line one way or the other." And Shoreham had become "truly the largest nuclear case of its kind that's ever been in the country."

He told the legislators they had had a string of victories. He cited the decisions in state and federal courts and on the NRC licensing board level, and predicted they would not be overturned in the courts. The courts, Brown said, would not tolerate "the federal government demanding that local government imperil the safety of its own citizens when local government has acted responsibly." He said "the other side" claimed in Washington that Suffolk County was against Shoreham for "obstructionist" reasons, when the county's opposition concerned "good government, what American is supposed to be about."

He quoted LILCO's own chairman, saying a "guerrilla war" had begun. "This is not for the fainthearted," said Brown.

And he told the legislators that Suffolk should prepare for "something very dramatic" coming out of Washington.

That came in the form of a series of mysterious meetings involving Lyn Nofziger, William Catacosinos and Peter Cohalan, and intense financial pressure applied on Suffolk County officials by LILCO and financial institutions. These events preceded a dramatic turnabout by Cohalan on Shoreham in June 1985. Cohalan announced that he was directing county agencies to cooperate in a drill of the LILCO Shoreham evacuation plan. (He also tried to fire Herbert Brown's law firm.) The Suffolk Legislature took his evacuation directive to court, where it was ruled an abuse of his powers as an administrator. The court ruled he was required to carry out the policies set by the county's governing body, the legislature.

The legislature vigorously continued to fight Shoreham. LILCO conducted a massive campaign to change the makeup of the legislature through the 1984 election, a move that failed. Even a stronger anti-Shoreham legislature was elected, and Gregory Blass became its presiding officer.

Meanwhile, there were new severe legal setbacks for LILCO. The same NRC licensing board that in April decided that the LILCO evacuation plan was "unlawful" issued a new ruling on August 26 declaring that no Shoreham operating license would be issued to LILCO because of continuing county and state opposition to the plan. "Even if we had found that LILCO had the necessary legal authority to implement the proposed plan, the plan would remain inadequate because of the ramifications of the refusal of the state and county to participate," the board ruled.

And on October 18, an NRC appeals board supported the lower board's findings that the LILCO evacuation plan was legally deficient. It also said, "There is simply no reasonable basis for assuming that the state or county could realistically step in at the last moment and execute the LILCO plan."

Nevertheless, on October 29, FEMA announced, following a request by an NRC majority, that it would conduct a drill of the LILCO evacuation plan. Three days later, FEMA revealed that it had hired a consultant to provide people who, along with federal personnel, would "simulate the roles of key state or local officials unable or unwilling to participate" in the drill. No people would actually be evacuated in the drill, which would be basically an exercise of the LILCO's "command and control" structure.

The Reagan administration was now moving to overcome the key block before LILCO could be given a license by the NRC to operate Shoreham—a drill, and then a ruling by the NRC on the LILCO evacuation plan.

Noting that the LILCO plan "has been found by the courts and the NRC's own licensing boards to be devoid of legal authority," Representative Markey opened a hearing in Washington on November 14, 1985, on the new Reagan administration Shoreham push. "According to the courts and the NRC's licensing boards, only state and local governments possess the legal authority and police powers necessary to implement an emergency plan."[34]

Markey continued: "The central question before the committee today is: Given these circumstances and conditions, why are the NRC and FEMA willing to conduct an exercise of LILCO's emergency plan? Spending scarce federal dollars to conduct a test of an emergency plan adjudged lacking in legality . . . is absolutely incredible."

He declared:

It is hard to ignore the hypocrisy revealed by this action. The Reagan administration, more than any other in recent memory, espouses state's rights. Yet FEMA and the NRC now propose to run roughshod over the expressed interests of New York State and Suffolk County. Similarly, this administration has given great lip service to the importance of law and order. Yet this exercise is being undertaken in the face of a decision by the New York State Supreme Court that the LILCO emergency plan is illegal. The unfortunate but inevitable conclusion is that this administration does not believe in getting the government off of the people's backs when it comes to the Shoreham nuclear power plant on Long Island.

However, Representative Carlos Moorhead of California, a Republican and ranking minority member on the Subcommittee on Energy Conservation and Power, said, "I want to applaud NRC's efforts to move forward on the issue of emergency preparedness at Shoreham." Moorhead said "a multi-billion dollar plant which is ready to operate" was being held hostage by local government, so there were broad national implications.

Some 200 people were present at the session in the Rayburn House Office Building: reporters from around the nation, many Congressional staffers, employees of the NRC, FEMA and other federal agencies, observers from the nuclear industry, and a large delegation from LILCO.

"At issue here today is the proper and legal role of the federal government in the face of compelling state and local concerns," declared Representative Robert Mrazek, a Democrat from Long Island. "The question is not the brilliance of LILCO's management, a management deficient in the past. We're not here to determine whether it was a wise decision for LILCO to be the only utility in the United States to invest in a uranium mine with Jimmy 'The Weasel' Frattiano. That is not why we're here today. We're here to discuss emergency evacuation planning."

He went on:

There is a fairly unique situation on Long Island and particularly in Suffolk County. LILCO has developed a plan. The plan is illegal, according to the courts, yet we are about to embark with a great deal of taxpayer money on an exercise to implement this plan. Now LILCO's plan has some rather unique components.

People who have been contaminated by radioactivity will drive their cars to the Nassau Coliseum where the Islanders [hockey team] may be playing, and they are going to drive into the parking lot where there are going to be people with Handiwipes to wipe off the radioactive dust on the automobiles. LILCO spent a million dollars for this plan and now it would appear that the NRC has decided it's time to implement it. And they have chosen FEMA to implement it.

FEMA, we all know, has its own remarkable planning background. It was FEMA that told us that in the event of a nuclear attack, there's a simple and safe and effective answer for every American, and that is to dig a big hole in the backyard, take off the back door and put it over the hole, and then cover the door with two feet of dirt. And Mr. T. K. Jones testified before Congress and said, "If there are enough shovels to go around, everybody is going to make it."

Well, the bottom line is a lot of taxpayers' dollars, in my view, has been wasted on some very unfortunate planning, and we have two NRC licensing boards that say this particular plan is illegal. If the NRC is simply committed to seeing this plant go on line and simply wants to have a piece of paper to look at—and say, "Look, the exercise was carried out. We spent $200,000 to carry out the exercise on this illegal plan. Now the plant can go on line, we can go to the next step"—then don't waste the $200,000 in taxpayers' money. Just step forward and say, "This plant ought to go on line regardless of whether state and local police powers are involved in the test."

Concluded Mrazek: "I would hope that we could get to the bottom of what the motivation is behind this particular decision, so that the kind of precedent that this will establish can be considered by members of Congress in terms of every other nuclear power plant in the U.S."

Representatives Norman Lent and William Carney, meanwhile, defended the drill. Lent decried the "local yokels in Suffolk County" government who were opposing Shoreham.

Carney said: "I think there are a lot of Long Islanders including myself who would like to know whether we can evacuate Long Island. Let's be honest. If the decision is that we cannot evacuate Long Island without the cooperation of state or local government, then the Shoreham question has finally come to an end. It will not operate and it will never operate under those circumstances."

"I think there is a misperception about what these exercises do," James Asselstine told Carney. This evacuation drill—any nuclear plant evacuation drill—does not involve the movement of people, he stressed. "They don't go out and move members of the public. What they do is they say, 'Who's responsible for making police decisions? Who's responsible for closing off roads and directing traffic? If you notify them, do they answer their phones? Do they know what they're supposed to do? . . . Who makes recommendations for evacuation? Who makes decisions for people to leave their homes or to stay in their homes and remain sheltered?' " Meanwhile, he said, the underlying question remains whether LILCO has the necessary authority to manage the situation.

Norman Lent and Carlos Moorhead, who earlier in the year had both demanded that FEMA use "its authority" and with LILCO implement a Shoreham evacuation plan, challenged Asselstine. "Isn't the real point here national energy policy and national security? If we allow a plant to be shut down simply because local officials don't want to participate in the process after the plant has been completed, do we not encourage other communities to do the same thing?"

Moorhead demanded: "Would you like to see this plant open?"

Asselstine replied: "I think my job on the commission is to make a decision whether the plant is safe to operate." He reviewed how after the Three Mile Island accident, the emergency planning requirement was established—and how it was still in force. "I think there should be adequate emergency planning for a plant, and if that cannot be provided, by whatever means, then I don't think the plant should operate."

Louis Giuffrida, meanwhile, had two months before resigned as FEMA director following several investigations into mismanagement and contracting fraud in his agency. Samuel Speck, an associate FEMA director, appeared in his stead. Speck testified that there is no movement of people in a drill of an evacuation plan for a nuclear plant because "an exercise is not meant to disrupt the public's normal routine."

Frederick Bernthal defended the drill. The NRC, he said, has a "broad mandate" under the Atomic Energy Act. He noted that the act says the NRC "shall issue on a non-exclusive basis" licenses for nuclear plants.

I would just emphasize the use of the words, "shall on a non-exclusive basis." When the commission's requirements and regulations are met, it is not an optional position for this commission to issue a license. It's required to issue a license. It's required by law to do so. Second, as to what might be achieved here, I think that Congressman Carney has gotten to the heart of the issue in his comment that it is most important to learn whether we can really evacuate Long Island.

Lando W. Zech (a former nuclear submarine commander and aide to Admiral Hyman Rickover), who four months earlier had been appointed by Reagan to the NRC during a Congressional adjournment—so, critics said, Zech could avoid being questioned by the Senate—also defended the NRC action. "It's my judgment that we're not doing anything at all illegal," said Zech.

Zech was named by President Reagan on January 24, 1986, to replace Nunzio Palladino as NRC chairman. The week before that appointment was to take place, Zech, a nuclear power enthusiast, told the Edison Electric Institute Governmental Affairs Conference that nuclear power "regulators need to provide" the nuclear industry with "an environment of more stability and more predictability, administratively where possible and through legislation where necessary." He also told the industry executives:

> Emergency planning and preparedness has become a potentially major obstruction in the road leading to the future of nuclear power. Local or state governments have off-site emergency authorities and responsibilities which neither the federal government nor the nuclear industry currently control. Thus they are in a position to obstruct operation of a nearby nuclear plant if they wish to do so. We seem to be able to do very little about this matter since we regulate only the nuclear industry in our efforts to achieve adequate off-site emergency preparedness. . . . Both industry and the government must seek creative solutions.[35]

And Zech declared that 2,000 new power plants will be needed by the turn of the century. "This means that at least one new large power plant, either coal or nuclear, will be needed in our country each month for the next 15 years."

In a break in the hearing, out in a hallway, Herbert Brown commented: "The NRC is going to throw itself into a volcano, even if it has to be consumed in the process to let this plant go on line."

He spoke of LILCO management's "strategy of assuming that the federal government, at all costs, will bail them out and take care of them," and LILCO's argument and those of others pushing for Shoreham that "Shoreham is the flagship of the nuclear fleet, and if Shoreham sinks, the entire fleet goes down, and we'll never have a nuclear plant."

Brown reflected on the process of how nuclear plants are allowed to be built and to operate.

I don't have confidence in the regulatory structure that regulates nuclear power. It's not a system which is truly predicated on the impression it gives to the public. It gives the impression to the public that safety and safety first is what it cares about. . . . But, in reality, that is not how the process works. The process is one that creates a cloak of legitimacy and due process. As the process works its way through and you participate, you see that due process is given a definition which is not openness, not objectivity, and not seeking a fair and full resolution of contested issues.

Back in the hearing room, as representatives and the NRC commissioners returned to their seats, James Asselstine commented to me: "It's as if Three Mile Island has been forgotten."

Letters of protest to the drill from Governor Cuomo and county and local officials were distributed to subcommittee members and put into the record of the hearing. The letter from Southampton Supervisor Martin Lang, a Republican, declared that the move for the drill "smacks of a conspiracy to impose an emergency plan on the residents of Suffolk County. It is a waste of the taxpayer's money, and it flies directly in the face of assurances given by President Reagan that the sovereignty of state and local officials over emergency planning for Shoreham would be respected."

In the next several months, there were several attempts to prevent the drill.

The Suffolk Legislature passed several resolutions in opposition and also placed a full-page advertisement in *The Washington Post*, on February 3, 1986. Headed "Letter to President Reagan," it asked for

your personal intervention to prevent agencies of your Administration from betraying your promise to the people of Suffolk
County. . . . Our views, Mr. President, are without regard to
politics or party. We are united as Republicans, Democrats,
and Conservatives on this issue of compelling public importance. We ask only that you honor your words of October 11,
1984, and that you prevent your subordinates from dishonoring
them by aiding LILCO's illegal emergency plan.

The letter also complained of how

Federal agency personnel are committed to pretend that they
are state and local government officials, and intend to play the
roles of such officials, over the objections of the very State and
local government officials whose roles the Federal personnel
intend to impersonate. Such role playing by Federal personnel
is not less objectionable—no less distasteful—than if we, in our
official governmental capacity, acted as pretenders to the Presidency and represented our conduct to be yours.

The legislature also passed a law making it illegal for anybody to
"perform or simulate Suffolk County roles or governmental functions"
in an emergency drill of which the legislature does not approve. The
law said such simulation would be "inconsistent" with the county's
"police powers and its duty to prevent such powers from being
usurped."

At a public hearing, Leon Campo testified:

How unfortunate that this county was compelled to pass
legislation which protects its very interests and therefore the
rights of the citizens. This circumstance is created by the desire
of corporate and governmental agencies determined to usurp,
impair and replace the police powers of Suffolk County with
powers which reside within their organizations and for their
own benefit and profit—all at the expense of the welfare of the
people.

LILCO and the federal government challenged the law in federal
court. The Department of Justice charged the county with "violating

the supremacy of the United States of America." U.S. District Court Judge Leonard Wexler struck down the statute. He ruled that although "this court . . . neither proclaims a renewed faith in nuclear power nor confers a blessing on LILCO or its Shoreham facility," Suffolk had "impermissibly intruded into a sphere of authority reserved exclusively to the federal government" on the "narrow question before this court" of whether "the acts made criminal by Suffolk County"—federal personnel simulating county and state officials in a drill—could be made illegal.[36]

Representative Markey charged FEMA with "apparent illegality" and "serious procurement irregularity which bears striking similarity to the scandals of the past" in its signing a "non-competitive, sole source contract" with a California firm to provide stand-ins for county and state officials.[37] The firm was Theodore Barry and Associates of Los Angeles, the same company that served as a consultant to the New York PSC in its investigation of the prudency of Shoreham costs. FEMA denied any illegality while also admitting that it selected the company after discussing "the acceptability of the firm with Messrs. John A. Weismantle and Freilicher of LILCO." The contract between FEMA and Theodore Barry and Associates also said: "LILCO will develop the basic exercise scenario."

Governor Cuomo said of the proposed drill: "It's wrong, it's absurd, it's cynical. We will oppose it every way we can." It would be a "make-believe charade," a "breach of faith with Long Islanders" and a violation of state and local sovereignty.[38]

Senator Daniel Patrick Moynihan of New York, a Democrat, complained to FEMA that "this sort of an exercise would not allow FEMA to make a finding on the adequacy of emergency plans for Shoreham. To proceed would only allow others with less expertise to draw ill-informed and misleading conclusions from a fundamentally flawed test."[39]

Senator Alfonse D'Amato of New York, a Republican, sent a letter to Reagan asking him to have FEMA cancel the drill because it would "usurp state and local government rights. . . . We cannot expect local residents to have confidence in an evacuation plan which was prepared over their objections."[40]

Many Long Island newspapers editorialized against the drill. *Suffolk Life* declared:

> Consider this: LILCO will help develop the scenario for the test which will evaluate them and their plan; the "test" will

only focus on a limited aspect of the total evacuation proposal; local governments will not participate, with outsiders in their place; no people will be moved. . . . There will be no scared residents on the roadways fleeing a plume of radiation. There will be no young children, evacuated from school, sitting in an empty house while their neighbors scurry to safety. There will be no movement of elderly from nursing homes, or patients from hospitals. There will be no actual traffic jams, people rushing around trying to gather members of their families, cars out of gas, breakdowns, accidents other than make believe mishaps in a computer. The fatal flaw is the fact that the portion that simply can't work will not be tested.[41]

But there was no stopping the federal government. FEMA arranged with DOE to provide it with 30 staff members from DOE's Argonne National Laboratory to serve as "evaluators." It was "clearly a conflict of interest," said Herbert Brown's associate Lawrence Lanpher, to have DOE personnel grade the exercise. "For the past year and a half, the department has worked behind closed doors to help get the plant open. To ask anyone to believe that DOE could be an impartial observer is just not credible."[42]

The day before the February 13, 1986, drill, FEMA held a press conference at a motel in Medford, Long Island.[43] Legislator Wayne Prospect, Herbert Brown and Fabian Palamino, Governor Cuomo's special counsel, were there. "To ask the public to believe what's going on in this room, you'd have to check your sanity at the door because this has all the appearance of a Dr. Strangelove exercise," said Prospect.

It indeed was Dr. Strangelove come to Long Island. Roger Kowielski, chairman of FEMA's Regional Assistance Committee, who came from Washington to supervise the exercise, had been the main briefing officer, speaking in a thick, difficult-to-understand Eastern European accent. His delivery was a cross between Peter Sellers' rendition of Dr. Strangelove and the fictional Czechoslovakian brothers made famous by John Belushi and Dan Ackroyd on "Saturday Night Live." He rambled on defending the drill and speaking about how LILCO "decision makers and managers will be making the decisions."

Prospect went on: "What we have here is some kind of event in which the bureaucracy is being greased for LILCO. This transcends the issue of Shoreham. It threatens at the very heart of democracy."

Brown also confronted Kowielski and the other FEMA officials. The NRC, said Brown, had become "the most discredited agency in Washington, and your agency has now become discredited, too." FEMA, he said, "is trying to cover up for LILCO."

Palamino scored the "charade" of the drill. He stressed that "we're talking about the health and welfare" of huge numbers of people.

The next day the drill was conducted. The *Newsday* (February 14, 1986) account stated:

Long Island Lighting Co. simulated a major accident at the Shoreham nuclear power plant. . . . More than 1,000 LILCO workers participated in the drill, which was observed by federal officials as part of the utility's effort to win an operating license for the controversial plant. LILCO employees conducted mock news conferences, drove cars along bus evacuation routes, pretended to notify 13 school districts to call off classes. . . . No warning signals really sounded, no homeowners were actually evacuated and no schoolchildren were sent home. Company officials, appearing at press briefings in a Ronkonkoma hotel throughout the day, issued statements about the imaginary accident but refused to answer questions about what LILCO workers were actually doing.

Giving the briefing of the press in Ronkonkoma was Elaine Robinson, a former Suffolk County legislator who, defeated for reelection, immediately went to work for LILCO doing lobbying as LILCO associate director of public affairs. (She subsequently commented: "I am making more money than I ever made.")

She would make announcements such as: "There is no panic. All evacuees are moving quickly and smoothly to the Nassau Coliseum. The accident will soon be under control. I repeat: There is no aberrant behavior. There is no panic."

She and other LILCO briefers would only answer questions that were termed "in scenario." Questions had to conform to the make-believe nature of the drill. If the questions were about real events during the drill, not about the make-believe bulletins concerning areas being successfully evacuated, traffic flowing well, and so on, the questions were ruled "out of scenario" and not answered. As it became apparent to newspeople that they were being used to fulfill a component of the evacuation drill requiring LILCO to brief the press, some walked out.

"This is not the real world—this is an exercise," declared FEMA regional director Frank Petrone.

"It was one of the most absurd things I've ever witnessed," commented Stephen Latham, attorney for Southampton Town, after observing the drill. "It's so unbelievably startling to think that someone will make a decision that will affect millions of people and have ramifications in the billions of dollars based on a charade. . . . The thing was so surreal. Here you had these LILCO and NRC and FEMA people running around with color-coded T-shirts play-acting on a life-and-death matter, knowing full well that this exercise was being done strictly so the NRC can concoct some idiot rationale for giving Shoreham a license. It made me sad and sick and enraged. It was the worst example of government decision making I've ever seen."[44]

NOTES

1. Herbert Brown in an interview with the author, March 1984.
2. From a speech made at a Nuclear Power Assembly, May 8, 1985, in Washington, D.C.
3. Campaign contributions from LILCO PAC to Carney and Lent are listed by the Federal Election Commission.
4. Reported in *Newsday*, March 18, 1984.
5. *Newsday*, March 18, 1984.
6. "Nofziger a $100,000 LILCO Advocate," *Newsday*, June 24, 1985.
7. Comments made in an interview with the author, November 1984.
8. John Wydler in an interview with the author, February 1986. LILCO PAC campaign contributions to Wydler are listed with the Federal Elections Committee. Contributions include those for the years 1979–1980. Wydler left Congress in 1980, and his name first appears on LILCO's filing with the Federal Energy Regulatory Commission of annual expenditures for "year ended December 31, 1982." He was paid $6,196, according to the filing, for "Services in Connection with the Evacuation Plan for Shoreham."
9. Statements by Reagan on nuclear power: "Nuclear power is the cleanest . . ." from campaign speech, August 1980; "The total radioactivity the people and the animals . . ." from radio address, May 1979; "To put things in focus . . ." from radio address, August 1979; "All the waste in a year from . . ." *Burlington Free Press*, February 15, 1980.
10. Quoted in *The Wall Street Journal*, December 15, 1980.
11. *The Wall Street Journal*, December 15, 1980.
12. "Statement by the President," issued by the White House, October 8, 1981.
13. This speech was made before the DOE/NRC Club of Sigma Xi, May 18, 1983.
14. "Factors Affecting the Nuclear Future," made at the Presidential Breakfast of the American Nuclear Society, June 14, 1983.

15. The speech was entitled "Nuclear Power: A Look Ahead" and was made at the International ENS/ANS Conference in Brussels, Belgium, on April 27, 1982.
16. Thomas Roberts' comments and vote on Palo Verde were reported August 31, 1985, in a *New York Times* article by David Burnham.
17. Quoted in *Reagan's Ruling Class, Portraits of the President's Top 100 Officials*, by Ronald Brownstein and Nina Easton, with an introduction by Ralph Nader, published by Presidential Accountability Group, 1982.
18. Ibid.
19. *Newsday*, May 7, 1984.
20. Michael Mariotte in an interview with the author, April 1986.
21. *Newsday*, April 16, 1983.
22. *Newsday*, February 24, 1986.
23. Blass in an interview with the author, March 1986.
24. The author was present at the Subcommittee on Oversight and Investigations hearing.
25. *The New York Times*, May 18, 1984.
26. The Union of Concerned Scientists report was issued in February 1985.
27. *The New York Times*, December 8, 1985.
28. Frank Jones in an interview with the author, April 1984.
29. Nora Bredes in an interview with the author, April 1984.
30. George Hochbrueckner in interview with the author, April 1984.
31. Press release dated April 27, 1984.
32. Maurice Barbash in an interview with the author, July 1984.
33. Richard Webb in an interview with the author, March 1984.
34. The author was present at the Markey subcommittee hearing.
35. Lando Zech's speech before the group, meeting January 16, 1986, on Marco Island, Florida, was entitled "U.S. Nuclear Power Plants: A Regulator's Perspective."
36. Judge Wexler issued his decision on February 11, 1986.
37. Rep. Edward Markey in a letter to Julius W. Becton, director of FEMA, December 10, 1985.
38. *Newsday*, November 14, 1985.
39. Sen. Daniel Patrick Moynihan in a letter to Becton, January 13, 1986.
40. Sen. Alfonse D'Amato in a press release, January 13, 1986.
41. *Suffolk Life*, November 20, 1985.
42. *Newsday*, January 13, 1986.
43. All the following comments made at FEMA press conference are from a tape recording of the event.
44. Stephen Latham in an interview with the author, February 1986.

8

GOVERNMENT BY LILCO

The way LILCO has been bulldozing its way around Washington, D.C., is just the way it has conducted itself for years with government on its home territory on Long Island.

"I would characterize LILCO as a classic case in which an economic power has been able to bury its long tentacles into the political process and thereby shape decisions," Suffolk Legislator Wayne Prospect said.[1] A high school social studies teacher before being elected to the legislature in 1980, he saw LILCO at work on government first-hand once he was in office. "Textbooks do not focus attention on how powerful economic interests buy influence in government," Prospect said. "LILCO's influence is deep and insidious. LILCO and its conduits in the Long Island Association [of Commerce and Industry] and the construction trade unions—all major contributors to both political parties and to political candidates—managed to buy silence from town and county governments."

Only a few legislators, according to Prospect, forcefully addressed LILCO issues. He regards "community groups coming down to the legislature and demanding legislators confront LILCO on Shoreham" as a pivotal development. "The only way tentacles like those of a company like LILCO can be chopped off is for the citizenry to get involved in their government and the political apparatus. That is what citizens did on Shoreham," he noted, causing "the Suffolk Legislature to become completely liberated from the LILCO octopus. Citizens helped liberate it."

Legislator Gregory Blass, a Republican, said: "LILCO represents the antithesis of the democratic process. It tries to undermine the will of the people through the constant repetition of the Big Lie. LILCO says it often and expensively enough that some people actually believe it. LILCO has been involved in the most clumsy intrigues. It has interfered with our elections. It has very close contact with the highest levels of government through its own activities and those of its allies and due to its close relationship with the banking industry. Money has been a main reason why Shoreham has been brought so far. LILCO and the financial interests behind it are hellbent on a hefty profit at our expense. LILCO has become a big-money, big-time operator, always working behind the scenes attempting to corrupt the atmosphere of government."[2]

Blass added, "Ironically, the harder they have been trying, the less successful they have been. They didn't give people credit for intelligence. And an overwhelming majority of the people are against Shoreham and supportive of public power."

LILCO is what led Blass into politics. He had just left the Navy in 1978 where he had been an officer in the Judge Advocate General's Corps. Finding that LILCO planned to build two nuclear plants in the small community where he settled, Jamesport, he went to meetings of the local town board. There, at the Riverhead board meetings, he saw "LILCO's corrupting effect staring me in the face. Town officials were blindly in support of Jamesport, mesmerized by LILCO's promises of tax money." So Blass organized a townwide referendum linked to the Jamesport project, and the vote was three-to-one against the nuclear project.

"I received threats as soon as I started pushing for the referendum," Blass said. Once Blass got elected to office and continued his opposition to LILCO, the threats continued. "There have been many anonymous phone calls from people telling me if I want to stay healthy, I had better lay off Shoreham or that my days are numbered." In January 1986, Blass became head of Suffolk County's governing body, its legislature, and the intense pressure on him persists today.

Often, the heavy hand of LILCO attempting to manipulate politics and government on Long Island and on a state level is painfully obvious.

"Lobbyist's Folder with Checks Found in Albany," was a headline in The New York Times (July 23, 1982). The Newsday (also July 23) headline stated: "Lobby Episode Raises Eyebrows." Henry Doebler, LILCO's lobbyist in the New York State capital, had left behind in a state senator's office in the capitol building, a folder containing LILCO Political Action Committee checks made out to five state legislators. The discovery of the checks came amid heavy LILCO lobbying against a bill designed to limit rate increases resulting from Shoreham construction.

State Senator James Lack, a Republican from Northport, Long Island, said: "Considering the juxtaposition—LILCO's dire attempt to kill the Shoreham rate phases-in at the same time its lobbyist is walking around and holding PAC checks—I think it's reprehensible."[3]

It is illegal to give campaign contributions on New York State property. Doebler, the son of a former LILCO chairman, insisted that he was not distributing the checks by hand but carrying them around prior to their being mailed. "All our checks are mailed," he said. "We don't deliver checks. It's illegal to deliver checks in a state building."[4]

Then there was LILCO's 1985 attempt to alter the makeup of the Suffolk Legislature. Rather than using LILCO PAC money to promote candidates, this time LILCO tried a different tactic. It hired Winner/Wagner, a California-based advertising and public relations firm that has specialized in defeating anti-nuclear power referenda, to set up an entity called Citizens to Open Shoreham. This was then used as a vehicle to campaign against anti-Shoreham candidates and for pro-Shoreham ones.

The air waves were saturated with commercials announcing that Citizens to Open Shoreham was "a grassroots committee . . . in favor of opening the completed Shoreham nuclear plant." Using LILCO's mailing list of ratepayers, a series of mass mailings from Citizens to Open Shoreham was made. (A New York PSC judge later ruled that LILCO "was in violation of the spirit and intent of the law" for allowing its mailing list to be used.[5])

Jim Blew, the Winner/Wagner executive in charge of the Citizens to Open Shoreham project, admitted that two thirds of its $750,000 1985 budget came from LILCO. The remaining money, he said, was from companies in the nuclear establishment including GE and Westinghouse, the Edison Electric Institute, companies that worked on Shoreham, including Stone & Webster and L. K. Comstock, and a number of banks, including Citibank. "The banks are the ones that lent LILCO the $4 billion for Shoreham. They naturally have an interest in getting it back," Blew said.[6]

Listed as the co-chairpersons of the entity were Santoz Abrilz, a Long Island industrialist and long-time promoter of Shoreham, now chairman of the Stony Brook Foundation, and Eena-Mai Franz, a Brookhaven National Laboratory scientist.

Blew, during the 1985 election, also set up Democrats to Open Shoreham as a "subcommittee" of Citizens to Open Shoreham. Listed as a co-chairperson of this group was a George Pack. Although Pack was not available to the press, a Long Island Democrat did get through to him. Rosemary Parsons of East Moriches said, "He told me he is retired, has LILCO stock, and is living on it. This is really a hoax. It has nothing to do with Democrats."[7]

In an attempt to remove Jane Devine of Huntington, the anti-Shoreham Democratic leader of the Suffolk Legislature, from the Democratic ticket, there were mass mailings in her district in the name of Democrats to Open Shoreham for her pro-Shoreham Democratic primary rival. "It's one thing," said Devine, "for LILCO to lobby for a return on its bad business risk. It's quite another to single out enrolled Democrats to write a letter which contains the 'platform' of my Democratic primary opponent and provide him with what constitutes a districtwide mailing." Also said Devine, LILCO employees, including lobbyist Elaine Robinson, assisted her opponent.[8] Devine won the primary by a five-to-one majority, and went on to handily win the general election.

Fraud was involved in Citizens to Open Shoreham mailings. Legislator John Foley, at a legislative meeting, displayed a Citizens to Open Shoreham item that was being circulated in his district.[9] Foley, a Blue Point Democrat, said:

> Paragraph 1 says, "Representatives from Citizens to Open Shoreham have met *several* times recently with our county Legislator John Foley to discuss his position regarding the opening of Shoreham." Fact: No such meetings have taken place— neither with individual representatives nor a group thereof. . . . Despite the fact that said hearings have NOT taken place, this completely misleading memorandum continues to build its strawman by saying, "Mr. Foley did not have reasoned responses to our facts. We think he is just playing politics with Shoreham." Fact: Since the meeting has not taken place, how could there be any type of response?

LILCO through its Citizens to Open Shoreham was "using name calling and the smear approach" and "the personal big lie . . . with this important issue," Foley said.

Other legislators then said their constituents were being sent identical mailings—except their names were substituted for Foley's. And they, too, had never met with any person from Citizens to Open Shoreham.

At another legislative session, Jane Devine charged that "LILCO and its surrogates are trying to take over control of Suffolk County government and they are willing to distort democracy in the process. This representative government is not for sale."

Also at that meeting, Legislator Philip Nolan, an Islip Democrat, said: "LILCO has decided to throw unlimited amounts of money— ratepayers' money—into its scheme to take over Suffolk government."

There were calls for investigations by State Consumer Protection Board Director Richard Kessel, among others, because the LILCO-created entities had not filed as political committees with the Suffolk Board of Elections. New York State law requires, said Peter DeNegris, the board's finance director, that any group trying to promote the success or defeat of a political candidate must register with the board before spending money.[10]

Kessel called on the New York PSC to prevent LILCO from spending ratepayers' money on such activities. "I think it takes real gall for LILCO to plead poverty, eliminate 1,000 jobs and say they are in desperate financial straits, and then use money for something like this."[11]

In the end, the big LILCO 1985 Suffolk elections push backfired. Voter sentiment was strongly anti-LILCO and anti-Shoreham. Indeed, candidates ran declarations in their advertisements such as: "SHE IS NOT THE VOICE OF LILCO." A Ratepayers Against LILCO line polled more votes than any but the Republican and Democratic tickets.

In 1986, the name of Citizens to Open Shoreham was changed to Citizens for Shoreham Electricity. The air waves were saturated with pro-Shoreham commercials in which Brookhaven National Laboratory scientists appeared, a series largely paid for by LILCO.

LILCO, with the onset of its ambitious nuclear power program, focused special political attention on Suffolk County because that is where the many nuclear plants it planned would go.

From the time LILCO unveiled its Shoreham project in 1966 until it announced its twin-plant Jamesport undertaking in 1974 it was given no difficulty by Suffolk government. The Suffolk County execu-

tive at that time, John V. N. Klein, moved to have the county participate as a neutral intervenor in NRC hearings on Jamesport, and he
hired attorney Irving Like to represent the county. "I chose Like because of his experience with the Lloyd Harbor Study Group and his
knowledge of the processes of the proceedings," recounted Klein, a
Republican. This irked LILCO. "Charlie Pierce told me that Like was
an obstructionist and I made a bad choice, all of which convinced me
that I probably made the right choice."[12]

The utility became more upset after the election of 1975 when,
principally due to the effects of the Watergate scandal, a Democratic
majority was elected to take over the legislature in heavily Republican
Suffolk, and legislative activity on nuclear issues started.

"I got a call from the Long Island Farm Bureau right after I took
office in January '76," said Joyce Burland, a Democrat from Sagaponack elected to represent the East End of Suffolk where LILCO
wanted to build numerous plants. "The farmers were up in arms over
the Jamesport project and transmission lines from Jamesport breaking
up farmland," recalled Burland. "I got them in touch with Tom Twomey. I told them I knew a public interest lawyer."[13]

Twomey began representing the farmers' organization, immediately stressing that the situation was bigger than transmission lines,
bigger than even Jamesport. The first press release Twomey and the
Farm Bureau issued on January 27, 1976 cited the 1974 PSC study of
19 potential nuclear plant sites on eastern Long Island and the 1975
Eco Systems analysis done for LILCO examining 11 sites. Twomey
charged in the statement that Long Island was being eyed as a base
for a large number of nuclear plants providing electricity to the "entire Northeast." He raised the issue of Eastern Long Island being
targeted as the site of what federal officials described as a "nuclear
park." The statement warned of the destruction of the character of
Long Island if it was used for such an undertaking. The Farm Bureau
intervened in hearings on Jamesport, and Twomey organized a coalition to work with it in fighting the plant that included over 30 organizations from the North Fork Audubon Society to the Tuckahoe
Taxpayers to the Southampton Baymen's Association.

Burland prepared a bill opposing Jamesport. Floyd Linton, a
former teacher (now a member of the New York State Board of Re-
gents), had become the legislature's presiding officer. Linton, a Democrat from Miller Place, recounted how Burland asked him to help

"get the votes together. She arranged a meeting with members of the Lloyd Harbor Study Group to discuss nuclear power. I remember Ann Carl was there."[14]

Irving Like was probing into whether there was a need for Jamesport. Harris Fischer, an ecologist with the county's Department of Environmental Control, had arranged for a comprehensive study to be done by the consulting firm of Dubin-Mindell-Bloome Associates of Manhattan. It would analyze existing and future Long Island energy use, with an evaluation of alternative energy sources. Its 1975 report was entitled, *A Study of Existing Energy Usage on Long Island and the Impact of Energy Conservation, Solar Energy, Total Energy and Wind Systems on Future Requirements.* It challenged—completely accurately, as it turned out—LILCO's claim of continuing sharply rising electrical use. It found that Long Island was extremely well-situated to take advantage of solar and wind energy. These along with co-generation, conversion of solid waste to energy, among other energy forms, and energy efficiency, could substitute for the electricity that would be produced by Jamesport and other new nuclear plants, the study found. Like made extensive use of the analysis.

In May 1976, the Burland anti-Jamesport resolution was approved by the legislature. All eleven Democrats (including soon-to-be LILCO lobbyist Elaine Robinson) voted for it. Republicans abstained or voted no. A passage in the bill read: "LILCO's recent sale to upstate New York of half of the power to be generated at these plants confirmed the county's Dubin Report that LILCO would not need the power produced."

After the measure passed, "We were ripped apart," recalled Linton.

The unions—the steamfitters, the laborers, the carpenters—made quite a lot of noise. *Newsday* came on heavy and accused the Democrats of being Luddites [members of a 19th-century English group that protested the Industrial Revolution by destroying machinery]. Lou Tempera [then the Suffolk labor commissioner, later convicted and jailed for taking pay-offs] told me that the Democratic majority was in real trouble with the unions. The unions also went to the [Democratic] political leadership and they came back saying we had made a terrible mistake and labor support would not be around.

John Klein vetoed the bill. Still, the Democratic majority continued the county's involvement with nuclear issues. In 1977, a resolution passed (and was supported by Klein) providing for Suffolk to become a neutral intervenor in NRC hearings beginning on Shoreham. Klein also had Like represent the county on Shoreham. Meanwhile, Klein changed his mind on Jamesport. "We had accumulated clear evidence that the anticipated demand was nonexistent. We got into a struggle in earnest on Jamesport. We shifted from being neutral to in opposition."

In the elections of 1977, the Democrats lost control of the legislature to a Republican majority led by a presiding officer strongly supportive of LILCO. LILCO and its backers were focusing heavy attention on the legislature and Suffolk County government. Elaine Robinson, after her defeat, was hired by LILCO as a LILCO lobbyist. She continued attending every legislative session, literally working out of a back room in the legislative chambers. Legislators would move in and out of the room during meetings. She was assisted by other LILCO lobbyists. Unions sent lobbyists to the meetings. Among them was Richard Harkin, representing Local #638 of the Enterprise Association of Steamfitters, who has been lobbying on behalf of nuclear power on Long Island at virtually every session of the legislature from that period to the present day. Explaining his presence, Harkin told me: "We believe in the technology."

Newsday regularly ran editorials boosting LILCO and its Shoreham and Jamesport projects. LILCO's business supporters got involved. Brookhaven National Laboratory scientists were quite visible. Lou Howard, who was to subsequently become a legislative presiding officer, would declare that he discounted that a serious nuclear plant accident could cause injury or death because BNL scientists "told me that even in the worst case scenario, a meltdown, all people would have to do is to get rid of their clothing and take a shower to wash off the radioactivity. I believe the Brookhaven scientists."[15]

There were many attempts to fire Irving Like and also MHB Technical Associates, hired by the county as consultants. Kevin Rooney, a LILCO lobbyist, commented after one discharge of MHB that if the firm was involved in the county's intervention on Shoreham, "we'd end up with a nuclear plant in Shoreham and no operating license."

Meanwhile, public demonstrations against LILCO's nuclear projects had begun. They would grow massive on Long Island in the years ahead, particularly after the Three Mile Island accident. Led by the SHAD (Sound and Hudson against Atomic Development) Alliance and involving other groups, they ultimately would involve thousands of people and civil disobedience—often going "over the fence" at Shoreham or blocking its main gate—resulting in mass arrests.

"Watch out for the three B's—big government, big business, big science—they're out to control our lives," Lorna Salzman, Mid-Atlantic representative of Friends of the Earth, declared at a 1977 demonstration at the Shoreham plant site.[16] It was time for "direct action," she said, "to let the politicians know that nuclear power is not acceptable in a democracy."

Dr. Charles Raebeck, co-chairman of Suffolk for Safe Energy and a former professor of education, called nuclear technology "the single most important issue facing modern society." Pointing to the dome of Shoreham, he said "that dome, when finished, will be like a tombstone."

Jan Hickman, a LILCO public relations person, watched from a distance and said of the rally: "It keeps people off the streets. I think the people here would be better off in a classroom learning about nuclear power."

Vera Parisi, regional director of the State Division of Human Rights for Suffolk County, was among 40 persons arrested for going "over the fence" at Shoreham in a 1978 demonstration. "People are not being considered when decisions to build nuclear plants are made," she said. "Nuclear plants manufacture products to destroy civilization in the present, and they may begin the destruction of the future."

Training in nonviolence was given to those seeking to making a statement by being arrested during anti-LILCO demonstrations. They divided up in "affinity groups" for their actions. "Even though public sentiment is against nuclear power, LILCO's wealth is still above the public health," said a flier those arrested with Parisi in 1978 distributed.

A stronger statement must be made directly to LILCO by the people. The potential victims of nuclear power have every right and obligation to step outside the laws which protect corporations and utilities which endanger the environment and human life. By our non-violent and humane actions we seek to expose the violence and inhumanity of the nuclear industry. Non-violent civil disobedience is the most powerful statement of conscience possible.

The protesters included a wide range of people, among them Kathleen Boylan, the wife of LILCO vice president Hugh Boylan. The daughter of a New York City police lieutenant, she was arrested three times for civil disobedience in connection with Shoreham demonstrations, and spent time in jail.

She related that she "began learning about nuclear power" in the late 1970s. "I felt very responsible, that I was participating because our finances were coming from LILCO. This was something immoral and dangerous to my children and to everybody else."[17]

Active in the Long Island Catholic Peace Fellowship, Boylan became deeply upset about the dangers of generating electricity from nuclear power and also

the connection between nuclear power and nuclear war. The system of nuclear power was set in place to maintain nuclear weapons development in our country. The amount of nuclear weapons that the government has in mind for the future would require vast amounts of plutonium that commercial nuclear power plants could provide. It's all tied together. Also, as well as a meltdown releasing the radioactive poisons in a nuclear plant, it could also happen if a nuclear plant was attacked by a plane dropping a conventional bomb blowing the plant apart. The radioactivity that would come out, in either instance, after a year's operation of a plant, could be a thousand times more than was released by the atomic bomb dropped on Hiroshima.

Boylan said, "I decided to say no to these things."

First, she tried to influence people connected with LILCO. Kathleen Boylan, the mother of five, spoke of "LILCO inviting all the executives' wives" to the Shoreham plant for a tour in 1978. She stood up in a conference room in which the women were being addressed and, in an attempt to "rewrite the agenda, I said, 'I am an opponent of what we are doing.' I was immediately surrounded by very big men. The rest of the women were ushered out. Nobody said, 'Let her speak.' I was in tears. One woman silently pointed to herself going out, the only gesture that somebody was with me." She found that LILCO officials "really knew very little about the consequences of nuclear power, and they didn't want to try to find out."

Then, she joined in direct action. Her conflict with her husband over nuclear power has been "the most difficult journey I've been on." Hugh Boylan finally resigned from LILCO.

"Not only is nuclear power anti-life," said Nobel Prize winner George Wald at the June 1979 demonstration at Shoreham, which drew 15,000 people and led to the arrest of 600, but despite "constant industry and government propaganda . . . it's an economic disaster, and the whole game now is to lay all its major costs on the people." Dr. Wald, a Harvard University biology professor, said the anti-nuclear movement "is people talking back to government" and "insisting on taking their lives in their own hands."

Folksinger Pete Seeger arrived at the demonstration, the largest ever held on Long Island, on the sloop *Clearwater* and, following Wald, sang an old song with new lyrics: "No nukes is good nukes/ we shall not be moved. Split wood not atoms/ we shall not be moved." The massive crowd sang along. Seeger said in an interview later that the U.S. "could run on solar energy," but energy choices had become political, not technological questions. He compared the anti-nuclear movement "to the struggle to get America out of the Vietnam war. Sooner or later . . . politicians will have to listen."

Dr. Ted Goldfarb, professor of chemistry at the State University at Stony Brook and a leader of the group, Science for the People, declared: "We have an uprising against corporations and monopolies who want to do us in, push us down the road to nuclear disaster."

LILCO's strategy has continually been one of denying any problems in connection with its nuclear projects or nuclear power in general. It also has attempted to intimidate demonstrators with litigation.

At the company's annual shareowners meeting,[18] for example, in April 1979, three weeks after the Three Mile Island accident, demonstrators marched outside carrying signs such as "OUR CHILDREN'S FUTURE BEFORE CORPORATE GREED." Inside, LILCO Chairman Charles Pierce proclaimed LILCO's continued faith in nuclear power. He called it "economical, environmentally benign, least harmful to public health." As for "What does Three Mile Island signify?" Pierce said, "It raises the question in the public mind . . . as to whether our prior assessment of reactor safety is valid." But, he asserted, "The superb safety record of nuclear reactors cannot be lightly dismissed."

In a December 13, 1979, letter to *The News-Review* of Riverhead, LILCO Vice President for Engineering Matthew C. Cordaro wrote:

Even if the worst credible accident happened at Shoreham, and the decision were made to evacuate, people would not be forced to stay away from their homes for long periods of time. In fact, they could return shortly after the accident had been terminated. Any emissions to the atmosphere following the loss-of-coolant accident described above would form a plume, similar to smoke from a chimney. . . . Once the plume passed, it would be safe to come back to the area.

LILCO's litigation against opponents has been cited in the 1985 book *The Big Chill*[19] as an example of "the use of litigation to halt political expression." The book noted LILCO's $2 million 1980 damage suit against Shoreham protesters. "LILCO served legal summonses on people and groups whose names appeared on SHAD literature as well as people who had attended only one SHAD meeting, and had not taken part in any demonstrations."

Victor Rabinowitz, an attorney with the National Emergency Civil Liberties Committee that represented those sued, charged at the time that LILCO was "attempting to terrorize and intimidate people from participating in the anti-Shoreham movement generally."[20]

Through the court, LILCO sought the names of contributors to SHAD and signers of its petitions. It claimed that SHAD was interfering with its property rights.

National Emergency Civil Liberties Committee lawyers alleged that LILCO had engaged in improper surveillance, and countersued, demanding that LILCO executives testify about surveillance of SHAD members and supporters. A settlement was arranged in which LILCO dropped its financial demand in return for an injunction barring future demonstrations involving people entering "onto the Shoreham property" or blocking access to it.

Before future demonstrations in recent years, LILCO has sent—by registered mail—hundreds of copies of this injunction to people arrested in early demonstrations, and to those whose names appeared on written material opposing Shoreham.

The formation of the People's Action Coalition, in the wake of the Three Mile Island accident, came at a time when LILCO had a grip on the Suffolk Legislature. The coalition decided to concentrate its efforts, which included demonstrations, on the legislature.

Up until then, many legislators "unfairly stereotyped" those who had come before it to complain about LILCO and its nuclear projects, noted Wayne Prospect. "They could not stereotype Leon Campo's Group. Here were middle-class Americans: Leon in his three-piece suit, with other men like him, and married women coming to meetings with their children. The legislators saw these people, and they couldn't write them off as just 'anti-nuke.' These people were the heart of the voting public of Suffolk County. This meant the legislators had to take Shoreham as a political issue—in the best sense of the word. Increasingly, citizens in Suffolk County had become interested in LILCO and Shoreham, and they were sending the message that if legislators were not sensitive to their concerns, they would be replaced by legislators who would be."[21]

Campo recounted, "We did not start with a conclusion." The group was formed after the Three Mile Island accident largely by people who had "accepted the official viewpoint as espoused by the company. After the accident, we asked questions, independently. We had no connection with one another. We had the same agenda of questions, and we met at various public forums. It was an alliance of citizens that came about naturally. Our questions were not being addressed by LILCO. Our inquisitiveness was met by the company stonewalling, not telling the truth. That caused the inquisitiveness to change to suspicion. The more we investigated, the more horrified we were. There were blockbuster revelations: for instance, that when LILCO 'upsized' the reactor it didn't 'upsize' the size of the plant it was put into, and so maintenance—to this day—is impossible in many parts of the plant; or that the plant was built on top of an artesian well."[22]

Campo, a school district administrator in East Meadow, Long Island, said, "Our common perspective was that what was necessary for this plant to be stopped was to focus our attention on government and the purpose of government: to magnify the public good and reflect the will of the citizens and not the corporations. What was necessary was to cause people on the county level to stand up and make the case for the citizenry, to address the issue and espouse the truth. We felt the county was the first line of defense."

He said, "Some people in public office react by seeing the light. More often, they do the right thing when they feel the heat. Once this light-and-heat principle is understood by citizens, they can do a great deal. In the absence of citizen action, that void is filled with vested interests. When we started, LILCO had a stranglehold on local government. The position of presiding officer of the legislature was

LILCO's outpost, its home-away-from-home. We reclaimed the citizenry's proper place in Suffolk's political process. It is also important for citizens not to be co-opted by any party label. It is important to realize that this is a cause that transcends politics. It's a matter of safety which affects everyone."

Suffolk, meanwhile, was to undergo a change in county executives. It came as John Klein began having serious doubts on Shoreham. After the Three Mile Island accident, he went to Harrisburg and, upon returning, sent a mailgram (May 9, 1979) to then New York State Governor Hugh Carey that said: "My visit to Harrisburg and my conversations with those involved in the Three Mile Island incident made it inescapably clear that it would be absolutely unthinkable to permit the Shoreham facility to go on line under the circumstances and conditions which exist today."

He cited the "appalling state of uncertainty and confusion" among officials as to what to do after the accident, and how

> state officials claim that they were given false, inaccurate and misleading information by the Nuclear Regulatory Commission. . . . Please keep in mind that at the Three Mile Island area the government officials have the capability of effecting an evacuation in a 360-degree configuration via an elaborate and extensive system of interstate, state and local highways. Evacuation from Suffolk County under similar circumstances is a thousand times more difficult and complex. . . . I further submit to you that based upon the geographic and population characteristics of Suffolk County and Long Island, it may, in fact, be impossible to develop such a plan which could adequately respond to a nuclear accident of any significant magnitude, and we, therefore, may well conclude that it is not possible to permit Shoreham to open.

Peter Cohalan won over Klein in a Republican primary because of scandal involving a large sewer project in the county. Cohalan took a position against Shoreham in the ensuing general election campaign while his opponent, Democrat Martin Feldman, appeared to support it. (Feldman's name later was to show up on the steering committee for Citizens to Open Shoreham.)

From the outset, however, Cohalan's behavior was erratic. As one of his early acts upon taking office as county executive in 1980, he fired Irving Like as the county's special counsel on LILCO and nuclear matters. This came just as the Jamesport project was killed by a New York State power plant siting board following county opposition led by Like and the challenges of the Long Island Farm Bureau and others. There were strong public protests to Cohalan's firing Like and legislative attempts to override his move.

In 1981, Cohalan attempted to work out a "settlement" with LILCO through which the county would withhold most objections to the project at NRC hearings in return for an inspection. LILCO would only agree to an initial inspection of two of the plant's systems, yet the county executive's office agreed to the deal.

Groups opposing Shoreham went *en masse* to legislative meetings to protest.[23] "LILCO has pulled all the plugs to try to railroad this through," charged Leon Campo.

Like told the legislators that they had a personal responsibility. From the "standpoint of conscience as well as common sense," he said they should reject the settlement.

"LILCO hasn't offered anything meaningful. It's buying the county off cheap," charged Stephen Latham, speaking for the Shoreham Opponents Coalition. The county executive's office was agreeing to a "political sellout. . . . It's a pattern of the county essentially deciding to toss in its lot with the utility rather than have any meaningful scrutiny of the safety of the plant, and I think that's unconscionable."

The legislature rejected the deal, what Wayne Prospect called a would-be "Faustian relationship with LILCO." It then scheduled a referendum on whether the county should "actively oppose" the NRC granting Shoreham a license pending "a complete physical inspection" of Shoreham. This never got on a ballot because of a lawsuit brought by Brookhaven National Laboratory scientists organized as Citizens for an Orderly Energy Policy.

In February 1982, after a nationwide search, Cohalan hired Herbert Brown's law firm to replace Irving Like. In March, the legislature authorized the work that led to the conclusion the following year that a successful evacuation would be impossible in the event of a serious Shoreham accident.

In May 1982, LILCO sent to state officials a report in binders marked "Suffolk County Radiological Emergency Response Plan" for their approval as the required Shoreham evacuation plan. During the settlement talks, LILCO had given Suffolk $245,000 to formulate a plan. Preliminary study began, but then was stopped and the money returned after the deal fell through. LILCO's presentation included some of this data.

The LILCO move outraged Cohalan.[24] At a special legislative session, he said,

> Both legislators and the executive together face an unwarranted action on the part of the Long Island Lighting Company. The purpose of LILCO's action is to operate the Shoreham nuclear plant before Suffolk County develops and implements a radiological emergency response plan—that is, before the county will be able to protect its citizens. . . . Last week, in what can be termed only an act of brazen arrogance, LILCO packaged various materials into binders entitled "Suffolk County Radiological Emergency Response Plan." LILCO transmitted these materials to officials of the State of New York, and LILCO requested the state officials to review and approve such materials as the radiological emergency plan of Suffolk County.
>
> The power to act for the people of Suffolk County is by law vested only in the county government. LILCO, by its presumptuous recent actions, has arrogated to itself that governmental power. This fact was confirmed in last Friday's newspaper where a high-level LILCO official justified his company's action with the following quoted words, "When government refuses to act responsibly, as a government, then we must do so for the government."

Cohalan later also declared his flat opposition to Shoreham after the conclusions of the county's consultants were issued in February 1983 and the legislature endorsed them.

"This county means a great deal to me," Cohalan told me as he looked out the window of his ninth floor office in Hauppauge, a panorama of suburban homes and green lawns below, parkland in the distance. "This is where I am from." He was preparing to sign the resolution passed by the legislature that said that because "no local radiological emergency plan" could protect residents, no plan would be "adopted or implemented."

"It's logic," said Cohalan, his gaze returning to his office. "There's no way anyone can tell me there's a way you can have an emergency plan for a plant sited where Shoreham is. There's no way the people who live east of the plant would move through the radioactive plume and escape. We have studied the issue very closely, and that is clear. The likelihood of a serious accident may be remote, but still, we cannot play the wheel of fortune with peoples' lives. Because people could not escape if there would be an accident at that plant, it cannot go into operation."

Cohalan's formal statement on Shoreham stated:

> The unique local conditions of Long Island make it *impossible* to protect the public safety if there were a serious accident at the Shoreham plant. In short, there never can be emergency preparedness to protect our citizens. . . . The result of no emergency preparedness is that Shoreham should never operate. LILCO voluntarily—or the NRC through its mandate—should immediately bring a halt to the Shoreham project.

Shoreham was the central issue in the 1983 election for Suffolk County executive. The Democratic candidate, State Assemblyman Patrick Halpin, insisted that the operation of Shoreham was "inevitable," so the county should stop fighting it.

"Tonight's victory is a victory for the people against those who would do LILCO's bidding," declared a winning Peter Cohalan on election night. "I had the backing of the people," and to those supporting LILCO on Shoreham, "I say, 'Wake up and listen to the people. Get out of your ivory towers.' " He went on, "Shoreham should be abandoned and abandoned now!" He promised he would "continue to fight to the bitter end" against the NRC, the New York PSC, FEMA and "anybody else trying to shove this $4.5 billion fiasco down our throats. I pledge to you I will continue this and we shall win."

Why Cohalan suddenly backed off two years later is still shrouded in mystery. His change in position was preceded by meetings in February and March 1985 with William Catacosinos and Lyn Nofziger. They were held at the Sayville, Long Island, home of a Cohalan friend, Walter M. Conlon, a former New York State tax commissioner until he was indicted in 1967 for engaging in illegal land deals in his prior position as Islip Town attorney. He was convicted for accepting unlawful fees while a public officer and jailed. Cohalan's first job in government was working for Conlon as an assistant Islip Town attorney. Conlon, in recent years, has been a principal advisor to Suffolk Republican Chairman William (Mike) Blake.

What transpired at those meetings has never been made public. Soon, however, Cohalan suddenly seemed equivocal about the fight against Shoreham.

The summer before, there had been talk of intense Reagan administration and nuclear industry pressure on Cohalan and Blake over Shoreham occurring at the Republican National Convention in Dallas. They were delegates to the convention at which Reagan was nominated to run for reelection. Gregory Blass said, "Several friends in Washington told me that Cohalan and Blake were literally collared, and high Reagan administration officials and nuclear industry representatives laid down the law to them: The county executive had to drop his opposition to Shoreham."[25] The reports of this pressure led the legislature to widen its involvement in Shoreham matters in the event there was a change by Cohalan.

Also, in early 1984, LILCO began withholding $52 million a year in property taxes owed to the school district in which the plant is located, Brookhaven Town, and the county, in protest to the county's position on Shoreham. The county's bond rating was being lowered. And representatives of rating companies, in meetings with county officials over bonds, pressed them on the Shoreham issue. Said Suffolk Budget Director Edward Boughal: "We were telling them what a good situation we had—our economy was fine—and they kept coming back with, 'Is the county's position on Shoreham going to change?' "[26]

Wayne Prospect charged: "The barons of Wall Street are conspiring to put the financial screws to Suffolk County." Still, he said, "what is involved in a manageable cash flow problem."[27]

Indeed, in his budget message accompanying the county's 1985 budget, Cohalan scored LILCO's "illegal" withholding of taxes and said, as a result, he had instituted "cost-cutting measures" and that "this belt-tightening program has worked."

Also, in early 1985, the State Legislature was getting set to act on legislation—subsequently passed—that would force LILCO to pay its back taxes or forfeit the Shoreham property immediately.

Early clues of a Cohalan change came in March when he met with Santoz Abrilz, Long Island Association of Commerce and Industry President Walter Oberstebrink and other Shoreham backers on LILCO rates. Subsequently, his deputy county executive, Howard

DeMartini, appeared with LILCO lobbyist Elaine Robinson before local officials to outline a rate "phase-in" program that LILCO and the county executive's office were trying to develop. In April, Cohalan's office sent Herbert Brown a letter saying Kirkpatrick & Lockhart should limit its legal work on Shoreham to "emergency planning and safety issues" and not to engage in a "litigation campaign against the federal government."[28]

Cohalan's change came on May 30. He issued "Executive Order Number 1—1985" arranging county support of a drill of LILCO's evacuation plan by ordering that "agents of the County of Suffolk assume the function of command and control" in such a drill. He said, "You could extrapolate I've dropped my opposition to the plant as long as the results of the drill are positive." Then he added, *"Alea jacta est . . .* the die is cast."

Late that night, LILCO delivered checks totaling $130 million for its back taxes.

Cohalan notified officials in Suffolk with telephone calls made at around midnight and then in the early morning hours, between 6:00 and 7:00 A.M.

Gregory Blass, notified at midnight, said Cohalan sounded "frayed and edgy, very tense" and "appeared to be reading something to me." He said Cohalan told him "the county needs leadership. I replied, 'The county needs leadership, not capitulation.' "[29]

He said Cohalan went on that LILCO would "pay its taxes." Blass said he replied that, nevertheless, "the long-term economic effects of Shoreham will be devastating." He said Cohalan then abruptly told him "Good night," and hung up.

On May 31, Cohalan sent a telegram to Ronald Reagan. "Dear Mr. President: I want to let you know that as County Executive, I have issued an Executive Order which directs Suffolk County officials to assume the County's responsibilities with respect to emergency response planning for the Shoreham Nuclear Power Station."

The reaction to Cohalan's change in position was very strong. There were weeks of demonstrations including sit-ins at his office leading to arrests.[30] Amid signs posted in the lobby to Cohalan's office such as "RESIGN COHALAN" and "BETRAYED LONG ISLAND," Susanne Katz, who moved to East Hampton on Long Island from Woodward, Pennsylvania, as a result of the Three Mile Island accident, said: "He's been bought out."

Monica Dolan of Great River said: "People should really wake up to the fact that the utilities have gotten much too much power. They are another form of government, forming public policy."

Leon Campo left a meeting with a Cohalan aide reporting: "We continue to demand to meet with the county executive. We'd like to know what the *quid quo pro* was. The public safety was put up for sale." Cohalan was refusing to "face us. He does not want to look at us eyeball to eyeball. He is saying to the people of Suffolk County, literally and figuratively: drop dead."

Zuliekah Gallagher was arrested after hanging an effigy of Cohalan in front of her Sayville flower shop. "I just bought a great house. I'm in love with my business, my house, my life on Long Island. But how can I stay when they turn that thing on?"[31]

Governor Cuomo, in a prepared statement issued May 31, 1985, said:

My position on Shoreham is clear and unequivocal. My paramount concern is and has always been the safety of the people of Long Island. It is abundantly clear to me that Long Island's unique geographical configuration and limited east/west roadway network makes it virtually impossible to evacuate the area surrounding Shoreham in the event of an accident. Nothing has changed in the past few days to convince me otherwise.

The governor commented to reporters that Cohalan "started by saying that evacuation was simply impossible. What's changed? Did the island shrink? Are roads wider? Were bridges built? None of that changed."

There were numerous calls for Cohalan's resignation, including one from Southampton Town Supervisor Martin Lang at a special meeting of county and town officials.[32] He said: "Suffolk County is in a state of emergency. The health and safety of its million and a half residents—as well as the very existence of its democratic form of government—are in peril. A renegade county executive, recklessly abandoning law and order, has taken the powers of government into his own hands."

Wayne Prospect called Cohalan's move "an act of treachery that has sealed his fate in history as the Benedict Arnold of Suffolk County."

William Catacosinos said, "This is fantastic, it's great."[33]

And John Herrington, from Washington, said that "if Shoreham had not opened, it would have been a major setback to the industry. . . . And I don't feel that local politics can be allowed to fly against national security."[34]

In a year-end interview in 1985, Cohalan stressed the financial issue for his switch in position. "We needed the money badly," he said of LILCO's back taxes.[35]

But a widely held view on Long Island is that he was pressured along other lines. *Suffolk Life* raised the possibility of blackmail, among other reasons. After the Cohalan switch, it ran an editorial on June 5, 1985, that noted how Cohalan tried to run as the Republican candidate for lieutenant governor of New York in 1983 and had gone to the state Republican convention in Manhattan expecting to be nominated on a ticket led by Lewis Lehrman. But, said the editorial, "an envelope arrived at the Lehrman headquarters that allegedly concerned Cohalan." After the contents of the letter were discussed, "Cohalan went to bed" and gave up his try to run for lieutenant governor.

Indeed, immediately after that convention Cohalan did not return to work but went into seclusion at his beach house on Fire Island for several weeks while accounts circulated—and several were published—that he was considering leaving his office.

Gregory Blass in his weekly newspaper column also spoke of "payoffs, blackmail, Oval Office overtures and hushed messages delivered by a noisy helicopter" as elements in the switch. He subsequently said the reference to "hushed messages" and a helicopter referred to "Nofziger moving around by helicopter with messages. It was an incredible turnaround, a 180-degree reversal, and I think the reasons put forth by Cohalan are bogus. I think the long tentacles of LILCO and the banks and Washington managed to have their way."

Wayne Prospect believes that Cohalan "took a dive." It was "a classic sellout by a politician. He played let's-make-a-deal with LILCO and various vested interests associated with LILCO, but there's no way of knowing what kind of prize was behind the curtain because whatever deal he cut for himself collapsed when his executive order was challenged by the legislature and declared illegal. He was never able to deliver his part of the bargain."[36]

The challenge by 12 county legislators of Cohalan's executive order was supported by four East End Suffolk towns and the state.[37]

The group of lawyers involved included Irving Like, Stephen Latham and Fabian Palamino. Like argued that Cohalan had played "Roman emperor for a day, dictator for a day" in attempting to "dismantle" county policy against Shoreham. This was "the stuff which totalitarianism regimes use as their stock and trade."

The county attorney's office conceded that the question of the legality of the Cohalan executive order was researched by LILCO. Assistant County Attorney Arlene Lindsay, as she defended the order in court, continually received notes passed by a LILCO lawyer in the front row of the spectators' gallery.

New York State Supreme Court Justice Robert W. Doyle ruled the Cohalan order an illegal usurpation of the powers of the policy-making body of the county, its legislature, and issued a permanent injunction prohibiting it from being carried out. The judgment was upheld by the Appellate Division and New York's highest court, the Court of Appeals.

John V. N. Klein, in private law practice, was hired by LILCO in 1983 to help in the development of the utility's plan to withhold taxes. He said he thought this could be LILCO's "trump card" over Suffolk.[38] He said he was amazed to find out in 1985, when he no longer was retained by LILCO, that the company was planning to "give away" its leverage—to pay the taxes—with the issuance of an evacuation plan directive by Cohalan. Klein recounted that he met Catacosinos at a breakfast gathering of the Long Island Association three days before LILCO paid its taxes and Cohalan issued his executive order, and Catacosinos told him about the arrangement in the works. "I told him that making a deal with the county executive is not going to solve the problem. I explained that the county executive is not the policymaker, the county legislature is, that the county executive does not have the final word." But, he said, Catacosinos "ignored" his advice and went ahead with the deal anyway, which like so many other LILCO ventures backfired.

"LILCO," said Klein, "is Murphy's Law moved into the utility business on Long Island and running rampant ever since."

Cohalan quickly became, in the words of State Assemblyman John Behan, "politically dead meat"[39] because of his Shoreham turnaround. As the *Southampton Press* editorialized, "Either by stupidity or sheer deceit, Mr. Cohalan has made himself forever unbelievable, a political Jonah. Either he was lying when he opposed Shoreham, or he's lying now."[40] The political and public furor has not subsided, and

Cohalan is regarded as unelectable on Long Island and just filling out the remainder of his term.

Gregory Blass was elected presiding officer of the legislature in 1986 as part of a bipartisan coalition based on the Shoreham issue. "The looming threat of an unsafe, unwanted and economically debilitating Shoreham nuclear power plant has galvanized this legislative body," he said in his acceptance speech.[41] "In an alliance with our governor, and most of our state and federal representatives, we stand strongly united against a concerted effort by LILCO, the nuclear power industry and elements of the federal bureaucracy to force this boondoggle down the throats of the people of this county."

He charged that "with unbridled arrogance," LILCO "has used millions of dollars wrung from the rate-paying public, in a cynical attempt to influence the election of this legislature and manipulate the views of public officials, as part of a master strategy to get Shoreham on line and force the public to pay for it. LILCO views the operation of Shoreham as the company's only hope for bailing itself out of self-inflicted financial disaster. In its effort to license Shoreham at any cost to the public, LILCO has emerged as a bad neighbor and a deserving target of public scorn. Hurricane Gloria and its aftermath revealed, in detail, the extent to which LILCO has abdicated its management obligations, particularly in the area of disaster preparedness. Its corporate resources are consumed by the obsession to get its nuclear meal ticket licensed."

Blass declared, "I am committed, with my legislative colleagues, to make 1986 the year in which we extricate Suffolk County from the debris of LILCO's irresponsible management and begin a constructive search for alternatives, in order to build a foundation for a safe and economical utility service in Suffolk's future."

While LILCO's hold on government in Suffolk was broken, its grip on Nassau County government remains.

"In Nassau County government there doesn't seem to be any contradiction between what's good for Nassau County and what's good for LILCO," said Marge Harrison.[42] For nearly a decade, she has led a citizens group in Nassau that has attempted to cause Nassau government "to take an independent position and course of action from LILCO." She has also been working for the replacement of LILCO by a municipally owned utility. Harrison has been active, too, in Democratic politics and is a vice chairman of the New York State Democratic Committee. And, she was a member of the New York State Fact Finding Panel on the Shoreham Nuclear Power Facility.

"There seems to be an operational agreement on energy issues between the Republican administrations of Nassau and LILCO," Harrison said. "They work in unison."

She went on: "For years we've had a joke, that with the county executive building on West Street off Old Country Road in Mineola and LILCO's corporate headquarters on the other side of Old Country Road, there is a tunnel under Old Country Road where [Nassau County Executive] Purcell would meet regularly with Catacosinos to coordinate their strategies. Purcell has cooperated with LILCO as long as I can remember. Nassau County has never taken any step independent of LILCO at all, even though such steps have been sought by citizens."

A high school teacher, she has an extensive collection of newspaper clippings and other material concerning Nassau government and LILCO at her home in Baldwin.

She pulled out one clipping. It was a March 19, 1984, *Newsday* story beginning,

> Mineola—Nassau County Executive Francis T. Purcell yesterday pulled his county out of a coalition formed to fight utility rate hikes and threw his support behind the 21 percent increase the Long Island Lighting Co. is seeking. Purcell also said he will be in Washington today and tomorrow to lobby on behalf of LILCO, which has been seeking federal help to solve its current financial problems and be allowed to open the Shoreham nuclear plant. Purcell said he would join LILCO chairman William Catacosinos for a Tuesday lunch with the Long Island congressional delegation.

Harrison said: "This is just another example of where the supposed representatives of the public in the county are acting as LILCO lobbyists."

Then, there was a *Newsday* clipping from January 22, 1985, involving Purcell's offer to make Nassau County facilities available for evacuees from Suffolk in the event of a Shoreham accident. Purcell was quoted as saying: "If LILCO asks for it, I would volunteer the [Nassau Community] college or any other facilities we have—including my own office."

Commented Harrison: "Purcell will admittedly do anything he can for LILCO."

She became involved with Long Island Citizens in Action in 1978, and with members of the group she has continually gone to meetings of the Nassau Board of Supervisors attempting to get action on LILCO issues, to no avail. She noted a January 22, 1983, *Newsday* article that reported on members of her group stressing at a board meeting that "radiation wouldn't stop at the county line."

But, said Harrison, "then and always, the officials have absolutely denied any problem, tried desperately to make the LILCO issue a nonissue. They try to pretend the problems don't exist."

Part of the reason is the intimacy between Nassau's Republican officials and LILCO officials through the years, she said, and their "commonality of views." Part of it, too, is that Nassau government officials also run an "expensive operation," he added. "Property taxes in Nassau are the highest in the United States. And then there are LILCO rates, second highest in the nation. People are hurting; there are many people with fixed incomes who have real difficulty paying these bills."

Harrison has repeatedly pointed to the two public power companies in Nassau, in Freeport and Rockville Centre, as examples of "municipal systems that are cheaper than LILCO and offer far superior service. Nassau officials refuse to take the legally needed steps to permit a serious movement forward on public power."

The handling, or lack of handling, of the LILCO issue in Nassau County is best viewed within the political environment of Nassau. Unlike Suffolk, which, although Republican-dominated, has had frequent changes in political balance in town and county offices in recent years, Nassau has become very much a one-party county with a Republican organization that is among the largest and most well-disciplined of any political organization in the United States.

The Nassau Republican Party has often been compared to the Democratic machine of the late Mayor Richard Daley in Chicago. It still bears the imprint of Joseph Margiotta, who took it over in 1968 and ran it with an iron fist until he resigned upon going to jail in 1982. During most of those years, he was also a New York state assemblyman. When he quit, he was described by *Newsday* as "the nation's strongest politician." He had been convicted of federal charges of fraud and extortion for forcing the county's insurance agent to kick back $680,000 to political cronies and himself. Republican officials from Nassau, including Purcell and Representative Norman Lent, supported Margiotta remaining on after his conviction.

Among those signing a letter to raise funds for Margiotta's defense was CIA Director William Casey, a Nassau Republican.[43]

At Margiotta's sentencing, U.S. Attorney Edward Korman urged a jail term because Margiotta "presides over a system of corruption so institutionalized and so subtle that effective criminal prosecution is often difficult, if not impossible." U.S. District Court Judge Charles Lifton described Nassau as having "a sad history of official misconduct."[44]

In 1985, Democrat John Matthews ran for Nassau County executive on the LILCO issue. "LILCO and the Republican Party have been running Nassau County as their own fiefdom," charged Matthews, calling for a change.[45]

Matthews went after Francis Purcell on the county executive's move to assist LILCO in finding an evacuation center for its Shoreham evacuation plan. LILCO desperately needed such a federally required center after administrators of schools and colleges, and representatives of churches, approached by LILCO, refused to let their facilities be used by LILCO. Purcell arranged for the utility to use the Nassau Veterans Memorial Coliseum. (The general manager of the coliseum, however, stressed that the agreement provided only that LILCO could have "reasonable access" and that LILCO would not be able to use the facility for evacuees while events such as the circus, ice shows or Islander hockey games were going on. "We couldn't for example, preempt the circus," said E. B. Summerlin, Jr.[46])

Matthews took Purcell to court on September 27, 1985, charging that his coliseum deal was "unauthorized and illegal." His suit alleged: "Unless immediate injunction relief is granted, the respondent (Purcell) will effectively destroy the Nassau County Charter form of government and will become the unauthorized accomplice of LILCO in allowing the Shoreham plant to operate by improperly allowing unauthorized use of Nassau facilities and personnel contrary to law." He cited the decision in the Cohalan Shoreham executive order case. State Supreme Court Justice Francis X. Becker dismissed the action, and Matthews brought an appeal, which is still pending. Meanwhile, months after the election, in April 1986, the Nassau County attorney's office also questioned the arrangement, "verifying what I said," declared Matthews.

Matthews purchased 100 shares of LILCO preferred stock to force a shareowners' meeting to elect new LILCO directors to replace Catacosinos and other LILCO directors who were up for reelection. The Matthews slate included the dean of special business programs at Adelphi University, a retired executive of the Brooklyn Union Gas Co., and the chairman of Central Federal Savings & Loan Association in Nassau. The challenge so upset LILCO officials that they spent $1.5 million in advertising and related expenses to fight it.

One LILCO mailing to shareowners was a memorandum headed with "IMPORTANT" and signed by Catacosinos. It charged, under "ABOUT MR. MATTHEWS," that he was "a local insulation contractor and politician. . . . YOU SHOULD KNOW THAT: Matthews is an avowed **public power advocate**." The Catacosinos memorandum went on that Matthews had "no employment activity other than his family run business." It scored his "printed propaganda with such hostile slogans as 'LILCO Must Go,' 'Goodbye LILCO,' and 'The Problem Is LILCO.' "

LILCO brought suit against Matthews in federal court as part of a broad legal action against Citizens to Replace LILCO, a group formed in 1985 to push for public power. LILCO charged that Matthews was connected with the group, which he wasn't, although he also advocated public power. LILCO's suit demanded both that the group cease its advertising calling for the replacement of LILCO by public power and that Matthews stop speaking about his attempt to get new LILCO directors elected. LILCO claimed that the advertising and Matthews' comments were violations of rules of the U.S. Securities and Exchange Commission. The suit was dismissed by U.S. District Court Judge Jack Weinstein. The free speech questions it raised resulted in the New York Civil Liberties Union coming into the situation.

These and other Matthews actions, at long last, made LILCO a critical political issue in Nassau—and the public responded forcefully.

"Until he took on LILCO," a *Newsday* political analysis declared, John Matthews' candidacy was not strong. But Matthews "suddenly has found credibility and publicity in the LILCO issue. People, he said recently, are telling him to 'keep it up.' And that is just what he is doing."[47]

Purcell protested: "It's easy to attack LILCO because LILCO is the enemy of the people, and people don't like their bills. But I think people understand that the county government does not run LILCO."[48]

A Matthews campaign advertisement labeled Purcell "LILCO'S CHOICE" under which were statements by Purcell supporting LILCO. Matthews was described as "CONSUMERS' CHOICE" and the advertisement contained sharply critical comments by him about LILCO. It asked that voters back Matthews and "SAY 'NO' TO LILCO."

Matthews lost to Purcell in the election, but his margin of 20,000 votes was substantially smaller than it was in 1981, when he also ran against Purcell and lost by 90,000 votes—and both he and Purcell attributed the reduced margin to the LILCO issue.

Matthews also was not able to unseat the LILCO directors. At a December 12, shareowners' meeting, he declared that when he asked that the meeting be held,

> It was my intention, and remains my intention, to focus on the issues: Shoreham, and should it open as a nuclear plant? Will it cost more to open Shoreham than to abandon it? I said no and still say no. Is Shoreham safe? Judging from the track record of those who built it, I said no and still say no. Could Long Island be safely evacuated in the event of a radiological disaster? I said no and still say no. Will Shoreham ever open in light of the opposition to this plant by the governor of New York State, the legislature of Suffolk County and the people of Long Island? I said no and still say no. Is the evacuation plan which brings evacuees from Suffolk to the Nassau Coliseum feasible and legitimate? I said no and still say no.

LILCO management, Matthews said, "has bet this company on Shoreham," and he urged a vote for his alternate board slate for "the future and safety of Long Island."[49]

Catacosinos insisted that "Long Island needs Shoreham's power and needs it today," and that it was time the area turned its attention from nuclear power to the issues of garbage disposal and water pollution.

Afterwards, Matthews said: "Today is not the end of the war."

LILCO has continued legal action against him. It appealed the Weinstein decision and has been attempting, said Matthews, to get him to "promise I never again will try to unseat the LILCO board. Of course I will not agree."

Matthews said he intends to continue to press the LILCO issue in Nassau politics—despite the expense of defending himself against LILCO litigation, and in the face of threats.

"I was supposed to speak last night with Marge Harrison about LILCO at the Great Neck Public Library," said Matthews in April 1986. "The event was well publicized, a lot of people were expected. But it was canceled because the library received a bomb threat."

Matthews, of Long Beach, said, "We're going to continue to fight against LILCO, and we don't expect it to be easy—it has never been easy."

In Nassau, said Matthews, county government "marches in lock step with LILCO. LILCO officials have been extremely close personally with Margiotta and Purcell. LILCO and its employees have supported Nassau Republican candidates for years with campaign contributions."

But he sees this coming to an end some day. "One party—no matter what the party is—cannot remain in power forever. One-party government can only lead to corruption because an arrogance develops." He expects that Nassau County government's domination by a Republican Party closely linked with LILCO will end possibly with revelations of scandal comparable to "the scandal we've been seeing rocking New York City."

A product of the Nassau Republican Party involved in the long close relationship between LILCO and the party, and through it Nassau government, is Edward P. Larkin. Larkin has also been in a position for the past 25 years to assist LILCO greatly on the state level.

Since 1961, he has been a member—a consistently pro-LILCO member—of the agency that regulates LILCO and other utilities in New York: the Public Service Commission.

Defending his consistent advocacy of rate hikes for LILCO, Larkin said: "If we don't give them [LILCO] the money, the lights will go out. We're obligated to give them the money they need."[50]

Before being appointed to the PSC, he was a state senator, a state assemblyman, presiding supervisor of the largest town in Nassau, Hempstead, and earlier in lesser positions in Nassau.

Of the relationship between LILCO and Nassau officials: "Of course there is a relationship between a big corporate entity and government. LILCO pays a lot of taxes. LILCO's a big factor in our county," said Larkin. "Yes, there's a relationship. Yes, LILCO has played a large part in the life of our county. I've known presidents and chief executive officers of LILCO over the years. These are all men who have been involved in promoting county ventures, public works, county improvements."

But, Larkin insisted: "I've been twenty-five years on the PSC and twenty-five years in politics, and in all those years no company has ever suggested to me to do anything out of order. Nobody has come to bribe me. Nobody has attempted to color my opinion."

Larkin has always been a sure and consistent vote for LILCO and the PSC. Even more critical has been the strong support of LILCO by PSC chairmen, for it is with the office of the PSC chairman that principal control over the PSC lies.

Vastly increased powers for the PSC chairman were engineered in the 1970s, said PSC member Ann Mead, when Joseph Swidler "was brought to New York by Rockefeller" to head the agency. "The statute was changed to give the chairman almost czar-like powers. All staff appointments are made by the chairman. The budget is prepared by the people who work for the chairman. The chairman picks the chief administrative law judge, who picks the judges who hear cases. Policies are basically made by the chairman. The members of the commission are just there to vote on cases after they have gone through the regular hearing process."[51]

The support of LILCO by the current PSC chairman, Paul L. Gioia, who joined state government in 1973 as an assistant counsel to Governor Nelson A. Rockefeller, has resulted in a number of calls for his resignation.

In January 1986, for example, after a PSC majority led by Gioia granted LILCO the entire $68.7 million rate hike it was seeking, State Assemblymen Joseph Sawicki, a Republican from Cutchogue, and John Behan charged that Gioia "has continually turned his back on the people of Long Island while being LILCO's staunch defender." They called on Governor Cuomo to "demand the resignation" of Gioia.

Gioia has made it clear through the years that his first concern is LILCO's financial health. After the PSC granted LILCO a $245 million rate hike in 1984, he said it would send a "positive signal to the financial community that we are providing cash to keep the company financially viable."[52] Governor Cuomo said he was "disappointed" because "both businesses and consumers will suffer as they are forced to pay for LILCO's past mistakes."

Although he has the power, Cuomo has never moved to replace Gioia as PSC chairman.

If there were any questions about Gioia's stand on LILCO and Shoreham, they were dispelled in March 1986 when, as the headline of the Long Island Association's newsletter declared: "Gioia defends LILCO rates, affirms Shoreham need." The story reported on a closed-door "candid two-hour session" Gioia had with the Long Island Association's energy committee, led by Shoreham advocate Santoz Abrilz. The PSC chairman was described in the account as saying that Shoreham was needed to deal with what he saw as a shortage of electricity on Long Island. "Shoreham would immediately provide sufficient capacity," he was quoted as saying.

In 1985, Gioia urged the New York State Energy Research Development Authority, on which as PSC chairman he has a seat, to approve tax exempt status on $500 million in loans to LILCO—money that banks said they would lend LILCO contingent on it being granted rate increases by the PSC. "Gioia was in conflict of interest," said Irving Like. "What Gioia was doing was pushing this kind of loan in his role on ERDA knowing that as PSC chairman he would, in turn, have to approve rate increases to pay for the loan."[53]

Gioia has surrounded himself with persons with similar views. He selected as the PSC general counsel, David E. Blabey, from the extremely pro-utility New York State Senate Energy Committee. His executive deputy is Lester Stuzin, who as early as 1971 was claiming that Shoreham was needed to deal with electric shortages. In that year, Stuzin asserted at a New York State Department of Environmental Conservation hearing on environmental effects of Shoreham, that "for the years 1977 through 1980, the [electricity] situation becomes critical, not merely for Long Island but for the entire New York Power Pool"[54] if Shoreham didn't go into operation. The years 1977 to 1980 came and went; Shoreham didn't go into operation, and that didn't mean a thing to the electric supply of Long Island or New York State.

The claim that nuclear plants are needed or brownouts and blackouts would occur has long been a central theme of LILCO—and echoed by the PSC.

A LILCO press release, sent out August 16, 1977, began:

A Long Island Lighting Company official warned today that if opponents succeed in stopping the construction of the Jamesport nuclear generating station, dire consequences could result for Long Island in the 1980's, including frequent blackouts of large areas of the Island during periods of high demand and eventual curbs on the amount of electricity that customers would be allowed to use.

The official, Wilfred Uhl, was quoted as going on to say that "the need to build a nuclear electric generation plant at Jamesport is clearly supported by all the evidence."

Jamesport was never built, and the electricity it would have produced was not missed on Long Island. There were no "dire consequences," no blackouts.

Before the summer of 1985 the PSC warned that there could be brownouts ahead. Earlier, Adam Madsen, LILCO's vice president for planning, told the Suffolk Legislature that Long Island faced six to twelve brownouts a year unless Shoreham opened.[55] Richard Kessell then accused LILCO of purposely trying to cause brownouts or blackouts by keeping a power plant in Far Rockway mothballed. "LILCO is playing a dangerous game of Russian roulette trying to use its system and customers in an effort to lobby for Shoreham."[56]

The summer of 1985 came and went and—and despite the threats by LILCO and the PSC—there were no brownouts.

The PSC had an especially critical role on the LILCO Jamesport nuclear plant project. This was because when LILCO began seeking a federal permit to build the twin plants in 1974, New York State had established a parallel licensing procedure to that of the federal government. (The system came too late to apply to Shoreham.)

A power plant's "environmental compatibility" would first be considered by a board presided over by a PSC administrative law judge sitting with an "associate examiner," a representative of the State Department of Environmental Conservation. Then a state siting board chaired by the PSC commissioner and composed of representatives of three other state agencies and the public would make a final determination. The second board, called the New York State Board on Electric Generation Siting and the Environment, would be advised by staff from the PSC.

In 1978, the PSC chair of the first board to consider the Jamesport application, Frederick T. Suss, supported the LILCO application for two nuclear plants at Jamesport. The DEC representative, Sidney A. Schwartz, voted for one.

An NRC licensing board, meanwhile, had followed NRC tradition and approved the Jamesport project.

The final state board seemed to have a majority which would support Jamesport. It included: PSC chairman Charles Zielinski; Goldie Watkins, a health physicist with the AEC between 1963 and 1968 who was the State Health Department's representative; William Seymour, who served under Rickover in the nuclear Navy and was listed in "Who's Who in Atoms" and was the State Commerce Department's representative; and William Johnke, the public representative. Johnke was an architect from Nassau appointed to the board by former New York Governor Malcolm Wilson, a Republican.

"Johnke said he has long been active in the Nassau Republican Party, and believed he had been recommended to the spot by Nassau Republican Leader Joseph Margiotta, who Johnke said was a personal friend he had known for years," reported John Rather of *The Long Island Traveler-Watchman* (September 7, 1978), a Southold newspaper. Johnke also said he had designed public buildings in Nassau, Rather noted.

The Long Island Farm Bureau tried unsuccessfully to get Johnke removed from the siting board for conflict of interest after it was discovered that he was the architect of a bank that would be the closest financial institution to the Jamesport site and would thus profit from it being built.

The Farm Bureau also protested briefings given by PSC staff members advising the board. It cited a "final briefing memo" prepared for the board by Cornelius Milmoe, a PSC staff adviser, which claimed that Jamesport's power was needed. "Pro-industry insiders within the PSC should not be entitled to submit the final biased briefing to the siting board," charged Tom Twomey. Milmoe subsequently left the PSC for a position at GE's silicon division.

At a meeting shortly before the board voted in January 1980, one advisor suggested that evacuation in the event of a serious Jamesport accident might be handled by people escaping Long Island by boat. "With Long Island they say boating is a big thing and . . . with so many boats around there is a possibility," said Bob Vessels.[57]

The days and weeks before the board met were full of intense activity by Jamesport opponents. "I went from town hall to town hall on Long Island gathering signatures of local officials on a letter that was presented to the governor," said John Mullen, an advertising man who at no fee "devoted four years of my life" to battling Jamesport.[58] He recounted that one signature he was unable to get on the letter was from the person then in Larkin's old job of Hempstead presiding supervisor, Alfonse D'Amato, who would go on and become a U.S.

senator. "Considering D'Amato's close relationship with Margiotta, we were not surprised."

The rejection of Jamesport by the siting board was a major surprise for LILCO. It was widely believed afterwards that Governor Carey—who in 1978, amid broad public pressure directed at him, had declared that "Jamesport is dead"—finally got personally involved and spoke to the siting board members, all of whom were gubernatorial appointees. He had said earlier that he would not get involved in the board's deliberations.

"Jamesport was a heavyweight championship fight that was won in the last seconds of the fifteenth round after a tremendous battle—a tremendous effort by many people—to get to the fifteenth round," said Mullen. "Then the governor, after vacillating, made a decision at the last minute to back up his stand against Jamesport."

Tom Twomey said, "The citizens on Long Island eventually, over a six-year period, finally got their feelings to the local political leaders and elected officials, and they, in turn, convinced Governor Carey that nuclear power was not the way to proceed." This came, said Twomey, despite obstacles created by the PSC. He added that "among the PSC staff and some of the commissioners, there were very good people: Ann Mead, for example, and Joel Blau. But I found the PSC, overall, to be a regulatory agency captured by the industry it is supposed to regulate."[59]

Indeed, it was work by Blau that was highly important in ending the Jamesport project—work done in the face of stern disapproval by some at the PSC.

Blau filed a series of briefs urging the final siting board reject the recommendations of the earlier board and support no nuclear plants at Jamesport. The briefs pointed to new forecasts by the PSC, a grouping of New York utilities called the New York State Power Pool, as well as by LILCO and the company it had brought into the Jamesport project, the New York State Electric and Gas Corporation. They showed, as Blau and a fellow PSC lawyer, Jeffrey E. Stockholm, declared in a 1979 PSC staff Brief on Exceptions, that earlier forecasts of electric capacity required on Long Island by LILCO and upstate New York by NYSEG had "decreased drastically." So in terms of need, "there is no need to certify the proposed facilities."

The brief also charged that LILCO's forecasts, although reduced, were still far too high. Among "reasons for LILCO's continuing overestimates of energy and demand growth," it said, was "the company's wholly judgmental assumption that 96 percent of new single family residences will utilize electric space heating." This was even though "as of 1977, only 2 percent of LILCO's single family residential customers had electric space heating, the lowest saturation rate of any company [in New York] other than Con Edison." The brief questioned LILCO's assumption "that the addition of nuclear power to its generation mix will cause a real price decrease in electricity" causing widespread use of electric heat.

It cited the financial load on ratepayers if the plants were constructed.

It is clear that the construction of a large scale nuclear project such as one or both Jamesport units would impose substantial financial burdens on the applicants and their ratepayers. If the units are needed to serve capacity requirements, those financial burdens must be incurred. It is an entirely different matter where the facilities are not required to meet forecasted needs.

It further noted how "capital costs for nuclear units have risen sharply," and discussed Shoreham.

The brief faulted Frederick Suss, the PSC administrative law judge on the first Jamesport board, for claiming that the state was preempted from considering radiological issues.

While the states are prevented from substituting their own radiological standards for those of the NRC, it does not follow, however, that they are precluded from considering radiological impacts premised on NRC standards in evaluating the relevant environmental impacts of alternative modes of generation.

It also said that Suss was "plainly erroneous" in asserting that the state board could not consider emergency planning because of federal preemption. The brief cited the "serious side-specific questions regarding the feasibility of developing an adequate evacuation procedure for the Jamesport facility" on Long Island. It said the Three Mile Island accident "underscores the need for adequate evacuation plans" because it "indicates that serious nuclear accidents may be more likely than previously thought. . . . A certificate for a nuclear facility in this proceeding should not be granted unless, at a minimum, a determination is made that it is feasible to develop and implement an effective evacuation plan."

Jamesport was only finally pronounced dead in November 1983 when the Long Island Farm Bureau and Suffolk County brought court actions entitled "Long Island Farm Bureau against Paul L. Gioia, etc. et al." and "County of Suffolk against Paul L. Gioia, etc. et al." contesting LILCO's request to keep pending a Jamesport power plant application before the siting board. The Appellate Division of New York State Supreme Court agreed with the contention that LILCO could not extend siting board proceedings "indefinitely."

The kind of pro-utility attitude of Suss—who projected an odd image by often wearing sunglasses while he conducted proceedings in the dark basement of a Holiday Inn in Riverhead—is typical of PSC administrative law judges.

Frank S. Robinson, in particular, has faced sharp public and political criticism for his LILCO decisions. He still, however, continues to be assigned by the PSC to LILCO cases. In April 1984, Robinson was scored for ruling that LILCO did not have to pass on to ratepayers any savings from its $100 million austerity program. "It looks like Christmas has come early for LILCO," said Deputy Suffolk Executive Frank Jones.[60]

Robinson in April 1984 recommended that LILCO receive a $190 million rate hike because it needed the money "to help avert bankruptcy" due to Shoreham.[61] That decision, said Richard Kessel, "would allow the company to continue to stonewall a decision on Shoreham."[62]

Paul Gioia has justified special treatment by the PSC to assist LILCO in avoiding bankruptcy over Shoreham by claiming that a LILCO bankruptcy would be would "counterproductive." He told a gathering of state legislators from Long Island in 1984 that "I don't know what would happen" if LILCO went bankrupt. "I don't think anybody knows what would happen."

State Assemblyman Paul Harenberg, a Democrat from Bayport, challenged Gioia on this point, indeed called upon him to have the PSC commissioners "exercise their responsibility under the Public Service Law to direct LILCO to file for bankruptcy."[63] Harenberg said: "It is time to recognize that LILCO management has failed, that the energy needs of Long Island can be met without activating Shoreham and the protection of the ratepayers must now be your primary duty."

He cited Section 119 of the State Public Service Law that states "upon determining . . . that the public interest requires that such corporation be reorganized in order to enable it . . . to render adequate public service at reasonable rates . . . the commission may, by order, direct the officers and directors to file a petition for bankruptcy."

Harenberg told Gioia: "Surely, there must be a threshold of Shoreham cost and a degree of LILCO mismanagement at which a majority of PSC members will exercise their responsibility under Section 119 and put LILCO into bankruptcy. Unless there is a point at which the PSC will finally vote to protect the ratepayers, including the directing of LILCO bankruptcy, then utility regulation is a sham, because the utility will eventually win and the ratepayers will always lose."

The split in dealing with LILCO on the New York PSC is often political. Public Service Law requires that no more than four members of the seven-member PSC be of one party. The PSC currently includes three Democrats, including Ann Mead, who tend to vote against LILCO requests. Its three Republicans, including Edward Larkin, virtually always support LILCO. Gioia, who says he is a "political independent," votes with the Republican commissioners.

There is enormous pro-utility sentiment in the New York State Senate, which has a majority of Republicans. "By way of philosophy, they are not consumer oriented but oriented toward big business, and utilities are big business," said Harenberg.[64] The State Assembly has a Democratic majority, which is generally pro-consumer, said Harenberg, and thus critical of utilities. There are exceptions, he noted, such as former State Assemblyman Angelo Orazio, a Nassau Democrat, an electrical engineer who led the Assembly's energy committee, "and was he pro-nuclear!"

"Utilities have massive clout with the State Senate," said Harenberg's senior counsel, Steven Liss. "Just look at the number of utility reforms initiated by the Assembly which died on the vine in the State Senate."[65]

The Senate Republican majority also projects its philosophy on utilities through its involvement in which Republicans are appointed to the PSC and the confirmation process for all PSC members. The Senate GOP leadership insisted in 1983 that Cuomo reappoint Larkin, leading to one of the early political tussles with the Senate in his governorship. It then refused to act in 1984 on Cuomo's appointment to the PSC of Democrat Gail Garfield Schwartz, who, it was expected, would support his positions on issues involving LILCO and Shoreham coming before it. The GOP leadership held up confirmation for months while the PSC considered the LILCO $245 million rate hike request.

The majority leader of the New York Senate is Warren Anderson of Binghamton, who has long been highly supportive of utilities, including LILCO, and has campaigned for the opening of Shoreham. An issue has been raised on occasion about Anderson's law firm representing utilities, including LILCO's would-be partner on Jamesport, NYSEG. Anderson's Senate office conceded that the Binghamton firm has utilities as clients, including NYSEG, but, said Charles Dumas, Anderson's press aide, the "implication is insulting" that Anderson favors utilities as a result.[66]

Gary Lavine, a counsel to the Republican minority in the State Assembly and its specialist on energy issues, said: "It is impossible to separate political considerations from regulation of gas and electric utilities. It has always been a political concern, particularly in this state."[67] He related how the first central electric generating station opened on Pearl Street in Manhattan in 1882, a project of Thomas Edison, and how with electricity spreading, states considered how to deal with the new industry. The attitude of New York State Republicans going back to the turn of the century, he said, was that "utilities are a natural monopoly," and they should be kept in private hands and regulated. Among Democrats in New York State, the tendency has long been to support municipal ownership or public power, he said. He chronicled numerous gubernatorial contests through the early years of the twentieth century in which the two approaches clashed, and of the 1920s when "the Niagara-Hudson Power Trust effectively controlled" the state's Republican organization.

He spoke of W. Kingsland Macy, the Suffolk County Republican chairman and state and later national GOP power, "wresting control" of the New York GOP in the 1930s and stopping it from being "a tool of the trust." He spoke of the governorship of Democrat Franklin D. Roosevelt during which a New York power authority began, which the Roosevelt New Deal's Tennessee Valley Authority was "modeled after." Then there was the post-World War II situation in which "there was a change in utility economics. Generating plants got bigger, rates got cheaper." Then came "the sorry tale of nuclear power, the technology that never caught up with the promise. Institutions that were very competent at building fossil-fuel plants had to grapple with a very alien technology. Some could handle it, some could not." Said Lavine: "LILCO is a product of 80 years of history of utility regulation and management."

A channel of communications about contemporary New York State government history, including news concerning state government action on utilities, is *Inside Albany*. It is a TV program syndicated on New York's Public Broadcasting Service stations and gets half its funding from the Energy Association of New York State, the trade association of New York's seven utilities, including LILCO.

Paul Harenberg, an advocate of LILCO being replaced by public power, charges that because of the source of its funding, "You can never expect *Inside Albany* to give you a fair shake on public power. It gives short shrift to any discussions of public power."[68]

This was denied by David Hepp, the executive producer of the program, which is organized at WMHT-TV in Schenectady. "We have never been approached by any lobbyist for LILCO or the energy association to lay off this or do this."[69]

Although there is dispute about whether LILCO and other utilities have influence on *Inside Albany*, there is no question that in the New York Metropolitan Area LILCO has extraordinary clout with a vital adjunct to government—the media, both regional and national.

Frances Cerra resigned from her job as a reporter at *The New York Times* as a result of LILCO and Shoreham. That occurred because the paper would not publish a story she did on how LILCO was facing bankruptcy because of the nuclear plant project, and it then barred her from any further LILCO coverage.

Cerra made known why she had to make "the difficult decision last year to leave" the paper, after nine years as a *Times* reporter, in a letter to *The Quill*, the monthly magazine of Sigma Delta Chi, the national fraternity of journalists. "What directly led to that decision was a story that I was asked to do in the summer of 1982, a status report on the Long Island Lighting Company and the Shoreham nuclear plant," she wrote. "The lead of the story I wrote said that the cost overruns and other problems LILCO was encountering in trying to finish the plant could lead to its financial demise."[70]

She continued,

> The story never ran. My editor accused me of bias so deep-seated that the story could not be edited or revised. He indicated further that for the *Times* to print such a story

prominently could adversely affect LILCO's financial well-being. He further told me that I—at the time covering Long
Island for the paper—should in the future consider LILCO out
of my beat. When I told him this was unacceptable, I was
punished by being removed from Long Island coverage and left
to dangle, uncomfortably, without portfolio and anything of
substance to work on.

It was soon clear that LILCO was at the brink of bankruptcy
because of Shoreham, she noted. She had known that was coming
because of "ten years of covering consumer issues and Long Island
issues which often had me focusing on LILCO. It came from living on
the Island and knowing the geography of the Shoreham site, which
Suffolk County later flatly stated would prevent evacuation." And, it
came from having studied analyses "of the financial straits which
LILCO was approaching."

Cerra commented later to me that the paper has been concerned
that critical coverage of Shoreham could "cause the stock market to
react. You could see their point of view because they can cause a
company to go bankrupt. On the other hand, at what point does the
responsibility to be very careful conflict with the duty to call the
public's attention to a problem? That's a fine call. So in my opinion,
they erred on the side of too much prudence."[71]

She continued that she understands that *The New York Times*
"carries such tremendous weight that writing about a company in a
bad light can cause them grave financial distress, and it's not to be
taken lightly. And I don't take that lightly, either. . . . But in my case
they were blind to the reality of the situation."

The Times has written numerous editorials supporting LILCO on
Shoreham—far disproportionate to the attention it has given to other
utilities outside of the New York City area and their nuclear projects.

"Long Island Goes Nuclear or Bust," was the title of a lead editorial in 1983.

> Some people believe the risks of nuclear reactors are intoler-
> able at any cost. Some people believe that Lilco should be
> broken financially for its management of the construction, even
> if Long Island must bear much of the burden. Most New York-
> ers and their leaders, however, should not be so quick to scuttle
> this huge investment.

A lead editorial in 1984 was titled "Mr. Cuomo's Test at Shoreham." In this, it called the governor's argument that "the safety issue is paramount" at Shoreham, "a charade." *The Times* said, "The intrinsic safety of Shoreham has been definitively assessed by the Federal Atomic Safety and Licensing Board."

A 1985 editorial was titled "Shoreham: Undamned? Undammed?" The piece, reacting to Cohalan's "astonishing reversal," declared: "Mr. Cohalan's change of heart begins a constructive process. The Governor's cooperation can complete it."

"The Low Road to Shoreham" was the title of a 1986 editorial. This one came after the FEMA drill of the LILCO evacuation plan and announced: "People who live near LILCO's dormant nuclear plant at Shoreham on Long Island can be safely evacuated in the event of an emergency. That much was proved by the evacuation exercise held this month under Federal supervision."

"I built a full-time career on covering nuclear horror stories *The New York Times* neglected," said Anna Mayo, a writer for *The Village Voice*.[72] She said she believes that the support of LILCO and Shoreham by *The Times* is related to common financial sources. "I've been told that the financing of *The Times* has involved Chase Manhattan, Citibank, that the Rockefellers have become more involved. These records are not public, so there is no way of knowing." She said through the years *Times* reporters seeking to investigate nuclear issues have told her about being "shifted off" these stories, and she has been given material that *Times* reporters "could not use."

Mayo has also had experience with another daily newspaper which has been a major booster of LILCO and its nuclear plants, *Newsday*. Based on Long Island, it has recently been expanding westward seeking to become a major New York region newspaper with its *New York Newsday* edition.

In the 1960s, said Mayo, she was asked to do "articles on nuclear power for *Newsday* for their 'Viewpoints' page. One, which proved to be a prophecy, dealt with evacuation." Another, a 1970 piece headlined "Mark Nuclear Energy as Your Worst Buy," began: "It is amazing how tenaciously American utilities cling to the belief that they can fool all of the people all of the time. While it is becoming very clear that nuclear power is prohibitively expensive for the ratepayer, the power companies continue to claim that it is the best buy available."

Then, she said, she was told that "LILCO executives were around at *Newsday*, they were there a lot, going into conferences. It was all very friendly. Then I did a piece on Hiroshima Day and it was rejected, and I did not write for *Newsday* again."

Former *Newsday* national editor Ernest Volkman wrote an article on *Newsday*'s approach to LILCO in the November 1980 issue of *Media People*.

> There are people on Long Island who suggest that, when viewed as a whole in the context of its support for the Shoreham nuclear plant, *Newsday*'s performance proved the power of a big utility to get favorable coverage in a major daily. A big advertising contract, this argument runs, is all LILCO needs to keep *Newsday* in line. But they are wrong. In fact, the relationship between LILCO and *Newsday* is more complicated.

Volkman said that *Newsday*, founded in 1940, went through a "profound shift" in 1970 with its sale to the Times-Mirror Co. media conglomerate.

> Life was not the same. The first clue was the firing of Bill Moyers, *Newsday*'s publisher, who had helped to build the paper's national journalistic reputation. . . . Traditionally, *Newsday* regarded itself as totally independent—an us-against-them posture aided by the paper's financial success. But Times-Mirror, a company obsessed with growth, saw *Newsday* as only on the threshold of a major expansion, and made it clear to the next executives that their jobs depended on greater profit.
>
> [That] dictum has been translated into an editorial philosophy that might be summarized as More Growth. Reduced to its essentials, the new thrust at *Newsday* has been to encourage greater growth on Long Island—and, coincidentally, greater growth in *Newsday* profits. Growth, in simple terms, meant more business, more industry, more homes, more income, more readers. To meet this goal, *Newsday* began an extensive courtship of the Long Island business community—a group it had openly antagonized in the old days—to mobilize a crusade for industrial expansion and greater commercial development. Capstone of this effort was a *Newsday* brainchild called the Long Island Action Committee, a coalition of business and industry leaders—including *Newsday*'s publisher—to lobby for development of Long Island.

How do LILCO and Shoreham fit into all this? To support its vision of great growth for Long Island—especially on its eastern end—*Newsday* has also argued that Long Island needs more electrical generating power—namely, nuclear power. LILCO's nuclear power plans are key to *Newsday*'s growth vision, since without power, the grand design of industrial and commercial development cannot take place. Indeed, LILCO and *Newsday* have recently contracted for the utility to buy *Newsday*'s headquarters building. The relationship between LILCO and *Newsday* smacks more of two business partners.

Volkman then explored the *Newsday*-created Long Island Action Committee and its links to LILCO, including the facts that committee's executive director is the son of LILCO's founder and its board includes LILCO's chairman.

He examined *Newsday* coverage of Shoreham, declaring that

virtually without comment, *Newsday* recorded the various problems at Shoreham . . . and has sought to downplay them. At the same time, it has kept up a drumfire of support for the project. Shortly after the Three Mile Island accident, for example, the paper prepared a lengthy editorial insert headlined, "Choices: The Future of Energy on Long Island." The insert, ostensibly an objective account of the problems of energy in the context of Three Mile Island, was so favorable to LILCO that the utility reproduced it and circulated it throughout Long Island. In case reporters working on the project didn't get the idea, one memo from the editors instructed them on how to proceed: "Keep comments from anti-nuclear activists succinct."

Volkman declared:

Newsday's efforts on behalf of Shoreham have not proven very persuasive. Put bluntly, many of its readers no longer trust the paper's coverage of the issue. . . . This is a sad performance, and illustrates once again the fatal lure of that perennial delusion that often afflicts newspaper owners and editors—the delusion that they can somehow mesh their commercial self-interests with their own editorial interests and still emerge clean. It cannot be done. Ultimately, such disrespect for the public interest and intelligence carries a heavy price: Credibility. *Newsday* will learn—to its cost—in the final analysis that readers will exact that price.

The titles of recent *Newsday* editorials in the constant stream boosting LILCO and Shoreham include: "Feeding the Public's Fears about Shoreham" (July 29, 1985); "Any Leadership Left for Shoreham?" (May 20, 1985); "Suffolk's LILCO Takeover Plan Is Half-Baked" (March 10, 1985); "Why Not Test the Shoreham Evacuation Plan?" (March 1, 1985); "Without Shoreham, Expect More Brownouts" (December 23, 1984); "Suffolk's Cost Overruns in Fighting Shoreham" (September 6, 1984); "Cuomo Should Try to Break the Shoreham Impasse" (March 14, 1983); "Stop the Bickering and Get On with Shoreham" (February 7, 1983).

Many of the editorials are written by Elizabett Van Nostrand, who occasionally breaks into a personal column. She began one (January 22, 1983), headlined "Suffolk Legislators and Shoreham," with: "If ignorance is bliss, the Suffolk County Legislature must have been close to heaven Tuesday. The thought that this body may be in charge of making decisions on emergency planning for the Shoreham nuclear plant would be laughable if it weren't so alarming."

Newsday associate editor William Sexton regularly champions LILCO and Shoreham, too. Wrote Sexton on October 22, 1985, "Now Three Mile Island is back in operation, while fear—not the cost of Shoreham, but the blind, unfounded fear of it . . . grips people in Suffolk."

The long *Newsday* campaign resulted in bumper stickers being distributed by the People's Action Coalition: "*Newsday* Loves LILCO."

And, with regularity, the *Newsday* "Letters" page contains objections. "*Newsday*'s pro-Shoreham editorials just keep coming and coming," wrote Legislator Wayne Prospect (March 15, 1985).

It is time for "Newsday" to acknowledge that the county's and the governor's opposition is based on conviction and a genuine concern for public safety. It has become monotonous to see "Newsday" repeatedly characterize the opposition to Shoreham as obstructionist. Does disagreement with "Newsday" qualify one as an obstructionist? One might well argue that the "obstructionist" label better suits "Newsday" itself, since "Newsday" has done everything within its power to sabotage the efforts of elected government to protect the public interest on the Shoreham question."

New York State Energy Commissioner William D. Cotter accused *Newsday* of "simply spouting the LILCO line" in a May 20, 1984, letter.

Your recent series of editorials regarding Shoreham and the Long Island Lighting Co. were poorly analyzed and misleading. . . . In effect you disregard the question of safety, giving it only lip service in a single sentence in the first editorial of the series. Thereafter, in carping language about the governor's failure to agree with your editorial wisdom, you suggest the governor is wrong for not pretending that he can evacuate the endangered residents in the event of an accident. And why should he ignore people's health, safety and perhaps a danger to their lives? Because in the judgement of your editorial writer, it is necessary for LILCO's sake, and in some unspecified way for the "economy."

A *Newsday* reporter, asking to remain anonymous, explained the situation as "an example of how higher echelons at *Newsday* can be just as elitist as executives of U.S. Steel. The publisher of *Newsday* doesn't join Mr. and Mrs. Brentwood or Mr. and Mrs. Center Moriches at cocktails. *Newsday* is a big, rich outfit and those who run *Newsday* gravitate to other big money interests. High-salaried top executives anywhere pretty much have the same mindset and look at each other with approval. *Newsday*, meanwhile, is supposedly representing the public, the people, and in many ways we are. We get into many things, exposing things. But on the Shoreham issue, I think it's an abberation. It's insanity."

Weekly newspapers on Long Island have also led in the challenge to LILCO. These include *The East Hampton Star*, *The Southampton Press*, the *Hampton Chronicle-News*, *The Suffolk Times*, *The News-Review*, and *Suffolk Life*. However, for media daring to challenge LILCO there has been a cost.

David Wilmott, editor and publisher of *Suffolk Life*, said: "We have felt the pressure and the message has been clear: change your position on LILCO and Shoreham and life can be a lot easier. In most cases, it was conveyed subtly, in casual conversation. Other times it came directly."[73] Often at stake was potential advertising, particularly from financial institutions. "We have been told: We will not advertise with you unless you alter your position on LILCO." In 1985, when *Suffolk Life* prepared to move into new expanded headquarters in Riverhead, sudden difficulties in bank financing of the new building popped up, and again the message was passed: The problems would vanish "if we backed off LILCO." Wilmott has refused to be intimidated. "I think people are too damn valuable," said Wilmott, who was a member of the New York State Fact-Finding Panel on the Shoreham Nuclear Power Facility.

Said Lou Grasso, the managing editor of *Suffolk Life*: "We will not let the public down. We will not let the profession down."[74]

Former Suffolk Republican Chairman Edwin M. (Buzz) Schwenk said LILCO hired him in 1979 specifically to try to "convince Wilmott that Shoreham was necessary and constructed properly and to get off the Shoreham kick and talk about other things." Schwenk said he had no success in that. Meanwhile, he found the LILCO public relations operation flabbergasting. "These people do about the poorest job of public relations I've ever seen. They spend millions of dollars with their high pressure. They don't understand people. They haven't accomplished anything other than to become an adversary and confront the populace."[75]

Joel Martin was fired in 1984 from his long stand as host of a popular Long Island radio talk show—a show that regularly focused on LILCO—after continuous pressure by LILCO. "The first time I ever talked about LILCO on radio was in 1973. I met Richie Kessel [then a Long Island consumer activist] and had him on the show and he talked about his drive to 'Say NO to LILCO.' Then I called LILCO up and spoke to June Bruce, the PR person, asking whether they would be interested in an opportunity to speak on the radio in reaction to Kessel. She said, 'I don't know how long you have been doing this, but if you were a professional journalist, you would know better than having Richard Kessel on the air, let alone asking us to respond to him. How dare you! We will have to consider whether to go to the management of the station about this.' "[76]

Martin said he went to the management of station WBAB-FM in Babylon first and told them what happened, and they were not concerned.

He continued to feature shows on LILCO and its nuclear plant projects, and the LILCO PR department took an increasingly more belligerent stance. For example, after a 1980 program that included Kessel, Wayne Prospect, Victor Yannacone and this writer, Martin said LILCO PR person Jan Hickman called declaring: " 'I'd like to speak to you about the show that was on the air last night. Who the fuck are you to pull that shit on us? You had no right to have those people on and that's going to the management!' Those were her exact words."

Meanwhile, said Martin, he was told that LILCO "was monitoring" his program. He got that information, he said, from the man doing the monitoring, Eric Peters of Albertson, Long Island. "He just called one night."

Peters confirmed in an interview that he monitored the Joel Martin Show for LILCO, and that he continues to monitor the airwaves for LILCO. Peters said he was the "Long Island representative" for a company called Radio TV Reports based in Manhattan. He said the company has had LILCO as an account for "I would say twenty years." Peters said, "I hear Nora Bredes of the Shoreham Opponents Coalition all day long. And John Matthews. What happened to Marge Harrison? She never talks anymore. I think all these people are fighting a losing battle. They won't admit the fact that Shoreham will open in a year, particularly if Cuomo decides to run for President. Then Kessel will have to leave the country."[77]

Martin said despite the "LILCO intimidation," the owners of WBAB, Sol and Muriel Horenstein, "stood with me." Then the station was sold in 1983, and the new owners promptly sent a note asking for "the most recent programs about LILCO." Several weeks later, Joel Martin was told he was fired. He also received numerous threatening calls at home, including death threats. His house was vandalized, the tires of his car were slashed, and he was physically attacked and beaten. There were demonstrations at WBAB protesting his being fired.

"It was the only nightly talk show on an FM contemporary music station in America," said Martin. "It was very highly rated. In the spring of '83 we were seven point four for a midnight to two time slot, twice the station's general rating. It had nothing to do with ratings. LILCO was after me for a decade, for reaching a young adult audience and letting them know what LILCO was up to."

NOTES

1. Wayne Prospect in an interview with the author, April 1986.
2. Gregory Blass in an interview with the author, April 1986.
3. Quoted in *Newsday*, July 23, 1982.
4. Quoted in *The New York Times*, July 23, 1982.
5. This comment by Administrative Judge Vincent Furlong was reported in *Newsday*, August 3, 1982.
6. Jim Blew in an interview with the author, January 1986.
7. *Suffolk Life*, August 11, 1985.
8. Jane Devine in an interview with the author, August 1985.
9. The author was present at this and subsequent legislative sessions when legislators commented on the matter.
10. Reported in *Newsday*, August 17, 1985.
11. Quoted in *Newsday*, March 25, 1985.
12. John Klein in an interview with the author, April 1986.
13. Joyce Burland in an interview with the author, April 1986.
14. Floyd Linton in an interview with the author, April 1986.
15. Lou Howard's comment was made, in various forms, to fellow legislators and the author numerous times.
16. The author was present at the demonstrations noted here.
17. Kathleen Boylan in an interview with the author, April 1986.
18. The author was present at the annual LILCO shareowners meeting.
19. Eve Pell, *The Big Chill: How the Reagan Administration, Corporate America, and Religious Conservatives Are Subverting Free Speech and the Public's Right to Know*. Boston: Beacon Press, 1985.
20. *The East Hampton Star*, January 23, 1981.
21. Wayne Prospect in an interview with the author, February 1986.
22. Leon Campo in an interview with the author, February 1986.
23. The author was at Suffolk Legislature meetings at which Campo, Like and Latham spoke.
24. The author was present at the special legislative session on May 18, 1982, which dealt with LILCO's sending the report to the state.
25. Gregory Blass in an interview with the author, August 1984.
26. Edward Boughal in an interview with the author, December 1984.
27. Wayne Prospect in an interview with the author, December 1984.
28. The letter was signed by Chief Deputy County Executive John Gallagher.
29. Gregory Blass in an interview with the author, June 1985.
30. The author was present at demonstrations at Cohalan's office.
31. Quoted in *Newsday*, June 2, 1985.
32. The author was present at the special meeting of county and town officials.
33. Quoted in *Newsday*, June 1, 1985.
34. Quoted in *The New York Times*, June 1, 1985.
35. This interview with Cohalan was published in *Newsday*, December 31, 1985.
36. Wayne Prospect in an interview with the author, April 1984.
37. The author was present at the court proceeding at which the Cohalan executive order was challenged.
38. John V. N. Klein's comments were made in an interview with the author, March 1986.
39. John Behan in an interview with the author, June 1986.
40. *Southampton Press* editorial, June 6, 1985.

41. The author was present at legislative session at which Blass gave his acceptance speech.
42. Comments here and following by Marge Harrison were made in an interview with the author, April 1986.
43. *The New York Times*, December 26, 1980. The story was headlined: "Margiotta's Defense Fund: G.O.P. Leader in Kickback Case Finds No Dearth of Noted Politicians to Chip In for His Legal Fees."
44. Comments made at Margiotta's sentencing are from *Newsday*, January 22, 1982.
45. Comments here and following by John Matthews were made in interviews with the author, January and April 1986.
46. *Newsday*, September 20, 1985.
47. *Newsday*, October 28, 1985.
48. *Newsday*, October 28, 1985.
49. John Matthews' comments and the comments following by William Catacosinos at shareowners' meeting were reported in *The New York Times*, *Newsday*, and *The Daily News*, all December 13, 1985.
50. Edward Larkin in an interview with the author, December 1985.
51. Ann Mead in an interview with the author, December 1985.
52. *Newsday*, August 16, 1984.
53. Irving Like in an interview with the author, April 1986.
54. *The New York Times*, December 19, 1971.
55. Adam Madsen's statement was reported in *Newsday*, May 17, 1985.
56. Richard Kessel's statement, ibid.
57. *The East Hampton Star*, January 10, 1985.
58. The comments by John Mullen were made in an interview with the author, April 1986.
59. Tom Twomey in an interview with the author, April 1986.
60. Quoted in *Newsday*, April 11, 1984.
61. Frank Robinson's decision story appeared in *The New York Times*, June 12, 1984, with the headline: "11% RISE IN RATES IS URGED FOR LILCO, Hearing Officer Bids P.S.C. Act to Avert Utility Bankruptcy."
62. *Newsday*, June 13, 1984.
63. Paul Harenberg's comments, and those following, were made in a letter to Gioia and in a public statement reported in, among other publications, the *Review* newspapers in a story with a headline: "Harenberg to PSC: 'There is life after LILCO.' "
64. Paul Harenberg in an interview with the author, March 1986.
65. Steven Liss in an interview with the author, March 1986.
66. Charles Dumas' comment on Anderson's law firm representing utilities was made to the author, February 1986.
67. Gary Lavine in an interview with the author, February 1986.
68. Paul Harenberg in an interview with the author, March 1986.
69. David Hepp in an interview with the author, March 1986.
70. *The Quill*, March 1984.
71. Frances Cerra in an interview with the author, December 1984.
72. Anna Mayo in an interview with the author, March 1986.
73. David Wilmott in an interview with the author, January 1986.
74. Lou Grasso in an interview with the author, January 1986.
75. Edwin (Buzz) Schwenk in an interview with the author, December 1985.
76. Joel Martin in an interview with the author, December 1985.
77. Eric Peters in an interview with the author, April 1986.

9

WHAT COULD HAVE BEEN
AND STILL CAN BE

"WE ALL LIVE IN CHERNOBYL," declared the banner as people gathered near LILCO's Shoreham nuclear plant to stress that the disaster that occurred in the Soviet Union could happen at Shoreham.[1]

The bright blossoms of early May on the trees and shrubs smelled sweet. The waters of the Long Island Sound glistened in the spring sun.

"We said a long time ago," declared Nora Bredes of the Shoreham Opponents Coalition, "that the answer could come blowing in the wind." It had—out of Russia, she said.

Two protesters dressed in the black robes of the grim reaper stood on both sides of the banner about Chernobyl. There were other signs, too, including one about a U.S. technological catastrophe: "SHORE-HAM—AS SAFE AS THE SHUTTLE," it read. Black balloons were released to indicate where radioactivity from a Shoreham accident would be carried in the wind.

Bredes cited the projections of the NRC's 1982 report, undertaken by Sandia National Laboratories, that a core meltdown at Shoreham could leave 40,000 "early fatalities," 75,000 "early injuries," 35,000 "cancer deaths" and $157 billion in property damage. "Being right here, we would be those 40,000 dead!" said Bredes. The dome of Shoreham could be seen in the distance.

The disaster at Chernobyl strengthened the feeling on Long Island against LILCO and its nuclear plans. It showed that catastrophic nuclear plant accidents are no impossibility: they can happen, and have devastating and long-lasting consequences.

Joe Paparatto of the SHAD Alliance, which organized the 150 protesters, said: "This is a critical time! Now is the time to put more pressure on than ever!" After he spoke, he said he was "encouraged that there are a lot of new faces here today."

Legislator Wayne Prospect commented earlier in the week: "As a result of that tragedy, only a card-carrying fanatic in the atomic brotherhood would now deny that serious accidents can occur with commercial nuclear power plants."[2]

It had been a week that revealed not only how the people of the Soviet Union were being lied to about nuclear power, but how people in the U.S.—including those on Long Island—were not being told the truth either, and still weren't.

"By Design, It Can't Happen Here," declared a headline in *Newsday* (April 30, 1986) above a story in which it was claimed that the containment domes on U.S. reactors could hold in the radioactivity released in any accident—a claim which *Newsday* accepted uncritically. (Later, the NRC would say that the Chernobyl reactor did have a containment dome.[3])

Brian McCaffrey, assistant to the vice president of nuclear operations of LILCO, was quoted as saying that the Shoreham "design assumes an accident has taken place, and the containment is made to handle the consequences."

Said Andrew Hull of Brookhaven National Laboratory: "Our containments are built to withstand pressure by a factor of two to three times of any accident."

Dr. Richard Webb stressed, meanwhile, what he has said for years, that "containments—at Shoreham or any U.S. nuclear plant—are not designed for the worst accident possibilities." They are built just to contain a small loss-of-coolant accident, he explained, and not to withstand the pressures of steam explosions that would occur during a serious core meltdown, or a massive instantaneous steam explosion occurring during a power excursion or nuclear runaway. "Do we have to wait until the huge catastrophe happens here?" Webb asked.[4]

The Sandia National Laboratories' analysis expected a bursting of the containment dome in severe core meltdown accidents in making its projections of death, injuries, cancer and property damage at Shoreham—or at any other nuclear plant under construction or in operation in the U.S.

The study,[5] the most recent comprehensive government analysis of the consequences of nuclear plant accidents, described five "groups" of nuclear plant accidents in a list of "accident spectrums."

The least serious, an "SST-5" (SST for "Siting Source Terms") would involve "limited core damage . . . the containment functions as designed." An "SST-4" would involve "modest core damage. Containment systems operate in a degraded mode." There would be "severe core damage" in an SST-3 and "containment fails by basemat melt-through," the "China syndrome." Then, in an "SST-2" there would be "severe core damage. Containment fails to isolate. Fission products release, mitigating systems (e.g., sprays, suppression pool, fan coolers) operate to reduce release." Finally, in an "SST-1" there would be "severe core damage" and "severe direct breach of containment."

Consequences of an "SST-1" for the Indian Point 3 nuclear plant, just north of New York City, were estimated by the study as being as high as 50,000 "early fatalities," 167,000 "early injuries," 14,000 "cancer deaths" and $314 billion in property damage. For the Salem 2 nuclear plant in New Jersey, it projected 100,000 "early fatalities," 75,000 "early injuries" 14,000 "cancer deaths" and $150 billion in property damage. Assessments in the analysis of "early fatalities," "early injuries," "cancer deaths" and property damage differ from plant to plant based on where they are sited, metereology, anticipated speed of evacuating the public, and other factors.

As to chances of an "SST-1" with "severe breach of containment" occurring, the analysis cited NRC estimates—what were called "probabilistic risk assessments"—of 1-in-100,000 "per reactor year." The chances of an "SST-2" are put at 2-in-100,000 per reactor year. And the chances of an "SST-3" are put at 1-in-10,000 per reactor year.

Webb said there could be worse accidents than the type of core meltdown that the Sandia analysis regarded as the most serious nuclear plant accident. He said he had made a thorough study of the Sandia report, interviewed the scientists who prepared it, and examined the data they used. The study did not consider a "massive reactor explosion"—including the major instantaneous steam explosion that could happen in a nuclear runaway. Further, he said, the Sandia report concluded that in the most serious accident it considered, the "SST-1," "only 16 percent" of the radioactive poisons in a nuclear plant would be released. It "simply accepted" NRC "source terms" premised on the belief that most of the other radioactive poisons would get "tied up in the reactor."[6]

He stressed that in an explosive "bursting" of a nuclear plant, much more radioactive poisons could be expected to be released. He also said the report did not adequately calculate the effect of plutonium fallout.

He said the report's researchers told him they estimated that up to 10,000 square miles of land could face "abandonment" in the wake of a serious nuclear plant accident. Webb said the more accurate estimate, based on the toxicity of the radioactive materials released and the area on which they could fall, could be 100,000 square miles.

Also, he said, the Sandia report "did not consider site radiation levels requiring evacuation of all the other reactors on the site. It didn't consider whether people would stay at adjacent reactors to obtain a safe shutdown mode." If they could not, he said, a catastrophic accident at one nuclear plant resulting in evacuation of all people from a site could lead to a major accident at a second or third nuclear plant at the same site—the sort of nuclear domino effect feared at Chernobyl.

In addition, said Webb, the evacuation of all people from the site could affect what is called the "spent fuel storage pool" at the site. This is a large swimming pool-like structure in which radioactive waste is stored. Water must constantly be kept circulating in the pool to dissipate the heat of the radioactive waste. Otherwise it would erupt, said Webb, with catastrophic consequences in what is termed a "loss of water" accident. Spent fuel storage pools, further, have only sheet metal roofs so there would be no stopping a release to the atmosphere. Webb said that in the event of a severe reactor accident, when personnel would have to flee for their lives and leave the storage pool unattended, there is a strong possibility that the pool's pumps would not be able to continue to function automatically. Thus, a "loss of water" accident in the nuclear waste pool could follow a major plant accident.

Webb also said that in terms of the deaths in the general population from the plume of radioactivity released in a severe nuclear plant accident (a plume he said would be roughly one mile wide and 75 miles long), as high as the estimates in the Sandia report were, they could be much higher. He said that "if the plume moved on New York City, the number of deaths could be many fold greater than the estimate in the Sandia report. There could be several hundred thousand deaths or maybe close to a million."

Jack Hickman, manager of the department at Sandia that prepared the report, had confirmed earlier that it did not take into account nuclear runaways and the other accident scenarios that Webb projected as causing a massive reactor explosion.[7]

Further, Hickman said the steam explosions that were considered would occur several hours into a loss-of-coolant accident. "They wouldn't affect the warning time period," said Hickman. (Thus evacuation could still be considered a possibility.)

He said that Sandia based its analysis on scenarios for a nuclear plant accident as given in a 1974 AEC report entitled *Reactor Safety Study: An Assessment of Accident Risks in U.S. Commercial Nuclear Power Plants*, which was given a serial number of WASH-1400.

This report provided the least negative picture on the likelihood and consequences of nuclear plant accidents since the WASH-740. The chairman of the study group that prepared it was Dr. Norman C. Rasmussen, a nuclear physicist at the Massachusetts Institute of Technology and a leading advocate of nuclear power.

It projected that with 100 nuclear plants operating in the U.S., one core meltdown "would occur, on the average, every one and three quarters centuries."

In 1985, in reply to a request from Representative Edward Markey, the NRC changed those odds drastically. Markey asked, "What does the Commission and NRC staff believe the likelihood of a severe core melt in the next twenty years for those reactors now operating and those expected to operate during that time?"

The NRC's official response—"In a population of 100 reactors operating over a period of 20 years, the crude cumulative probability of such an accident would be 45%."[8]

But abstract numbers weren't the issue in the wake of Chernobyl on Long Island. In the February 1986 issue of *Soviet Life* there was an article about nuclear power in Russia, with special attention given the Chernobyl nuclear facility. It was accompanied by an interview with the minister of power and electricity in the Ukraine, Vitali Sklyarov. Amid color photos meant to present Russian nuclear power in the best possible light, in the article Sklyarov was asked: "Nuclear plants are being built close to big cities and resort areas. How safe are they?" He replied, "The odds of a meltdown are one in 10,000 years."[9]

On Long Island and all over the world, the clouds of radioactivity that erupted from the Chernobyl accident and descended over Europe are imprinted in the public mind.

Cesium-137 had descended in massive amounts, the radioisotope that attacks the gonads, ovaries and muscle systems and has a half-life of 30 years or a hazardous lifetime of 600 years. (Dr. Irving Lyon of Bennington College had testified about cesium-137 at the AEC Shoreham construction permit hearings. He told how it substituted for potassium in the soft tissues and muscles of fish and concentrated with a "factor of 6,500.") Strontium-90, the radioisotope that attacks the bone marrow and causes leukemia, also fell out in large amounts. Strontium-90 has a half-life of 28 years and so a hazardous lifetime (hazardous lifetimes are determined by multiplying half-lives by 20) of 560 years. Then there were massive amounts of iodine-131 that attacks the thyroid and causes thyroid cancer. It is relatively short-lived with a half-life of eight days and a hazardous lifetime of 160 days. And there were many other fission products—lethal twins of safe and stable elements in nature—released, some with extremely long hazardous lifetimes.

It was not clear in the wake of Chernobyl how many people died immediately, but it was becoming clearer that an epidemic of disease and death would follow and continue for many years. This was the sort of nightmare that nuclear power could *really* cause.

Some Long Island news accounts noted that Shoreham was a mere 60 miles from midtown Manhattan, the geographical center of a metropolitan area with nearly 20 million people, and Chernobyl was 60 miles from Kiev.

Meanwhile, another major incident of LILCO mismanagement was revealed in the weeks prior to Chernobyl, along with a major example of the Reagan administration's promotion of Shoreham.

"It's a very serious problem" said NRC inspector John Berry.[10] A member of the Shoreham Radiochemistry Department came to him, he said, claiming "something wasn't right" in the department. That led to an NRC investigation and, for the NRC, amazingly strong criticism of LILCO.

"The result of this inspection raises serious concerns regarding the quality and management of the Radiochemistry Program at Shoreham and the attentiveness of Senior Management to identified program deficiencies," wrote Richard W. Starostecki, director of the NRC's regional division of reactor projects, to LILCO.[11]

An NRC report said that in preparing people for the positions in that critical department—it is supposed to determine the amount of radioactivity released from the plant—"No formal training for technicians was offered, nor was training review of qualification records evident." Further, "Some of the problems noted with the improper use of control charts and graphs appear not to be due to a deliberate attempt by technicians and foremen to ignore trends or indicators, but rather indicate that they in fact were unaware of the purpose of these graphs and charts."

The report continued: "Numerous instances were found where individuals had been certified as technicians without having completed the required initial program." LILCO was involved in the sort of thing Ronald Stanchfield had spoken of a year earlier; they had "qualified the chemistry technicians on procedures by giving open book exams."

The NRC also spoke of poor physical conditions in the department, it being in "a general state of clutter and disarray."

As a result of its probe into the Radiochemistry Department, the NRC said it would delay giving permission to LILCO to resume low-power testing of Shoreham.

Then, on April 14, Frank Petrone, the regional director of FEMA, resigned after refusing to remove a line he included in FEMA's report on the February LILCO evacuation plan drill. The line said that "since the plan cannot be implemented without state and local participation, FEMA cannot give reasonable assurance . . . that the public health and safety can be protected."

Petrone declared at a press conference that FEMA Director Julius Becton told him to alter the report or be fired. "I had no choice," he said. "They wanted me to change my report."[12]

Petrone also charged that FEMA had been under "tremendous pressure" from the NRC, the DOE, and other federal agencies—and the White House—to assist in getting Shoreham licensed to operate.

In his letter of resignation, Petrone wrote: "I believe the credibility of the agency is endangered when the national office moves to overturn critical regional decisions, particularly where the courts have ruled on their issues."

Governor Cuomo praised Petrone's "courage and integrity."[13]

Herbert Brown called the situation "FEMAgate."

Legislator Wayne Prospect said: "FEMA is exhibiting outright contempt for the people of Suffolk County."[14]

Legislator Tony Bullock, an East Hampton Democrat, said: "It's a tangible manifestation of what we know to be happening—the heavy-handedness of FEMA and the collusion between the federal agencies and LILCO."[15]

Meanwhile, a move to try to get rid of LILCO had been proceeding under full steam.

During the winter before the Chernobyl accident, a mile from the waterfall on Sumpwams Creek in Babylon Village—the source of energy for the first utility on Long Island, the Babylon Electric Light Company—Maurice Barbash was sitting in his office, coordinating Citizens to Replace LILCO.

"It's unbelievable!" said Barbash. "The phones are jumping off the hooks. I've never seen an issue that has generated more public response on Long Island."[16]

The group had just run a full-page advertisement in Long Island newspapers and the response had been strong. A dummy of the advertisement was hanging near his desk.

"THE PROBLEM ISN'T JUST SHOREHAM. THE PROBLEM IS LILCO!" it declared. "The problem isn't just whether Shoreham is safe, nor just whether hundreds of thousands of men, women and children can get off Long Island quickly and safely in case of accident . . . all legitimate fears. The real problem is LILCO."

Under the heading, "LILCO'S MANAGEMENT," the advertisement spoke of how "LILCO's mismanagement is staggering." It noted the huge Shoreham cost overrun, the $1.395 billion PSC penalty against LILCO, how the company "neglected vital services like storm damage prevention." The Chairman of Grumman, Long Island's largest employer, summed it up: "The cost of Shoreham now threatens to destroy the economy of Long Island."

It went on: "BUT THAT'S NOT ALL. Now LILCO wants you to foot the bill for their foul-ups." It spoke of LILCO attempting to have its ratepayer pay the PSC penalty, the penalties incurred for its refusal to pay property taxes, and the cost of damages during Hurricane Gloria "aggravated" by LILCO. "Gov. Cuomo called LILCO's proposals a scheme to save itself at public expense. Right! In fact, LILCO wants to lock us all into their higher rates and safety problems. Forever. Isn't there a better way? You bet there is!"

It cited the municipally owned Rockville Centre public power utility on Long Island where people pay "less than half of what the rest of us (who are in LILCO's clutches) pay."

The way to deal with LILCO, said the advertisement, is to "REPLACE LILCO WITH A LONG ISLAND POWER AUTHORITY. Financial experts confirm it: replacing LILCO with a Long Island Power Authority will cost a lot less than bailing LILCO out."

Further, it declared,

A L.I. POWER AUTHORITY WOULD PROTECT OUR SAFETY. Here's the plain fact: LILCO's life depends on opening Shoreham—and making all of us pay for it. And this despite Shoreham's safety problems. That's why they're spending a fortune on propaganda while we put up with terrible service. A Long Island Power Authority would close Shoreham, keep it out of the rate base and supply dependable, safe power at far lower cost. Simple as that.

The advertisement closed with

LILCO, THE MANIPULATOR. LILCO has taken other steps to bamboozle us, intimidate our legislators and manipulate local elections. They've hired California and Washington PR hotshots and are planning to spend whatever is necessary to hype us by flooding the newspapers and airwaves with their slick propaganda. . . . If you've had it with incompetence and arrogance, if you resent LILCO's attempts to take over our local governments, if you're fed up with one of the country's worst utilities—join us now.

Hanging up on a far wall was a bumper sticker from the group Barbash earlier led, Citizens Committee for a Fire Island National Seashore. "This dwarfs the Fire Island issue, on an economical level, on an environmental level," he commented. "I have had a long affair going with Long Island. I think it's the greatest place to live. My way of life is here. My family is here. I love it here, and don't want to move. LILCO is a terrible threat—economically and environmentally. Either way, it can destroy us."

He explained the strategy: New York State in conjunction with Long Island's counties, rather than condemning LILCO's assets and taking over the company in this way, would buy LILCO's depressed stock, take over the company and dissolve it, and establish a public power authority in its stead. The authority's first priority would be to abandon Shoreham. The authority would be run by "an elected non-partisan board, like a school board. It would be—unlike LILCO—accountable to the people."

He spoke of how, without Shoreham, a "major threat to life" would be removed, and with LILCO being replaced by a public power entity, "our rates could become reasonable."

Barbash stressed, "We've done our homework." He pulled out a report prepared for Citizens to Replace LILCO by the Energy Systems Research Group of Boston. "The central conclusion of the analysis here," said the report, "is that the public power alternative does, indeed, promise substantial benefits to electric customers. Further, "the authority would not share LILCO's corporate imperative that Shoreham operate," and because "it is likely that the operation of the Shoreham facility would not make economic sense to an authority, rendering the safety and emergency evacuation issues moot." It made a comparison of rates between LILCO and public power, and in its conclusion said:

> It appears that Long Island ratepayers would fare considerably better under power provision by a public authority than under the continued operation of LILCO. Rates are likely to be of the order of 25–35 percent less, the Shoreham issue can be finally resolved, and, with more progressive utility management, new sources of electricity and demand-side savings can be pursued.

Several weeks later, the steering committee of Citizens to Replace LILCO was having a meeting.[17]

A broad-based panel, it included former Suffolk County Republican chairman Anthony Prudenti; Arthur Metzger, the leader of a business group upset about LILCO rates; Nassau financier Norman Blankman; Dan Gluck, head of the New York Community Action Network, a community-advocacy group; Judith Sneddon, director of Guild Hall, an arts and theatre center in East Hampton; Nancy Nagle Kelley, president of the Group for the South Fork, an environmental organization—and old anti-LILCO hands—Leon Campo, Nora Bredes, Tom Twomey, Irving Like, and Bill Chaleff, chair of the East End Shoreham Opponents.

Results of a recent poll commissioned by *Newsday* on Shoreham were being discussed. The November 1985 poll found, as *Newsday* phrased it,

> opposition to the Shoreham nuclear power plant has reached an all-time high of 71 percent, as confidence in LILCO's man-

agement has continued to decline. . . . The poll also found
that seven out of 10 Long Islanders believe Shoreham's owners,
Long Island Lighting Co., should be taken over and run by
local government as a publicly owned utility.

The poll found, "in Suffolk County, 77 percent of residents oppose
Shoreham, while only 15 percent favor its operation. In Nassau, the
breakdown is 65 percent opposed and 26 percent in favor." On replacement of LILCO by public power, 71 percent said they were in
favor, 20 percent said they were opposed and the remaining 12 percent
were undecided.

"This is a movement of the people by the people for the people,"
said Campo.

Twomey spoke about "contacting every elected official on Long
Island" to get support for the public power drive—a page from the
Jamesport campaign.

The discussion turned to the proposed FEMA drill of the LILCO
evacuation plan. "They're really trying to ram this down the throats of
the people of Long Island," said Barbash.

Prudenti said he planned to "get in touch with the Republican
National Committee . . . the president, the vice president. They're
going to know what the people of Long Island think about this!"

The Suffolk Legislature at its first meeting of the new year passed
a resolution supporting replacement of LILCO by a public power
authority. The bill began: "Whereas, the Long Island Lighting Company, through years of mismanagement, arrogance, and indifference
to the interests of the people and economy of Suffolk County, has lost
the public's confidence . . ."

Suffolk's town supervisors declared their support for the bill.

Even Nassau County Executive Francis Purcell found himself
forced to put together a commission, on which he asked Maurice
Barbash to serve, to consider the issue. However, others named to the
panel included long-term Shoreham supporter and former secretary
to Governor Nelson Rockefeller William Ronan; John Donohue, second vice-president of Chase Manhattan; and, in an ex-officio capacity, Deputy Nassau County Executive Owen Smith, a son-in-law of
CIA director William Casey.

And then, surprisingly, the state senators from both Suffolk and
Nassau—all Republicans—announced they would support a takeover

of LILCO by a public power authority. "We believe that a public agency would be able to best meet Long Islanders' energy needs at reasonable rates," they said.[18]

Harenberg introduced enabling legislation in the State Assembly. It began:

> The legislature hereby finds and declares that an economic emergency exists in the Long Island Lighting Company franchise area. Mismanagement and imprudent decisions by LILCO have caused constantly escalating and intolerable costs of electricity in the franchise area thereby posing a serious threat to the economic well-being of the residents and commerce of the area. Such actions have further impaired and weakened the capability of LILCO to meet the energy needs of the people in a reliable, efficient and economic manner. In addition, they have diverted resources from beneficial investments in energy conservation, improved energy efficiency, improved transmission capability and alternative sources of energy supply to investments in projects which threaten the economy and business climate in the Long Island area. The investment in the Shoreham nuclear power plant has created significant rate increases, intolerable to the Long Island ratepayers, and will require further extraordinary rate increases should the plant go into service.

Governor Cuomo declared: "I very much like the idea of public power generally. It's been enormously successful. It means you don't have shareholders to give your dividends to. And LILCO has trouble."[19]

Cuomo formed a commission to study the issue led, oddly enough, by former U.S. Deputy Energy Secretary John Sawhill, a former member of the board of Con Edison, which, through the years, has fought off several public takeover attempts.

Sawhill was also co-author of a key strategy document on nuclear power. Entitled *Energy: Managing the Transition*, it was prepared in the form of a book published in 1978 by the Trilateral Commission, the group of U.S., Western Europe and Japanese government leaders and business executives organized in the early 1970s by David Rockefeller.

It placed great faith in nuclear power:

> Nuclear plants are large, highly capital-intense energy
> sources primarily useful for providing base load generating ca-
> pacity, and in some countries, they will undoubtedly play an
> increasingly important role in this sector of the electric utility
> industry. Yet, citizens groups in almost every one of the Trilat-
> eral countries have raised serious questions about their govern-
> ment's nuclear program, claiming that the current generation
> of fission reactors creates certain undesirable environmental
> effects and has the added disadvantage of producing a highly
> radioactive waste that must be stored for thousands of years.
> Some of these protests have been quite vocal and have had the
> effect of limiting the number of sites available for future plants,
> increasing the time required to build new plants, and, as a
> consequence, increasing the cost and reducing the potential
> economic benefits of nuclear energy.

Energy: Managing the Transition, which Sawhill wrote with a
Japanese professor of nuclear engineering and the European secretary
of The Trilateral Commission, notes, "This 'social constraint' is a
relatively new dimension in the nuclear equation that governments
must take into account in evaluating their future nuclear plants." And
it concludes:

> The existence of such a constraint will make it increasingly
> necessary for governments to encourage open discussion and
> debate on nuclear issues and to disseminate as widely as possi-
> ble correct information on the benefits and safety of nuclear
> power in comparison with the risks associated with it.

The strategy of *Energy: Managing the Transition* was followed by
the Carter administration, which, it has been frequently noted, had a
close connection with the Trilateral Commission. Trilateral Commission members before taking office were President Carter himself, Vice
President Walter Mondale, Secretary of State Cyrus Vance, Secretary
of State Harold Brown, National Security Advisor Zbigniew Brezinski
(who ran the commission before going to Washington), and other top
Carter administration officials.

But The Trilateral Commission is also strongly linked with the
Reagan administration. Vice President George Bush and Defense Sec-

retary Weinberger, among other top Reagan administration officials, were members.

Sawhill, a Trilateral member, too, was also formerly head of the Federal Energy Office in the Nixon administration and a deputy undersecretary of Carter administration.

Another Cuomo appointee to the panel considering a LILCO takeover was Alfred Kahn, chairman of the New York PSC from 1974 to 1977. During this time LILCO, with virtually no objection from the PSC, received $140 million in rate hikes and the cost of Shoreham doubled to $1 billion. Kahn, before his PSC chairmanship, was a consultant to the utility-funded Electric Power Research Institute and afterwards a consultant to the National Economic Research Association, a private group that does work for utilities including LILCO. Kahn was also a member of the New York State Fact-Finding Panel on the Shoreham Nuclear Power Facility and joined in the minority "Clarification of Views" of Dr. Herbert Kouts and William J. Ronan, long-time secretary to Governor Rockefeller, taking issue with the majority report and holding that nuclear plant accidents "were extremely unlikely" and "the effects of such accidents were very much overestimated."

Another member of the Cuomo panel was William W. Hogan. In addition to being a professor at Harvard, he has been a consultant to the Electric Power Research Institute, as well as the utility industry trade group, the Edison Electric Institute, one of the organizations that helped fund Citizens for Shoreham Electricity. Also, Hogan was a consultant between 1981 to 1983 to General Public Utilities, the parent company of Metropolitan Edison, the owner of Three Mile Island; in 1983 to Public Service of New Hampshire, the principal owner of the Seabrook nuclear facility; and in 1983 and 1984 consultant on corporate strategy studies for various electric and gas utilities.

Several theories were advanced in Albany as to why Cuomo, a solid critic of LILCO and Shoreham, appointed such members to the LILCO panel. One held that Cuomo thought it was important that the powerful financial institutions that support utilities and the utility industry knew that a panel involved in considering a LILCO public takeover plan included people on it with close links to the industry. Another theory was that Cuomo was unaware of the close links of these members.

Also appointed by Cuomo, however, to the panel was John Bierwirth, Grumman Corporation chairman who had been taking a strong position for public power, and against Shoreham. In testimony earlier in 1985 before the State Consumer Protection Board, Bierwirth said: "By now, I think it is obvious to all of us that Shoreham is a catastrophe. It is a catastrophe for LILCO, for Grumman and all the other energy users on Long Island—which means all of us as individuals." In a letter later that year to *Newsday*, Bierwirth wrote, "The time has come to seriously consider the option of public power. . . . Public power may offer Long Island an opportunity to preserve our healthy economy."[20]

LILCO rates have indeed been causing companies to flee Long Island. The Regional Energy Action Coalition, the group led by Metzger, reported to the New York PSC in 1984 that some 28 energy-intensive Long Island firms employing 4,000 persons were actively considering moving elsewhere due to rising LILCO rates. "New Jersey electric rates are already 25 percent cheaper," said Metzger, who runs Amco Plastics Materials, Inc. of Farmingdale. "We don't want to move, but we may be forced to."[21]

Most of the firms were involved in plastics, printing, packaging and electroplating. Gerald Zimand, president of one of them, Plastcal Corp. of Farmingdale, said: "I've had it. I simply cannot compete."

Two major Long Island companies announced they were moving their manufacturing operations off Long Island because of high LILCO rates. They were Rosco Tools Inc., a screwdriver maker with plants in Smithtown and Central Islip, and New York Twist Drill Corp., a cutting-tool maker, with a plant in Melville.

Jim Van Bramer, industrial relations director of New York Twist Drill, said, "We need to stay in the East to retain expertise, but we don't need to be in LILCO territory."[22]

Public power on Long Island has long been aggressively fought by LILCO—and the utility continues to attack it with great energy. LILCO vice president Ira Freilicher candidly told me, during a major push for public power in 1981 in Suffolk, why he was against it.

As Freilicher stood at the doorway to the Suffolk Legislature's meeting room watching proceedings on public power, I kidded him: "What are you worried about? You may end up the vice president of TVA on Long Island."

Freilicher noted quickly, "I checked into how much they made at the TVA," and he found that David Freeman, then the chairman of the Tennessee Valley Authority, the nation's biggest publicly owned utility, "makes only $52,000 a year."[23] At that point, as chief of

LILCO public relations and affairs, Freilicher was making $78,000, almost 40 percent more than the head of the vast TVA.

Also on hand at the meeting lobbying against public power were other LILCO representatives, busy weaving through legislative hallways and in and out of legislative offices caucusing with legislators. They included Elaine Robinson, George Soos, and Mike Patterson, former press secretary to Governor Carey. (LILCO has made use of a wide variety of public relations practitioners including, for some time, noted media consultant David Garth.)

The scene at that 1981 meeting shocked Dorothy Wolosin, the president of the then newly formed People's Action Coalition. "I'm very disappointed. I've heard about things like this but never saw it with my own eyes. LILCO has complete access to the county legislature. It is very obvious that LILCO has enough power to dictate exactly what it wants.[24]

After the takeover legislation failed to gain sufficient votes to pass, Gregory Blass declared: "It shows once again that LILCO is far more than an innocent utility in Suffolk County. It is a major political power and there continues a close and unhealthy relationship between LILCO and county government."[25]

Wayne Prospect declared: "This is the most brazen show of lobbying I've ever seen."[26] He called some of LILCO's tactics "despicable." The utility sent out 3,600 mailgrams to legislators in the names of its employees, he charged, many identically worded including misspellings such as, "The attempt . . . is pure folley."

LILCO has always insisted public power is not workable. "This is a high risk venture with little or no benefit to the consumers," Catacosinos insisted in 1984 as the Suffolk Legislature again considered a countywide takeover of LILCO.[27]

At that hearing Perry Cohen, representing the Long Island Public Power Project, spoke and stressed the principal motivation for public power on Long Island: LILCO.

Has not the present utility management consistently, over a period of many years, conducted its decision-making process through secrecy, closed meetings, misrepresentation, refusals to allow independent inspections at Shoreham, a "me first" profit motive, and the absolute elimination of public, democratic input into the decision-making process? Are not LILCO's policies having a devastating impact upon the lives and fortunes of all Long Island residents—particularly Suffolk's? Are they not demanding that we be *prepared* to abandon our homes and businesses at a moment's notice—and face the certain chaos that would surely follow such an attempt? Are they not demanding we all make highly destructive economic sacrifices so that those same managers can continue to line their own golden pockets?

He further spoke of a "disease which seems to consume the management of LILCO—arrogance, cynicism, deception, coercion, and personal greed. . . . Damage has already been done. But we can stop any further damage and begin to take the steps that will lead to the permanent healing and health of our entire community."

Always the public power models of Freeport, Rockville Centre and Greenport—the municipal utility hold-outs to LILCO—have been close at hand.

In 1899, the village of Greenport inaugurated its public power system by purchasing a power plant from a company that was started a dozen years before.

James Monsell, Greenport superintendent of public utilities, regularly speaks of providing electricity as a service, not as a business. The Greenport public power company, he has said, provides electricity for street lights, the fire station, for public buildings—for free.[28] Monsell, a local person born and raised in Greenport, has been with the village public power company for over 30 years, working his way up. The utility services 3,000 customers with rates half of those that LILCO charges.

While the Committee to Replace LILCO in recent months has led the largest drive yet for public power on Long Island, moves toward public power in particular areas of Long Island were also pushed forward.

In the election of 1985, voters in Southampton Town by a margin of four-to-one approved the creation of the Hampton Electric Power Company to serve the Tiana Shores section of Hampton Bays. Town officials saw it as a test of the feasibility of a townwide municipal utility. "Everyone I've talked to has said they're going to vote yes," said Marie Louise Pratz, one of HEPCO's leaders. "They say nothing can be worse than LILCO."[29]

In Patchogue, the location of the Patchogue Electric Lighting Company, the last local utility LILCO took over (in 1964), there was a call to "bring back PELCO." In the *Long Island Advance* of Patchogue, Robert F. Logan wrote a column about LILCO bills being "astronomical, service is indifferent . . . and given a chance, I believe they will kill us with Shoreham, and not just financially."[30]

Indeed, publicly controlled utilities would enable, it has been emphasized, the people of Long Island to choose safe forms of energy production rather than the nuclear power that LILCO favors.

Long Island is especially well-suited to harvest safe, renewable energy. With great regularity, the winds blow off the surrounding sea. The sun shines strongly on this island that is on the same latitude as Madrid in Spain. Powerful ocean waves hit the shores of Long Island and the tides move up and down constantly. There are other energy sources close at hand.

This was true in 1975 when the firm of Dubin-Mindell-Bloome Associates did a comprehensive analysis for Suffolk County of existing and future Long Island energy use, and evaluated alternative energy sources, and it is true now.

The person who directed the study was no idle dreamer. Fred S. Dubin, president of the company of consulting engineers and planners, was a graduate of the Carnegie Institute of Technology and a registered professional engineer in 25 states. He had been a full professor at both Columbia University and the University of Southern California. In addition, he had been involved in design and systems analyses of more than 7,000 projects, among them college campuses, redevelopment projects and new towns.

The conclusions of the study included:

• Long Island "energy requirements will not follow the historical trends, but will undergo marked changes, particularly after 1980." Events would "markedly reduce the growth rate of both electrical consumption and demand."

• "Opportunities available now to conserve energy and reduce peak electrical demands with commercially available equipment" would, "if they were implemented," sharply reduce peak demands and annual electricity consumption.

• "Meteorological and climatic conditions, including available solar radiation, are favorable for the utilization of solar energy on Long Island. Equipment is commercially available now for solar space heating, domestic hot water and cooling. . . . In Long Island, solar energy can be used for existing buildings as well as for new structures.

About 75 percent of all existing dwelling units and 100 percent of all existing non-residential buildings could be retrofitted with solar collectors for heating domestic hot water, and about 25 percent of all existing dwelling units and 50 percent of all non-residential buildings could utilize solar energy, with solar collectors for space heating."

• "There are additional opportunities to reduce electrical peak demand with a vigorous program of load management including time-of-day metering."

• De-centralized "total energy systems"—systems of co-generation—could "reduce the peak power demand and annual electrical requirements of central utility plants by reducing the transmission and system losses."

• "Wind energy could supply a major part of all energy required for Long Island with a combination of on-shore and off-shore wind generating plants. There are a vast number of options employing wind generators from 40 to 1,500 kilowatts in size . . . at costs which appear to be more economic than central utility plants."

Dr. William Heronemus, the specialist in wind energy who testified at the Shoreham construction permit hearings, contributed to the study. He declared in it, "Windpower alone, but preferably windpower carefully joined to solar collector systems and total energy systems could free the entire region from all of the problems associated with proliferation of fossil or nuclear central power plants, and would create thousands of employment opportunities."

There have been several studies that have specifically concluded that any electricity that Shoreham would produce could be substituted by energy conservation—and produce substantial financial savings and jobs as well.

In 1981, the New York City-based Council on Economic Priorities presented such an analysis to the New York PSC as LILCO sought a $228 million rate hike largely to pay for Shoreham. The council maintained that "a comprehensive conservation program in LILCO's service area can save about as much electricity as Shoreham would generate as well as large amounts of oil and gas used for heating in buildings, thereby producing billions of dollars in net savings for LILCO's customers over the next twenty years and creating thousands of new jobs in the Long Island region each year."

The jobs would be created in the retrofitting of structures and other activities involved in directing money that would be used for Shoreham for improving energy efficiency on Long Island—and thus eliminating the need for energy from the nuclear plant.

A study by the Energy Systems Research Group, Inc. of Boston, done in 1980 and entitled, *The Conservation Alternative to the Power Plant at Shoreham, Long Island*, concluded that "on grounds of technology availability, scarce fuel savings, cost attractiveness, and long-term system reliability, a conservation alternative to completing Shoreham is not only feasible, it is far superior."

Dr. Ralph Herbert, professor of environmental studies at the Southampton Campus of Long Island University, has written extensively on both the conservation alternative to Shoreham and how just one form of alternative energy—electricity produced directly from sunlight through photovoltaic cells—would be cheaper than the electricity that Shoreham could provide with nuclear power.

He has done analyses showing that the average Long Island resident could easily reduce electrical use by half, and expanded this into a 1984 book, *How to Knock 50% Off Your LILCO Electric Bill*. (In 1986, a national version of that book—telling people through the U.S. how they could save this percentage on their electric bills—was published entitled, *Cut Your Electric Bills in Half*.)

"Electricity is the most expensive form of energy used in your home, yet for many tasks it is either unnecessary or used wastefully," Herbert begins in *How to Knock 50% Off Your LILCO Electric Bill*. "LILCO electric rates are currently about 11 cents per kilowatt hour. Over the next several years this rate will probably climb to at least 15 cents per kwh." The "typical Long Island family" using 600 kwh per month of electric power in 1986 would be paying $90 a month for it. Those who heated their water electrically paid another $70 a month. Herbert projected that by 1987 many LILCO customers would be paying $2,000-a-year electric bills, unless they took "the necessary steps toward reducing their consumption of electricity now." (LILCO customers with all-electric homes would have bills radically higher.)

Herbert wrote about how

> many people on Long Island and around the country are beginning to realize that there are simple, cheap ways to save on electricity and that in some cases the switch to alternative fuels and new equipment can save them substantial amounts of money over the long run. Today there is a major transition going on in this country. Literally millions of people are curtailing their use of electric power through the use of conservation techniques and by shifting to high efficiency appliances and renewable energy sources.

Herbert continued in the book that "contrary to earlier projections" by LILCO and other U.S. electric utilities

of annual rises in demand for power of 7% each year, demand
has remained relatively stable since the mid-1970s, and a
downward trend is anticipated over the next two decades.
Some experts now foresee the need for 25% less electricity at
the end of this century than we use today. Hence the irony of
projects like the Shoreham nuclear power plant that were begun many years ago and are now being completed at a time
when their power is not needed. Ratepayers have seen their
dollars sunk into these projects and are fed up. They may be
profitable for the stockholders but are driving householders to
the poor house.

Herbert declared:

The reality is that Shoreham's electrical power will never be
needed by Long Islanders. LILCO projections of future demand for additional power have become fantasies. Conservation and the shift to renewable sources of energy will make
Shoreham's power superfluous. In fact, it is likely that one or
several of LILCO's other [conventionally powered] plants may
also have to cease operation during the next decade as the
demand for LILCO power slides ever downward.

Herbert's *How to Knock 50% Off Your LILCO Electric Bill* and
its 1986 successor prescribed how that could be simply done. Recommendations included: for hot water—reduce the temperature setting
on a water heater's thermostat, insulate the hot water tank, use flow
restricters to reduce the amount of hot water used, insulate pipes, put
a timer or manual switch on the water heater, go to tankless water
heating, install a solar hot water system; lights—substitute more efficient light bulbs for less efficient ones, install light dimmers; refrigera-
tion—do a "conservation retrofit" on a refrigerator or buy "a more
efficient unit"; cooking—convert to smaller, energy saving appliances
such as pressure cookers, convert to an "energy-efficient gas range";
cooling—make your existing air conditioner "more efficient" or convert to "more efficient" room or even better, central air conditioning,

add insulation to a house, install "shading devices" to reduce sunlight coming in; heating—insulate above ceilings and under floors, add insulation to walls, install storm windows and doors and insulating shutters or drapes, add weather stripping and caulking, install a "passive-solar attached greenhouse."

Herbert gave specific savings figures in both books, suggested models of equipment to purchase for maximum efficiency, and stressed how one could cut an electric bill in half by eliminating half, or more, of electric needs "without lowering your quality of life."

Photovoltaic cells converting sunlight directly to electricity have come into wide use on satellites—replacing nuclear power that the Atomic Energy Commission insisted in the late 1950s and 1960s would be a wonderful way to power satellites. That was until the SNAP-9A nuclear powered satellite underwent a mishap in 1964 and burned up in the atmosphere, releasing radioactive materials. Alternative energy sources were sought, and photovoltaics were developed. Through the years, their price has come plunging down and they are now in wide use—whether it is on calculators or providing large amounts of electricity.

Ralph Herbert has noted that the cost of electricity from photovoltaic cells is 10 cents per kilowatt hour and by the mid-1990s is expected to be "as low as 3 cents per kilowatt hour." They are thus already lower in cost than LILCO electricity and, in future years, far, far lower than LILCO electric rates if Shoreham is allowed to go into operation.

"The real economic competitors to Shoreham are not oil or coal but conservation, co-generation, wind, solar and hydropower," wrote Herbert in a rebuttal in *Newsday* to a claim by a LILCO official that Shoreham electricity was "the only alternative." Herbert added, "Of these the cheapest is conservation, which can displace new power at less than the operating and fuel costs of new plants."[31]

Many co-generation projects are now underway on Long Island. The chairman of one of the largest firms in the world in co-generation, Richard H. Nelson,[32] is a Southampton, Long Island, resident and received some of his inspiration for starting Cogenic Energy Systems, Inc., which is based in Manhattan, on the energy debacle he witnessed with LILCO on Long Island.

Long Island "lends itself beautifully" to co-generation, said Nelson, who describes co-generation as "the simultaneous production of

two energy forms from a common fuel," in this instance the "simultaneous production of electricity and heat from the same fuel source at
the same time."

Nelson, formerly an investment banker and for seven years a
White House assistant, said, "I think we've seen the end of central
power plants as an era in this country." The production of electricity
in recent decades in the United States, mainly in big central power
plants, has meant that most of the heat created to boil the water to
make the stream to turn the turbines in such plants has been wasted—
vented out smokestacks. "Over 75 percent of the heat is expelled," said
Nelson. "Most utilities operate on approximately 25 percent efficiency
no matter what the fuel source."

Through co-generation, he said, "we can generate electricity and
recover heat and bring the fuel source up to 90 percent efficiency."

Co-generation was, in fact, widespread in the U.S. at the turn of
the century, said Nelson. Factories and mills would routinely co-gen-
erate electricity from heat which otherwise would be wasted in industrial processes. In the era of cheap fossil fuel, utilities went to
centralized facilities and co-generation faded. "Now with utility bills
escalating monthly, it behooves us to find alternative ways," said Nelson, and "we're just coming into the excitement of what co-generation
can do."

Co-generation projects now underway on Long Island include
those at county correctional facilities in Yaphank and Riverhead.
They are expected to produce excess electricity at night—when on-site
electric needs are down. There is a connection to LILCO lines, and
the utility is required by state law to purchase that surplus electricity.
The utility first balked at agreeing to accept the excess electricity, but
finally agreed. "It's about time," said Legislator Joseph Rizzo, a Republican of Islip Terrace, who pushed for the installation of the units,
produced by Cogenic Energy Stems, Inc. "Maybe it's because it was
the first time they had to deal with this kind of thing."[33] Rizzo estimated that each $100,000 co-generation unit (both set up by Nelson's
firm) would save Suffolk taxpayers $50,000 a year in heating and
electrical costs and thus pay for itself in two years.

The Grumman Corporation announced in 1985 that it would
build a 25 megawatt co-generation system at its main facility in Beth-
page to produce most of the electricity needed—thus enabling Grumman to all but cut itself off from LILCO. (The cost would be 5 cents
per kilowatt hour.)

Even Brookhaven National Laboratory announced in 1985 that it was going ahead with a co-generation plant to produce electricity for the laboratory. Vincent O'Leary, associate director of the laboratory, said that through co-generation, heat would be generated along with electricity that would cost "about 4 cents" per kilowatt hour for the laboratory to produce, less than half the cost of LILCO electricity.[34]

Original settlers on Long Island generated power from the wind. Some of these centuries-old windmills can be seen today in communities on Long Island's East End.

Now appearing are new windmills. Among these is a 60-foot high unit at the East Hampton home of Donald Miller. It generates enough electricity to light and heat the Miller home, as well as providing surplus power that LILCO must purchase. "I guess it's the Scotsman in me," said Miller as to why he installed a windmill. He saw it as the way to avoid rising LILCO rates.[35]

Don Duffy established Wind Energy Systems in Kings Park in 1978 and traveled across the nation to find wind turbines appropriate for Long Island. In 1986, Duffy was saying "the potentials for windpower are tremendous on Long Island. We have the wind. Being on the coast, being on this island, we have plenty of wind. We're above twelve and a half miles per hour average. I would say it's around the fourth or fifth best location in the United States."[36]

The machines his company sells for Long Island are produced in upstate New York, the midwest, and Canada and "are basic fiberglass-bladed, salt resistent, maintenance free, and can provide anywhere from 5 kilowatts up to 500 kilowatts. They can produce enough electricity for an average electrically heated home up to a factory."

Duffy said a big problem has been "LILCO trying to undercut me. There was a man in Asharoken Village who really wanted to install a wind turbine. But his request was challenged in court, and I am sure that LILCO was behind that. Asharoken receives 60 percent of its tax monies from LILCO generating plants, and so LILCO has pull with the village and fought me. LILCO doesn't want to see energy harvested from the wind. It doesn't want to see any alternatives."

The cheapest source of energy in the world today is hydropower—the U.S. generated 12 percent of its electric power from hydropower in 1985; New York State, 20 percent.

Canada has surplus hydropower. It could easily provide Long Island with large amounts of hydroelectricity. In 1984, a contract between Hydro-Quebec, the largest utility in Canada, and New York State went into effect under which Hydro-Quebec began supplying 111 million megawatt hours of hydroelectricity annually. The contract guarantees that the purchase price will be 20 percent less than the average cost of fuel used to produce electricity by coal, oil, and natural gas in New York State.[37]

Some Canadian hydroelectricity already comes to Long Island through the LILCO system. With a new transmission line (called Marcy-South), now in the process of being built, and a second cable under the Long Island Sound to the Island, slated to be completed in 1991, 1,000 megawatts of Canadian hydroelectric power can come to Long Island—more than Shoreham would produce, and at a dramatically cheaper price.

And Hydro-Quebec has more power it would like to sell. "We still have 40,000 megawatts of untapped resources," said Jacques Guevremont, vice president of export sales and marketing for Hydro-Quebec, in 1985.[38]

"I'm not concerned about losing the power," Governor Cuomo said about Shoreham in 1984, pointing to the availability of cheap, abundant Canadian hydropower.[39]

Noted energy expert Amory Lovins, on a 1983 visit to Long Island, where he met with Shoreham opponents, said of the consequences of abandoning the plant: "It would save money and people could sleep a lot better."[40]

Lovins, who coined the phrase "soft energy" and is a physicist and author of numerous books on energy (World Energy Strategies, Soft Energy Paths, Energy/War: Breaking the Nuclear Link, and Brittle Power) said, "Once you build a reactor it is cheaper not to run it than to run it."

When considering energy, he stressed in an interview, "You have to start by asking what energy needs are. What do you need the energy for? It is only a means to an end, not an end in itself."

He rolled off statistics about "total end use energy" and its elements. Some 58 percent of energy is "for heat, mainly at low temperature." Nuclear power has no use here, said Lovins, repeating his often quoted statement that using nuclear power-generated electricity for electric resistance heating "is like cutting butter with a chain saw."

He said that heat, the major use of energy, can be well provided through "passive and active solar technology."

"Another 34 percent of energy needs are liquid fuels for vehicles," he went on. These can be obtained "through farm and forestry wastes" converted to alcohol and methane.

That leaves 8 percent of total energy as involving electricity. And this, he said, could be "appropriately" provided through hydro and wind power, photovoltaic cells and co-generation. He stressed that energy efficiency could be achieved "with no change in life style."

As to the argument of LILCO that Shoreham is necessary to "displace" oil, Lovins said: "You would save a lot more oil faster and cheaper by making buildings and cars energy efficient. If saving oil is a goal—and I think it is a good goal—building a nuclear power plant won't do it. That is a last priority, the slowest and costliest way to save oil."

Said Lovins: "No, Shoreham is not needed at all."

The simple figures of LILCO's generating capacity, Long Island's energy use, and the amount of electricity that Shoreham would *really* provide demonstrate further why the plant is not needed. LILCO—without Shoreham—has a total generating capacity of 3,714 megawatts. The greatest use of the LILCO system in 1985, its "peak," was 3,365 megawatts in August. (LILCO is described as a "summer peaking" utility—air-conditioner use on Long Island brings electric use up. Summer is, of course, the time of year when the sun is the strongest, and there have been major advances in recent years in the development of solar-powered air-conditioning systems.)

That August peak, meanwhile, came while LILCO was keeping shut its 112-megawatt Far Rockaway plant in an attempt, charged Richard Kessel before the Suffolk Legislature two months before, "to create a power shortage which might weaken opposition to Shoreham."[41] And it was with LILCO trying—as it continues to attempt—to discourage alternatives to the power it provides.

Although the Shoreham plant is generally described as an 820-megawatt facility, after the electricity it would produce that is needed to operate the plant itself—for equipment, controls, lights—is subtracted, the net capacity of the plant is 809 megawatts.

Meanwhile, Adam Madsen, LILCO's vice president of planning, divulged at a meeting of the Suffolk County Supervisors Association in May 1985 that LILCO would not run Shoreham at more than 45 percent of that capacity for the first five of its hoped-for thirty-year life. LILCO, he said, wanted to very slowly bring the plant up to full capacity.

Forty-five percent of 809 is 364 megawatts. That's 9 percent of LILCO's capacity. Energy efficiency, wind power, co-generation, hydropower, among other things, could easily eliminate the need for this electricity.

But beyond this, there is the matter of "capacity factor"—the percentage of rated power actually generated by a power plant considering shutdowns. In the case of nuclear plants, they must be shut down during refueling, and there is an extraordinary amount of shutdowns due to breakdowns and for repairs. In the case of Shoreham, considering its construction, the downtime for repairs is likely to be even greater than normal for nuclear plants. Whether Shoreham could even come close to the rather dismal 50 percent average "capacity factor" of U.S. nuclear plants is questionable. Thus the 9 percent Shoreham contribution would seem to more likely be 4 or 5 percent of the overall LILCO generating capacity.

The abandonment of Shoreham would have no impact on Long Island energy needs—it makes economic sense, according to an extensive analysis conducted in 1985.

Done by the Energy Systems Research Group of Boston for the New York State Consumer Protection Board, the analysis determined that it would cost LILCO customers $450 million more to operate Shoreham than to abandon it. "Recent decreases in oil prices, as well as LILCO's higher estimates of Shoreham operating costs and capital additions, indicate that there is now no economic advantage in operating the plant," said the report.

Declared Kessel: "This study means that the last thread of reason for opening Shoreham has been unraveled."[42]

A 1983 report on Shoreham abandonment by the same group for Suffolk County concluded: "LILCO customers need not pay higher electric rates than they would if the facility were to operate."

As to that LILCO oil claim—made regularly—that Shoreham is important because it would substitute for oil, LILCO likes to project the notion that its electrical system is dependent on expensive oil of uncertain supply.

In general, the "oil displacement" argument for nuclear power is questionable. The Department of Energy's most recent statistics show that of 219 billion kilowatt hours of electricity used in the U.S. in December 1985, only 11.2 billion kilowatt hours were from oil-fired generation, about 5 percent of the total.[43] The push for nuclear power has thus very little to do with cutting down oil use. (Coal-fired generation was 127.8 billion kilowatt hours, nuclear was 33.8 billion, hydroelectric was 25.3 billion, natural gas-fired was 20 billion.)

Unlike virtually all the rest of the utilities in the U.S., LILCO does generate all its electricity from oil, but it is not an uncertain supply. It is mainly residual oil from Venezuela.

Figures from the American Petroleum Institute, an industrial trade group, show that, in general, oil imported into the U.S. is not as large an amount as many Americans believe, and little of that is from the volatile Persian Gulf nations. According to the American Petroleum Institute, in 1985 the U.S. imported only 30 percent of its oil, and less than 9 percent of that (less than 3 percent of the total) was from Persian Gulf countries.

The American Petroleum Institute lists the following top six nations that provided the U.S. with oil in 1985 and the percentage of the U.S. supply they provided: 1. Mexico, 5.3 percent; 2. Canada, 4.8 percent; 3. Venezuela, 3.9 percent; 4. United Kingdom, 2 percent; 5. Indonesia, 2 percent; 6. Nigeria, 1.8 percent. Saudia Arabia is way down in ninth place with .8 percent.[44]

Further, the residual oil LILCO uses has always been the most available oil there is. It's the gunky, thick residue left after gasoline and other petroleum products are refined away. Even before the glut of oil the world now is experiencing—and predictions are that we will be in the midst of the surplus for years ahead—there was no shortage of residual oil. And Long Island, in the sea off busy tanker lanes, is in a prime position to obtain oil.

Who would pay for Shoreham if it is abandoned?

Article 9, Section 1-f of the Constitution of the State of New York, Section 72 of the New York Public Service Law, and Section 61.5 of Title 16 of the New York Code of Rules and Regulations all cite the "used and useful" principle. If a facility fails to operate, that failure is the financial responsibility of those who took the risk of building the facility, the doctrine holds.

The report of the 1936 New York State Joint Legislative Committee to Investigate Public Utilities stated:

> In the process of rate-making it has been the practice of the Public Service Commission of this State and regulatory bodies generally throughout the United States to deduct from the property values of the particular utility involved, the value of

property found not used and useful in the industry. Such property, which is not serving the public, may be included in the category of unnecessary facilities, and commissions and courts would not countenance a rate based upon assets held in idleness or not useful in the public interest.

The New York State Legislature in 1986 passed bills that would affirm the "used and useful" principle in the state, in the wake of a court decision challenging it.[45]

Jerrold Oppenheim, an assistant attorney general in charge of energy and utilities, testified before the New York State Fact-Finding Panel on the Shoreham Nuclear Power Facility in 1983 that if Shoreham was abandoned, state law demands that LILCO and its investors pay the full price—not LILCO ratepayers.[46]

There is also the possibility of converting Shoreham to run with a non-nuclear energy source. Shoreham's twin, the Zimmer plant near Cincinnati, abandoned as a nuclear facility during "Black January" in 1984, even though it was 97 percent completed, is being converted to generate electricity from coal.

"I sense a feeling of relief," said Mayor Arnold Bortz of Cincinnati after the announcement by Cincinnati Gas and Electric of that plan. "The issues of Zimmer as a nuclear plant can be put behind us. I think the decision is a victory for common sense."[47]

In 1979, the Suffolk Legislature called for an investigation into the conversion of Shoreham to a coal-fired plant—with anti-pollution "scrubbers." LILCO insisted a conversion to coal would be too expensive. Madsen said that $1.4 billion would be lost.[48] That $1.4 billion, of course, is but a quarter of Shoreham's apparent eventual price tag.

Another option is conversion of Shoreham to operate on natural gas. Gregory Blass directed Suffolk County to investigate that possibility in 1986. He noted that such a conversion was being considered by the Consumers Power Company of Michigan for its abandoned Midland nuclear plant. Some $4.2 billion was invested in Midland before this project was scrapped, "a situation not dissimilar to the one residents here on Long Island find themselves in," he said. Consumers Power, he noted, conducted a study that included analyses of abandonment, conversion of Midland to coal-fire, and conversion to natural gas-fire, and "concluded that gas would be the most efficient alternative with the best chance of being completed on time and within budget. Most importantly, gas was the best choice from an environmental standpoint."

In any event, the colossal risk of running Shoreham absolutely need not be taken. There are many alternatives.

And certainly after Chernobyl, the collosal risk—not the theoretical but the real risk—is obvious.

Former LILCO Chairman Charles Pierce told the Suffolk Legislature in 1983 that the probability of a major nuclear plant accident at Shoreham was once every 500 million years. Dr. Vance Sailor, a Brookhaven National Laboratory scientist who headed the original group of BNL scientists working with LILCO in promoting nuclear power, Suffolk Scientists for Cleaner Power & Safer Environment and has been active in successor groups, also testified. These were the hearings the legislature conducted into evacuation planning. He said the possibility of a catastrophic accident at Shoreham was once every 50 million years. Their numbers were even stranger than Ukranian Minister Sklyarov's one in 10,000 years.[49]

But, as noted at the outset of this book, LILCO and Shoreham is a study *in extremis*—why the situation so clearly demonstrates the forces at work today throughout the U.S. utility industry.

On Long Island, where people fought three centuries ago for self-determination, a new fight involving the same principle has been going on. It has been a second Battle of Long Island, and it provides a dramatic picture of the conflict that has been raging nationally as a federal government attempts to impose its will on people in America—something that is not supposed to happen here.

"A little over three hundred years ago, this nation was born out of a crucible of conflict that hinged over the questions of fairness, due process, and local determination of destiny," said Suffolk Legislator Steven Englebright in early 1986 as he paralleled the federal government's push for Shoreham to the oppression by England that led to the American Revolution. The scene was the special meeting of the Suffolk Legislature called for a vote on the appeal to President Reagan to block the FEMA drill of LILCO's evacuation plan.[50]

"Suffolk County was literally a battleground in the war that ensued, but the Revolution established these rights and they were codified into law," he continued.

The right of self-determination is today our Constitutional right, and it is our moral imperative to defend it as Suffolk's soil is once again the site of a struggle against tyranny. This time the tyrant is clearly the LILCO monopoly. However, our contemporary tyranny may also again be that of a governmental entity remote from the actual people who are governed, remote from local determination of destiny. In the circumstances that we now find ourselves in, King George was to the Stamp Act as the federal government is to LILCO's proposed test of an evacuation plan for Shoreham. Now, as then, there will be resistance to tyranny by citizens of this county. We will resist in whatever form it takes, and from whatever quarter it comes.

The blindness, the arrogance, of the federal government has been constant. Donald Hodel, in 1984, dismissed concerns about evacuation on Long Island after a nuclear plant accident by saying, "It sounds as though there are millions of people who must be moved across bridges. Take a look at a Long Island map and you will see there are no bridges that need to be crossed in order to have an evacuation."[51]

That's just the point: There are no bridges off Long Island except a few and a couple of tunnels on one end of its 120-mile length. Its residents would be trapped.

After the Chernobyl catastrophe, White House Chief of Staff Donald Regan was quoted in a *Newsday* (May 1, 1986) article as saying that nuclear plants must be built in the U.S. Datelined Bali, Indonesia, the story said, "In a poolside interview with reporters from Newsday and a handful of other newspapers, Regan said the disaster near Kiev shouldn't concern American citizens." It also said, "On the same subject, a top presidential aide who declined to be identified"— often the way White House officials like Regan make statements— "discussed the continuing problems over opening Long Island Lighting Co.'s nuclear plant at Shoreham, which he called 'a political fight' and not one over safety. 'No one has ever said that Shoreham is unsafe,' he said, dismissing concerns that residents couldn't be evacuated in case of an accident. They couldn't be evacuated even without an accident, he explained. 'You try to get off Long Island anytime, whether there's a disaster or not.' "

Then, on the *Meet the Press* television program four days later, Regan—he couldn't ask to be called "a top presidential aide who declined to be identified" while on live television—said, "There's no way to get off Long Island on a Sunday afternoon." He suggested a bridge be built across Long Island Sound to assist in an evacuation in the event of an accident at Shoreham.[52]

Governor Cuomo, at a news conference later that day, said Regan's statement was further evidence that Shoreham should not open: that the federal government was conceding that there could be no successful evacuation of Long Island. "The significance of the statement couldn't be any more profound. Even the White House has agreed that an effective evacuation plan for Shoreham, a statutory requirement pre-requisite to licensing, is impossible," said Cuomo. "Here is the White House saying evacuation is not possible . . . that you need a bridge. There is no bridge, therefore you cannot have an evacuation."

Cuomo added: "As a matter of common sense, as a matter of morality, it [Shoreham] has to be prevented from opening. The President can do that. We call upon him to do that."[53]

It will be some time before the final chapter of the LILCO and Shoreham story will indeed be written.

Up until the Chernobyl catastrophe, the expectation was that the NRC would approve LILCO's evacuation plan and give LILCO a license, and the fight would then go to the courts. The NRC might still do that, but not as fast. The NRC could break its long tradition of never having denied a license to a nuclear plant. If that happens, it will be a monumental event.

NRC approval of Shoreham's operation will, meanwhile, lead to an extended court challenge.

If Shoreham is "shoved down the throats of the people of Long Island," said Wayne Prospect, "it proves that our system of government can't function when big money is at stake." If Shoreham is stopped, "it proves that when people organize in a democracy, citizen power can defeat financial power."[54]

If the federal government allows Shoreham to operate, said Gregory Blass, it shows that "money still wins over public health and safety." If Shoreham is stopped, "it will be a victory for the people of Long Island and future generations and save us from a terrible, terrible risk."[55] (In May 1986, Suffolk Republican Party leaders refused to support Carney for a fifth term in Congress because of what they called his vulnerability on the Shoreham issue. On June 4, Blass was designated to run instead. Suffolk Democrats chose Hochbrueckner as their candidate.)

What happens to Shoreham will have great impact on the future of nuclear power. "If it is licensed," said Michael Mariotte of the Nuclear Information Resource and Service, "it will show that the industry can overcome almost any opposition. If it doesn't, it'll show just the opposite."[56]

If it is allowed to operate, there will be a great impact on the lives of millions of people. Here will be an outrageously constructed nuclear plant sitting in the center of one of the world's densest areas of population—right in the middle of Long Island, New York City to the immediate west, Connecticut to the north, densely packed New Jersey to the southwest. And, as we have learned from Chernobyl, radioactivity from a nuclear plant accident goes much farther than that. If there is to be an event in America like Chernobyl, Shoreham—if it is permitted to operate—is a prime candidate.

Barbash, after a *Newsday* report about a letter written by a Chernobyl manager a month before the accident criticizing corruption and incompetence at the plant,[57] compared the points the manager made with what the New York PSC investigation into Shoreham construction found.

The manager, in her letter published in a Kiev newspaper on March 28, spoke of defects in the plant's construction. She wrote: "In citing these facts, I would like to draw attention to the unacceptability of deficiencies in building atomic power stations in general. Each structure must conform to a certain standard, each cubic meter of reinforced concrete must guarantee reliability and, thus, safety," and at Chernobyl, "this is exactly what is lacking."

Barbash, in a May 22 letter to the editor of *Newsday*, noted that the Chernobyl letter cited "substandard construction and workmanship . . . along with thefts and bureaucratic incompetence." Meanwhile, the PSC report on Shoreham charged, said Barbash, that "LILCO wasted more than 10 million man hours on the construction of Shoreham . . . and allowed workers to drink and use drugs on the job as well as steal."

The letter about Chernobyl, he went on, spoke of how "lack of organization weakened not only discipline but also responsibility of each person for the overall result of the work. The impossibility and unwillingness of engineers to organize teamwork resulted in lower standards." The PSC reported: "Engineering drawings barely kept pace with construction and sometimes lagged behind . . . drawings were sometimes sent incomplete to construction crews so equipment was put in the wrong place or the drawings had to be revised. . . . Many of the engineering drawings were virtually useless . . . the engineers kept finding errors and making changes on their drawings after equipment was already installed, so it had be be ripped out and redone."

The letter about Chernobyl said, "As they tried to fulfill an unrealistic quota, it led to disorganization of the construction and a complete failure of the overall plan." The PSC report on Shoreham, Barbash continued, determined that "LILCO developed unrealistic schedules for work at Shoreham, causing inefficiencies and congestion problems so severe that they sometimes prevented crews from working at all. . . . LILCO effectively lost management of the project."

Declared Barbash: "If you blacked out the names, the descriptions are actually interchangeable. Things are actually not so different here as they are in Russia. Chernobyl and Shoreham, despite some design differences, evidently experienced the same construction management failure. Prophetically, the Russian engineer who wrote the letter said that the Chernobyl failure 'will be repaid over the decades to come.' . . . Who in his right mind still wants to open Shoreham?"

Statements about Chernobyl in the *Soviet Life* article and declarations by LILCO about Shoreham in issues of *Keeping Current*, a bulletin mailed monthly by LILCO to "neighbors of Shoreham," were compared by the Shoreham Opponents Coalition in an April-May "Shoreham Update."

Of the claim in *Soviet Life* of the odds of a meltdown being "one in 10,000 years," the coalition cited a LILCO claim in a January 1983 issue of *Keeping Current*: "Shoreham was designed and built with many back-up systems in the event of a malfunction so it is highly unlikely that an accident would occur."

Soviet Life wrote of the effect on the local environment: "Even before the first unit was started up, mobile labs recorded natural radiation background within 50 km of the plant. . . . The reactors have in no way affected the health of the environment. The station is ecologically pure." LILCO in an April 1983 issue of *Keeping Current* asserted, "Well before construction began on Shoreham, experts were studying the sea life around the plant. . . . The careful watch will continue for as long as Shoreham operates . . . and is designed to make sure the production of electricity doesn't upset the delicate environmental balance near the plant."

In its profile of Chernobyl workers, *Soviet Life* featured "Boris Chernov, 29, a steam turbine operator. . . . He states, 'I wasn't afraid to take a job at a nuclear power plant. There is more emotion in fear of nuclear power plants than real danger." LILCO in a June 1983 issue of *Keeping Current* featured "Shoreham profile: Robert Loper, Station Technical Support Manager. 'Radiation can be highly beneficial to mankind,' Bob says, and he's working to bring about these beneficial effects at the Shoreham Nuclear Power Station. He adds, 'People learn that nuclear energy is a workable method of producing electricity as nuclear plants continue to operate with good safety records.' "

Of health risks, *Soviet Life* said, "Thorough studies conducted in the Soviet Union have proved completely that nuclear power plants do not affect the health of the population." The November/December 1983 of LILCO's *Keeping Current* said: "An emergency preparedness plan for residents surrounding a nuclear plant is required by federal law, even though the likelihood of an accident necessitating action by the public is very small."

The Shoreham Opponents Coalition said of "Chernobyl and Shoreham: LILCO and the Soviets share more than a love of nuclear propaganda. Methods to calculate the chances of major accidents have been developed cooperatively, critical assumptions shared. Experts on both sides once agreed TMI was improbable, Chernobyl impossible. Above all, Soviet and U.S. experts share a fatal pride. It convinced them that men and technology could absolutely, always *control* nuclear power and so avert disaster. The question is whether even an accident of Chernobyl's dimensions—one that has spread radiation worldwide—will be enough to humble the 'experts.' "

In the weeks before Chernobyl, the Shoreham Opponents Coalition used humor in challenging the TV commercial blitz by Brookhaven National Laboratory scientists insisting that Shoreham was safe.

Their commercial, aired free of charge under the "fair time" provisions of the Federal Communications Commission's Fairness Doctrine, featured a puppet by the name of Dr. Radius T. Murphy. In the advertisement, Dr. Murphy, "father of Murphy's Law," tells viewers that he and a number of his colleagues have found that "the safety of the plant is clearly determined by multiplying the rate of neutron absorption by twice the length of the Long Island Expressway." He assures viewers that the result is an accident probability of "2.9 billion to one." As Dr. Murphy continues, however, he trips over his feet, spills coffee, and inadvertently knocks apart the set. At the close of the advertisement, a voice reminds viewers that "scientists are only people and people make mistakes."

On May 15, 1986, Governor Cuomo formally asked the NRC to "forthwith terminate the pending proceedings for a license to operate the Shoreham nuclear facility." In a letter to Palladino, Cuomo cited the statements by Regan and a "top presidential aide" which he said confirmed "the validity of what New York State and Suffolk County have been asserting in proceedings before the Nuclear Regulatory Commission, namely that there can be no safe offsite evacuation plan for the Shoreham nuclear plant."

The NRC, the governor stressed, "is charged with the legal responsibility for regulation of the commercial nuclear power industry. The objective of such regulation is to assure that the public health and welfare are adequately protected. That objection cannot be satisfied, by your own regulations, without an acceptable emergency preparedness plan, an impossibility in this situation, which even senior White House officials now acknowledge. Your insistence to proceed with this licensing proceeding, if you so desire, can only raise new and serious questions about the independence of the Commission and its dedication to the protection of the public health and safety of the residents in the vicinity of the proposed Shoreham facility."

The Cuomo letter was released by Kessel as he appeared before the Suffolk Legislature on May 15 and urged wide government support for the governor's call.

"It is important that all of Long Island's elected officials join Governor Cuomo publicly in seeking the final abandonment of Shoreham," said Kessel. "Long Island can no longer afford public officials and political candidates who 'flip-flop' on the Shoreham issue. Chernobyl should have taught all of us that evacuation is the key issue in the area of nuclear safety. The public must be safely evacuated from an area in the event that an accident occurs. Everyone who lives on Long Island knows that evacuation is impossible because of the Island's unique geographic configuration."

Kessel said the governor's action was "consistent with his pledge to make sure that the safety of the people of Long Island is not compromised for the needs of LILCO and the nuclear industry."

The same day, Cuomo criticized the New York Public Service Commission for having voted to allow LILCO rates to double to pay for Shoreham if the plant went into operation. Cuomo charged that "the Public Service Commission decision ignores the world-wide importance of events at Chernobyl, which makes it improbable that Shoreham will ever operate. The commission also ignored the fact that both houses of the state legislature have passed 'used and useful' bills which will prevent LILCO from passing the costs of a non-operating plant on to Long Island ratepayers."

The rate increase was approved by the PSC on May 14 in what has become its usual four-to-three split on Shoreham, with PSC chairman Paul Gioia leading the majority. Gioia said the "phase-in" proposal doubling LILCO's rates to pay for Shoreham would help LILCO "regain its financial health."

Cuomo noted that "for the past three years, I have proposed sweeping reform of the Public Service Commission—to make it a public agency that serves the public and not the utility industry; for the past three years, the state senate Republicans have thwarted our efforts to make the PSC responsive to consumers. Now, maybe they will find the necessity to act."

Tom Twomey believes that if Shoreham gets the go-ahead, LILCO could quite easily be back on its drive for more nuclear plants. "If NRC and LILCO break the backs of the state and local government, it's very possible LILCO will resurrect its plans for additional nuclear plants," he said. "There's no question in my mind that its officials would do so if they received support. It's clear, in view of the way LILCO under Catacosinos has dealt with the people of Long Island in the last year, that they still have a manifest destiny image of themselves. They harbor ambitions to become one of the largest utilities in the U.S., one of the largest corporations in the country, and they feel the way to do that is to get into the wholesale business and supply the entire Northeast with nuclear-powered electricity." Twomey added, "Corporate madness still grips LILCO."[58]

There is a huge problem of vested interests.[59] This book has examined the links between federal officials and the nuclear industry, the links involving banks, the U.S. energy "establishment," state and local figures and institutions. The LILCO and Shoreham situation brings this all out starkly.

There are legal difficulties. "These people's problem is with the Atomic Energy Act," Frederick Shon complained during a break in an NRC hearing on Shoreham in 1983. "That's what governs this proceeding." Shon, for many years a nuclear engineer with the AEC and the NRC, and before that an engineer in the nuclear industry, was an administrative judge at the session. With him was Dr. Jerry Kline, another NRC administrative judge, who had formerly been a radiation ecologist on the NRC staff, and before that had been with national nuclear laboratories. The Atomic Energy Act, they said, dictated government encouragement of nuclear power. They said they were just following that edict.[60]

"This is mad," said Peggy McKinnon Clark of Shoreham, back in the hearing room. "We're not only talking about nuclear power. We're talking about the erosion of the democratic process. This is supposed to be a free country where people have the right to life, liberty and the pursuit of happiness. This is a beautiful island. I don't see the point of jeopardizing life on it because of these people in the nuclear industry."[61]

Arthur McComb, a veteran of the Shoreham battle, was distributing a statement he had written:

> Why must we continue this charade? Prejudgment is painfully clear . . . Home rule, due process, has been ignominiously massacred by our own federal bureaucracy, by non-resident, non-elective judges, on a licensing board appointed by appointees. . . . This three-judge licensing board of the NRC has made a farce of home rule, due process. This mockery has made fools of the people of New York State.

There is a Constitutional problem. The founders of this nation drafted a marvelous document designed precisely to prevent a usurpation of power by individuals or groups.

Richard Webb is a highly patriotic man; he joined the nuclear Navy and then Rickover's staff building the first commercial nuclear plant in the U.S. because he thought nuclear power "was a clean source of energy for America."[62] Upon comprehending its true risks and consequences, he began an exploration into what Constitutional right the federal government had to promote nuclear power. He found it had none. The federal government, Webb has written, has violated the most fundamental instrument of governance in the U.S., its Constitution. Researching the legislative history of the Atomic Energy Act, he found its authority is based on the "so-called welfare and commerce clauses of the Constitution." They are included in Article 1, Section 8 of the Constitution.

Article 1, Section 8 says, "The Congress shall have Power To lay and collect Taxes, Duties, and Excises, to pay the Debts and provide for the common Defense and general Welfare of the United States . . ." It goes on to declare that Congress shall have the power "to regulate Commerce with foreign nations, and among the several States . . ."

Webb has argued, "It can be clearly demonstrated that these clauses of the Constitution were not intended by the makers of the Constitution to confer a general power to the federal government 'to provide for the general welfare' as the government has assumed in promoting nuclear energy." Nor, he has maintained, do they give the federal government "a general power to regulate industry within a State."

With the Atomic Energy Act, "the Federal Government has unconstitutionally assumed the power to govern the internal, domestic affairs of the states (thus preempting state and local laws and resolutions)" when, in fact, "the federal government was established by the Constitution basically to manage only the external affairs of the states."

Webb wrote in a "proposed legal action" against Shoreham:

This breakdown of constitutional government, therefore, explains our nuclear predicament, including the thwarted efforts and the frustrations of the state and county governments to protect the people of New York from the accident dangers of the Shoreham reactor, and, I think, explains many other big problems facing America."

Suffolk County officials to whom Webb gave his plan were interested but concerned about undertaking such a broad challenge. Webb conceded this in his proposal:

True, the ramifications of overturning the federal government's assumptions of power under the welfare and commerce clauses are enormous. But I say, this is all to the good; for surely it is better to have democratic government—government close to the people—and not central government remote from the people. . . . It is time—long overdue—to restore constitutional government, which is to say, to restore the principle and the practice that the government gets its powers from the consent of the people. We should start with the Shoreham case; for what could be more of a reason than to protect the public against catastrophic accidents.

There has been no end to LILCO arrogance and deceit.

In 1985, for example, browsing in the document room of the Shoreham-Wading River Public Library, Jane Alcorn of CLOSE came upon a previously unknown element of LILCO's evacuation plan. She read testimony by Dr. Thomas Urbanik II, representing the NRC staff, on LILCO's intention in the event of a Shoreham accident to use vehicles to tie up the Long Island Expressway to prevent people from Long Island's dead-ended East End from fleeing west.

Urbanik said:

We're going to have a management strategy that will deploy vehicles on the LIE that will make the LIE appear to people from the east not to be a six-lane freeway. We're going to have vehicles that are going to be parked in the roadway and it's going to quickly become congested, in one sense because we've restricted the capacity, and those folks from the East End, if they wanted to, are going to see a congested freeway. . . . If we take a Long Island Long Company utility truck and park it in the outside lane of the freeway, that freeway does no longer have three lanes. It only has two lanes. So the demand downstream of that artificially induced bottleneck cannot exceed the capacity that we artificially induced at that bottleneck. So those folks cannot preempt all of the capacity downstream. We have taken it away from them.[63]

On May 24, 1986, the Suffolk Legislature approved a measure to have Suffolk County bring a lawsuit against LILCO under the Federal Racketeer Influenced and Corrupt Organizations Act, (RICO). The suit would seek to force LILCO to pay $5.4 billion in damages.

Legal papers on which the suit is to be based, prepared by the Manhattan law firm of Hill, Betts & Nash, of which former federal organized crime prosecutor Kenneth McCallion is a partner, charged:[64]

> There appears to be substantial evidence that, over the last 15 years, LILCO officials have engaged in a systematic scheme to defraud the State of New York and Long Island ratepayers by issuing false public statements and witholding critical facts regarding the Shoreham nuclear power plant. This scheme involves a continuing cover-up of faulty design and construction deficiencies; false statements and knowing misrepresentations of time and cost projections to both the Public Service Commission, the Nuclear Regulatory Commission and the public in general; falsification of testing procedures and critical records; collusion and conflicts of interest in the granting of construction contracts; and materially false representations in rate increase applications to the PSC.
>
> This deceptive scheme by LILCO is so massive and multi-faceted that the most appropriate legal remedy for governmental entities, ratepayers and other victims of this fraud is under the federal racketeering (RICO) statute.
>
> [Because] approximately $1.8 billion in [Shoreham] costs have already been passed on to the ratepayers, the damages sought would be approximately $5.4 billion.

The legal papers charged that LILCO had engaged in what the RICO statute defines as "racketeering activities" or "two or more 'predicate acts,'" including federal offenses such as mail, wire and securities fraud, as well as the state offenses of bribery and extortion."

They said,

> The theory of the case would be that, since at least 1977, LILCO officials knew that the [Shoreham] project was mismanaged and poorly constructed, and that despite this knowledge—or perhaps because of it—they consistently issued false public statements that painted a falsely optimistic picture of the project's progress. . . . From 1977 to 1983, when it finally admitted that the situation was desperate and that bankruptcy was imminent, LILCO continued to issue optimistic forecasts even though it knew its cost and time projections could not be met and that the project continued to be plagued with problems. . . . LILCO's primary intention was to hide the true

facts about Shoreham from public scrutiny so that it could continue to raise money for the project through rate increases and securities offerings. The consequences of LILCO's deception are staggering. . . .

Even more significantly, LILCO's conduct has gone beyond a mere cover-up of its management. In a desperate attempt to move the project towards completion, or "critical path" as it was referred to, LILCO cut serious corners in the construction of the plant, and it attempted to cover up its shoddy and even dangerous practices by falsifying procedures and records. In effect, LILCO's conduct has caused serious safety, as well as financial consequences.

Deceit and cover-up have been part and parcel of the push for nuclear power since its beginning.

"The lies we have been fed about nuclear power have been as cunningly handcrafted as the masterpieces of Benvenuto Cellini," the writer Kurt Vonnegut, who has a home in Sagaponack, Long Island, has said. "If we let them, they will kill everything on this lovely blue-green planet with their rebuttals . . . with their vicious stupid lies." Americans are now in a position of having to protect themselves "against our own government and our own industries."[65]

When the truth—what Henrik Ibsen called "a lion in the street"—comes out about nuclear power, people change their minds quickly.

Ann Carl, who with her husband, William, began the fight on Long Island against nuclear power, was recalling from the couple's present home in Virginia recently how she learned about nuclear power. "I was a writer in the early 1960s, on conservation issues, and had just done a column that said we should go to clean nuclear power. I got a bunch of letters from people saying, 'You don't know what you are talking about.' So I explored the issue. I went all over the country, interviewing people, attending meetings, gathering information and studying it. The more I learned, the more I was convinced of the great dangers of nuclear power."[66]

When she started writing pieces in the *Long Island Commercial Review* critical of LILCO and its nuclear power plans, "to alert people to the facts," she said, the paper's publisher "was approached by LILCO and I was fired."

William Carl noted how he was an engineer, a designer of hydrofoil boats. He went to Grumman when his company was acquired by Grumman, which still produces the hydrofoils. As his wife began examining nuclear power, he also began studying it and came to the same conclusions as she did.

Why don't fellow engineers, in the nuclear industry, comprehend what he realized? "A lot of them don't go into it far enough. They think that everything is going to work. Things just don't always work."

In the late 1970s, William Carl retired and the couple bought a sailboat, sold their Long Island home, fulfilled a lifelong dream of sailing to Europe, and then cruised for two years. They didn't forget about nuclear issues. From the boat, William Carl noted, they took samples of seawater for Woods Hole Oceanographic Institute, which wanted to test it for plutonium.

Of the dispersal of radioactivity all over the world, "The only thing that helps," he said, "is that I'm sixty-nine years old now. It takes five to ten years for a small amount to do damage. It's the youth of the world I'm worried about, and the unborn."

On Long Island, through the U.S. and the world, people were not informed about nuclear power from its outset. They were not told, and this was done on purpose. Keeping the public in the dark was deemed necessary by the promoters of nuclear power if it was to succeed. Those in government, science and private industry who have been pushing nuclear power knew that if people were given the facts, if they knew the consequences of nuclear power, they would not stand for it. They hoped that when the deaths and cancer and mutations began happening, it would be too late. By then there'd be a dependence on nuclear power, and the fall-back public relations line would be used: well, 50,000 people get killed on U.S. roads in auto accidents each year—are we to outlaw cars?

Indeed, one of the pieces of propaganda LILCO has distributed is a booklet entitled *The Moral Implications of Energy*. It declared:

> Nevertheless, even if (God forbid) there were to be a meltdown accident that took as many as 10,000 lives (immediate and delayed) and that this were to happen once every 10 years, we would still lose only about one-fifth as many lives from a nuclear accident in each 10-year period as automobile accidents now kill every year on American highways and streets.

There is, in fact, no comparison. Traveling in a car entails a degree of danger, but it is a risk taken voluntarily, and there is little choice if one wants to get from place to place.

But there is a clear choice in humanity determining how energy is to be provided. It can take the admittedly lethal nuclear energy road or the path of safe, renewable energy sources. We do not need to take the mammoth risk of nuclear power that threatens our very survival, and the survival of those who are to come after us. For nothing less than survival is at stake.

Admiral Hyman Rickover himself admitted this when in 1982 he made a farewell address before a committee of Congress and said:

I'll be philosophical. Until about two billion years ago, it was impossible to have any life on earth; that is, there was so much radiation on earth you couldn't have any life—fish or anything. Gradually, about two billion years ago, the amount of radiation on this planet and probably in the entire system reduced and made it possible for some form of life to begin. . . . Now when we go back to using nuclear power, we are creating something which nature tried to destroy to make life possible. . . . Everytime you produce radiation, you produce something that has life, in some cases for billions of years, and I think there the human race is going to wreck itself, and it's far more important that we get control of this horrible force and try to eliminate it. I do not believe that nuclear power is worth it if it creates radiation.[67]

Rickover recommended that "we outlaw nuclear reactors." (It would have been more helpful if Rickover, so personally responsible for the development of nuclear technology in the U.S., would have mentioned this not in 1982, but in 1962 or 1952.)

Maybe Rickover didn't realize what he was involved in then. Maybe he was too caught up in it. "These people owe their positions and livelihoods to the nuclear establishment," Lorna Salzman of Friends of the Earth has said. "They're not going to make an objective assessment of the problems of nuclear power. They accept science as an article of faith, a religion. They think science and technology will solve all our problems. And if they're wrong, a lot of people are going to die."

Religion and morality have much to do with the situation.

"We're talking about a religious problem—and it's time religious people wake up," Father Bill Brisotti told a citizens' town meeting in 1979 at an orphanage that is one mile from the Shoreham site.[68] "We've been building golden calves long enough," the Catholic priest said to the 350 people who overflowed the institution's chapel. "Each time people build golden calves we're brought to our knees. The tragic potential of a nuclear power plant catastrophe is immense. And what for? Fifty percent of the energy produced in the U.S. is wasted. Do we intend to leave a legacy of thousands upon thousands of years of managing radioactive waste so people now can run hair dryers? We're talking about something very deep, about the way we live."

"What about morality?" asked Ronald Gumbert in 1981, as a Suffolk legislative committee was considering the negotiations then underway between LILCO and Peter Cohalan on a settlement on Shoreham.[69] "We cannot afford to deal with this as business as usual. Shoreham has the potential to destroy this whole island." A psychologist and father of four from Rocky Point, three miles from Shoreham, he said the nuclear plant was "being forced down our throats by the federal government and corporations. . . . You must take a moral or personal decision on this issue. Our lives are at stake!"

Albert Einstein, in the end, very much regretted what he had wrought with that letter from Peconic, just a few miles east of Shoreham. "If I had known that the Germans would not succeed in constructing the atom bomb, I never would have moved a finger," he declared in his book, *Out of My Later Years*. He wrote, "Since I do not foresee that atomic energy is to be a great boon for a long time, I have to say that for the present time it is a menace."

It would be deserving, and is a matter of life and death, that the menace of the nearby nuclear plant at Shoreham be ended, and then the entire nuclear scourge that has been unleashed should be eliminated.

NOTES

1. The author was present at this demonstration on May 3, 1986.
2. Wayne Prospect in an interview with the author, April 1986.
3. *Newsday* reporter John McDonald reported on May 9, 1986, in a story headlined "NRC: Plant Had Some Containment Features" that, "The Soviet nuclear disaster at Chernobyl occurred in a reactor that was outfitted with a system designed to prevent radiation from entering the atmosphere in the case of an accident, according to NRC documents and officials. Since the accident, U.S. nuclear industry spokesmen have downplayed its relevance to U.S. reactor safety, arguing that the Chernobyl reactor had no containment structure at all. . . . While there are still major gaps in the information that the U.S. officials have on the damaged Chenobyl reactor, it is clear that it 'has

some containment features,' said Joseph Fouchard, a spokesman for the Nuclear Regulatory Commission." The story went on to quote testimony earlier in the week by NRC Commissioner Asselstine before Markey's subcommittee that the containment structure surrounding the reactor was "rated stronger" than those surrounding some U.S. reactors.

4. Richard Webb's comments were made in an interview with the author, April 1986.
5. Technical Guidance for Siting Criteria Development, Sandia National Laboratories, Albuquerque, New Mexico, for the U.S. Nuclear Regulatory Commission, 1982. (NUREG/CR-2239)
6. These and the following comments by Webb were made in interviews with the author, 1985–1986.
7. Jack Hickman's comments were made in an interview with the author, December 1985.
8. The NRC assessment appears in a document entitled, "NRC Response to Chairman Markey for 4/17/85 NRC Authorization Hearing."
9. *Soviet Life*, February 1986, No. 2. The magazine is published monthly by the Soviets in the U.S. under what its masthead explains is a "reciprocal agreement" with the U.S. through which the U.S. government publishes a magazine called *America* in the Soviet Union. In a May 6, 1986, letter to *Newsday*, James B. Brennan of Rocky Point wrote of the Russian minister's predictions of a meltdown occurring once in 10,000 years:

How reassuring all this must have been to the Soviet citizens. How hauntingly familiar these claims must sound to Long Islanders. I seem to have heard similar claims from the Long Island Lighting Co. and other representatives of the nuclear industry. I wonder if LILCO and the Soviet nuclear industry have hired the same public relations firms. I also wonder if it is a great comfort for the survivors of the accident in Chernobyl that they are not likely to experience another meltdown for another 9,999 years.

In a briefing given by the NRC, reported by *Suffolk Life* on May 15, 1986, NRC commissioners were told that Chernobyl had a containment dome able to withstand an explosive force of 27 pounds of pressure per square inch. This is about the same pressure that the Shoreham plant would be able to withstand, according to Dr. Michio Kaku. Kaku said that the Shoreham containment dome is only able to withstand 30 pounds of pressure per square inch, "or about the pressure that's in your car's tires."

New York Times reporter Stuart Diamond reported in a page one story on May 19, 1986, that

the nuclear power plant that exploded in the Soviet Union last month had more safety features and was closer to American reactor design than Western experts had assumed in the days soon after the accident, nuclear experts say. . . . The conclusions are based on technical drawings and other information obtained through Government and international scientific sources by American nuclear experts in recent days. The experts say it has become clear that a large structure of heavy steel and concrete surrounded the No. 4 reactor at Chernobyl, and that at least some of the containment structure was designed to withstand pressure similar to those in many American reactors.

group Public Citizen placed an ad signed by leaders of the Union of Concerned Scientists which declared: "IN CASE YOU THINK THE RUSSIANS ARE THE ONLY ONES COVERING UP NUCLEAR DANGERS, JUST

READ THESE MEMOS." The memos, some of which were pictured, were from the U.S. Atomic Energy Commission and concerned anxieties over containment domes produced by General Electric—the company that made the containment dome at Shoreham. In one 1971 memo, Dr. Stephen Hanauer, a top federal nuclear official, said of fears that GE containment buildings may rupture in a major accident: "GE wants us . . . not to mention the problem publicly."

The advertisement also included a memo from Dr. Joseph Hendrie, a long-time Brookhaven National Laboratory nuclear scientist and, later, top NRC official. Hendrie rejected a "ban" on GE containment design. Such a ban could raise too many embarrassing safety questions about existing GE nuclear plants, he said, and "could well be the end of nuclear power." Hendrie went on to become the chairman of the NRC.

The Public Citizen ad continued: "Why do we call attention to these particular memos today? Because the Chernobyl nuclear plant, contrary to earlier reports, did have a containment building. Indeed, the design used by the Russians bears a striking resemblance to the long-suspect design used by General Electric. In the aftermath of the Chernobyl nuclear disaster, our own government's thirty-year cover-up of nuclear safety dangers raises a life-and-death issue to which Americans must respond."

10. Reported in *Suffolk Life*, March 12, 1986.
11. From a letter by Richard W. Starostecki, to LILCO Vice President John Leonard, March 14, 1986. The report that was attached had an NRC number of 50–322–86–03.
12. Reported in *Newsday*, April 15, 1986.
13. Reported in *Newsday*, Ibid.
14. Wayne Prospect in an interview with the author, April 1986.
15. Tony Bullock in an interview with the author, April 1986.
16. Maurice Barbash's comments here and following, were made in an interview with the author, December 1985.
17. The author was present at the meeting of steering committee of Citizens to Replace LILCO, December 1985.
18. "State Takeover of LILCO Urged by Republicans," *The New York Times*, January 7, 1985.
19. *Newsday*, October 24, 1985.
20. "Consider Public Power," a letter to *Newsday*, November 21, 1985.
21. "28 Firms Consider Leaving LI," *Newsday*, March 9, 1984.
22. *Newsday*, August 24, 1984.
23. Ira Freilicher in an interview with the author, July 1981.
24. Dorothy Wolosin in an interview with the author, July 1981.
25. Gregory Blass in an interview with the author, July 1981.
26. Wayne Prospect in an interview with the author, July 1981.
27. The author was present at this hearing.
28. James Monsell in an interview with the author, May 1979.
29. *The Southampton Press*, October 24, 1985.
30. "Bring Back PELCO," *Long Island Advance*, October 31, 1985.
31. Ralph Herbert, "Conserve Electricity, Kill Shoreham," *Newsday*, January 31, 1985.
32. Richard Nelson was a White House assistant under President Lyndon Johnson. His comments were made in an interview with the author, December 1981.
33. Reported in *Newsday*, September 17, 1985.

34. Reported in *Newsday*, October 8, 1985.
35. Donald Miller's comments were reported in "Now It's 'Power from the People,' " *Newsday*, December 4, 1985.
36. Don Duffy in an interview with the author, May 1986.
37. Canadian hydropower figures are from Larry Frech of the New York Power Authority's information office, in interviews with the author, May 1986.
38. Reported in *The New York Times*, October 15, 1985.
39. Reported in "Sez Shoreham's Washed Up, Cuomo on Nuke Plant: Let LILCO Take a Bath," New York *Daily News*, February 3, 1984.
40. Amory Lovins in an interview with the author, May 1983.
41. Statement of Richard Kessel before the legislature on June 11, 1985.
42. Reported in *Newsday*, October 14, 1985.
43. Department of Energy statistics are from *Monthly Energy Review*, December 1985 (DOE/EIA–0035 85/12).
44. American Petroleum Institute figures are from the association's February 1986 report *Estimated Crude and Product Imports by the U.S. from Leading Supplier Countries*.
45. The decision was made by the Court of Appeals on March 25 and involved a $41 million investment by Con Edison in a power plant project, which Con Edison subsequently abandoned. The PSC had approved allowing Con Edison to pass the cost on to ratepayers. Shoreham opponents have argued that the case of Shoreham is different.
46. Reported in *Newsday*, October 1, 1983.
47. *The New York Times*, January 22, 1984.
48. Reported in *Newsday*, June 5, 1979.
49. The author was present when Charles Pierce and Vance Sailor made their projections of the possibility of a major nuclear plant accident at Shoreham, January 1983.
50. The author was present at this meeting.
51. Reported in *The New York Times*, May 9, 1984.
52. *Meet the Press* broadcast on May 4, 1986.
53. Reported in *Newsday*, May 5, 1986.
54. Wayne Prospect in an interview with the author, April 1986.
55. Gregory Blass in an interview with the author, April 1986.
56. Michael Mariotte in an interview with the author, April 1986.
57. *Newsday*, May 2, 1986: "Worker Criticized Plant's Safety a Month before Nuclear Accident."
58. Tom Twomey in an interview with the author, March 1986.
59. William J. Nohejl, director of the Long Island Farm Bureau and chairman of its Jamesport nuclear plant committee, spoke on that point before the Suffolk Legislature on November 29, 1977, when he said:

    Farmers are generally noted for their common sense and conservative approach to any proposal they are dealing with. The Farm Bureau has spent thousands of hours studying the proposed Jamesport plants. We have no axe to grind, and we have come to the conclusion that the Jamesport plants are nothing but a technological can of worms. LILCO has paraded one witness after another, paid very highly, to argue that the plants are needed, that the electricity they will produce will cost less, and that they will present no environmental dangers or safety threats to the land and residents of Suffolk County. The Long Island Farm Bureau, at great expense, has retained experts of national renown to present a more balanced picture of just what LILCO is up to. We have hired individuals from the academic and consulting community who in no way stood to gain from the construction of the Jamesport plants. They were not dependent upon the nuclear industry for their jobs. They are honest and decent citizens who delved into the problems of nuclear power and came to conclusions very, very different from LILCO. . . . LILCO's case for Jamesport is built upon the testimony of men who have spent most of their lives in the nuclear or utility industry and have a great deal to *lose* if the Jamesport plants are not constructed. Yet, on the other side of the coin, the Suffolk County residents have a great deal to lose if the plants are constructed.

60. Frederick Shon's and Jerry Kline's comments were made in an interview with the author, December 1983.
61. Peggy Clark in an interview with the author, December 1983.
62. Richard Webb's comments, here and following, were made in interviews with the author, 1985–1986.
63. Thomas Urbanik's testimony was given on January 26, 1984, before NRC board in Riverhead.
64. Charges were contained in legal papers entitled "Potential Civil Action against LILCO."
65. Kurt Vonnegut's comments were made in a program produced by WNET-TV in New York, entitled "The Creative Edge," and broadcast on August 10, 1985.
66. Ann and William Carl's comments were made in interviews with the author, May 1986.
67. Hyman Rickover made his comments to the Joint Economic Committee of Congress, January 28, 1982.
68. The author was present at event on April 5, 1979, at which Father Brisotti spoke.
69. The author was present at the hearing on August 4, 1981, at which Gumbert spoke.

Index

Selected Grove Press Paperbacks

62334-7   ACKER, KATHY / Blood and Guts in High School / $7.95
62480-7   ACKER, KATHY / Great Expectations: A Novel / $6.95
62192-1   ALIFANO, ROBERTO / Twenty-four Conversations with Borges, 1980-1983 / $8.95
17458-5   ALLEN, DONALD & BUTTERICK, GEORGE F., eds. / The Postmoderns: The New American Poetry Revised 1945-1960 / $9.95
17801-7   ALLEN, DONALD M., & TALLMAN, WARREN, eds. / Poetics of the New American Poetry / $12.50
17061-X   ARDEN, JOHN / Arden: Plays One (Sergeant Musgrave's Dance, The Workhouse Donkey, Armstrong's Last Goodnight) / $4.95
17657-X   ARSAN, EMMANUELLE / Emmanuelle / $3.95
17213-2   ARTAUD, ANTONIN / The Theater and Its Double / $6.95
62433-5   BARASH, D. and LIPTON, J. / Stop Nuclear War! A Handbook / $7.95
62056-9   BARRY, TOM, WOOD, BETH & PREUSCH, DEB / The Other Side of Paradise: Foreign Control in the Caribbean / $9.95
17087-3   BARNES, JOHN / Evita—First Lady: A Biography of Eva Peron / $4.95
17928-5   BECKETT, SAMUEL / Company / $3.95
62489-0   BECKETT, SAMUEL / Disjecta: Miscellaneous Writings and a Dramatic Fragment, ed. Cohn, Ruby / $5.95
17208-6   BECKETT, SAMUEL / Endgame / $3.50
17953-6   BECKETT, SAMUEL / Ill Seen Ill Said / $4.95
62061-5   BECKETT, SAMUEL / Ohio Impromptu, Catastrophe, and What Where: Three Plays / $4.95
17924-2   BECKETT, SAMUEL / Rockababy and Other Short Pieces / $3.95
17299-X   BECKETT, SAMUEL / Three Novels: Molloy, Malone Dies and The Unnamable / $6.95
17204-3   BECKETT, SAMUEL / Waiting for Godot / $3.50
62418-1   BERLIN, NORMAND / Eugene O'Neill / $9.95
17237-X   BIELY, ANDREW / St. Petersburg / $12.50
17252-3   BIRCH, CYRIL & KEENE, DONALD, eds. / Anthology of Chinese Literature,Vvol. I: From Early Times to the 14th Century / $17.50
17766-5   BIRCH, CYRIL, ed. / Anthology of Chinese Literature, Vol. II: From the 14th Century to the Present / $12.95
62104-2   BLOCH, DOROTHY / "So the Witch Won't Eat Me," Fantasy and the Child's Fear of Infanticide / $7.95
17244-2   BORGES, JORGE LUIS / Ficciones / $6.95
17270-1   BORGES, JORGE LUIS / A Personal Anthology / $6.95

17258-2 BRECHT, BERTOLT / The Caucasian Chalk Circle / $4.95

17109-8 BRECHT, BERTOLT / The Good Woman of Setzuan / $3.95

17112-8 BRECHT, BERTOLT / Galileo / $3.95

17065-2 BRECHT, BERTOLT / The Mother / $2.95

17106-3 BRECHT, BERTOLT / Mother Courage and Her Children / $2.95

17472-0 BRECHT, BERTOLT / Threepenny Opera / $2.45

17393-7 BRETON ANDRE / Nadja / $6.95

17439-9 BULGAKOV, MIKHAIL / The Master and Margarita / $5.95

17108-X BURROUGHS, WILLIAM S. / Naked Lunch / $4.95

17749-5 BURROUGHS, WILLIAM S. / The Soft Machine, Nova Express, The Wild Boys: Three Novels / $5.95

62488-2 CLARK, AL, ed. / The Film Year Book 1984 / $12.95

17038-5 CLEARY, THOMAS / The Original Face: An Anthology of Rinzai Zen / $4.95

17735-5 CLEVE, JOHN / The Crusader Books I and II / $4.95

17411-9 CLURMAN, HAROLD (Ed.) / Nine Plays of the Modern Theater (Waiting for Godot by Samuel Beckett, The Visit by Friedrich Durrenmatt, Tango by Slawomir Mrozek, The Caucasian Chalk Circle by Bertolt Brecht, The Balcony by Jean Genet, Rhinoceros by Eugene Ionesco, American Buffalo by David Mamet, The Birthday Party by Harold Pinter, Rosencrantz and Guildenstern Are Dead by Tom Stoppard) / $14.95

17962-5 COHN, RUBY / New American Dramatists: 1960-1980 / $7.95

17971-4 COOVER, ROBERT / Spanking the Maid / $4.95

17535-2 COWARD, NOEL / Three Plays by Noel Coward (Private Lives, Hay Fever, Blithe Spirit) / $7.95

17740-1 CRAFTS, KATHY & HAUTHER, BRENDA / How To Beat the System: The Student's Guide to Good Grades / $3.95

17219-1 CUMMINGS, E.E. / 100 Selected Poems / $3.95

17329-5 DOOLITTLE, HILDA / Selected Poems of H.D. / $8.95

17863-7 DOSS, MARGOT PATTERSON / San Francisco at Your Feet (Second Revised Edition) / $8.95

17398-8 DOYLE, RODGER, & REDDING, JAMES / The Complete Food Handbook (revised any updated edition) / $3.50

17219-1 DURAS, MARGUERITE / Four Novels: The Afternoon of Mr. Andesmas; 10:30 on a Summer Night; Moderato Cantabile; The Square) / $9.95

17246-9 DURRENMATT, FRIEDRICH / The Physicists / $6.95

17239-6 DURRENMATT, FRIEDRICH / The Visit / $4.95

17990-0 FANON, FRANZ / Black Skin, White Masks / $8.95

17327-9 FANON, FRANZ / The Wretched of the Earth / $4.95

17754-1 FAWCETT, ANTHONY / John Lennon: One Day At A Time, A Personal Biography (Revised Edition) / $8.95

17902-1 FEUERSTEIN, GEORG / The Essence of Yoga / $3.95

62455-6   FRIED, GETTLEMAN, LEVENSON & PECKENHAM, eds. /
          Guatemala in Rebellion: Unfinished History / $8.95
17483-6   FROMM, ERICH / The Forgotten Language / $6.95
62073-9   GARWOOD, DARRELL / Under Cover: Thirty-five Years of CIA
          Deception / $3.95
17222-1   GELBER, JACK / The Connection / $3.95
17390-2   GENET, JEAN / The Maids and Deathwatch: Two Plays / $8.95
17470-4   GENET, JEAN / The Miracle of the Rose / $7.95
17903-X   GENET, JEAN / Our Lady of the Flowers / $3.95
17956-0   GETTLEMAN, LACEFIELD, MENASHE, MERMELSTEIN, &
          RADOSH, eds. / El Salvador: Central America in the New Cold
          War / $9.95
17994-3   GIBBS, LOIS MARIE / Love Canal: My Story / $6.95
17648-0   GIRODIAS, MAURICE, ed. / The Olympia Reader / $5.95
17067-9   GOMBROWICZ, WITOLD / Three Novels: Ferdydurke, Pornografia
          and Cosmos / $12.50
17764-9   GOVER, ROBERT / One Hundred Dollar Misunderstanding / $2.95
17832-7   GREENE, GERALD and CAROLINE / SM: The Last Taboo / $2.95
62490-4   GUITAR PLAYER MAGAZINE / The Guitar Player Book (Revised
          and Updated Edition) $11.95
17124-1   HARRIS, FRANK / My Life and Loves / $9.95
17936-6   HARWOOD, RONALD / The Dresser / $5.95
17653-7   HAVEL, VACLAV, The Memorandum / $5.95
17022-9   HAYMAN, RONALD / How To Read A Play / $6.95
17125-X   HOCHHUTH, ROLF / The Deputy / $7.95
62115-8   HOLMES, BURTON / The Olympian Games in Athens: The First
          Modern Olympics, 1896 / $6.95
17241-8   HUMPHREY, DORIS / The Art of Making Dances / $9.95
17075-X   INGE, WILLIAM / Four Plays (Come Back, Little Sheba; Picnic;
          Bus Stop; The Dark at the Top of the Stairs) / $7.95
62199-9   IONESCO, EUGENE / Exit the King, The Killer, Macbeth / $9.95
17209-4   IONESCO, EUGENE / Four Plays (The Bald Soprano, The Lesson,
          The Chairs, and Jack or The Submission) / $6.95
17226-4   IONESCO, EUGENE / Rhinoceros and Other Plays / $5.95
17485-2   JARRY, ALFRED / The Ubu Plays (Ubu Rex, Ubu Cuckolded,
          Ubu Enchained) / $9.95
62123-9   JOHNSON, CHARLES / Oxherding Tale / $6.95
62124-7   JORGENSEN, ELIZABETH WATIKINS & HENRY IRVIN / Eric
          Berne, Master Gamesman: A Transactional Biography / $9.95
17200-0   KEENE, DONALD, ed. / Japanese Literature: An Introduction for
          Western Readers-$2.25
17221-3   KEENE, DONALD, ed. / Anthology of Japanese Literature:
          Earliest Era to Mid-19th Century / $12.50

17278-7   KEROUAC, JACK / Dr. Sax / $5.95
17171-3   KEROUAC, JACK / Lonesome Traveler / $5.95
17287-6   KEROUAC, JACK / Mexico City Blues / $7.95
17437-2   KEROUAC, JACK / Satori in Paris / $4.95
17035-0   KERR, CARMEN / Sex for Women Who Want to Have Fun and
          Loving Relationships With Equals / $9.95
17981-1   KINGSLEY, PHILIP / The Complete Hair Book: The Ultimate
          Guide to Your Hair's Health and Beauty / $10.95
62424-6   LAWRENCE, D.H. / Lady Chatterley's Lover / $3.95
17178-0   LESTER, JULIUS / Black Folktales / $4.95
17481-X   LEWIS, MATTHEW / The Monk / $8.95
17391-0   LINSSEN, ROBERT / Living Zen / $12.50
17114-4   MALCOLM X (Breitman., ed.) / Malcolm X Speaks / $5.95
17023-7   MALRAUX, ANDRE/The Conquerors/$3.95
17068-7   MALRAUX, ANDRE/Lazarus/$2.95
17093-8   MALRAUX, ANDRE / Man's Hope / $12.50
17016-4   MAMET, DAVID / American Buffalo / $4.95
62049-6   MAMET, DAVID / Glengarry Glenn Ross / $6.95
17040-7   MAMET, DAVID / A Life in the Theatre / $6.95
17043-1   MAMET, DAVID / Sexual Perversity in Chicago & The Duck
          Variations / $6.95
17471-2   MILLER, HENRY / Black Spring / $4.95
17760-6   MILLER, HENRY / Tropic of Cancer / $4.95
17295-7   MILLER, HENRY / Tropic of Capricorn / $3.95
17933-1   MROZEK, SLAWOMIR / Three Plays: Striptease, Tango,
          Vatzlav / $12.50
17869-6   NERUDA, PABLO / Five Decades: Poems 1925-1970.
          bilingual ed. / $12.50
62243-X   NICOSIA, GERALD / Memory Babe: A Critical Biography of Jack
          Kerouac
17092-X   ODETS, CLIFFORD / Six Plays (Waiting for Lefty, Awake and
          Sing, Golden Boy, Rocket to the Moon, Till the Day I Die,
          Paradise Lost) / $7.95
17650-2   OE, KENZABURO / A Personal Matter / $6.95
17002-4   OE, KENZABURO / Teach Us To Outgrow Our Madness (The
          Day He Himself Shall Wipe My Tears Away; Prize Stock; Teach
          Us to Outgrow Our Madness; Aghwee The Sky Monster) / $4.95
17242-6   PAZ, OCTAVIO / The Labyrinth of Solitude / $9.95
17084-9   PINTER, HAROLD / Betrayal / $6.95
17232-9   PINTER, HAROLD / The Birthday Party & The Room / $6.95
17251-5   PINTER, HAROLD / The Homecoming / $5.95
17539-5   POMERANCE / The Elephant Man / $5.95
62013-5   PORTWOOD, DORIS / Common Sense Suicide: The Final
          Right / $8.00

17658-8	REAGE, PAULINE / The Story of O, Part II; Return to the Chateau / $3.95
62169-7	RECHY, JOHN / City of Night / $4.50
62171-9	RECHY, JOHN / Numbers / $8.95
17983-8	ROBBE-GRILLET, ALAIN / Djinn / $4.95
62423-8	ROBBE—GRILLET, ALAIN / For a New Novel: Essays on Fiction / $9.95
17119-5	ROBBE-GRILLET, ALAIN / The Voyeur / 4.95
17490-9	ROSSET, BARNEY, ed. / Evergreen Review Reader: 1962-1967 / $12.50
62498-X	ROSSET, PETER and VANDERMEER, JOHN / The Nicaragua Reader: Documents of a Revolution under Fire / $9.95
17446-1	RULFO, JUAN / Pedro Paramo / $3.95
17123-3	SADE, MARQUIS DE / Justine; Philosophy in the Bedroom; Eugenie de Franval; and Other Writings / $12.50
17979-X	SANTINI, ROSEMARIE / The Secret Fire: How Women Live Their Sexual Fantasies / $3.95
62495-5	SCHEFFLER, LINDA / Help Thy Neighbor: How Counseling Works and When It Doesn't / $7.95
62438-6	SCHNEEBAUM, TOBIAS / Keep the River on Your Right / $12.50
17467-4	SELBY, HUBERT, JR. / Last Exit to Brooklyn / $3.95
17948-X	SHAWN, WALLACE, & GREGORY, ANDRE / My Dinner with Andre / $6.95
62496-3	SIEGAL AND SIEGAL / AIDS: The Medical Mystery / $7.95
17887-4	SINGH, KHUSHWANT / Train to Pakistan / $4.50
17797-5	SNOW, EDGAR / Red Star Over China / $9.95
17939-0	SRI NISARGADATA MAHARAJ / Seeds of Consciousness / $9.95
17923-4	STEINER, CLAUDE / Healing Alcoholism / $6.95
17926-9	STEINER, CLAUDE / The Other Side of Power / $6.95
17866-1	STOPPARD, TOM / Jumpers / $4.95
17260-4	STOPPARD, TOM / Rosencrantz and Guildenstern Are Dead / $3.95
17884-X	STOPPARD, TOM / Travesties / $3.95
17912-9	STRYK, LUCIEN, ed. / The Crane's Bill: Zen Poems of China and Japan / $4.95
17474-7	SUZUKI, D.T. / Introduction to Zen Buddhism / $3.95
17224-8	SUZUKI, D.T. / Manual of Zen Buddhism / $7.95
17599-9	THELWELL, MICHAEL / The Harder They Come: A Novel about Jamaica / $7.95
17969-2	TOOLE, JOHN KENNEDY / A Confederacy of Dunces / $4.50
17403-8	TROCCHI, ALEXANDER / Cain's Book / $3.50
62168-9	TUTUOLA, AMOS / The Palm-Wine Drinkard / $4.50
62189-1	UNGERER, TOMI / Far Out Isn't Far Enough (Illus.) / $12.95
17560-3	VITHOULKAS, GEORGE / The Science of Homeopathy / $12.50

17331-7   WALEY, ARTHUR / The Book of Songs / $9.95
17211-6   WALEY, ARTHUR / Monkey / $8.95
17207-8   WALEY, ARTHUR / The Way and Its Power: A Study of the Tao
          Te Ching and Its Place in Chinese Thought / $8.95
17418-6   WATTS, ALAN W. / The Spirit of Zen / $3.95
62031-3   WORTH, KATHERINE / Oscar Wilde / $8.95
17739-8   WYCKOFF, HOGIE / Solving Problems Together / $7.95

Grove Press, Inc., 920 Broadway, New York, N.Y. 10010